MINUTES OF THE COMMISSIONERS FOR DETECTING AND DEFEATING CONSPIRACIES IN THE STATE OF NEW YORK

ALBANY COUNTY SESSIONS

VOLUMES II–III
1780–1781
ANALYTICAL INDEX

A Da Capo Press Reprint Series

THE ERA OF THE AMERICAN REVOLUTION

GENERAL EDITOR: LEONARD W. LEVY

Claremont Graduate School

MINUTES OF THE COMMISSIONERS FOR DETECTING AND DEFEATING CONSPIRACIES IN THE STATE OF NEW YORK

ALBANY COUNTY SESSIONS, 1778-1781

Edited with an Introduction by Victor H. Paltsits

VOLUMES II-III
1780–1781
ANALYTICAL INDEX

DA CAPO PRESS • NEW YORK • 1972

Library of Congress Cataloging in Publication Data

New York (State). Commission for Detecting and
  Defeating Conspiracies, 1777-1778.
  Minutes of the Commissioners for Detecting and
Defeating Conspiracies in the State of New York.

  (The Era of the American Revolution)
  Reprint in 2 v. of the 3 v. first ed. published in
Albany in 1909-1910.
    CONTENTS: v. 1. 1778-1779. — v.2. 1780-1781.
Analytical index.
    1. U.S — History — Revolution — Committees of safety.
2. New York (State) — History — Revolution — Sources.
I. Paltsits, Victor Hugo, 1867-1952, ed.

E263.N6N425 1972   973.3   72-1835
ISBN 0-306-70504-4

This Da Capo Press edition of *Minutes of the Commissioners
for Detecting and Defeating Conspiracies in the State of New
York* is an unabridged republication in two volumes of the three-
volume first edition published in Albany, New York in 1909-1910.
Volume III of the original edition is reprinted with permission
from a copy in the collections of the Brooklyn Public Library.

Published by Da Capo Press, Inc.
A Subsidiary of the Plenum Publishing Corporation
227 West 17th Street, New York, New York 10017

MINUTES OF THE COMMISSIONERS FOR DETECTING AND DEFEATING CONSPIRACIES IN THE STATE OF NEW YORK

ALBANY COUNTY SESSIONS

VOLUME II
1780–1781

MINUTES

of

Commissioners

for

Conspiracies

Met Albany 29th June 1779.

Present

John M. Beekman   Isaac D. Fonda.
Jeremiah Van Rensselaer

Joseph Concklin of New Town having been apprehended for declaring that he was a friend to the King of Great Britain and making use of other expressions which plainly discovered his disaffection to the American cause Attachment to the Crown of the said Joseph Concklin having at this Time he was liberated from Confinement entered into a Recognizance whereby he engaged to appear before any one of the Members of this Board when called upon and the said Joseph Concklin having complied with the Terms of his said Recognizance it is therefore Ordered that the said Joseph Concklin pay the sum of £100 he therefore secure his Recognizance and that he be remain till for his appearance and be committed and for him and that a Mittimus be made out for the Goaler to take him into his Custody.

Angus McIntosh having some Time since been taken a Prisoner somewhere near the Head of Delaware River and confined in Goal was brought before the Board and it appearing to us from the candid Confession of the said Angus that he be the Board being of opinion that his going at large will therefore that he be liberated on his entering into a Recognizance with a sufficient Security for his future good Behaviour and appearance before any one of the Commissioners of Conspiracies when called upon until Discharged by this B.
Angus McIntosh on Recognizance in — — — — £200.0.0
James Bell his Bail in — — — — — £200.0.0

The Board then adjourned

Met Albany 30th June 1779.

Present

John M. Beekman   Isaac D. Fonda
Jeremiah Van Rensselaer

James Flaherty Deserter from Burgoynes Army residing with James Hutchinson at the Hosack Hill having been apprehended on Suspicion of being privy to the Robberies lately committed at the Helderberg was brought before the Board and it having appeared to us that the Suspicion examining him ill founded therefore resolved that he be liberated on his entering into a Recognizance for his good Behaviour in future

Rough Draft of Minutes (an insert), with
Emendations by Gansevoort

(One-half reduced)

MINUTES *of the*

Commissioners for detecting and defeating *Conspiracies*

IN THE STATE OF NEW YORK

ALBANY COUNTY SESSIONS, 1778–1781

Edited by VICTOR HUGO PALTSITS, *State Historian*

VOLUME II : 1780–1781

PUBLISHED *by the* STATE OF NEW YORK, ALBANY, 1909

Met Albany 3ᵈ January 1780
Present

John M Beeckman ⎱ ⎰ Mathew Visscher
Isaac D Fonda ⎰ ⎱

Isaac Lamb for whose Apprehension a Warrant [was] issued
on the 31ˢᵗ Ultimo having been Apprehended was brought
before the Board on being Examined he says that in the year
1777 he went to Burgoyne to which he was persuaded by Mose
Dormen and others that he after wards went to New York
where he has remained since that Thomas Wiltsie is come
with him from New York his Examination [128] is in the
following Words (to wit) (see Examination on the File)

Resolved that the said Isaac Lamb be committed and that
a Mittimus be made for him —

Adjourned

Met Albany 5 January 1780
Present

Jeremiah Van Renselaer ⎱ ⎰ Mathew Visscher
Isaac D Fonda ⎰ ⎱

Whereas it has appeared to this Board that Rudolfh
Schoenmaker, Johan Jost Schoenmaker and a Negro Man
Slave of the said Rudolfh Schoenmaker have been lately
committed to the Custody of Anthony Van Veghten Esqʳ
high Sheriff of the County of Tryon by Virtue of a certain
Instrument in Writing under the Hands of Wᵐ Petry Hendrick
Herchemer and Peter Ballinger Esqʳˢ for Crimes supposed
to be committed by the said Rudolfh Schoenmaker & Johan
Jost Schoenmaker in the year 1777 & as the said Rudolfh
Schoenmaker has lately for the same sopposed Crimes

been bound by us in a Recognizance to appear at the next Court of Oyer & Terminer to be held in the County of Tryon and permitted in Consequence thereof to go at large & as it appears to us as well from the said Instrument in Writing as other Information that the supposed Crimes w[h]erewith the said Johan Jost Schoenmaker and the said Negro Man Slave are groundless —

It is therefore resolved that an Order be made out to the said Anthony Van Veghten Esqʳ to discharge from his Custody the said Rudolph Schoonmaker, Johan Jost Schoenmaker and the said Negro Man Slave —

Adjourned —

           Met Albany 14ᵗʰ January 1780
Present

John M Beekman ⎫   ⎰ Isaac D Fonda
Mathew Vischer ⎭   ⎱

Philip Empey appeared before the Board and requested our Permission to go & visit his Family at Bowman's Kill —

[129] Resolved that they [sic] said Philip Empey have permission Granted him for that purpose and that he return to the Place to which he is restricted by his Recognizance in one Forthnight from this Day —

Isaac Lamb who was one the 3ᵈ Instant confined was brought before the Board resolved that he be discharged from his Confinement on entering into a Recognizance for his good Behaviour Appearing before us on the first Day of February next and also appearing before the Board when thereunto required

Isaac Lamb on Recognizance in......... £1000
David Sprague his Bail ......in......... £ 500
John Cormichael also his Bail in........ £ 500

Resolved that Alexander Squire enter into a Recognizance
for his good Behaviour & appearing on the first Day of
February next or when required —

    Alexander Squire on Recognizance in...... £5000
    Gurdin Squire his Bail ....in...... £5000—

Adjourned —

          Met Albany 21ˢᵗ January 1780
  Present

    John M Beekman ⎱ ⎰ Isaac D Fonda
    Mathew Vischer ⎰ ⎱

Jacob Merkle of Tryon County confined for disaffection
was brought before the Board   resolved that be be Discharged
from Confinement on entering into a Recognizance with a
sufficient Surety for his future good Behaviour and appearing
before any three of the Commiss.ʳˢ for Conspiracies when
Called upon —

    Jacob Merkle of Tryon CountyFarmer in. £1000
    John Breadfrick of Stonerabia in Tryon
      County Farmer his Bail in............. £ 500

Adjourned —

[130]   Met Albany 26ᵗʰ January 1780
  Present

    John M Beeckman ⎱ ⎰ Mathew Vischer
    Isaac D Fonda ⎰ ⎱

The Board having received Information that William
True of Kinderhook is a person whose going at Large may
prove dangerous to the Safety of the State & that it is
necessary he Should be Confined —
It is therefore resolved that a Warrant be made out

directed to Lieu^t Reuben Murry to take to his Assistance two Men & apprehend the said William True and forthwith bring him before us —

Adjourned

Met Albany 1st February 1780
              Present

Jeremiah Van Renselaer ⎫ ⎧ Isaac D Fonda
Mathew Visscher   ⎭ ⎩

Resolved that Andrew Squire who was taken Prisoner at Stoney Point be permitted to go at large in the District of Schaactikoke untill Called upon to be Exchanged on Entering into a Recognizance to appear before the Commissary of Prisoners or any other Authority of this State when called upon —

Andrew Squire on Recognizance in........ £500
Gurdin Squire his Bail ....in........ £500

William True alias Comfort Carpenter for whose Apprehension a Warrant was made out on the 26th Ultimo was brought before the Board   Resolved that he be confined & that a Mittimus be made out for him —

Resolved that Stephen Astin be discharged on entering into Recognizance for his Appearance at the Next Supreme Court of Judicature to be held at the City Hall in this City on the third Tuesday in April next and that in the same time be of Good Behaviour

Stephen Astin on Recognizance in........ £1000
Isaac Shelden his bail ....in........ £ 500
Hosea Hamilton also his Bail ..in........ £ 500

Adjourned

[131]   Met Albany 2nd February 1780

    Present

    John M Beekman   }   { Isaac D. Fonda
    Jeremiah V. Renselaer }   {

Edward Finn who was some time ago Liberated from
Confinement on entering into a Recognizance with D^r
George Smith as his Surety laid Before the board a Petition
wherein he sets forth the Difficulties he Labours under from
his being restricted to these & requesting Permission to
go to Ballstown for the Purpose of Keeping a School, and
the said George Smith appearing before us and requesting
to be Discharged from the Recognizance by him entered
into for the said Edward Finn —

Resolved that the Said Edward Finn be informed that
the Board will take the said Petition into Consideration
and will give him an answer to the Same on the 5th Instant

Also Resolved that Dr George Smith be discharged from
his Recognizance as Surety for the said Edward Finn —

    Adjourned —

        Met Albany 5th February 1780

    John M Beekman   }   { Mathew Visscher
    Jeremiah Van Renselaer }   {

Edward Finn who was ordered to attend the Board this
Day to receive an answer to the Petition presented to us on
the 2nd Instant appeared agreeable to the said Order —

Whereupon it is resolved that the said Edward Finn have
Permission to go to Ballstown on his entering into a Recognizance to remain in the District of Ballstown until Called
upon by us and not to Depart the said Limits without Leave

obtained for that Purpose from Col! James Gordon and to
behave himself peaceably and as a good Subject of the
State —

>   Edward Finn Schoolmaster on Recognizance
>   in.................................. £500

Adjourned

[132]   Met Albany 6ᵗʰ February 1780
          Present

          John M Beekman ⎱   ⎰ Isaac D Fonda
          Mathew Vissher ⎰   ⎱

Alexander Hubs appeared according to an order of this
Board and being examined in the Respect to Benjamin
Davis Andries Ten Eyck Junʳ & Christian Legrange saith
as follows (to wit) (see Examination on the File)
   Resolved in Consequence of the above Examination that
the sᵈ Christian Legrange enter into a Recognizance with
a Sufficient Surety for his Appearance at the next Supreme
Court of Judicature to be held at the City Hall in this City
on the Third Tuesday in April next & in the mean time
be of the good Behaviour towards all and every the liege
Subjects of this State

>   Christian Legrange on Recognizance in..... £500
>   Thomas Lottridge his Bail......... in..... £200

Resolved that the above Mentioned Andries Ten Eyck
Junʳ enter into a Recognizance & that he be bound in every
like Respect [as] Christian Legrange

>   Andries Ten Eyck Junʳ On Recognizance in £500
>   William Burnside his Bail............. in £250

Adjourned

Met Albany 7th February 1780

Present

John M Beekman }
Mathew Visscher }   } Isaac D Fonda

Resolved that Isaac Lamb be discharged from Confinement on entering into a Recognizance to appear before
any three of the Commissioners for Conspiracies when called
upon or before any other Judicial Authority if required &
do his Duty & be of the good Behaviour towards all the
liege Subjects of this State for and during the Continuance
of three Years

Isaac Lamb on Recognizance in........... £600
David Sprauge [sic] his Bail in........... £300
Alexander Hubs also his Bail in.......... £300

Resolved that William True Alias Comfort Carpenter be
discharged from Confinement on his entering into a Recognizance with Sufficient Sureties for his Appearance at the
next Supreme Court of Judi- [133] cature to be held at the
City Hall in this City on the third Tuesday in April next
& not to Depart the Court without Leave and also for his
appearing before any three of the Commissioners for Conspiracies when thereunto required and for his good and
peaceable Behaviour

William True on Kinderhook District Physi-
  cian in............................... £1000
Elijah Hudson of Kings District his Bail in. £ 500
Henry Bush of the same Place also his Bail
  in................................... £ 500
Jesse White of the same Place also Bail in. £ 500

Adjourned

Met Albany 8th February 1780

Present

John M Beeckman ⎱   ⎰ Isaac D. Fonda
Mathew Visscher ⎰   ⎱

The Board having been informed that Mathew Brown James Brown & James Brown Junr are able to give some very Material Information respecting the Conduct of John Dunbar at the time when General Burgoyne came down with his Army resolved that the said Mathew Brown James Brown & James Brown Junr be Severally cited forthwith to appear before this Board they may be examined as to the above

The Board having also received Information that Gerrit Van Ness is able to prove that Lieu.^t Col.^l Daniel B. Bradt did furnish some of the Enemy with Arms when Burgoyne came down with his Army

It is therefore resolved that the said Gerrit Van Ness be cited forthwith to appear before this Board in Order that he may be examined as to the same

Adjourned

Met Albany 9th February 1780

Present

Jeremiah Van Renselaer ⎱   ⎰ Mathew Visscher
Isaac D Fonda ⎰   ⎱

As the Act of the Legislature of this State[1] by which the Powers vested in this Board will in a few days expire and as it is uncertain whether the said Act will be continued It is therefore Resolved that all such Persons who have been employed to perform Services by Order of this Board be

---

[1] The reference is to the act of October 1, 1779. By an act of March 13, 1780, any two justices could enlarge deserters from the British. The commissioners were revived by an act of June 14, 1780. See Appendix I: Laws.

notifyed to deliver in their Accounts that the[y] may be paid 1780
Feb. 9.

[134] Resolved that the Secretary to this Board pay to Lieut: Thomas Ismay the sum of £91 " 19ˢ " 6ᵈ being the full Amount of the Pay and Subsistance Roll of the Party of Militia under the command of the said Thomas Ismay

Resolved that the Secretary also pay to John Fonda Junʳ the sum of £74 being for beef Provided by him for the use of the State Prisoners —[1]

Adjourned

Met Albany 14ᵗʰ February 1780 1780
Feb. 14.
Present

John M Beekman } { Isaac D Fonda
Mathew Visscher } {

Resolved that Robert Davis be discharged on entering into a Recognizance for his future good Behaviour doing his Duty as a good & faithfull Subject of the State & appearing before any three of the Commissioners for Conspiracies and remaining within the following Limits (to wit) West the Mill of Colᴸ Veeder, South the Creek East and north the Hill —

Robert Davis on Recognizance in. £500

Met Albany 22 April 1781 [sic for 1780] 1780
Apr. 22.
Present

John M Beeckman } { Isaac D. Fonda
Mathew Vischer } {

Resolved that Abraham Hoogteling be discharged from Confinement on entering into a Recogᵉ for his good Be-

---

[1] The original voucher is in *Revolutionary Manuscripts*, vol. 40, p. 173, dated February 28, 1780, State Comptroller's office.

haviour & appearance before any one of the Commissioners for Conspiracies when called upon until discharged by this Board

> Abraham Hoogteling of the West District of
> the Manor of Renselaerwyck Yeoman in. £100
> Joseph Salsbury of the same Place Yeoman
> his Bail in............................ £100

[135]   Albany 28th June 1780

An Act having been passed by the Legislature of this State on the 14th Day of June 1780 entitled An Act to revive the Laws appointing Commissioners for detecting and defeating Conspiracies in the words following (to wit)[1]

Whereas the Act " for appointing Commissioners for detecting and defeating Conspiracies and declaring their Powers " passed the fifth day of February 1778 and the Act " for encreasing the number of Commissioners for detecting and defeating Conspiracies within this State " passed the third day of April 1778 are expired   And whereas there is good reason to apprehend that Emissaries from the Enemy are lurking in different parts of the State, and that the Disaffected Inhabitants are conspiring against the public peace and safety: by reason whereof it hath become Necessary to revive the Powers of the said Commissioners —

Be it therefore enacted by the people of the State of New York, represented in Senate and Assembly, and it is hereby enacted by the Authority of the same; that the said two Acts, & the Powers and authorities by them or either of them granted to the Commissioners appointed or to be appointed by Virtue of the said Acts, or any and every three of them, shall be and are hereby revived, and shall

---

[1] Appendix I: Laws, June 14, 1780.

136

sum of Fourteen Shillings of the Money to be issued agreeable
to the Resolutions of Congress of the Eighteenth day of March last
and that the Treasurer of this State shall out of any monies
which may be in the Treasury, advance to the said Commiss-
-ioners or any three of them such sum or sums as they shall
from time to time require to defray the Expence of the Busi-
-ness hereby committed to them, not exceeding in the whole
the sum of two thousand pounds of like Money aforesaid

      I do hereby certify that the foregoing is a true
Copy of the Original Law now lodged in the Secretary's Office
of this State. Given at Kingston June 20th 1700—
               Robert Harpur Depy Secy

      In Consequence of which Act the following
Members Met Vizt
John M. Beekman ——— } Isaac D. Fonda
Jeremiah Van Rensselaer } Mat. Vischer

      Resolved that Leonard Gansevoort Junr be appointed
as Secretary to this Board and that his pay be the same as is
allowed to the Secretary of the Board of Commissioners for Con-
-spiracies sitting at Poughkeepsie—

      Ordered that Jacob Hedney be appointed as
Door Keeper to this Board and that he have an Allowance for
each Day he shall be actually employed in and about that
Business the sum of 6/ per Day—

      Ordered that the Secretary lay before the Board
as soon as conveniently may be an exact List of such Perso

Clean Copy of Minutes
exhibiting Gansevoort's reappointment

(One-half reduced)

Continue and be in full force during the Continuance of the present War with Great Britain. That each Commissioner shall be allowed for each day he shall be actually employed in the Execution of the said Office, the [136] sum of Fourteen Shillings of the Money to be issued agreeable to the Resolutions of Congress of the Eighteenth day of March last and that the Treasurer of this State shall out of any monies which may be in the Treasury, advance to the said Commissioners or any three of them such sum or sums as they shall from time to time require to defray the Expence of the Business hereby committed to them, not exceeding in the whole the sum of two thousand pounds of like Money aforesaid —

1780
June 28.

I do hereby certify that the foregoing is a true Copy of the Original Law now lodged in the Secretary's Office of this State. Given at Kingston June 20th 1780 —
Robert Harpur Dep^y Secr^y —

In Consequence of which Act the following Members Met Viz^t

John M. Beeckman   Isaac D. Fonda
Jeremiah Van Rensselaer   Mat: Visscher

Resolved that Leonard Gansevoort Junr be appointed as Secretary to this Board and that his pay be the same as is allowed to the Secretary of the Board of Commissioners for Conspiracies sitting at Poughkeepsie —

Ordered that Jacob Kidney be appointed as Door Keeper to this Board and that he have an Allowance for each Day he shall be actually employed in and about that Business the sum of 6/ per Day —

Ordered that the Secretary lay before the Board as soon as conveniently may be an exact List of such Persons [137] as have been bound by Recognizance's from time to time by the Board of Commissioners for Conspiracies heretofore

1780
June 28.

acting Specifying the Days when they were discharged and the sums in which they have been respectively bound —

Adjourned

1780
June 29.

Met Albany 29ᵗʰ June 1780

Present

John M. Beeckman   } { Isaac D. Fonda
Jeremiah Van Rensselaer } { Mathew Visscher

Major Jacob Schermerhorn appeared before the Board and informed that the cause of Commitment of Hendrick Kittle and Nicholas Van Valkenburgh is as follows (to wit)

Hendrick Kittle for insulting the Court Martial appointed to try him for neglect of Militia Duty and for Saying he would not be tried by them —

Nicholas Van Valkenburgh for drinking the Kings Health and damning every one that opposed the King's Laws —

It is ordered that Jan Devoe Junʳ who is Bail for the Appearance and good Behaviour of William Sanders be ordered to bring the said William Sanders before this Board on Saturday the first day of July next and that in Case of Failure the Recognizance entered into by the said Jan Devoe Junʳ will be prosecuted —

John Blackley having been confined by order of the Magistrates of this City for attempting to go off to the Enemy and it appearing to us that the Proof against him is not so clear as to render his Confinement any Longer necessary do therefore order that he be Liberated from his Confinement [138] on his entering into a Recognizance with sufficient Sureties for his appearance when called upon before the Board of Commissioners for Conspiracies or any Civil authority in this State & for his future good Behaviour during the Continuance of the present War with Great Britain —

John Blackley of the City of Albany Taylor
on Recognizance in.................. £2000
Nicholas Halenbeeck of the City of Albany
Carpenter his Bail in.................. £1000
Colin Gibson of the same place Taylor
also his Bail in...................... £1000

The Board having received Information that Henry Simpson Living on the Schenectady Road is of a Suspicious Character and that as a Tavern Keeper it is Necessary he should be laid under Restrictions therefore ordered that a warrant be made out Directed to Jacob Kidney the Door Keeper to apprehend the said Henry Simpson and forthwith bring him before us —

It is ordered that the Goaler lay before this Board a true List of all such Persons as are now in Confinement together with the cause of their Commitment and the Names of the Magistrates by whom committed —

Adjourned —

Met Albany 30th June 1780 —

Present

| Jeremiah Van Rensselaer | Mathew Visscher |
| Isaac D Fonda | John M. Beeckman |

Whereas from the Disturbances occasioned by the dis-affected Inhabitants of this County and from the [139] pressing Necessity at this Juncture of enforcing a due Observance to the Laws and punishing such as transgress against them and for the more speedy apprehension of such suspicious Persons as may be lurking about the Country it is thought necessary to have a Number of Men in differ-ent Parts of this County to carry into Execution such orders as may from time to time be issued by this Board and that

the Parties so to be employed be raised on the East and
west side of the River and Lieu.^t Philip Staats of Col.^l Killian Van Rensselaer's Regiment having been applied to in
order to take the Command of one of the said Parties and
he declaring his willingness to except [*sic*] the same —

Be it therefore ordered that a warrant be made out Directed to the said Lieu.^t Philip Staats to engage to the Number of about ten men who are to Provide themselves with
a good Horse & proper Arms and Accoutrements and who
are to be allowed the same Pay given to the Cavalry of the
Army of the United States and to have an allowance made
them for Horse hire and Subsistance —

Jacob Kidney attended and informed that he had apprehended Henry Simpson who being brought before the Board
and examined and the Charge against him not appearing
to be such as to merit a Commitment therefore resolved
that he enter into a Recognizance with two Sureties himself in £1000 and the Sureties each in £500 for his personal
appearance before the Board or either of the Commissioners when thereunto required to be of the good Behaviour
do his duty as a good and faithful subject of the State ought
to do and to give Information to the said Commissioners
from time to time of all such [140] Matters and things
which may come to his Knowledge and which may tend in
any Manner to the Prejudice of the United State of America
during the Continuance of the present war with Great
Britain —

Henry Simpson of the City of Albany Inn-
keeper on Recognizance in............ £1000
Jesse Fairchild of the same Place Blacksmith
his Bail in......................... £ 500
William Charles of the same Place also his
Bail in........................... £ 500

A Return being made according to order by the Secretary of the different Persons who have been bound by Recognizance's ordered that Notice's be put up in different Parts of this County ordering such Persons to appear before this Board on the 20th day of July next —

Adjourned —

1780
June 30.

Met Albany 1st July 1780
Present

1780
July 1.

John M. Beeckman   Isaac D. Fonda
Jeremiah Van Rensselaer   Mathew Visscher

Whereas a number of suspicious Persons are daily passing through this County who on being apprehended & Questioned name Officers in the Militia under whose command they pretend to be by which Means many Villians go unpunished to prevent which in future it is resolved that Letters be wrote to the different Colonels or Commanding Officers of General Ten Broeck's Brigade requesting them as soon as possible to furnish this Board with the Names of every Person of their Regiment and the Companies to which they Belong —

[141] Jan Devoe Junr according to order appeared before the Board with William Sanders whom he requested Permission to Surrender in Discharge of himself —

Resolved that the said William Sanders be committed and that a Mittimus be made out to the Goaler to take him into his Custody — And also Resolved that Jan Devoe Junior his Bail be Discharged from his Recognizance —

Lidia Currey having been confined by order of the Magistrates of this City for assisting in concealing & harbouring Persons from the Enemy was brought before the Board & examined

Resolved that she be discharged from her Confinement

on Gerrit Bradt of the Hellebergh entering into a Recognizance for her future good Behaviour and Appearance before this Board when required —

> Gerrit Bradt of the Hellebergh in the County
> of Albany Yeoman on Recognizance as
> Bail for Lidia Currey in.............. £100

Leonard Gansevoort Jun.ʳ Secretary to this **Board** Exhibited to us an Account for Paper purchased by him for the use of this Board amounting to £144 Continental Money ordered that the same [be] paid —

Adjourned —

Met Albany 3ᵈ July 1780

    Present

    Jeremiah Van Rensselaer ⎱   ⎰ Isaac D. Fonda
    John M. Beeckman   ⎰   ⎱ Mathew Visscher

The Goaler laid before the Board a paper whereby he was requested to take into his Care the Body of John Armstrong of the Manor of Rensselaerwyck a Person Notoriously [142] disaffected to the American Cause and deliver him over to this Board —

Whereupon it is ordered that a Mittimus be made out to the Goaler to take the said John Armstrong into his Custody and Closely confine him —

Hendrick Appley having been committed to Goal by order of the Justices in this City on suspicion of his being privy to the secreting and harbouring a Party of the Enemy was brought before the Board and Enquiry being made into the Proofs in support of the same and the said Charge appearing in the Judgment of this [Board] unsupported but the said Hendrick Appley being a Disaffected Person —

Therefore resolved that he be discharged from Confinement on entering into Recognizance for his future good

Behaviour and appearance before any of the Commissioners for Conspiracies when called upon during the Continuance of the present war with Great Britain

> Hendrick Appley of the Hellebergh in the
> County of Albany Yeoman on Recog-
> nizance in........................... £100
> Andries Ward of the same place Yeoman his
> Bail in............................... £ 50
> John Waggoner of the same place Yeoman
> also his Bail in...................... £ 50

Simeon Griggs of Half Moon having attempted to go to Canada and join the Enemy and having been apprehended by order of the Magistrates of this City and by them suffered to return home at the request of Col. Van Schoonhoven to endeaviour to procure Bail for his future [143] good Conduct in Consequence thereof Alexander Griggs the Father of the said Simeon Griggs appeared before us and informed the Board that he was willing to enter into Recognizance for the said Simeon Griggs —

Whereupon resolved that the said Alexander Griggs enter into a Recognizance for the future good Behaviour of his son Simeon Griggs and for his appearance when called upon before any three of the Commissioners for Conspiracies and for his remaining within the Limits of the District of Half Moon unless when called upon to do Militia duty which recognizance to be in full force during the Continuance of the present war with Great Britain —

> Alexander Griggs of the Half Moon District
> in the County of Albany Yeoman on Recog-
> nizance as Bail for Simeon Griggs in....... £200

Evert Ostrander, John Frazer, and John Andrew having been apprehended on their way to Canada to join the Enemy

1780
July 3.

were brought before the Board and on being examined Confessing the Charge alledged against them and declaring an Intention of persisting in the like Conduct in future —

It is therefore resolved that the said Evert Ostrander, John Andrew, and John Frazer be confined and that a Mittimus be made out to the Goaler to take them into his Custody —

Adjourned —

1780
July 4.

Met Albany 4ᵗʰ July 1780 —
Present

Jeremiah Van Rensselaer }   { Isaac D. Fonda
John M. Beeckman   }   {

[144] Information having been given to this Board that a certain James Mellderon has lately come to this place who appears to be of a suspicious Character. It is therefore ordered that Jacob Kidney be commanded to apprehend the said James Mellderon and bring him forthwith before us—

Jacob Kidney appeared and informed that he had apprehended the said James Mellderon —

Whereupon resolved that he be brought before the Board on his Examination producing a Pass from a Justice of the Peace at Fredericksburgh it is Ordered that he be given in Charge to the Goaler till he shall give Surety for his producing to us proper Vouchers of his Character as a Friend to the American Cause —

Graudus J. Cluet having been on his way to join the Enemy and having returned and Voluntarily surrendered himself and being brought before us by his Father Jacob Cluet and on being examined appearing candid and open in his Confession and making Promises of future good Conduct therefore resolved on account of his Youth and the Intercession of the said Jacob Cluet his Father whose Atachmen to the American Cause has been evinced on several Occasions that he be permitted to return home —

Simeon Griggs for whom Alexander Griggs was on the 3$\underline{d}$ Instant bound by Recognizance appeared before the Board ordered that he enter into Recognizance for his future good Behaviour and for his appearance before [145] any three of the Commissioners for Conspiracies when called upon and for his remaining within the District of the Half-Moon unless called upon to do Military duty during the Continuance of the present war with Great Britain —

> Simeon Griggs of the District of the Half
> Moon in the County of Albany Yeoman on
> Recognizance in....................... £200

Abraham Peltz having been apprehended & confined by Major Ezekiel Taylor on Suspicion of being privy to a Party of Men going off to the Enemy and the Proof appearing rather ill founded but the said Abraham Peltz being a disaffected person it is therefore ordered that previous to his discharge be be bound by a Recognizance for his future good Behaviour and Appearance before any three of the Commissioners for Conspiracies when called upon during the Continuance of the present war with Great Britain —

> Abraham Peltz of New Town in the County
> of Albany Yeoman on Recognizance in.... £50
> Hendrick Peltz of Pougkeepsie in Dutchess
> County his Bail in..................... £50

Duncan M$\underline{c}$Dougall appearing before the Board and being willing to become surety for James Mellderon   It is ordered that the said Duncan M$\underline{c}$Dougall enter into a Recognizance for the said James Mellderon's transmitting to this Board a proper Certificate of his attachment to the American

Cause from four or more respectable Inhabitants of Dutchess County within One Month from this day —

James Mellderon of Fredericksburough in the County of Dutchess Yeoman on Recognizance in.............................. £50

[146] Duncan Mc̱Dougall of the City of Albany his Bail in............................. £50

Adjourned

Met Albany 5ᵗʰ July 1780 —

Present

John M. Beeckman } { Isaac D. Fonda
Mathew Visscher }

A Letter was laid before the Board from Coḻ Abraham Wemple at Schenectady informing us that he had some time ago committed to Goal a German formerly belonging to Burgoyne's Army from an Apprehension of his being an Enemy to the cause of America but that he having learned from various Circumstances that his suspicions were ill founded he therefore requests that he may be liberated from his Confinement —

On Consideration of which Letter it appearing that the said German is a Prisoner of war and that he comes properly under the direction of the Military power Therefore ordered that he be delivered over to Colonel Goose Van Schaick the Commanding Officer in this Place —

Adjourned —

Met Albany 6ᵗʰ July 1780

Present

John M. Beeckman } { Isaac D. Fonda
Mathew Visscher }

It being suggested to the Board that Francis Rawworth lately an Inhabitant of Johnstown in Tryon County can give

Information respecting the Conduct of Robert Adams at the time Sir John [147] Johnson destroyed Caughnawago —

1780
July 6.

Ordered therefore that the said Francis Rawworth be summoned to attend this Board immediately —

The said Francis Rawworth appeared and on his Examination says that he did not see Mr Adams during the time Sir John Johnson was at Johnstown and that he has understood the said Robert Adams was taken Prisoner by a Party of Men and carried to Sir John —

Marte Freligh having been heretofore bound by Recognizance for his good Behaviour and appearance before the Board of Commissioners for Conspiracies when thereunto required and also for his appearance on the last day of every Month before any one of the said Commissioners and the said Marte Freligh this day appearing pursuant to notification & it appearing from the Information of John M. Beeckman Esqr one of the Members of this Board that the said Marte Freligh has punctually appeared before him pursuant to the tenor of his said Recognizance —

Resolved therefore that he be discharged as to that part of his Recognizance which requires his appearance on the last day of every month but that the Remainder of the said Recognizance shall stand & remain in full force and Virtue during the Continuance of the present war with Great Britain —

Resolved that Major Henry Van Veghten be and he is hereby requested and fully Authorized & empowered to stop every Person whom he may find travelling through this City and whom he may conceive [148] from their appearance and Conversation to be of suspicious Character's and on his detecting any such person make report to us of the same as soon as conveniently may be —

Adjourned —

                    Met Albany 7ᵗʰ July 1780 —
          Present

          John M. Beeckman   )   (Mathew Visscher
          Jeremiah Van Rensselaer)   (Isaac D. Fonda

Received a letter from Math[e]w Adgate Esqʳ one of the
Justices of the Peace of this County dated Kings District
5ᵗʰ day of July Instant wherein he informs us that having received Information that Daniel Green, Joseph Potter and
David Darrow were collecting a Number of Sheep in King's
District with an intention of driving them to the westward
and as there is the greatest reason to suppose from their
disaffection to the American Cause that they mean to convey them to the Enemy or at least bring them so near the
Frontiers that the enemy may with safety take them that
therefore he had caused them to be apprehended & conveyed to us by Ensign Jones and the said Daniel Green
and Joseph Potter being brought before the Board and
Examined & proving Satisfactorily to us that they had no
intention of driving the said sheep to the Enemy were severally discharged but David Darrow on his examination
denying the Authority of this Board and all Civil Jurisdiction in this State and pretending that by his religious principles [149] he is restrained from taking up Arms in defence of the Country and that he does not intend to do any
kind of Military duty whatsoever nor does not in any instance intend to abide by the Laws of this State, and John
Hocknear of Nistageune and David Macham of New Lebanon appearing before us to Vindicate the cause and Justify
the Principles of the said David Darrow and acknowledging a Concurrence of Sentiment with him and declaring
that it was their determined Resolution never to take up
arms and to dissuade others from doing the same and as

such principles at the present day are highly pernicious and
of destructive tendency to the Freedom & Independence of
the United States of America —

It is therefore resolved that the said David Darrow, John
Hocknear and Joseph Macham stand severally committed
& that a Mittimus be made out for them —

M.ʳ Jones informed that a certain Jonah Case an Inhabitant of Goshen in the County of Litchfield in the state of
Connecticut who has been inimically disposed to the American Cause from the Commencement of the War and was
for his disaffection confined to his Farm has several times
passed through his place on his way to Nistageune for the
Purpose of associating with a set of people who call themselves shaking Quakers and that a certain Zadock Wright
a prisoner of war who has been by the Commissioners for
Conspiracies liberated from Confinement and by Parole
restricted to the Limits of Kings District also pretends to be
of the denomination of people called shaking Quakers and
that he dissuades people [150] from taking up Arms —

It is ordered in Consequence of the said Information that
a Letter be wrote to Mathew Adgate Esq.ʳ to have the said
Jonah Case apprehended and brought before us —

It is also ordered that the said Zadock Wright be cited
forthwith to appear before this Board —

Adjourned —

Met Albany 10.ᵗʰ July 1780 —

Present

John M. Beeckman }   { Isaac D. Fonda
Mathew Visscher   }   { [Samuel Stringer]

A Certificate signed by Robert Harpur Esq.ʳ Deputy Secretary of this State was laid before the Board whereby it

appears that Samuel Stringer Esqr was on the 1st day of July Instant appointed by the Council of appointment as a Commissioner for detecting and defeating Conspiracies within this State in Consequence of which Certificate the said Samuel Stringer took the Oath as prescribed in and by the ["] Act for appointing Commissioner for enquiring into detecting & defeating all Conspiracies which may be formed in this State against the Liberties of America" and also took his seat at the Board as a Member —

Edward Archer of this City appeared before the Board and informed that George Rodgers did Yesterday in his presence say that the French Fleet was come to carry off the Damned Rebel Officer Washington who was afraid he would he hanged and the Rebel Congress that the [151] Whigs were all a set of scoundrels and Rascals and that he was persuaded the British Troops would in a forthnight's time march through the City of Albany —

Ordered that a Letter be wrote to John Ryley to request him to appear before this Board to give Information respecting Nicholas Van Valkenburgh now confined in Goal —

The affidavit of John Coppernoll & John Vrooman respecting Jacob J. Truax was laid before the Board from which it appears that the said Jacob J. Truax is a person greatly disaffected to the American Cause whose going at large may prove dangerous to the Safety and wellfare of this State —

It is therefore resolved that a warrant be made out directed to Jacob Kidney to apprehend the said Jacob J. Truax and that the Goaler be ordered to receive him into his Custody and closely confine him —

A Number of Negroes having been apprehended at the Half Moon on suspicion of their intending to burn & destroy that Settlement and they having been severally examined by us denyed the Charge alledged against them but acknowledged that they had an intention of going to Canada to which they were induced by William Loucks a son in Law of Hans Roeliffse and a Hessian named Coonradt[1] living with William Waldron who told them that when they got to Canada they would be free and that the said William Loucks and Coonradt told them they would go with them —

I[n] Consequence of which Information it is ordered that a Letter be wrote to Colonel Van Schoonhoven[2] at Half Moon requesting him without delay to [have] the said William [152] Luycks and Coonradt apprehended and brought before us —

Ordered also that a Letter be wrote to Hendrick Van Schoonhoven requesting him immediately to send down his Negro wench who has given Information concerning the above mentioned Negroes in Order that she may be examined —

Adjourned —

Met Albany 11<u>th</u> July 1780 —

Present

John M. Beeckman }
Isaac D. Fonda   }   { Samuel Stringer

In Consequence of the Information Yesterday given to this Board by Edward Archer respecting George Rodgers

It is ordered that a warrant be made out Di[r]ect[ed] to Jacob Kidney as Constable to apprehend the said George Rodgers and that the Goaler be ordered to take into his Custody and closely confine him —

Israh Sanford was brought before the Board by Major

[1] Frederick Coonradt.
[2] Colonel Jacobus Van Schoonhoven.

1780
July 11.
Henry Van Veghten as a Person of a suspicious Character on examining him it appears that he is an inhabitant of the State of Massechusetts Bay and is also one of those persons who pretend that they are restrained by their religious principles to take up Arms in defence of the Country —

Ordered that he be discharged but that he be informed that if he is again found in this County he will be closely Confined —

James Patherton of Nestageune was also brought before the Board and on being questioned pretend- [153] ing that he is restrained by his Religious principles to take up Arms in defence of the State —

Resolved that the said James Patherton have Permission to go and procure a sufficient surety for his future good Behaviour and doing his duty as a faithful subject of the state —

Adjourned —

1780
July 12.
Met Albany 12th July 1780

Present

John M. Beeckman ⎱   ⎰ Isaac D. Fonda
Samuel Stringer ⎰   ⎱

A Letter from Lieu^t Col^l Henry Van Rensselaer dated 11th July Instant was laid before the Board containing the Charges alledged against Nicholas Kittle, John Armstrong, and Jacobus Moll, which Letter is in the words following (to wit)   (see Letter on the file)

Anthony Van Schaick Esqr made application to the Board in favour of Thomas Andrew a prisoner now confined [in Goal and on examining into the nature of his crime (he having been confined by order of the Magistrates of this City) and finding the charge alledged against him not properly supported —

Therefore resolved that the said Thomas Andrew be liberated from Confinement on his entering into a Recognizance with the said Anthony Van Schaick as his surety for his future good Behaviour & appearance before any three of the Commissioners for Conspiracies when thereunto required during the Continuance of the present war with Great Britain —

[154] Thomas Andrew of Newtown in the
County of Albany Yeoman on Recogni-
zance in.............................. £200
Anthony Van Schaick of the County of
Albany Esqr his Bail in................ £100

It having been represented to this Board that Peter Crapole a prisoner now confined in Goal who was apprehended on his way to the Enemy has been destitute of provisions for some days and being unable on Account of his poverty to purchase any it is therefore resolved that the Goaler be requested to furnish the said Peter Crapole with provisions for which the Board will allow him one shilling per day —

Colonel Jacobus Van Schoonhoven having at the request of this Board sent us Frederick Coonradt ordered on examining him that he procure surety for his Good behaviour and appearance when called upon —

Adjourned —

Met Albany 13<u>th</u> July 1780
Present

Mathew Visscher)   (Samuel Stringer
Isaac D. Fonda)   (John M. Beeckman

Whereas it has been suggested to this Board that Jacob A. Lansing of this County who was confined by the Magistrates of this City for assisting & encouraging the subjects of this State to go over & join the enemy and Robert Adams of Johnstown in Tryon County intend to remove themselves by writs of Habeas Corpus before the Honorable Robert Yates Esq⁙ [155] in order to their being bailed and as it is highly necessary at this time that they [the] said Jacob A. Lansing & Robert Adams should be continued in their present confinement —

Therefore ordered that a Mittimus be made out to the Goaler to detain and keep them in his Custody untill discharged by any three of the Commissioners for Conspiracies

The examination of Barnet Van Vranken and Flemin Highby taken by Col⁙ Van Schoonhoven were laid before the board respecting the conduct of the inhabitants of Newtown ordered that the same be filed —

Lieu⁙ Colonel Henry K. Van Rensselaer informed the Board that he last night had sent to Goal William Hutton as a Person whose going at large might be dangerous to the safety of the State that the said William Hutton has made use of threats against the Court Martial appointed to try him for Neglect of duty and says he is determined not to take up arms in defence of the country —

In Consequence of which information he was brought before the Board & examined and recommitted —

Lieu⁙ Col⁙ Rensselaer also informed the Board that he has confined John Armstrong, Thomas Blewer, Andries Stoll, Andries Weger, and Christian Crow, as dangerous and disaffected persons and prays that they may be continued in confinement —

Ordered that he be informed that this Board will not liberate them untill they have given Collonel Rensselaer a previous intimation of it —

Adjourned —

[156]   Met Albany 14th July 1780

Present

Samuel Stringer ⎱   ⎰ John M. Beeckman
Isaac D. Fonda ⎰   ⎱ Mathew Visscher

Frederick Bonestel having been by the former Board of
Commissioners for Conspiracies liberated from confinement
on entering into a Recognizance for his Good behaviour and
monthly appearance and the sum for which the said recognizance was taken being too small on account of the depreciation of the Continental Money —

It is therefore ordered that the said Frederick Bonestel
enter into a new recognizance with a sufficient surety for his
future good behaviour and appearance before any three of the
Commissioners for Conspiracies when thereunto required during the continuance of the Present war with Great Britain—

Frederick Bonestel of the Manor of Rens-
    selaerwyck in the County of Albany Weaver
    on recognizance in.................... £100
Anthony Abramse of the same place Yeoman
    his Bail in........................... £100

Adjourned —

                Met Albany 15th July 1780

Present

John M. Beeckman ⎱   ⎰ Samuel Stringer
Mathew Visscher ⎰   ⎱ Isaac D. Fonda

Christopher File having by the former Board of Commissioners for Conspiracies been liberated from [157] confinement on entering into a recognizance for his good behaviour & appearance on the last day of every month and the
sum for which the said recognizance was taken being insuffi-
cient on account of the depreciation of the Continental money

1780
July 15. and Melchart File the Father of the said Christopher File appearing this day before us and being desirous of becoming surety for his son —

It is therefore ordered that the said Melchart File enter into a recognizance for the future good Behaviour of the said Christopher File and for his appearance before any three of the Commissioners for Conspiracies when thereunto required during the continuance of the present war with Great Britain —

Melchart File of Manor of Rensselaerwyck in
the County of Albany Farmer as Bail for
his son Christopher File in.............. £100

Whereas from the frequent complaints that have been exhibited to this Board respecting the conduct of a number of the Inhabitants of Newtown it is become necessary that some rigerous measure should be adopted to bring them to a sence of their duty and to confine such of them as are most dangerous and as it is probable that the Board will receive better information respecting their conduct by opening a Board a[t] New Town —

It is therfore resolved that there be a meeting of the Board at Newtown and Stillwater on Tuesday next and that a Letter be wrote to Major Taylor informing him of the same & requesting his Attendence there at that time —

Adjourned —

1780
July 17. [158]   Met Albany 17$\underline{^{th}}$ July 1780 —
Present

John M. Beeckman ⎫   ⎰ Isaac D. Fond?
Samuel Stringer   ⎭   ⎱ Mathew Visscher

John Meyer having been heretofore bound by a recognizance for his good behaviour and appearance when called and appearing this day according to Notification —

Ordered that he enter into a new recognizance for his future good behaviour and appearance before any three of the Commissioners for Conspiracies when called upon during the continuance of the present war with Great Britain —-

John Meyer of East district of the Manor of
    Rensselaerwyck Labourer . . . . in £100
Jacob Springer of the same place his Bail in £100

Amaziah Winstone of Kings district appeared before the Board and informed that by virtue of a warrant directed to him by Mathew Adgate Esq⟨r⟩ ⟨;⟩ Justice of the peace he had apprehended Joel Pratt and Hezekiah Hammond whom he had ready to produce to the Board ordered that they be brought in and examined —

Joel Pratt and Hezekiah Hammond being examined say they mean not to take up arms in defence of the Country whereupon ordered that they be confined and that a Mittimus be made out to the Goaler to take them into his custody —

John Todd was brought before the Board and [159] examined and then recommitted —

Peter Crapole who was also examined and then recommitted —

Resolved that a letter be wrote to Mathew Adgate Esq⟨r⟩ suggesting to him a proper mode of conduct towards the people called shaking Quakers which letter is in the words following (to wit) (see copy letter on the file)

Received a letter from Mathew Adgate Esq⟨r⟩ Justice of the peace dated 14th day of July instant respecting Joel Pratt and Hezekiah Hammond which letter is in the words following (to wit) (see letter on the file)

Egbert Ostrander having been heretofore bound by recognizance and appearing this day according to notification to enter into a new recognizance —

Ordered that he enter into the same for his future good

behaviour and appearance before any three of the Commissioners for Conspiracies when called upon during the continuance of the present war with Great Britain —

> Egbert Ostrander of the East District of the
> Manor of Rensselaerwyck Yeoman in..... £100
> Jacob Ostrander of the same place Yeoman
> his Bail in............................. £100

Nicholas Van Valkenburgh, Hendrick Kittle, and Jacobus Moll having been committed for disaffection to the American cause and they having severally promised to be of good behaviour in future —

It is therefore resolved that they be severally discharged on entering into a Recognizance for their future good behaviour and appearance before any three [160] of the Commissioners for Conspiracies when thereunto required during the continuance of the present war with Great Britain and also for their appearance at the next supream Court of Judicature to be held at the City Hall in this City on the last [sic] in July instant (or wheresoever the said Court shall be held in the State of New York) and not depart the Court without Leave —

> Hendrick Kittle of Schodack Yeoman in..... £200
> Nicholas Van Valkenburgh of the same
> place Yeoman in...................... £200
> Jacobus A. Moll of D̲º̲ ....D̲º̲ £200
> Johannis Kittle of D̲º̲ ......Bail in....... £200
> Johannis J. Muller of D̲º̲ ....Bail in....... £200

Adjourned —

Met Albany 18ᵗʰ July 1780

Present

| John M. Beeckman | } | { | Isaac D. Fonda |
| Samuel Stringer | } | { | Mathew Visscher |

James Robbins appearing before the Board according to 1780
July 18. notification ordered that he appear as soon as possible with a sufficient person as his surety to enter into a recognizance —

James Akins having been heretofore bound by recognizance and appearing this day according to order with Neil McNeil as his surety —

Ordered that he enter into a recognizance of anew for his future good behaviour and appearance before any three of the Commissioners for Conspiracies when there unto required during the continuance of the present war   [161] with Great Britain —

James Atkins of Pits Town in the County of
    Albany Yeoman in.................... £100
Neil McNeil of the East District of the
    Manor of Rensselaerwyck Yeoman his Bail
    in................................. £100

Adjourned —

Met Albany 19th July 1780 — .   1780
July 19.
Present

John M. Beeckman)   (Isaac D. Fonda
Mathew Visscher   )   (Samuel Stringer

Martin Galer having been heretofore bound by recognizance and appearing this day according to notification to enter into a new recognizance —

Resolved that he enter into the same for his future good behaviour and appearance before any three of the Commissioners for Conspiracies when thereunto required during the continuance of the present war with Great Britain —

Martin Galer of the East District of the
    Manor of Rensselaerwyck Farmer in.... £100
John Shaver of the same place Farmer his Bail
    in................................. £100

1780 July 19.

Nicholas Michael having also been bound by recognizance & appearing this day to enter into a new recognizance

Ordered that he enter into the same for his future good Behaviour and appearance before any three of the Commissioners for Conspiracies when thereunto required during the Continuance of the present war with Great Britain —

Nicholas Michael of the East District of the
Manor of Rensselaerwyck Innkeeper ..in. £100
Jurie Michael of the same place his Bail in. £100

[162] Davis Michael also appearing to enter a new Recognizance —

Ordered that he enter into the same for his future good Behaviour and appearance before any three of the Commissioners for Conspiracies when thereunto required during the Continuance of the present war with Great Britain —

David Michael of the East District of the Manor
of Rensselaerwyck Labourer in......... £100
Nicholas Michael of the same place Innkeeper
his Bail in.......................... £100

Colin Gibson and Nicholas Halenbeeck who did on the 29th day of June last become surety for the good behaviour and appearance of John Blackley came this day and surrendered the said John Blackley in discharge of the recognizance by them entered into and the said John Blackley being desirous of engaging as a soldier in the three months service

It is resolved that the said Colin Gibson and Nicholas Halenbeeck be accordingly discharged from their Recognizance and that the said John Blackley have leave to enlist as aforesaid —

Adjourned —

Met Albany 21ˢᵗ July 1780

Present

John M. Beeckman }   { Jeremiah Van Rensselaer
Samuel Stringer   }   {

Received a Letter from Hugh Mitchell Esqʳ dated this day at Schenectady informing that a number of tories have been apprehended and brought to that [163] place and requesting a copy of the oath to be taken by the Commissioners for Conspiracies in order that Ryneir Mynderse & Abraham Outhout Esqʳˢ who have been lately appointed to that Office might be Qualified —

Ordered in consequence of the said Letter that a copy of the oath be made out & transmitted to the said Hugh Mitchell and that the said Commissioners be requested from time to time to transmit to this Board such information as they may receive & that this Board will afford them every assistance in their Power towards carrying into Execution such plans as they may think expedient to adopt to promote the public good —

Adjourned —

Met Albany 22ⁿᵈ July 1780 —·

Present

John M. Beeckman)   (Jeremiah Van Rensselaer
Isaac D. Fonda   }   { Samuel Stringer
Mathew Visscher   )   (

Jacob Kidney the door Keeper appearing informed us that agreeable to the warrant of this Board he had apprehended George Rodgers ordered that he be confined and hat a Mittimus be made out for him —

John Nightingale having been apprehended by order of this Board as a disaffected person ordered that a mittimus be made out for him —

1780
July 22.
The Board of Commissioners who by a resolution of this Board were to meet at Newtown or Stillwater having returned reported that the[y] had on the 19th Instant opened a Board at Stillwater which they had continued untill the [164] 20th Instant and that they had on the first day of the said Meeting Sent for Major's Taylor and Dickerson to consult what Persons to send for to be examined and which to apprehend — That upon consultation they agreed to summons Elias Delong, Flemon Higby, Barent Van Der Werken, William Williams, Jotham Bemus, John Bemus, Richard Collins, and Moses Hunter and accordingly made out summons's and delivered them to Major Taylor that they made out a warrant to apprehend Jacob Heemstraet, John Rose and Nathaniel James directed to Lieu^t Joseph Cook and delivered to Major Taylor —

That they examined the following persons (to wit) Moses Hunter, Jotham Bemus, Jaddiah Millard, William Williams, Peter Van Camp, Jacob Heemstraet, Flemon Higby, Marytie Scut, Barent Van Der Werken, Robert Todd, and Amos Moore and reduced their Examinations to writing and that they are in the following words (to wit)　(see Examinations on the file) —

That on the second day of said meeting being the 20th Instant they had bound the following Persons in Recognizance's for their good behaviour doing their duty and appearing before any three of the Commissioners for Conspiracies when thereunto required during the Continuance of the present war with Great Britain —

Stephen Hooper of New Town Farmer in... £100
Simon Van Camp of the same place Farmer
　　his Bail in............................ £100
John Hooper of New Town Farmer in..... £100
Francis Waggoner of the same place Farmer
　　his Bail in............................ £100

[165]   Joseph Devall of New Town Farmer in. £100

Stephen Hooper of the same place Farmer
his Bail in............................. £100

Joseph Conklin of New Town Farmer in... £100
Dirck Heemstraet Jun.ᵣ of the same place
Farmer his Bail in..................... £100

James Conklin of New Town Farmer in.... £100
Dirck Heemstraet of the same place Farmer
his Bail in............................ £100

John A. Conklin of New Town Farmer in.. £100
William Bartin of the same place Farmer his
Bail in................................ £100

Peter Van Campen of New Town Farmer in £100
Hendrick Brevoort of the same place Farmer
his Bail in............................ £ 50
Stephen Ladue of the same place Farmer also
his Bail......................... in..... £ 50

John Vincent of New Town Farmer in..... £100
Nicholas Teachout of the same place Farmer
his Bail......................... in..... £100

Amos Moore of New Town Farmer in..... £300
William Williams Jun.ᵣ of New Town Farmer
in £100
Williams Williams of the same place Farmer
his Bail in........................... £100

Ordered that a Letter[1] be wrote to his Excellency Governor Clinton inclosing him a copy of Peter Van Campen's Examination taken at Newtown which letter is in the following words (to wit)   (see draught Letter on the file)

Adjourned —

[1] In *George Clinton Papers*, no. 3094, archives of New York State Library

Met Albany 23ᵈ July 1780 —

Present

John M. Beeckman } { Samuel Stringer
Jeremiah Van Rensselaer }

Received a letter from Hugh Mitchell, Ryneir Mynderse, and Abraham Outhout Esqʳˢ Commissioners for Conspiracies at Schenectady dated the 22ⁿᵈ Instant wherein [166] they inform us that they send under Guard fourteen Persons some of whom they have had apprehended on their way to the enemy and others had forwarded and supplied them with provisions whose names are as follows Vizᵗ Josep[h] Warner, Jacob Ball, John Ball, Peter Snyder, Christian Sea, Christopher Warner, Nicholas Sea, Andrew Loucks, Richard Schermerhorn, Bartholemew Schermerhorn, Jacob Seybert, George Shamon, Frederick Wheeler, and John Broacham, which Letter is in the following words, (to wit) (see letter on the file) —

Ordered that a Mittimus be made out for the above mentioned Persons —

Received also another letter from the said Commissioners dated at Schenectady 22ⁿᵈ Instant wherein they inform us that they also send to us under Guard three other Persons who they have caused to be apprehend[ed] whose names are Jacob Man, William Loucks, and John Jost Warner which Letter is in the following words (to wit) (see letter on file)

Ordered that a Mittimus be made out for them

It having been suggested to this Board that James Ludlow who last Winter came from New York and is at present at Kinderhook by his conduct gives great reason to suspect that he is guilty of some evil Practice against the State therefore ordered that a Letter be wrote to Major Isaac Goes at Kinderhook requesting him immediately to send to this Board the said James Ludlow —

Adjourned —

Met Albany 24th July 1780

Present

[167] John M. Beeckman   } } Samuel Stringer
Jeremiah Van Rensselaer }

Whereas frequent complaints have been made by sundry
of the well affected inhabitants of this County that John
Partherton, William Lees, and Ann Standerren, by their
conduct and conversation disturb the publick peace and
are daily dissuading the friends to the American cause from
taking up Arms in defence of their Liberties —

Therefore ordered that a warrant be made out to Jacob
Kidney forthwith to apprehend the said John Partherton,
William Lees, and Ann Standerren and bring them before us
and that he be authorized in case of any resistance to call
to his assistance such a number of men as he may conceive
necessary to carry the said warrant into Execution —

The Board having received information that Thomas
Wood Junr who has been concerned in a number of robberies is lately come from New York and is now in and
about his place of abode —

Thereupon resolved that a letter be wrote to Capt Jacob
De Freest[1] requesting him to collect a Party of Men and
endeavour to apprehend the said Thomas Wood Junr —

Adjourned —

Met Albany 25th July 1780 —

Present

John M. Beeckman } } Isaac D. Fonda
Samuel Stringer   }

William Davis appeared before the Board and informed
us that in conversation with Mathewis Van Valkenburgh

---

[1] De Forest.

1780
July 25. [168] the said Valkenburgh professed himself a subject to King George and that he intended to remain so and said that his cause was a just one —

Ordered that the above information be reduced to writing and that the same be taken into consideration

It having been suggested to the Board by Lieut Coll Henry K Van Rensselaer that David Henry formerly an Officer in Coll Livingston's Regiment and now residing at the New City is able to give some very material Information concerning Abraham Ja: Lansing and some other disaffected Persons —

It is therefore resolved that a Citation be made out for the said David Henry to appear forthwith before this Board and that the said Citation be sent to Capt Christopher Tillman at New City in order to its being served —

Adjourned —

1780
July 26.   Met Albany 26th July 1780
Present

John M. Beeckman }   { Isaac D. Fonda
Samuel Stringer }

Jacob Kidney appeared before the Board and informed us that he had agreeable to the warrant issued to him on the 24th Instant apprehended John Partherton, William Lees, Ann Standerren and that he had also apprehended James Whiteacre, Calven Harlow, and Mary Parthington, whom he found in Company with them and it appearing that they have also been guilty of the like Practices with the above named Persons —

[169] It is therefore resolved that they be severally interrogated whether they are principled against taking up Arms in defence of the American cause and whether they have not endeavoured to influence other persons against taking up

arms to which Questions they having severally answered in the affirmative resolved thereupon that they be committed and that a Mittimus be made out for them —

Received a Letter[1] from his Excellency Governor Clinton dated Poughkeepsie the 24th Instant which Letter is in the following words (to wit) (see Letter on file)

James Bramley appeared before the Board & informed us that he had been ordered by the Commissioners for Conspiracies at Schenectady to remove his family to this place and Surrender himself up to this Board and he in Consequence of the said order appearing this day and avowing his principles as a person disaffected to the American cause —

Therefore ordered that the said James Bramley be informed that it is the determination of this Board that he procure by Friday next a Freeholder to become his Surety for his good Behaviour and appearance before us when called upon —

Adjourned —

Met Albany 27th July 1780 —

Present

Samuel Stringer } { John M. Beeckman
Isaac D. Fonda }

David Henry agreeable to the Citation sent to Capt Christopher Tillman this day appearing ordered [170] that he be examined as to the conduct of John Todd and John Gibson who are now confined in Goal —

The said David Henry being Examined saith as follows (to wit) (see Examination on file)

Ordered thereupon that the said David Henry be discharged —

Adjourned —

---

[1] In *George Clinton Papers*, no. 3094, archives of New York State Library

                    Met Albany 28th July 1780 —
          Present
          John M. Beeckman ⎱   ⎰ Hugh Mitchell
          Samuel Stringer   ⎰   ⎱

Hugh Mitchell Esqr. laid before the Board the examinations of the prisoners sent to Goal by the Schenectady Commissioners ordered that the same be filed —

A Letter was laid before the Board from Philip Pell
Esqr Commissary of State Prisoners dated 30th June 1780
respecting Henry Van Schaack, David Van Schaack, Lam-
bert Burgert, Mathew Goes Junr., John D. Goes, and Dirck
Gardinier which Letter is in the following words (to wit)
(see letter on file)

Ordered that the Subject of the above Letter be taken
into Consideration —

It having been suggested to this Board that Simon Viele
of the Manor of Rensselaerwyck is able to give some very
material information respecting Peter Cohoon who was some
time ago committed as a spy from the enemy   Ordered
therefore that he be sent for and examined —

Simon Viele appearing agreeable to order [171] and being
examined under oath saith as follows (see Examination on
file)

Ordered that the said Simon Viele enter into a Recognizance to appear at the next supream Court of Judicature
to be held at the City Hall in this City on the third Tuesday in October next (or wheresoever the said Court shall
then be held) to testify to such Matters as he may know
concerning Peter Cohoon and not to depart the Court without Leave —

Simon Viele of the west District of Manor
    of Rensselaerwyck Farmer in............ £400

It being the Opinion of this Board that the imprisonment
of Peter Ten Broeck and William Bowen Prisoners of war
(who have been heretofore released from confinement by a
former Board of Commissioners for Conspiracies) will tend
to expedite their Exchange —

Therefore resolved that an Order be made out & sent to
them to appear before us on Monday the 7$\underline{th}$ day of August
next —

Adjourned —

Met Albany 29th July 1780 —
Present

John M. Beeckman } { Isaac D. Fonda
Samuel Stringer   } {

Samuel Baker residing in the East District of the Manor
of Rensselaerwyck being suspected of having a connection
with some disaffected inhabitants of this County was ordered
to appear before the Board on his appearing and being
examined under Oath and declaring himself [172] innocent
of the charge therefore ordered that he be discharged —

Peter Seeger was sent for on information given to this
Board that he is able to give some Material Evidence concerning Peter Cohoon who is now confined in Goal as a
spy from the Enemy —

Ordered that he be examined and that his Examination
be reduced to writing which is in the words following (to
wit) (See Examination on file)

Ordered also that the said Peter Seeger enter into a Recognizance to appear at the next supream Court of Judicature
to be held at the City Hall in this City on the third Tuesday
in October next (or wheresoever the said Court shall be
held) to give Evidence on the Part of the people of this
State and not to depart the Court without leave —

Peter Seeger of the west District of the
Manor of Rensselaerwyck Labourer in. £400—

Adjourned —

Met Albany 30ᵗʰ July 1780 —
Present

Jeremiah Van Rensselaer ⎱ ⎰ Isaac D. Fonda
Mathew Visscher   ⎰ ⎱

Information having been exhibited to this Board by Gerrit
Heyer of this City that on Wednesday last three men came
up the River in a Batteau one of whom he supposed to be
Thomas Man the other the son of Patrick Ryan living on
the Green Island both of which persons have been with the
Enemy for some time past and there being a probability of
the said persons being at the House of [173] the said Patrick
Ryan —

Therefore ordered that a Letter be wrote to Capt Christopher Tillman requesting him to take a Party of Men and
endeavour to apprehend them —

Lucas Moore of Saragtoga having about a Year since made
his escape from the Goal in this City where he was confined
for having been with the Enemy and being apprehended &
brought before us on a suspicion of guiding a Party of
Tories from Newtown who were on their way to join the
Enemy and he professing himself a Prisoner of war therefore ordered that he be confined and that a mittimus be
made out to the Sheriff to take him into his Custody —

Adjourned —

Met Albany 31ˢᵗ July 1780
Present

John M. Beeckman ⎱ ⎰ Samuel Stringer
Isaac D. Fonda   ⎰ ⎱

Agreeable to the request made by this Board to Major Isaac Goes of Kinderhook on the 23^d instant to send to us for Examination James Ludlow and the said James Ludlow appearing and being Examined and having satisfied the Board that the charges alledged against him are without Foundation it is therefore ordered that he be discharged —

The Board proceeded to the consideration of an Affidavit of Susannah Parie taken before Johannis Van Deusen Esqr. wherein the said Susannah Parie charges Angus Mc Donald and Doctor Thompson of Livingston's Manor with having harboured British Officers from Canada on their [174] way to New York and secreting persons who had been concerned in Robberies which affidavit was transmitted to the former Board of Commissioners for Conspiracies —

Resolved on Consideration of the said Affidavit that Citations be made out for the said Doctor Thompson & Angus McDonald to appear before this Board on Monday the seventh day of August next and that the said Citations be inclosed in a Letter and sent to Johannis Van Dusen Esqr requesting him to have them served on the said McDonald and Doctor Thompson —

Application was made to the Board by John Lansing Junr Esqr in favour of Robert Adams of Johnstown now confined in Goal by an order of this Board requesting his liberation —

Ordered that he be informed that the Board cannot in the present critical situation of Public affairs consent to his Enlargement —

Isaac D. Fonda Esqr informed the Board that he has received information that Andrew Bowman, John F. Cluet, Hendrick Kerkner, Jacob Kerkner, and a certain man named Frederick a step son of Michael Huff all residing in the West District of the Manor of Rensselaerwyck are preparing to go Off and join the Enemy —

Resolved in Consequence of the said Information that a warrant be made out directed to Capt Ostrum Authorizing him forthwith to apprehend the said persons and bring them before us —

Adjourned —

[175]   Met Albany 1.st August 1780

Present

John M. Beeckman   }   } Samuel Stringer
Jeremiah Van Rensselaer }   {

Richard Langley a Prisoner of war taken at Stoney point who was some time ago confined in Goal by Richard Esselstyne Esqr was brought before the Board and examined his Examination is in the following words (to wit) (see examination on file)

The Board taking into consideration the Letter received from Philip Pell Esqr Commissary of state Prisoners on the 28.th Ultimo do in consequence thereof —

Resolve that an order be made out and sent to Henry Van Schaack, David Van Schaack, Lambert Burghert, Mathew Goes Junr John D. Goes, and Dirck Gardinier to prepare and hold themselves in readiness to be removed to the Goal in Goshen in Orange County by the 15.th day of this month where they are to remain as Prisoners untill exchanged for some of the inhabitants of this State at present in the power of the Enemy —

Also resolved that an order be sent to Peter Ten Broeck who was liberated from his confinement by the former Board of Commissioners for Conspiracies to prepare himself and be in readiness on the 15.th day of this month to be removed to the Goal in Goshen in the County of Orange —

Doctor George Smith of this City being charged with forwarding Peter Cohoon a spy from the Enemy through the Country and the said Peter Cohoon having under Oath [176] charged him therewith —

It is therefore ordered that Jacob Kidney be ordered forthwith to apprehend the said George Smith and convey him to the Goal in this City and that the Goaler be ordered to take him into his Custody and closely confine him —

Adjourned —

Met Albany 2<u>nd</u> August 1780 —

Present

John M. Beeckman } { Samuel Stringer
Mathew Visscher } { Jeremiah Van Rensselaer

A Letter from Philip Pell Esq<u>r</u> Commissary of state Prisoners was laid before the Board dated Poughkeepsie 27<u>th</u> Ultimo wherein he request's us to cause Henry Van Schaack, David Van Schaack, Cornelius Van Schaack, Lambert Burghart, John D. Goes, Mathew Goes Jun<u>r</u> Dirck Gardineir, & Jacob Legrange, to be sent down to Fishkill under the care of an Officer of the levies which letter is in the following words (to wit) (see letter on file) —

Ordered in consequence of the said letter that the resolutions of this Board of Yesterday with respect to Henry Van Schaack, David Van Schaack, Lambert Burghart, John D. Goes, Mathew Goes Jun<u>r</u> and Dirck Gardineir be rescinded and that they be severally ordered to appear before us on Saturday the fifth instant —

Also resolved that the resolution of Yesterday with respect

to Peter Ten Broeck be and is hereby rescinded and that the said Peter Ten Broeck be ordered to appear before this Board on Monday the 7th day of August Instant —

[177] Resolved that an Order be sent to Major Zadock Wright (a Prisoner of war who was confined by th s Board to Kings District) to appear before us on Saturday the 5th Instant in order that he may be removed to Fishkill to be there delivered over to Philip Pell Esqr Commissary of State Prisoners to be exchanged —

Resolved also that an order be sent to Martin Crum of Claverack who refused to take the oath tendered agreeable to an act of the Legislature of this State to persons of Neutral and Equivocal characters to appear before this Board on monday the 7th instant in order that he may be removed to Fishkill to be there delivered over to the Commissary of State Prisoners —

Andries Stoll who was some time ago committed to Goal as a dangerous and disaffected person was brought before the Board and we having certain information that his wife is in a very distressed situation without the benefit of any aid or assistance and expecting shortly to be brought to bed the Board do therefore on Consideration thereof resolve that the said Andries Stoll be released from his confinement on his entering into a Recognizance with a sufficient surety for his appearance when called upon by any three of the Commissioners for Conspiracies and for his good Behaviour and doing his duty as a good and faithfull subject of the State during the continuance of the present war with Great Britain

Andries Stoll of the East District of the Manor
of Rensselaerwyck Blacksmith in......... £100
Abram Robison of the same place Farmer
his Bail in.............................. £100

It having appeared to the Board that Alexander Outhout who was confined by the Magistrates of this [178] City for attempting to go off and join the Enemy was persuaded thereto by Doctor Johnson and others and that no danger is to be apprehended from him on account of his Youth & inexperience; therefore ordered that he be released on Alexander Bulson entering into a recognizance for the said Alexander Outhout's appearing before this Board when called upon & for his good behaviour and doing his duty as a good and faithful subject of the State during the continuance of the present war with Great Britain and also for his appearance at the next Supream Court of Judicature to be held at the City Hall in this City on the third Tuesday in October next and not to depart the Court without Leave —

> Alexander Bulson of the East District of the
> Manor of Rensselaerwyck on Recognizance
> as Bail for Alexander Outhout in........ £100

The Board having received information that Doctor George Smith who was Yesterday confined by order of this Board is dangerously ill and that a continuance of his present confinement may endanger his life —

It is therefore ordered that he be discharged on his entering into a Recognizance with a sufficient surety for his appearance before any three of the Commissioners for Conspiracies when thereunto required and for his good Behaviour untill discharged by this Board —

> George Smith of the City of Albany Phy-
> sician in.......................... £100
> Patrick Smith of the same place Merchant
> his Bail in.......................... £100

Adjourned —

[179]   Met Albany 3ᵈ August 1780

Present

John M. Beeckman ⎰   ⎰ Isaac D. Fonda
Mathew Visscher   ⎱   ⎱ Samuel Stringer

John Ryley appeared before the Board and informed that
he had apprehended Jacob Smith and Jacob Dymont for
Stealing two Horses from Frederick Barringar, that in his
way to said Barringar's he was overtaken by Marcus Dymont
who offered him a sum of money to let the said Jacob Smith
and Jacob Dymont make their Escape and that afterwards
the said Jacob Smith & Jacob Dymont struck him the said
John Ryley on the head and by that means made their escape
in which they were assisted by the said Marcus Dymont
and the said Marcus Dymont being a Person disaffected
to the American Cause Thereupon resolved that a warrant
be made out directed to Philip Herwig commanding him
with the assistance of six men to apprehend the said Jacob
Smith, Jacob Dymont, and Marcus Dymont and bring them
before us —

The said John Ryley was Examined as to Nicholas Van
Valkenburgh which Examination is in the following words
(to wit) (see examination on file)

It appearing probable to this Board from the intimacy
of Samuel Kitcham with Doctor Johnson that the said
Kitcham was knowing to the said Johnsons intention of
going off to the Enemy it is therefore ordered that he be
Examined under oath —

The said Samuel Kitcham being Examined and declaring
himself ignorant of the said Doctor Johnson's [180] intentions thereupon ordered that he be discharged —

Adjourned —

Met Albany 4th August 1780 —

Present

John M. Beeckman ⎱   ⎰ Samuel Stringer
Isaac D. Fonda   ⎰   ⎱

Samuel Stringer Esqr one of the Members of this Board informed that he had caused to be apprehended & brought before him a certain John Ryley as being a Suspicious person that he had examined him and on finding by his own Confession that he is a Prisoner of war had committed him to Goal Resolve[d] that the above procedure be approved of and that a mittimus be made out for the said John Ryley —

Christopher Warner one of the prisoners sent down by the Schenectady Commissioners was brought before the Board and examined —

Resolved that he be liberated from his confinement on Hendrick Warner of the Bever Dam entering into a recognizance for the good behaviour and personal appearance of the said Christopher Warner before any three of the Commissioners for Conspiracies and for doing his duty as a good and faithfull subject of this State during the continuance of the present War with Great Britain —

Hendrick Warner of the Bever Dam in the
County of Albany Farmer on Recognizance as Bail for Christopher Warner in £100

Adjourned —

[181]   Met Albany 5th August 1780

Present

John M. Beeckman ⎱   ⎰ Isaac D. Fonda
Mathew Visscher ⎰   ⎱ Jeremiah Van Rensselaer
Samuel Stringer ⎰   ⎱

Resolved that an order be made out and directed to John Decker Robison & Bastian Bearn of Livingston's Manor who became surety for the appearance of John Smith before this Board when called upon to deliver up to this board the said John Smith on or before the sixteenth day of August Instant and that they be informed that unless this order is complied with their recognizance will be prosecuted —

Major Zadock Wright appeared before the Board agreeable to the order of the 2nd Instant —

Resolved that the said Zadock Wright enter into a Parole to proceed to Fishkill and on the 15th Instant Surrender himself a Prisoner at that place to Philip Pell Esqr Commissary of State Prisoners which parole is in the following words (to wit) (see Parole on file) —

Henry Van Schaack, David Van Schaack and Mathew Goes Junr who on the 2nd instant was cited to appear before us appeared this day according to order —

It is resolved that they respectively enter into a Parole to repair to Fishkill and on the 1st [or 16th][1] day of September next surrender themselves prisoner's at that place to Philip Pell Esqr Commissary of State Prisoners which parole is in the following words (to wit) (see Parole on file)

Resolved that Jacobus Ostrander be liberated from [182] confinement on his entering into a Recognizance with sufficient sureties for his future good Behaviour for his appearance before any three of the Commissioners for Conspiracies when thereunto required and doing his duty as a faithful subject of the state during the Continuance of the present war with Great Britain

Jacobus Ostrander of Newtown in the County
of Albany Farmer in.................... £100

[1] Date altered and ambiguous.

Abraham Douw of the City of Albany Gentleman his Bail in .... £ 50

Abraham Bogart of the same place Cordwainer also his Bail in................. £ 50

Adjourned —

Met Albany 8th August 1780 —
Present

John M. Beeckman   ⎫   ⎧ Samuel Stringer
Jeremiah Van Rensselaer ⎬   ⎨
Mathew Visscher   ⎭   ⎩ Isaac D. Fonda

A Letter from Doctor George Smith dated the 7th instant
was laid before the Board wherein he request's to be sent to
New York or exchanged which letter is in the following
words (to wit) (see letter on file)

Ordered that he be informed that the subject of his
Letter will be taken into Consideration at some future day —

It having been represented to this Board that James
Halstead of Nistageuna is a Person who is disaffected to the
American cause and that he has harboured and secreted
persons going over to the Enemy —

Therefore resolved that a warrant be made out directed to
John Tillman to apprehend the Said James [183] Halstead
and forthwith bring him before us —

Resolved that John Ostrander be liberated from Confinement on his entering into a recognizance for his future good
behaviour doing his duty and appearing before any three of
the Commissioners for Conspiracies when called upon during
the continuance of the present war with Great Britain —

John Ostrander of Newtown in the County
of Albany Farmer in.................... £100

Jacob Heemstraet of the same place Farmer
his Bail in £100

1780
Aug. 8.
It having been represented to this Board that it will be necessary for Henry Van Schaack, David Van Schaack and Mathew Goes Jun.ʳ to be down at Fishkill at an earlier day than is specified by their Parole therefore resolved that they be ordered to be at Fishkill on the 20.ᵗʰ instant —

The Board having received information that there is at present at Newtown a Person who is industriously circulating reports through the Country tending to injure the American cause which Person is a son in Law to John Concklin —

Resolved that Major Ezekiel Taylor be requested to have him apprehended forthwith and sent to us —

Adjourned —

1780
Aug. 9.
Met Albany 9ᵗʰ August 1780 —
Present

John M. Beeckman   Mathew Visscher
Samuel Stringer   Hugh Mitchell
Isaac D. Fonda   Jeremiah Van Rensselaer

[184] Resolved that a Letter be wrote to Philip Pell Esq.ʳ Commissary of State Prisoners respecting Henry Van Schaack, David Van Schaack, and other prisoners of war which Letter is in the following words (to wit)   (see letter on file)

Richard Schermerhorn of Schenectady who was confined by the Commissioners of that place for being concerned with a party that intended to go off and join the enemy was brought before the Board and on his Examination appearing candid and open in his answers to the Questions proposed to him —

Therefore resolved that he be liberated from confinement on his entering into a recognizance with a sufficient surety for his good behaviour doing his duty when required and appearing before any three of the Commissioners for Conspiracies when called for during the continuance of the present war with Great Britain —

Richard Schermerhorn of Schenectady La-
  bourer in £500
Jacob Schermerhorn of the same place
  Farmer his Bail in.................... £500

Resolved that Christian Sea be liberated from Confinement
on his entering into a Recognizance with a sufficient surety
for his good behaviour doing his duty and appearing before
any three of the Commissioners for Conspiracies when
thereunto required during the continuance of the present
war with Great Britain —

Christian Sea of the Bever Dam in the County
  of Albany Farmer on recognizance in £100
William Dietz of the Hellebergh in the County
  aforesaid Farmer his Bail in............ £100

[185] John Tillman appeared before the Board and
informed us that he had apprehended James Halstead
agreeable to our warrant issued on the 10th instant and that
he had him ready to produce to us, whereupon resolved that
the said James Halstead be examined his Examination is in
the following words (to wit) (See Examination on file) —

Adjourned —

Met Albany 10th August 1780

Present

| John M. Beeckman | | Isaac D. Fonda |
| Jeremiah Van Rensselaer | | Mathew Visscher |

Resolved that Christian Cray be liberated from his confinement on entering into a recognizance with a surety
for his good behaviour doing his duty and appearing before
any three of the Commissioners for Conspiracies when
thereunto required during the continuance of the present war
with Great Britain —

1780 Aug. 10.

Christian Cray of the East District of the Mano[r] of Rensselaerwyck Farmer in... £100
Archilaus Lynd of the same place Farmer his Bail in............................ £100

Bartholemew Schermerhorn of Schenectady who was confined by order of the Commissioners for Conspiracies at Schenectady was brought before the Board and Hugh Mitchell Esq[r] one of the said Commissioners being of opinion that the said Bartholemew Schermerhorn may with safety be liberated from Confinement —

Therefore resolved that he be discharged on entering into a recognizance with a sufficient surety for his good behavi-[186]our doing his duty and appearing before any three of the Commissioners for Conspiracies when thereunto required during the Continuance of the present war with Great Britain —

Bartholemew Schermerhorn of Schenectady Farmer in............................ £500
Ryer Schermerhorn of the same place Farmer his Bail in............................ £500

Frederick Weller of the District of Schenectady having also been confined by the Commissioners for Conspiracies at Schenectady was brought before the Board ordered that he be discharged on entering into a recognizance with a sufficient surety for his good Behaviour doing his duty and appearing before any three of the Commissioners for Conspiracies when thereunto required during the continuance of the present war with Great Britain

Frederick Weller of the District of Schenectady Labourer in.................. £200
Johannis Weller of the same place Farmer his Bail in............................ £200

Resolved that John Broachim be liberated from confinement on entering into a Recognizance with a sufficient surety
for his good Behaviour doing his duty and appearing before
any three of the Commissioners for Conspiracies when
thereunto required during the continuance of the present war
with Great Britain —

> John Broachim of the District of Schenectady
>   Farmer in.......................... £200
> Ryer Schermerhorn of the same place Farmer
>   his Bail in............................ £200
> Johannis Weller of the same place Farmer
>   also his Bail in...................... £200

Adjourned —

[187]   Met Albany 11th August 1780 —
   Present

      John M. Beeckman   Samuel Stringer
      Jeremiah Van Rensselaer   Isaac D. Fonda
      Mathew Visscher

Abraham Jacob Lansing appeared before this Board
according to our order resolved that he enter into a recognizance for his good Behaviour doing his duty and appearing before any three of the Commissioners for Conspiracies
when thereunto required during the continuance of the
present war with Great Britain —

> Abraham Jacob Lansing of Lansingburgh
>   in the County of Albany Farmer in...... £500
> Jacob Van Derheyden of the East District
>   of the Manor of Rensselaerwyck his Bail
>   in................................. £500

Dr Joseph Young appeared before the Board and informed
us that he had received information from James Marr of

this City that a certain Peter Seeger who is now in Town has mentioned some circumstances respecting the attack of the enemy at Schohary from which he is led to suppose that the said Peter Seeger has connection with the Enemy —

Therefore ordered that Jacob Kidney immediately apprehend the said Peter Seeger and bring him before us —

Peter Seeger being brought before us and examined as to the above informed us in what manner he had received his information and the same being satisfactory ordered that he be discharged —

Resolved that Samuel Stringer Esq.ʳ be requested to propose John Tillman Jun.ʳ to raise and take the command of [188] a Ranger Company to be under the direction of this Board —

William Pemberton who is charged with harbouring and forwarding through the country Peter Cohoon a spy from the Enemy appeared before the Board according to our order and as the proof in support of the above charge is not so full as to render his confinement necessary —

Therefore ordered that he enter into a Recognizance with sufficient sureties for his good Behaviour doing his duty and appearing before any three of the Commissioners for Conspiracies when thereunto required during the Continuance of the present war with Great Britain —

William Pemberton of the City of Albany
Marriner in.......................... £500
William Charles of the same place Butcher
his Bail in........................... £250
Wheeler Douglass of the same place Innkeeper also his Bail in................. £250

Resolved that George Shannon be liberated from confinement on entering into a recognizance with a sufficient surety for his good Behaviour doing his duty and appearing before any three of the Commissioners for Conspiracies when called upon during the continuance of the present war with Great Britain —

George Shannon of the District of Schenec-
tady Farmer in........................ £200
Johannis Shoemaker of the same place
Farmer his Bail in.................... £200

John Nightingale who was confined for making use of expressions tending to injure the American cause and being of a suspicious character was brought before the Board and it appearing that his Family are greatly distressed by the [189] means of his confinement —

Therefore ordered that the said John Nigh[t]ingale be liberated from his confinement on entering into a recognizance with a sufficient surety for his appearance before any three of the Commissioners for Conspiracies when called upon for his good behaviour doing his duty and remaining within the following Limits (to wit) to the north from his house to the Schenectady Road to the west to Veeder's Mill's to the south to the Norman's Creek and to the East to Hudson's River during the continuance of the present war with Great Britain unless called upon to do Militia duty—

John Nightingale of the west District of the
Manor of Rensselaerwyck Yeoman in.... £100
Joshua Bloore of the City of Albany Merchant
his Bail in............................ £100

Adjourned —

Met Albany 12ᵗʰ August 1780

Present

John M. Beeckman		Mathew Visscher
Jeremiah Van Rensselaer		Samuel Stringer
Isaac D. Fonda		

1780
Aug. 12.
Resolved that Jacob Sybert be discharged from his con-
finement on entering into a Recognizance for his good
Behaviour doing his duty and appearing when called upon
before any three of the Commissioners for Conspiracies
during the continuance of the present war with Great
Britain —

> Jacob Sybert of the west District of the Manor
>   of Rensselaerwyck Labourer in.......... £100
> Peter Radliff of the same place Farmer his
>   Bail in............................... £100

Resolved that Peter Snyder be liberated from Con- [190]
finement on entering into a Recognizance for his good
Behaviour doing his duty and appearing before any three
of the Commissioners for Conspiracies when thereunto
required during the Continuance of the present war with
Great Britain —

> Peter Snyder of the west District of the Manor
>   of Rensselaerwyck Labourer in.......... £100
> Hendrick Snyder of the same place Farmer
>   his Bail in........................... £100

The Board having received certain information that
William True for whose appearance Col! Abraham Van
Alstyne became surety is gone off to the Enemy —
Resolved that an order be made out to Col⁻ Van Alstyne
to deliver up the said William True or pay the Amount of
the recognizance by him entered into for the said William
True —
Resolved that John Boyd who is surety for William
M⁵ Auley deliver up the said M⁵Auley in fourteen days from
this day —
The Board having received information that John Rodliff
and Arent Rodliff for whom Rykert Rodliff became surety

have refused to do Militia duty whereby they have forfeited their Recognizance's therefore resolved that the said Rykert Rodliff their Bail appear before this Board on Wednesday next to shew cause why the said Recognizance's should not be put in Suit —

It having been suggested to us that George Keneir of this City is able to give information respecting several persons that have lately gone off and joined the Enemy and the said George Keneir being sent for appeared was examined & then discharged —

[191] Resolved that Doctor George Smith and Joshua Bloore be ordered to deliver up to this Board on or before the 19th day of August instant Ebenezer Knap, Elisha Marsh, Nicholas Schuyler, Nathan Lull & Joseph Lull for whose appearance when called upon the said George Smith and Joshua Bloore have become surety —

Resolved also that Joshua Bloore be ordered to deliver up to this Board on or before the 19th day of August instant Barnabas Loughley for whose appearance the said Joshua Bloore is surety —

Resolved that James Caldwell deliver up to this Board on or before the 19th day of August instant Duncan McConnelly and John Maginness for whose appearance before us when called upon he has become surety —

Also further resolved that Lewis Fotie deliver up Henry J. Mesick on or before the 19th day of August instant agreeable to the Tenor of his Recognizance —

Adjourned —

Met Albany 13th August 1780

Present

John M. Beeckman }   { Samuel Stringer
Mathew Visscher   }

1780
Aug. 13.

Andries Bronck and [blank] Wells appeared before the Board and informed us that being out on a scout by order of Col! Van Bergen towards Beesink they had taken Prisoner a certain John Sheerman whom they suspected to be a spy from the Enemy and one of those Tories who have some time ago infested that part of the Country with continual Robberies and the said John Sheerman being brought in and examined says that he comes from Fishkill and was when he was apprehended [192] on his way to his Family who live near Schenectady   Ordered that he be committed and that a Mittimus be made out for him —

Adjourned

1780
Aug. 14.

Met Albany 14th August 1780

Present

John M. Beeckman } { Samuel Stringer
Mathew Visscher

Andries Loucks one of the Prisoners now confined in Goal by the Schenectady Commissioners was brought before the Board and Examined ordered that he be recommitted —

Resolved that Johan Jost Warner be liberated from confinement on his entering into a Recognizance for his good Behaviour and appearing before any three of the Commissioners for Conspiracies when called upon during the continuance of the present war with Great Britain and also for his appearance at the next supream Court of Judicature to be held on the third Tuesday in October next at the City Hall in this City (or wheresoever the said Court shall then be held) and not depart the Court without leave —

Johan Jost Warner of Schohary Farmer in.. £100
Christian Weaver of the same place Farmer
    his Bail in.............................. £100

Resolved that the said Johan Jost Warner enter into a 1780 Aug. 14.
recognizance for the appearance of his wife Margaret Warner
at the next Supream Court of Judicature to be held on the
third Tuesday in October next at the City Hall in this City
(or wheresoever the said Court shall then be held) and not
to depart the Court without leave —

> Johan Jost Warner of Schohary Farmer on
> Recogᵉ as Bail for his wife Margaret
> Warner in £200

Adjourned

[193]   Met Albany 15ᵗʰ August 1780   1780 Aug. 15.
    Present

    John M. Beeckman ⎫   ⎰ Isaac D. Fonda
    Mathew Visscher ⎭   ⎱ Samuel Stringer

Resolved that Robert Adams be discharged from confinement on his entering into a recognizance with sufficient
sureties for his future good Behaviour doing his duty and
appearing before any three of the Commissioners for Conspiracies when called upon during the continuance of the
present war with Great Britain —

> Robert Adams of Johnstown in Tryon County
> Merchant in........................... £200
> Thomas Shipboy of the City of Albany
> Merchant his Bail in................... £100
> James Caldwell of the same place also his
> Bail in............................... £100

Resolved that Leonard Weger be liberated from confini-
ment on entering into a recognizance with a surety for his
future good behaviour doing his duty and appearing before
any three of the Commissioners for Conspiracies wheneve[r]

called upon during the continuance of the present war with Great Britain —

> Leonard Weger of the East District of the
>   Manor of Rensselaerwyck Farmer in..... £100
> Jurie Francisko of Cooksborough in the
>   County of Albany Farmer his Bail in.... £100

The Board having received information that Christopher Hutt of the Bever Dam who is now in this City is by his conduct and conversation daily endeavouring to injure the American cause therefore resolved that he be immediately apprehended by the door Keeper & confined & that a Mittimus be made out for him —

Adjourned —

[194]   Met Albany 16th August 1780
          Present

> John M. Beeckman ⎱ ⎰ Isaac D. Fonda
> Samuel Stringer ⎰ ⎱

Resolved that an order be made out directed to Arent N. Van Patten who became Bail for the appearance of Johannis Staring of Tryon County to deliver up to this Board the said Johannis Staring on or before the 26th day of August instant —

Rykert Rodliff being on the 12th instant cited to appear before the Board to shew cause why the Recognizance entered into by the said Rykert Rodliff for his sons Arent Rodliff and John Rodliff should not be put in suit as they the said Arent and John Rodliff refused to do Militia duty and the said Rykert Rodliff appearing and denying the charge alledged against his sons therefore resolved that the said Arent Rodliff & John Rodliff appear before this Board

on Friday the 18th day of August instant in order that they
may be examined as to the same —

James Halstead having on his examination informed the
Board that a certain Samuel Kid or Tid living with John
Duncan near Schenectady is able to give some very Material
information respecting Letters received by the said John
Duncan from the Enemy —

Resolved that a letter be wrote to Capt Hendrick Ostrum to
have the said Samuel Kid apprehended and brought before us
as soon as possible that he may be Examined as to the above—

Adjourned —

[195]   Met Albany 17th August 1780
     Present

     John M. Beeckman }   { Isaac D. Fonda
     Samuel Stringer   }   {

Resolved that Joachim Van Slyck of Claverack who
became surety for the appearance of Bartholemew Van
Valkenburgh before this Board when called upon deliver up
the said Bartholemew Van Valkenburgh on or before the
23d day of August instant —

Lewis Fotie agreeable to the order of the 12 instant
appeared before the Board with Henry J. Mesick —

Resolved that the said Henry J. Mesick enter into a
recognizance of anew for his good Behaviour doing his duty
and appearing before any three of the Commissioners for
Conspiracies when thereunto required during the continuance
of the present war with Great Britain —

     Henry J. Mesick of the District of Claverack
       Farmer in............................. £500
     Lewis Fotie of the City of Albany Baker
       his Bail in £500

Resolved that Jacob M. Vosburgh of Claverack District who became surety for Dirck Vosburgh's appearance before this Board when called upon deliver up the said Dirck Vosburgh on or before the 23$^{\underline{d}}$ day of August instant —

Resolved that Peter Van Valkenburgh of Claverack District who became surety for Hendrick Skinkle's appearance before this Board when called upon deliver up the said Hendrick Skinkle on or before the 23$^{\underline{d}}$ day of August instant —

The Board being of opinion that John Kluck of this City is a dangerous and disaffected person and that his going at large may prove of dangerous consequences to the safety [196] of the State therefore resolved that Jacob Kidney be ordered forthwith to apprehend the said John Kluck and confine them —

There being reason to suspect that John McDole, Colin Farguson & Peter Muir of this City are knowing and accessary to several persons going off to the enemy therefore resolved that they be immediately sent for —

John McDonald, Colin Farguson, & Peter Muir appearing were examined on oath and returning Satisfactory Answers to the Questions proposed they were discharged —

Adjourned —

Met Albany 18$^{\underline{th}}$ August 1780

Present

John M. Beeckman   Samuel Stringer
Isaac D. Fonda   Mathew Visscher

Rykert Radliff agreeable to the order of the 16$^{\underline{th}}$ instant appeared before the Board with his sons Arent Radliff and John Radliff.

Resolved that the above mentioned John Radliff enter into a Recognizance with a sufficient surety for his good

1780
Aug. 18.

behaviour doing his duty and appearing before any three of the Commissioners for Conspiracies when thereunto required during the continuance of the present war with Great Britain —

John Radliff of the west District of the Manor
of Rensselaerwyck Labourer in £200
Rykert Radliff of the same place Farmer his
Bail in £200

The above mentioned Arent Radliff being under age resolved that his Father Rykert Radliff enter into [197] a Recognizance for him the same in every respect with that entered into by his Brother John Radliff —

Rykert Radliff of the west District of the
Manor of Rensselaerwyck Farmer on
Recognizance as Bail for his son Arent
Radliff in £200

Resolved that Jacob Halenbeeck Jun.ʳ of Klinkenbergh be ordered forthwith to appear before the Board with a sufficient surety to enter into a Recognizance of anew —

Resolved that Philip Cook, Peter Livingston Jun.ʳ, Wilhelmas Dillenbeeck, and Jacob Fraligh be ordered to appear before this Board on the 24ᵗʰ day of August instant agreeable to the Tenor of their several Recognizance's —

Adjourned —

Met Albany 19ᵗʰ August 1780
Present

1780
Aug. 19.

John M. Beeckman ⎱   ⎰ Samuel Stringer
Mathew Visscher ⎰   ⎱

Resolved that a letter be wrote to Hugh Mitchell Esq.ʳ one of the Commissioners for Conspiracies at Schenectady

requesting him to send down to this Board William Bowen a
Prisoner of war in order to his being sent down to the Commissary of state Prisoners for the purpose of an Exchange —

Bartholemewis Van Valkenburgh appearing according to
order to enter into a new Recognizance resolved that he be
bound for his good Behaviour doing his duty and appearing
before any three of the Commissioners for Conspiracies
when thereunto required during the continuance of the
present war with Great Britain —

> Bartholemewis Van Valkenburgh of the Dis-
> trict of Kinderhook Farmer in.......... £200
> [198] Joachim Van Slyck of the same place
> Farmer his Bail in £200

Information having been exhibited to this Board from
which they are of opinion that Isaac Ostrander of the Hellebergh is a dangerous and disaffected person and that by his
conversation he endeavours daily to injure the American
cause and he having been cited to appear before us appearing
this Day —

Resolved that he be confined and that a Mittimus be
made out for him —

Dirck Vosburgh of the District of Claverack having
been ordered to appear before us to enter into a recognizance
of anew and appearing this day agreeable to order —

Resolved that he be bound for his good Behaviour doing
his duty and appearing before any three of the Commissioners
for Conspiracies when thereunto required during the continuance of the present war with Great Britain —

> Dirck Vosburgh of the District of Claverack
> Farmer in £200

Resolved that a citation be made out directed to Doctor
Thompson and Angus McDonald of the Manor of Living-

1780
Aug. 19.

ston to appear before this Board on the 24th day of August instant to answer the charges alledged against them in an Affidavit of Susannah Parie taken before Johannis Van Deusen Esqr and that Capt Robison of Claverack District be requested to deliver the said citation to any Constable of Livingston's Manor to have the same served —

John Decker Robison of Claverack District appeared before the Board with John Smith for whose appearance before us when called uppon he some time since became surety —

[199] Resolved that the said John Smith enter into a Recognizance of anew for his good behaviour doing his duty and appearing before any three of the Commissioners for Conspiracies when thereunto required during the continuance of the present war with Great Britain and also for his remaining within the Limits of Livingston's Manor unless he shall be called upon to do Militia duty or obtain permission from this Board to leave the same and for his appearing before us on the 14th day of October next —

John Smith of Livingston's Manor Labourer
     in.. £1000
John Decker Robison of Claverack District
     his Bail in........................... £1000

Resolved that Thomas Weger be liberated from confinement on Samuel Kitcham's entering into a recognizance for his good behaviour doing his duty and appearing before any three of the Commissioners for Conspiracies whenever thereunto required during the continuance of the present war with Great Britain —

Samuel Kitchim of Lansingburgh Farmer on
     Recognizance as Bail for Thomas Weeger
     in.. £100

Adjourned —

Met Albany 22nd August 1780

Present

John M. Beeckman ⎱   ⎰ Mathew Visscher
Isaac D. Fonda   ⎰   ⎱ Samuel Stringer

Resolved that William Loucks be liberated from Confinement on his entering into a Recognizance with a sufficient surety for his good Behaviour doing his duty and appearing before any three of the Commissioners for Conspiracies when thereunto required during the continuance of the [200] present war with Great Britain —

William Loucks of Schohary Farmer in..... £100
Peter Borst of the same place Farmer his Bail
in £100

Resolved that a letter be wrote to Lieu^t Col^l Henry K. Van Rensselaer requesting him to furnish this Board with a List of the Names of the Persons who are able to prove the charges alledged against Thomas Blewer now confined in Goal

Adjourned

Met Albany 23^d August 1780

Present

John M. Beeckman ⎱   ⎰ Isaac D. Fonda
Samuel Stringer   ⎰   ⎱

Mathew Van Valkenburgh having heretofore been bound by a Recognizance and having been cited to appear before this Board to enter into a Recognizance of a new and appearing agreeable to Order —

Resolved that he enter into the same with a sufficient surety for his good Behaviour doing his duty and appearing before any three of the Commissioners for Conspiracies wheneve[r] thereunto required during the continuance of the present war with Great Britain —

> Mathew Van Valkenburgh of the East District of the Manor of Rensselaerwyck Blacksmith in.......................... £100
> Hendrick Skinkle of Claverack District Blacksmith his Bail in............... £100

Hendrick Skinkle of Claverack having also been cited to appear before this Board to enter into Recognizance of anew and appearing agreeable to Order —

[201] Resolved that he enter into a recognizance with a sufficient surety for his good Behaviour doing his duty and appearing before any three of the Commissioners for Conspiracies when thereunto required during the continuance of the present war with Great Britain —

> Hendrick Skinkle of Claverack District Blacksmith in.......................... £100
> Mathew Van Valkenburgh of the East District of the Manor of Rensselaerwyck Blacksmith his Bail in................. £100

Information being exhibited to this Board that there is at present in this City a certain person who calls himself James Van Zant who there is the greatest reason to suspect is an Emissary from the Enemy —

Whereupon resolved that the said Person be sent for & examined on his Examination he says he is last Come from Newport that he left Long Island about three Years ago that his Father has a farm there and that he was led by curiosity to see Albany and on his producing a proper Pass resolved that he be discharged —

Adjourned —

                    Met Albany 24ᵗʰ August 1780
          Present

          John M. Beeckman ⎰   ⎱ Isaac D. Fonda
          Mathew Visscher   ⎰   ⎱ Samuel Stringer

Jacob Man confined by the Commissioners for Conspiracies at Schenectady was brought before the Board and as no direct proof has as yet been exhibited against him and he offering a good surety for his future good conduct —

Therefore resolved that he enter into a recognizance for his good behaviour doing his duty and appearing before any three of the [202] Commissioners for Conspiracies whenever thereunto required during the continuance of the present war with Great Britain —

  Jacob Man of Schohary Farmer in......... £200
  William Man of the same place Farmer his
    Bail in.............................. £200

Philip Cook appearing before the Board according to order to enter into a Recognizance of anew —

Resolved that he [be] bound for his good behaviour doing his duty & appearing before any three of the Commissioners for Conspiracies when thereunto required during the continuance of the present war with Great Britain —

  Philip Cook of the west District of the Manor
    of Rensselaerwyck Taylor in............ £100
  Wilhelmas Dillenbagh of the same place
    Farmer his Bail in.................... £100

Wilhelmas Dillenbagh appearing before the Board to enter into Recognizance of anew —

Resolved that he enter into the same for his good behaviour doing his duty and appearing before any three of the Commissioners for Conspiracies when thereunto required during the continuance of the present war with Great Britain —

Wilhelmas Dillenbagh of the west District of
the Manor of Rensselaerwyck Farmer in.. £100
Philip Cook of the same place Taylor his
Bail in.............................. £100

On reading a Petition of Doctor George Smith setting
forth his situation as to Health and circumstances and
praying leave to go to Canada with his Family —

Resolved that Dr George Smith be informed that this
Board are well acquainted with his State of health & have
therefore no objections to his going to Canada but that it
is not [203] in the power of this Board to grant him the
Permission required and that an application of this nature
ought to be made to his Excellency Governor Clinton —

Adjourned —

        Met Albany 25th August 1780 —
Present

John M. Beeckman } { Samuel Stringer
Isaac D. Fonda   }

A Certificate was laid before the Board signed by Nathan
Pearce & several others of the Principal inhabitants of
Fredericksborough in Dutchess County setting forth that
Dr James Muldrum is a friend to the American Cause
and that he has behaved himself well for several years
past —

Resolved in Consequence of the said Certificate that Duncan Mc Dougall who became Bail for the said Dr James
Muldrum be discharged from the recognizance by him
entered into for the said James Muldrum —

Resolved that citations be made out for John Cuppernull
and John J. Vrooman of Tryon County to appear before
Hugh Mitchell Esqr at Schenectady on the sixth day of

September next to enter into Recognizance's for their appearance at the next supream Court and that the said citations
be inclosed in a letter to the said Hugh Mitchell to be forwarded to them —

Angus McDonald agreeable to the order of this Board of
the 19th instant appeared this day before us —

Resolved that he be committed and that a Mittimus be
made out for him —

Adjourned —

[204]   Met Albany 26th August 1780
          Present

          John M. Beeckman ⎱   ⎰ Isaac D. Fonda
          Mathew Visscher ⎰   ⎱ Samuel Stringer

Resolved that Ann Standerren and Mary Partherton (who
were some time ago confined for endeavouring to persuade
the subjects not to take up arms in defence of the American
cause) be sent down to the Commissioners for Conspiracies
at Poughkeepsie for the purpose of their being removed
within the Enemies Lines   And that a letter with respect
to them be wrote to the said Commissioners —

The board having taken into consideration the application of Jacob A. Lansing to be liberated from confinement
whereupon resolved that he be discharged from his said
Confinement on his taking an Oath that he will not directly
or indirectly by word or deed give or cause to be given any
aid comfort or intelligence to any of the enemies or opposers
of the united States of America and that he will make known
to the Commissioners for Conspiracies all conspiracies that
may be formed in this State against the liberties of America
and of all treasonable actings or doings that may come to
his Knowledge and entering into a recognizance with suffi-

cient sureties for his good Behaviour doing his duty and appearing before any three of the Commissioners for Conspiracies when thereunto required during the continuance of the present war with Great Britain —

Jacob A. Lansing of the East District of the
Manor of Rensselaerwyck Farmer in.... £500
[205] Abraham Ja: Lansing of Lansingburgh
Farmer his Bail in...................... £250
William Liverse of the East District of the
Manor of Rensselaerwyck Farmer also
his Bail in........................... £250

John Sherman was brought before the Board and Examined who says he deserted from the Batteau Service at Fish Kill resolved that the Quarter Master General be requested to send him down to Fish Kill—

Adjourned —

Met Albany 28<u>th</u> August 1780

Present

John M. Beeckman ⎱ ⎰ Samuel Stringer
Mathew Visscher ⎰ ⎱ Isaac D. Fonda

John Nightingale who was on the 11<u>th</u> instant released from confinement on entering into a Recognizance with Joshua Bloore as his surety appeared this day before the Board and requested that Abraham Veeder of the Norma[n]s Creek may be accepted as his Bail in the stead of the said Joshua Bloore —

Whereupon Resolved that the said Joshua Bloore be discharged from his recognizance and that the said Abraham Veeder enter into a recognizance for the said John Nightingale's conforming to the Terms of the recognizance by him entered into on the said 11<u>th</u> day of August instant —

Abraham Veeder of the Norma[n]s Creek
Farmer as Bail for John Nigh[t]ingale in £100

William Bowen a prisoner of war on Parole having been
cited to appear before the Board appeared this day according
to order

Resolved that he enter into Parole to proceed to Fish-
[206] Kill and by the fourth day of September next there
deliver himself up as a prisoner of war to Philip Pell Esqr
Commissary of state Prisoners which Parole is in the following
words (to wit) (see Parole on file)

Robert Davis having been cited to appear before this
Board appeared resolved that he enter into a recognizance
of anew for his good behaviour doing his duty and appearing
before any three of the Commissioners for Conspiracies when
thereunto required during the continuance of the present
war with Great Britain —

Robert Davis of the Normans Kill School-
master in.......................... £100
Volkert Veeder of the same place Farmer his
Bail in £100

Whereas Dirck Gardineir, Lambert Burghart and John D.
Goes of Kinderhook have been cited to appear before this
Board at a certain day now past and have neglected to appear
whereby they have severally broken their Parole

Therefore resolved that a warrant be made out directed to
John Tillman forthwith to apprehend and bring them
before us —

Martin Crom of Claverack District having also been cited
to appear before this Board and not appearing agreeable to
our order therefore resolved that the said John Tillman also
apprehend the said Martin Crom and bring him before us—

Received a letter from Mathew Adgate Esqr dated King

District 27$\underline{th}$ instant inclosing several Examinations respecting Major Zadock Wright which Letter and examinations are in the following words (to wit)   (see letter and examinations on file) —

[207]   Received another Letter from Mathew Adgate Esqr dated 27$\underline{th}$ instant informing that he sends to us under Guard Samuel Johnson who is going about the Country & dissuading people from taking up Arms in defence of the American cause which Letter is in the following words (to wit) (see Letter on file) —

Adjourned —

Met Albany 29$\underline{th}$ August 1780

Present

| John M. Beeckman | { | Mathew Visscher |
| Isaac D. Fonda | } | Samuel Stringer |

The Board having taken into consideration the Application of Jacob J. Truax to be liberated from confinement do thereupon resolve that he be discharged on his taking an Oath not to aid comfort or assist the enemies of the United States and to make known all Plots & conspiracies against this or any other of the United States of America & on his entering into a recognizance for his good behaviour doing his duty & appearing before any three of the Commissioners of Conspiracies whenever thereunto required during the Continuance of the present war with Great Britain —

Jacob J. Truax of the City of Albany Innkeeper in £500

Isaac Truax of the same place Innkeeper his Bail in. £250

Johannis Wyngart of the same place Yeoman also his Bail in £250

**1780
Aug. 29.**   Joseph Hawkins, Thomas Yarns, William Ball and William
Griffen having been apprehended by Order of Albert Baker,
John Moss & Noah Pain Esq⁻ˢ three of the Justices of [208] the
peace for the County of Charlotte were brought before the
Board under Guard and it appearing from the charges trans-
mitted by the said Justices that the said prisoners are dangerous
& disaffected Persons and that they have been with the enemy—

It is therefore resolved that they be committed and a
mittimus be made out for them —

Deborah Baker was brought before the board by Colⁱ
Henry K. Van Rensselaer as an evidence against Thomas
Blewer and the said Deborah Baker being examined saith as
follows (to wit) (see examination on file)

Adjourned —

**1780
Aug. 30.**   Met August 30ᵗʰ August 1780
                 Present

          John M. Beeckman ⎫   ⎰ Mathew Visscher
          Samuel Stringer ⎭   ⎱

An Act¹ for the Legislature of this State entitled " An Act¹
for the Removal of the Families of Persons who have joined
the enemy passed 1ˢᵗ day of July 1780 was laid before the
Board and as it is highly Necessary the said Act should be
put into immediate Execution and as there are not a sufficient
number of printed Copies for the different districts therefore
ordered that the secretary to this Board make copies of the
said Act for every district in this County and that the same
be forthwith transmitted to the Justices of the said district
in order that no delay may be occasioned in the Execution of
the same —

Adjourned —

¹ Appendix I· Laws, July 1, 1780.

[209]   Met Albany 31ˢᵗ August 1780

Present

John M. Beeckman ⎱   ⎰ Mathew Visscher
Samuel Stringer ⎰   ⎱

John Boyd Junᵣ appearing before the Board according
to order for the purpose of entering into a recognizance
of anew —

Resolved that he enter into the same with a sufficient
surety for his good behaviour doing his duty and appearing
before any three of the Commissioners for Conspiracies
when thereunto required during the continuance of the
present war with Great Britain—

John Boyd Junᵣ of Balltown Millwright in. £100
John Holmes of the same place Farmer his
    Bail in.............................. £100

Adjourned —

            Met Albany 1ˢᵗ September 1780

John M. Beeckman ⎱   ⎰ Mathew Visscher
Isaac D. Fonda   ⎰   ⎱ Samuel Stringer

Received a letter from Hugh Mitchell Esqʳ dated the
20ᵗʰ August last respecting John Cuppernull and John J.
Vrooman which is in the following words (to wit) (see letter
on file)

Agreeable to an order of this Board the following Persons
appeared to enter into new recognizance's (to wit) Coenrad
Clapper, David Finger, Martinus Schuck, Johannis Muller,
Andries Rees, Andries Rees Junᵣ Johannis Tatter, Solomon
Schutt, Nicholas Wheeler, Broer Witbeeck, Fite Miller,
Johannis Shaver, Jacob Hoofman, William Schuck,

Albartus Siemon, [210] Johannis Siemon, Jurie Lemon, &
John Concklin —

Resolved that they enter into the same and that they
be severally bound for their good Behaviour doing their
duty and appearing before any three of the Commissioners
for Conspiracies when thereunto required during the continuance of the present war with Great Britain —

Coenradt Clapper of Livingston's Manor
Farmer in.......................... £100
David Finger of the same place Farmer his
Bail in............................. £100

David Finger of Livingston's Manor Farmer
in................................. £100
Coenradt Clapper of the same place Farmer
his Bail in......................... £100

Martinus Schuck of Livingston's Manor
Labourer .... in. £100
Johannis Muller of the same place his Bail in. £100

Andries Rees Jun: of Livingston's Manor
Labourer in £100
Andries Rees of the same place Farmer his
Bail in............................. £100

Andries Rees of Livingstons Manor Farmer
in................................. £100
Andries Rees Jun: of the same place Labourer his Bail in.................. £100

Johannis Tater of Livingston's Manor
Farmer in £100
Solomon Schutt of the same place Labourer
his Bail in......................... £100

Solomon Schutt of Livingston's Manor
Labourer in.......................... £100

Johannis Tater of the same place Farmer
his Bail in............................ £100

Nicholas Wheeler of Livingston's Manor
Farmer in............................ £100
Broer Witbeeck of the same place Farmer
his Bail in............................ £100

Broer Witbeeck of Livingston's Manor
Farmer in............................ £100
Nicholas Wheeler of the same place his
Bail in............................... £100

Fite Miller of Livingstons Farmer....... in £100
Johannis Shaver of the same place his Bail in £100

Johannis Shaver of Livingston's Manor
Labourer......................... in £100
Fite Miller of the same place Farmer his Bail in £100

---

[211] Jacob Hoofman of Livingston's Manor
Farmer in............................ £100
William Schuck of the same place Farmer
his Bail in............................ £100

William Schuck of Livingston's Manor
Farmer in............................ £100
Jacob Hoofman of the same place Farmer
his Bail in £100

Albertus Siemon of Livingston's Manor
Farmer in............................. £100
Johannis Siemon of the same place Farmer
his Bail in £100

Johannis Siemon of Livingston's Manor
    Farmer in.......................... £100
Albertus Siemon of the same place Farmer
    his Bail in............................ £100

John Concklin of Livingston's Manor
    Farmer in............................ £100

Jurie Lemon of Livingston's Manor La-
    bourer in £100

Coenradt Cline of Livingston's Manor
    Farmer Bail for Peter Lampman in...... £100

John Tillman appeared before the Board and informed us
that he had agreeable to the warrant directed to him apprehended Lambert Burghart of the District of Kinderhook
and Martin Crom of Claverack District —

Lambert Burghart being brought before us says that he is
very willing to comply with any order of this Board respecting him but that he is at present in no situation to travel
to Fish Kill being indisposed occasioned by the Yaws which
he has had upon him for a year past and as we have been
Certified as to the truth of the same —

Therefore resolved that the said Lambert Burghart enter
into a parole to remain at his place of abode in Kinderhook
District untill called upon by any three of the Commissioners
for Conspiracies or the Commissary of State Prisoners —

Resolved that Martin Crom appear before the Board to
morrow Morning —

[212] The Board taking into consideration the application of John Bratt to be liberated from Confinement —

Resolved on account of his age & infirmeties that he be
released on his taking an oath not to comfort aid or assist
any of the enemies of the United States and to make known

to us all persons coming from the enemy who secrete themselves in the woods and also on his entering into a recognizance with a sufficient surety for his good Behaviour
doing his duty and appearing before any three of the Commissioners for Conspiracies when thereunto required during
the continuance of the present war with Great Britain —

John Bratt of the Hellebergh Farmer in.... £100
John Willson of Kinderhook Farmer his
    Bail in.............................. £100
Barent Van Alen of the City of Albany Mar-
    riner also his Bail in.................. £100

Adjourned —

Met Albany 2<u>nd</u> September 1780
Present

John M. Beeckman ⎱ ⎰ Samuel Stringer
Isaac D. Fonda   ⎰ ⎱ Mathew Visscher

Martin Crom who was ordered to appear before the Board
appeared and laid before us a Certificate signed by a number of Militia Officers and other of the principal and well
affected inhabitants of Claverack District Certifying that the
said Martin Crom has always since the present war conducted himself as a peaceable subject of the State and has
done his duty faithfully when called upon And the said
Martin Crom also laying before us two Letters [213] directed
to this Board the one from Major John M<u>c</u>Kinstrey & the
other from Joseph Clarke both dated 31<u>st</u> August last in
which said letters the said Major M<u>c</u>Kinstrey and Josep[h]
Clarke recommend to us the said Martin Crom as a faithfull
and leige subject of the State which Letters are in the following words (to wit) (see letters on the file)
Resolved on consideration of the above Certificate and

letters that Martin Crom return to his place of abode in
Claverack District and there remain till called upon by this
Board —

Jacob Halenbeeck Jun.ʳ appeared before the Board according to order to enter into recognizance of anew —

Resolved that he enter into the same with a sufficient
surety for his good behaviour doing his duty and appearing
before any three of the Commissioners for Conspiracies when
required during the continuance of the present war with
Great Britain —

Jacob Halenbeeck Jun.ʳ of Cooksakie District
Farmer in........................... £100
Adam Hilton of the same place Farmer his
Bail in.............................. £100

Adjourned —

Met Albany 4ᵗʰ September 1780
Present

John M. Beeckman } { Isaac D. Fonda
Mathew Visscher }

The Board having received information that John Cobham
is frequently going to the Northward & there being great
reason to suspect that he keeps up a correspondanc[e] with the
enemy — Therefore resolved that the said John Cobham
[214] be ordered forthwith to appear before this Board —

John Cobham appearing informed the Board that there are
several persons at Fort Edward & Saragtoga who are indebted to him in large sums of money and that he has been
endeavouring to collect the same and producing to the Board
several notes of hand for Money due to him thereupon resolved that the said John Cobham be discharged and that he
be cautioned against leaving this City in future without a Pass
from this Board —

Hazelton Spencer an Ensign in Sir John Johnsons Corps
having been apprehended at Danby in the County of Charlotte was brought before the Board and examined resolved that he be committed —

Resolved that Isaac Ostrander be liberated from his Confinement on entering into a recognizance for his good Behaviour doing his duty and appearing before any three of the Commissioners for Conspiracies when thereunto required during the Continuance of the present war with Great Britain —

Isaac Ostrander of the Hellebergh Farmer in.. £100
John Waley of the west District of the Manor
of Rensselaerwyck Farmer his Bail in..... £100

Capt Isaac Van Valkenburgh appeared before the Board and informed us that he and William Klauw had became surety before the Commissioners for Conspiracies at Pougkeepsie for John J. Van Valkenburgh and Mathew McCagge who lately came from New York that they the said John J. Van Valkenburgh and Mathew McCagge should in ten days [215] surrender themselves as prisoners to this Board and producing a Certificate of the same from the said Commissioners —

And the said John J. Van Valkenburgh being examin[e]d saith as follows (to wit) (see Examination on file) —

Resolved that the said John J. Van Valkenburgh be permitted to go to Kinderhook on his entering into a recognizance for his good Behaviour doing his duty and appearing before any three of the Commissioners for Conspiracies when thereunto required during the continuance of the present war with Great Britain —

John J. Van Valkenburgh of Kinderhook
Labourer in........................... £500
Jurry Van Valkenburgh of the same place
Farmer his Bail in.................... £500

Also resolved that Mathew M:Cagge be discharged on Peter L. Van Alen of Kinderhook entering into a Recognizance for the said Mathew M:Cagge's good Behaviour doing his duty and appearing before any three of the Commissioners for Conspiracies when thereunto required during the continuance of the present war with Great Britain —

> Peter L. Van Alen of Kinderhook Weaver as
> Bail for Mathew M: Cagge in £500

Adjourned —

Met Albany 5th September 1780
Present

> John M. Beeckman } { Isaac D. Fonda
> Samuel Stringer }

Lieutenant Thomas Ismay appeared before the Board and informed us that Benjamin Van Etten and his son John Van Etten of the Manor of Rensselaerwyck refuse to do [216] any Militia duty and say they will not take up Arms against the King that William Hooghtaling of the same place said he was a Kings man and that he would have nothing to do with the Rebels and that Adrian Bradt is greatly disaffected and that the Persons who are able to prove the above charges are Simeon Viele and Philip Radliff —

Resolved in consequence of the above information that citations be made out and sent to the said Simeon Viele and Philip Radliff commanding their appearance before us at the City Hall on the 7th instant —

The board being also informed that Ensign Ephraim Hudson is able to give information against several disaffected Persons resolved that a letter be wrote to the said Ephraim Hudson requesting his appearance before us as soon as possible —

Resolved that a citation be sent to Mrs Catharine Burlingham to appear before us on the 7th instant to give information respecting the conduct of several of the inhabitants of
New Scotland —

John Broachim who was on the 10th August last liberated
from Confinement appeared before the Board with David
Kittle as his surety —

Resolved that Ryer Schermerhorn and Johannis Weller
his former Bails be and they are hereby discharged and that
the said John Broachim enter into recognizance anew with the
said David Kittle as his surety for his good Behaviour doing
his duty & appearing before any three of the Commissioners
for Conspiracies when thereunto required [217] during the
continuance of the present was with Great Britain —

John Broachim of the District of Schenectady
    Farmer in............................ £200
David Kittle of the same place Farmer his
    Bail in £200
Adjourned —

Met Albany 6th September 1780

Present

John M. Beeckman } { Samuel Stringer
Isaac D. Fonda   } {

John Johnson of the State of Connecticut appeared before
the Board and laid before us a letter from Col^l William B.
Whiting of Kings District wherein the said Col^l Whiting
request's that Samuel Johnson who was the other day confined by Mathew Adgate Esqr for dissuading the inhabitants
of this State to take up Arms in defence of the Country may
be delivered over to the said John Johnson his Brother as he
beleives from the former character of the said Samuel John-

son that he is at present Insane   And that the said John Johnson producing also a letter from the said Mathew Adgate Esq? to this Board advising compliance with the above request —

Resolved in consequence of the above Letters that the said Samuel Johnson be delivered over to the said John Johnson and that he be cautioned against coming in this State whilst he persists in inculcating such dangerous and destructive Principles —

Resolved that the Secretary pay to Jesse Fairchilds[1] the sum of £162 — 16   Continental Money on account —

Hendrick Merkle appeared before the Board according to our order to enter into anew Recognizance —

[218] Resolved that he enter into the same for his good behaviour doing his duty and appearing before any three of the Commissioners for Conspiracies when thereunto required during the continuance of the present war with Great Britain —

> Hendrick Merkle of Tryon County Farmer in. £100
> John Roff of the City of Albany Merchant
>   his Bail in............................ £100

Adjourned —

Met Albany 7th September 1780
                Present

        John M. Beeckman }   { Isaac D. Fonda
        Mathew Visscher   }   { Samuel Stringer

Siemon Viele appeared before the Board according to our order of the 5th instant and was examined his examination is in the words following (to wit)   (see examination on file)

[1] He signed his name "Fairchild". See note under date of September 12, 1780.

Catharine Bullingham and Philip Radliff being also on the 5th instant cited to appear before the Board appeared and were examined their Examination's are as follows (to wit) (see examinations on file)

John Armstrong who was some time since confined by Col! Henry K. Van Rensselaer was brought before the Board —

Resolved that (agreeable to the request of the said Col! Rensselaer) the said John Armstrong be liberated from confinement on his entering into a recognizance for his future good behaviour doing his duty and appearing before any three of the Commissioners for Conspiracies [219] when thereunto required during the continuance of the present war with Great Britain —

John Armstrong of the East District of the
Manor of Rensselaerwyck Weaver in..... £100
John E. Lansing of the same place Farmer his
Bail in............................. £100

Adjourned —

Met Albany 8th September 1780

Present

| John M. Beeckman | } | { | Isaac D. Fonda |
| Mathew Visscher | | | Samuel Stringer |

Resolved that Jacob Ball Jun.r of the Bever Dam be discharged from confinement on entering into a recognizance for his good behaviour doing his duty and appearing before any three of the Commissioners for Conspiracies when thereunto required during the continuance of the present war with Great Britain —

Jacob Ball Jun.r of the Bever Dam Farmer in £100
Peter Man Jun.r of Schohary Farmer his Bail
in £100

Resolved also that John Ball Junr be discharged from confinement on entering into a Recognizance for his good behaviour doing his duty & appearing before any three of the Commissioners for Conspiracies when called upon during the continuance of the present war with Great Britain —

> John Ball Junr of the Bever Dam Labourer in £100
> William Man of Schohary Farmer his Bail in £100

Adjourned —

[220]   Met Albany 11th September 1780

Present

John M. Beeckman } { Mathew Visscher
Isaac D Fonda   } { Samuel Stringer

Resolved that George Rodgers be discharged from confinement on entering into a recognizance with a sufficient surety for his good behaviour doing his duty and appearing before any three of the Commissioners for Conspiracies when called upon during the continuance of the present war with Great Britain —

> George Rodgers of the City of Albany Weaver
> in £100
> Henry Van Wie of the same place Carpenter
> his Bail in........................... £100

Resolved that Mathias Rose, William Rodgers, John Stiles, Robert Brisben, and John McDole be severally cited to appear before this Board on the 24th day of September instant with sufficient sureties to enter into new recognizance's

A Letter directed to this Board from Capt Isaac Van Valkenburgh dated the 9th instant was laid before us wherein he requests a Certificate of John Van Valkenburgh's having entered into a recognizance before us for his good behaviour and appearance before us when called upon in order that 1780 Sept. 11. the said Isaac Van Valkenburgh may by producing the said certificate be enabled to get the Effects taken from him when he came from New York and which were detained by a Justice of the peace residing at Crompon in Dutchess County —

Resolved that in compliance with the above request a certificate be made out and transmitted to the [221] said Capt Van Valkenburgh —

Adjourned —

Met Albany 12th September 1780 1780 Sept. 12.

Present

John M. Beeckman } } Samuel Stringer
Mathew Visscher }

Resolved that Christopher Hutt be liberated from confinement on entering into a Recognizance for his good behaviour doing his duty and appearing before any three of the Commissioners for Conspiracies when thereunto required during the continuance of the present war with Great Britain —

Christopher Hutt of the west District of the
Manor of Rensselaerwyck Farmer in..... £100
William Monk of the Hellebergh Farmer his
Bail in £100

Resolved that the Secretary pay to Jesse Fairchild the sum of 282£ 16^s on account of services performed for this Board —[1]

Adjourned —

[1] The item ordered paid, on September 6, amounting to £162 „ 16s., and the above amount, making together the sum of £445 „ 12s., were paid together. The original voucher is in *Revolutionary Manuscripts*, vol. 40, p. 172, State Comptroller's Office.

                    Met Albany 13ᵗʰ September 1780
          Present
            John M. Beeckman ⎱ ⎰ Samuel Stringer
            Mathew Visscher ⎰ ⎱

Thomas Blewer having been committed to Goal by Colᴸ
Henry K. Van Rensselaer was brought before the Board
Resolved that he be liberated from Confinement on entering into a recognizance with a sufficient surety for his
good behaviour doing his duty & appearing before any
three of the Commissioners for Conspiracies when thereunto required during the Continuance of the present war
with Great Britain —

> [222] Thomas Blewer of the East District of
>   the Manor of Rensselaerwyck Farmer in . £100
>   David Groesbeeck of the City of Albany
>   Cordwainer his Bail in................ £100

Adjourned —

                    Met Albany 15ᵗʰ September 1780 —
          Present
            John M. Beeckman ⎱ ⎰ Samuel Stringer
            Isaac D. Fonda   ⎰ ⎱

William Klaw of Kline Kill appeared before the Board
and informed us that there is at present at Kinderhook a
certain woman who has lately been to New York that from
every circumstance there is the greatest reason to suppose
that she has been sent there by certain Tories at Kinderhook for the purpose of obtaining intelligence and it being
highly necessary that this Matter should be enquired into
and properly investigated —
Therefore Resolved that a Letter be wrote to Major Isaac

Goes requesting him to have the said woman apprehended and brought before him and to examine her as to the Names of the persons who sent her to New York and to send the said persons together with the said woman forthwith to us —

A Certificate dated 13th instant signed by John L. Bronk and Philip Conine Esq[rs] was laid before the Board wherein the[y] set forth that aggreeable to a Law of this State Entitled an Act for the removal of the Families " of persons who have joined the Enemy" they have warned the following persons to remove out of this State or to such parts of it as [223] are within the power of the enemy within twenty days from the date of the said Certificate Viz[t] Rachel Halenbeeck the wife of Casper P. Halenbeeck, Maria Jansen the wife of Johannis Jansen, Margaret Riemer the wife of Johannis Riemer, Maria Eckler the wife of William Eckleer, Engeltie Schram the wife of Frederick Schram and Cornelia Danials the wife of Dirck Danials, ordered that the said Certificate be filed —

A Certificate dated 9th September signed by Samuel Van Veghten Esq[r] one of the Justices of the peace for the County of Albany was laid before the Board wherein he sets forth that agreeable to the last mentioned act of the Legislature he has warned the following persons to remove out of this State or to such parts of it as are in the power of the enemy Viz[t] Catharine Dies the wife of Jacob Dies, Eva Dies the wife of Mathew Dies, Mary Van Garde the wife of Benjamin Van Garde, Elizabeth Lampman the wife of Wilhelmas Lampman, Gertruyd Dewitt the wife of Evert Dewitt, Jakemyntie Williams the wife of Frederick Williams, Jane Picksen the wife of John Picksen and Jane Straight the wife of Thomas Straight —

Adjourned —

                    Met Albany 16ᵗʰ September 1780
            Present

            John M. Beeckman ⎫   ⎰ Samuel Stringer
            Isaac D. Fonda   ⎭   ⎱ Mathew Visscher

James Parks who came from the enemy last spring having been apprehended was brought before the Board on
being Examined he saith as follows (to wit) (see Examination on file)

[224] Resolved that the said James Parks be confined and
that a mittimus be made out for him —

Johan Jurie Fought appearing according to our order to
enter into anew recognizance —

Resolved that he enter into the same for his good behaviour
doing his duty and appearing before any three of the Commissioners for Conspiracies when thereunto required during
the continuance of the present war with Great Britain —

    Johan Jurie Fought of Lonenburgh in the
        District of Coxsakie Farmer in.......... £100
    Sylvester Salsbury of the County of Albany
        Farmer his Bail in..................... £100

Resolved that an order be made out directed to Amos
Lucas forthwith to deliver up to this Board William Tyler
for whose appearance when called upon he became surety —

Resolved that citations be sent to John Wans, William
Jackson, Andrian Bradt, Benjamin Van Etten, and William
Hooghteling to appear before this Board on the 19ᵗʰ day of
September instant —

Also Resolved that a citation be sent to Dꭇ Thompson of
Livi[n]gston's Manor to appear before this Board on or before the first day of October next —

The board having received information that Major Zadock
Wright is at present with his Family in Cumberland County —

Resolved that a letter be wrote to Moses Wright (who entered into a bond to deliver up the said Zadock Wright [225] when called upon) forthwith to bring before the Board the said Zadock Wright —

Adjourned —

Met Albany 18th September 1780

Present

John M. Beeckman } { Samuel Stringer
Mathew Visscher }

Agreeable to the citation sent to Doctor Thompson on the 16th instant he appeared resolved that the said Dr Thompson be committed and that a Mittimus be made out to the Goaler to take him into his custody and closely confine him —

Cornelia Danials appeared before the Board and informed us that her Husband Dirck Danials had about four years ago gone off to the Enemy and that agreeable to a late Law John L. Bronk & Philip Conine Esq^{rs} two of the [Justices] of the Peace for this County had ordered her to leave this State or remove to such parts of it as are in the Power of the enemy And the said Cornelia Danials laying before the Board a Recommendation from the said Justices setting forth that she has always behaved herself in an unexceptionable Manner and recommending it to the Board to grant her a Permit to remain at her Habitation —

Resolved in Consequence of the said recommendation that a Permit be granted her accordingly —

John Stiles having been ordered to appear before the Board to enter into a new Recognizance appeared pursuant to the said Order —

Resolved that he enter into the same with a sufficient

surety for his good behaviour doing his duty and [226] appearing before any three of the Commissioners for Conspiracies when called upon during the continuance of the present war with Great Britain —

John Stiles of Palmertown in the County of
Albany Farmer in...................... £100
James Eldrige of Saragtoga in the County
aforesaid Farmer his Bail in............ £100

Seth Perry appeared before the Board and informed us that James Starks, Ephraim Knowlton & Philip Philips are endeavouring daily to instil into the minds of weak and ignorant people a persuasion that it is contrary to Scripture to take up Arms in defence of the Country and are otherwise by their conduct and conversation giving Offence to the friends of the American cause —

It is therefore resolved that the said James Starks, Ephraim Knowlton, and Philip Philips be cited to appear before this Board on Wednesday the 27$\underline{th}$ day of September instant to answer the above complaint and that the said Seth Perry be ordered to produce Witnesses in support of the said charge on that day —

Adjourned —

Met Albany 19$\underline{th}$ September 1780
                    Present

John M. Beeckman   }   { Isaac D. Fonda
Jeremiah Van Rensselaer }

Adrian Bradt, Benjamin Van Etten and William Jackson, having been cited to appear before this Board appeared —

Resolved on consideration of the charges alledged against them respectively that they be committed and that a [227] mittimus be made out directed to the Goaler to take them into his custody and safely keep them untill discharged by any three of the Commissioners for Conspiracies —

James Starke having been accused by Seth Perry and others with being a person disaffected to the American cause appeared before the board and requested that he might be permitted to bring Evidences before us to invalidate the said Charge whereupon resolved that the secretary to this Board furnish the said James Starke with citations for such persons as the said James Starke may think necessary to produce to disprove the said Charge —

Adjourned —

Met Albany 20<u>th</u> September 1780
Present

John M. Beeckman } { Samuel Stringer
Mathew Visscher } { Isaac D. Fonda

John M:Dole having been heretofore bound by recognizance appeared this day according to the order of this Board Resolved that he enter into Recognizance of anew with a sufficient surety for his future good behaviour doing his duty and appearing before any three of the Commissioners for Conspiracies when called upon during the continuance of the present war with Great Britain —

John M:Dole of Saragtoga in the County of
    Albany Farmer in..................... £100
John Mahoney of the same place Farmer his
    Bail in............................ £100

Daniel B. Bradt Esq<u>r</u> Supervisor for the District of Hosick in this County Certified to the Board that he had agreeable to the Law for the Removal of Families of Persons who have [228] gone off and joined the Enemy warned the following Weomen to depart the State or remove to such parts of it as are in the power of the enemy in twenty days from the time of such Notification (to wit) Rebecca Ruyter, Sarah Cammeron, Catharina Best, Elizabeth Ruyter, Hannah Simpson, Elizabeth Letcher, Ariantie Wies, Maria Young & Susannah Lantman —

A Certificate signed by Daniel B. Bradt, John Randell, and a Number of other Persons residing in Hosick District was laid before the Board wherein they set forth that Susannah Lantman and Maria Young whose Husbands are gone to the enemy and who have been lately notified to leave the State are desirous of remaining at their Habitations —

Resolved on considering the subject of the said Certificate that this Board can in no wise agree to grant Permits to the said Susannah Lantman & Maria Young for the above Purpose —

Adjourned —

         Met Albany 21ˢᵗ September 1780
        Present

| John M. Beeckman | | Isaac D. Fonda |
| Jeremiah Van Rensselaer | | Samuel Stringer |

The Board having received information that William Shanklin formerly an inhabitant of Cherry Valley and now residing in the East District of the Manor of Rensselaerwyck is a person who has always professed Principles Inimical to the American cause and who has at the destruction of Cherry Valley by the Indians assisted the Enemy in plundering and robbing the well affected [229] Inhabitants and the same having been attested to by John Willson and James Scott also formerly residing at Cherry Valley —

It is therefore resolved that the said William Shanklin be forthwith apprehended and confined and that a warrant be made out for that Purpose —

A Letter directed to this [Board] dated 19ᵗʰ instant from Johannis Lawyer and William Dietz Esqʳˢ two of the Justices of the Peace of this County was read setting forth that Sarah Zimmer of Schohary has agreeable to the Law for the Removal of the Families of persons who have gone over to the Enemy been warned to leave the State or remove to Such parts of it as are in the Power of the enemy and she is desirous of remaining at Home and having always conducted herself in an unexceptionable manner they request that Permission may be granted her for that Purpose —

1780
Sept. 21.

Resolved that the subject of the above Letter be taken into Consideration till to morrow —

Adjourned —

Met Albany 22nd September 1780

1780
Sept. 22.

Present

John M. Beeckman } { Mathew Visscher
Jeremiah Van Rensselaer } { Samuel Stringer

Noah Pain Esqr one of the Justices of the peace for the County of Charlotte appeared before the Board and laid before us several Examinations taken by him respecting Thomas Yarns and others now here confined in Goal which Examination's are in the following words (to wit) (see examinations on file) —

[230] The Board taking into consideration the Letter received from Johannis Lawyer and William Dietz Esq.^{rs} respecting Sarah Zimmer do resolve that a Permit be granted to the said Sarah Zimmer to remain at her Habitation —

Adjourned —

Met Albany 23^d September 1780

1780
Sept. 23.

Present

John M. Beeckman } { Mathew Visscher
Jeremiah Van Rensselaer } { Samuel Stringer

Resolved that Benjamin Van Etten be discharged from

Confinement on entering into a recognizance for his future
good Behaviour, doing his duty and appearing before any
three of the Commissioners for Conspiracies when thereunto required during the continuance of the present war
with Great Britain —

> Benjamin Van Etten of the West District of
> the Manor of Rensselaerwyck Farmer in.. £100
> Jacob Roseboom of the City of Albany Gen-
> tleman his Bail in.................... £100

Also resolved that Adrian Bradt be discharged from confinement on entering into a recognizance with a sufficient
surety for his good Behaviour doing his duty and appearing
before any three of the Commissioners for Conspiracies
when thereunto required during the continuance of the
present war with Great Britain —

> Adrian Bradt of the west District of the
> Manor of Rensselaerwyck Farmer in..... £100
> John Radliff of the City of Albany Carpenter
> his Bail in............................ £50
> Rykert Van Sante of the same place Car-
> penter also his Bail in................. £50

[231]   Resolved that William Jackson be discharged from
Confinement on entering into a recognizance with a sufficient surety for his good Behaviour doing his duty and appearing before any three of the Commissioners for Conspiracies when thereunto required during the continuance
of the present war with Great Britain —

> William Jackson of New Scotland in the west
> District of the Manor of Rensselaerwyck
> Farmer in............................. £100
> Mathew Watson of the City of Albany Mer-
> chant his Bail in £100

D.ʳ Thompson made application to the Board to be lib- 1780 Sept. 23. erated from confinement on account of the Illness of his wife and the distressed Situation of his Family and he producing an Affidavit of Jacob Power as to the truth of the above —

Resolved on the consideration thereof that the said Thomas Thompson be discharged from his confinement on entering into a recognizance with sufficient sureties for his appearance at the next Supream Court of Judicature to be held at the City Hall in this City on the third Tuesday in October next to answer to such charges as shall then and there be alledged against [him] and not to depart the Court without Leave and for his good behaviour in the mean time —

Thomas Thompson of the Manor of Livingston Physician in £500
Coenradt Rosman of the same place Farmer
  his Bail in £250
John Shuts of the same place Farmer also
  his Bail in........................... £250

Adjourned —

[232]   Met Albany 24.ᵗʰ September 1780   1780 Sept. 24.
  Present
    John M. Beeckman   ⎱ ⎰ Mathew Visscher
    Jeremiah Van Rensselaer ⎰ ⎱ Samuel Stringer

A Letter was laid before the Board dated the 23ᵈ Instant signed by Seth Perry, Samuel Hill and other well affected persons setting forth that Numbers of the Torys in New Bethlehem in the Manor of Rensselaerwyck are collecting in the night time and that there is great reason to suppose unless timely prevented they may injure some of the friends to

**1780
Sept. 24.** the American cause and requesting that a warrant may be granted for the Apprehension of the said persons —

On taking the subject of the above letter into consideration It is resolved that a warrant be made out directed to Seth Perry to apprehend all such disaffected persons as are above complained of and forthwith bring them before us —

Adjourned —

**1780
Sept. 25.**

Met Albany 25th September 1780

Present

Jeremiah Van Rensselaer ⎱   ⎰ Isaac D. Fonda
John M. Beeckman   ⎰   ⎱ Samuel Stringer

The Board having received information that Capt Isaac Lansing is able to give some material information against James Legrange of this City it is therefore ordered that the said Isaac Lansing be requested to attend this Board immediately —

Robert Brisben having been heretofore bound by [233] Recognizance appeared before us according to our order to enter into Recognizance of anew —

Resolved that he enter into the same with a sufficient surety for his good Behaviour doing his duty and appearing before any three of the Commissioners for Conspiracies when thereunto required during the continuance of the present war with Great Britain —

Robert Brisben of Saragtoga Farmer in..... £100
Jonathan Pettit of the City of Albany Cordwainer his Bail in £100

Isaac Lansing appearing according to our order was examined and his Examination is in the following words (to wit) (see examination on the file) —

Resolved in consequence of the said Examination as the

said James Legrange is under the age of Twenty one Years that he procure some person to become surety for his future good Behaviour —

Arie Legrange appearing before the Board and being willing to become surety for James Legrange It is resolved that he enter into a recognizance for the said James Legrange's future good behaviour doing his duty and appearing before any three of the Commissioners for Conspiracies when called upon during the continuance of the present war with Great Britain —

> Arie Legrange of the City of Albany Merchant
> as Bail for his son James Legrange in.... £100

Resolved that Philip Herwig be requested immediately to furnish this Board with the Crime of John McDorn & that he perticularly ascertain the time when the same was committed —

[234] John Tunnicliff appeared before the Board and requested Permission for himself and John Rawbottom to go to Tryon County for the purpose of seeing his Farm —

Resolved that Permission for that purpose be granted them on Joshua Bloore entering into a Recognizance for their returning within a reasonable Time to this place and behaving themselves during their Absence in a becoming Manner —

> Joshua Bloore of the City of Albany Merchant
> as surety for John Tunnicliff & John Raw-
> bottom in........................... £100

Adjourned —

Met Albany 26th September 1780
Present

| John M. Beeckman | Isaac D. Fonda |
| Samuel Stringer | Mathew Visscher |

1780
Sept. 26.   Lieutenant Ephraim Hudson having been cited to appear before the Board in order to his being examined with respect to sundry persons living at New Scotland appeared and being examined says —

That William Jackson is a person of weight & Influence in the part where he lives that he is certain that the Expresses from the Enemy which pass up & down the Country lodge at his House, that John Burnsides is a Tory and that the Party that robbed Lieu.^t Leonard went from Burnsides House — (See Examination on file) —

John Herrington and Ephraim Knowlton having been apprehended in consequence of a warrant issued on the 24th instant was brought before the Board —

[235] Resolved that they be confined and that a Mittimus be made out to the Goaler to take them into his Custody —

Adjourned —

1780
Sept. 27.   Met Albany 27th September 1780 —

Present

John M. Beeckman }   { Jeremiah Van Rensselaer
Samuel Stringer   }   { Mathew Visscher

The Board proceeded to the Examination of the Charge of disaffection to the American cause Exhibited by Seth Perry against James Starks, Ephraim Knowlton & Philip Philips and in support of the said charge the following persons were examined as witnesses (to wit) Benjamin Valentine, Mrs Skinner, Sarah Barnum, Mary Knowlton, Samuel Hill, Mrs Beagle, Elizabeth Barnum, Jabez Landers and John Lawrence their Examinations are as follows (to wit) (see Examinations of file)

In order to invalidate the charge above alledged the said James Starks requested that the following persons might be examined (to wit) Isaac Lawrence, Richard Lawrence, Mine Lawrence, William Barnum, Jacob Herrington, Lena Herrington, Robert Patrick, Nathaniel Culver, John Salsbury, Dirck Sluyter, & Henry Salsbury which Examination's are in the following words (to wit) (See examination's on the File)

1780
Sept. 27.

Resolved that the consideration of the above Examinations be postponed till to Morrow Morning —

Resolved that a letter be wrote to his Excellency Governor Clinton inclosing a copy of the Letter received from [236] John D. Goes which Letter is in the following words (to wit) (See Letter on the file)[1]

Adjourned —

Met Albany 28ᵗʰ September 1780
Present

1780
Sept. 28.

John M. Beeckman }   { Jeremiah Van Rensselaer
Samuel Stringer }   { Mathew Visscher

As no Particular charge has yet been exhibited against John Herrington therefore resolved that he be discharged from Confinement —

The Board having resumed the consideration of the Examinations Yesterday taken and the charge of disaffection against James Starke appearing to be well founded it is resolved that he enter into Recognizance with sufficient sureties to remain within the Limits of Kings District and not depart the same without leave obtained for that purpose from any three of the Commissioners for Conspiracies (unless it be to do Militia duty) and for his good Behaviour and appearance before any of the said Commissioners for Conspiracies when called upon during the continuance of the present war with Great Britain —

---

[1] In *George Clinton Papers*, no. 3242, and the letter of Goes, no. 3194, archives of New York State Library.

<table>
<tr><td>1780
Sept. 28.</td><td>James Starke of Kings District Labourer in... £100</td></tr>
</table>

1780
Sept. 28.

James Starke of Kings District Labourer in... £100
Nathaniel Culver of the same place Esq.ʳ his
Bail in.............................. £ 50
John Salsbury of the same place Farmer
also his Bail in........................ £ 50

Adjourned —

1780
Oct. 2.

Met Albany 2ⁿᵈ October 1780
Present

John M. Beeckman }
Mathew Visscher }   } Isaac D. Fonda

[237] Samuel Perry of Palmerton having been cited to appear before the Board to enter into a new Recognizance appeared for that purpose with a sufficient surety resolved that he enter into the same for his good behaviour doing his duty and appearing before any three of the Commissioners for Conspiracies when called upon during the continuance of the present war with Great Britain —

Samuel Perry of Palmertown in the District
of Saragtoga Farmer in................ £100
Rowland Perry of the same place Farmer his
Bail in............................... £100

John Perry having also been cited to appear before the Board to enter into a new Recognizance appearing resolved that he enter into the same for his good behaviour doing his duty and appearing before any three of the Commissioners for Conspiracies when called upon during the continuance of the present war with Great Britain —

John Perry of Palmertown in Saragtoga
District Farmer in..................... £100
Rowland Perry of the same place Farmer his
Bail in............................... £100

Adjourned —

Met Albany 3ᵈ October 1780

Present

John M. Beeckman } { Samuel Stringer
Mathew Visscher   } { Isaac D. Fonda

Mathias Rose having been cited to appear before this Board to enter into a new Recognizance appeared for that Purpose with a sufficient surety —

Resolved that he enter into the same for his good behaviour doing his duty and appearing before any three of the [238] Commissioners for Conspiracies when called upon during the Continuance of the present war with Great Britain —

Mathias Rose of Saragtoga District Labourer
   in.................................... £100
Freeman Barligh of the same [place] Farmer
   his Bail in........................... £100

Adjourned —

Met Albany 4ᵗʰ October 1780

Present

John M. Beeckman } { Jeremiah Van Rensselaer
Samuel Stringer   } { Mathew Visscher

A Petition of Ephraim Knowlton was laid before the Board whereby he request's to be released from Confinement and the same being taken into Consideration —

Resolved that he be released accordingly on entering into a recognizance for his good behaviour doing his duty and appearing before any three of the Commissioners for Conspiracies when called upon during the continuance of the present war with Great Britain and also for his appearance at the next Supream Court of Judicature to be held on the third Tuesday in October Instant at the City Hall in this

City (or wheresoever the said Court shall then be held in the State of New York) and not depart the Court without Leave —

> Ephraim Knowlton of the East District of
> the Manor of Rensselaerwyck Farmer in.. £100
> Thomas Knowlton of the same place Farmer
> his Bail in............................ £100
> Robert Patrick of the same place Farmer also
> his Bail in............................ £100

Adjourned —

[239]   Met Albany 5th October 1780

Present

> John M. Beeckman }   { Jeremiah Van Rensselaer
> Samuel Stringer   }

It appearing from the Examination of James Halstead that James Drummond of Nistageune has harboured and secreted Emissaries from the Enemy and has from the Commencement of the present Contest been esteemed as a person disaffected to the American cause —

It is therefore resolved that a citation be made out directed to the said James Drummond to appear before this Board on Saturday the seventh day of October instant to answer the above complaint —

It having been suggested to us that Philip Van Rensselaer Esqr has received a Letter from Coll Richard Varick (who was Aid De Camp to General Arnold at the time he went off to New York) which contains Expressions which would tend to discover some of the persons concerned with Arnold in his Villianous Plot —

It is therefore resolved that the said Philip Van Rensselaer be requested to attend this Board with the said Letter as soon as conveniently may be —

John Tunnicliff to whom a pass was granted by this Board to go to Tryon County appeared and requested that Joshua Bloore who became surety for his Return to this City might be discharged from the Recognizance entered into for him resolved that the said Joshua Bloore be discharged accordingly —

Adjourned —

[240]   Met Albany 6th October 1780

Present

John M. Beeckman } { Isaac D. Fonda
Samuel Stringer   }

The Board having received information that Hans Peter Snyder living on Fishkill at Saragtoga has and still keeps up a Correspondence with the enemy and harbours persons passing through the Country who are coming from the enemy —

It is therefore resolved that a warrant be made out for the immediate apprehension of the said Hans Peter Snyder and that the said warrant be inclosed in a Letter to Col! Cornelius Van Veghten and that he be requested to have the same served —

Abraham Hooghteling who was some time ago confined for having been with Brant and his Party and who broke Goal having been again apprehended was brought before the Board resolved that he be committed —

Adjourned —

Met Albany 7th October 1780

Present

Mathew Visscher } { Isaa[c] D. Fonda
John M. Beeckman } { Samuel Stringer

Nicholas Lake having been heretofore cited to appear before the Board appeared before us this day to enter into a new Recognizance resolved that he enter into the same with a sufficient surety and that he be bound for his good Behaviour, doing his duty, and appearing before any three of the Commissioners for Conspiracies whenever called [241] upon during the continuance of the present war with Great Britain —

Nicholas Lake of Cinkaick in the County of
Albany Farmer in...................... £100
Abraham Schuyler of the City of Albany
Merchant his Bail in £100

A Return signed by John Younglove Esq⁏ was laid before us wherein he specifies that he has agreeable to An Act of the Legislature for the Removal of the Families of Persons who have joined [the] enemy ordered the following persons to depart this State or remove to such parts of it as are in the power of the Enemy, (to wit) Elizabeth Hogle the wife of John Hogle, Jane Hogle wife of Francis Hogle and three Children of Simeon Covell ordered that the said return be filed —

Elizabeth Hogle one of the weomen named in the above return made by John Younglove Esq⁏ appeared before the Board and requested Permission to remain at her Habitation assigning as a reason that her Husband was killed at the Battle of Bennington and the same being certified to us by sundry well affected inhabitants of this County and that the said Elizabeth Hogle has since the going away of her Husband behaved herself in a becoming manner —

It is therefore resolved that a permit be granted to the said Elizabeth Hogle for the above purpose —

Resolved that Henry Van Corlaer who was heretofore bound in a recognizance for his good Behaviour and appear-

ance before this Board when called be cited to appear forthwith with a suffi- [242] cient surety to enter into Recognizance
of anew —

A Return signed by John Bebee Esq.ʳ one of the Justices
of the peace for this County was laid before the Board
wherein he specifies that agreeable to an Act of the Legislature of this State entitled an Act for the Removal of the
Families of Persons who have joined the enemy he has warned
the following persons to depart this State or remove to such
parts of it as are in the power of the Enemy, (to wit) Jerusha
Ingram wife of Benjamin Ingram Junʳ, Mary Mᶜ Carty wife
of Duncan Mᶜ Carty, Lucretia Woodward wife of David
Woodward & Abigail Woodward wife of Josiah Woodward –

Lucretia Woodward and Jerush[a] Ingraham two of the
women named in the above return appeared before the Board
and requested Permission to remain at their Habitations and
produced to the Board Certificates from sundry of the well
affected Inhabitants of this County of their good Character
and that their remaining in the Country will not be detrimental to the Freedom & independence of this and the
United States in consequence of which Certificates and
recommendations —

It is resolved that a permit be granted to the said Lucretia Woodward and Jerusha Ingraham —

John Tunnicliff appeared before the Board and requested
Permission to go to Tryon County in Search of some Horses
and other Effects that were unjustly taken from him and
converted to the Private use of several Individuals in the
said County —

Resolved that agreeable to the said request [243] the
said John Tunnicliff have Permission granted him to go to
Tryon County in search of the said Horses and Effects —

Captain Jarvis Mudge appeared before the Board & re-

1780
Oct. 7.

quested that his son in Law David Darrow now here confined in Goal may be liberated from his confinement on
account of the Illness of his wife —

Resolved in consequence of the said Application that the
said David Darrow have Permission to go and see his wife
on his entering into a Recognizance for his Surrendering
himself up to this Board as a prisoner on or before the 28th
Instant and for his good and peaceable Behaviour during
that time —

David Darrow of New Lebanon Kings Dis-
trict Farmer in........................ £100
Jarvis Mudge of the same place Farmer his
Bail in............................... £100

Adjourned —

1780
Oct. 8.

Met Albany 8th October 1780
Present

John M. Beeckman ⎱   ⎰ Samuel Stringer
Mathew Visscher   ⎰   ⎱

John Drummond having been adjudged a person of a
Suspicious Character and dangerous to the safety of the
State and being [sic] in consequence thereof been ordered
to appear before this Board and he appearing this day and
being charged with the above and denying the same but at
the same time professing his principles in Favour of the
Crown of Great Britain and declaring his intention of not
taking up Arms in Defence of the American Cause —

Therefore resolved that he be committed and that a Mittimus be made out for him —

[244] Cornelius Viele appeared and requested that the
above mentioned John Drummond might on account of the
distressed situation of his Family be permitted to go Home

for a few days and the said Cornelius Viele being an approved friend to the Country —

Therefore resolved that his Request be complied with
and that the said John Drummond have Permission to return home and surrendering himself as a Prisoner to this
Board on or before the 11ᵗʰ instant and in the mean time
be of the good Behaviour —

John Drummond of Nistageune in the County
of Albany Farmer in.................. £100
Cornelius Viele of the same place Farmer his
Bail in £100

Adjourned —

Met Albany 9ᵗʰ October 1780 —
Present

John M. Beeckman ⎞ ⎰ Samuel Stringer
Isaac D. Fonda   ⎠ ⎱ Mathew Visscher

Isabel Clark of Cooksborough appeared before the Board
and laid before us a Certificate signed by Lieuᵗ Jacob Halenbeeck and a number of other well affected Inhabitants of
this County setting forth that the said Isabel Clark has
received an order from a Justice of the Peace to depart
the State or remove to such parts of it as are in the Power
of the Enemy in consequence of her Husband's having gone
off to the Enemy and they further Certify that the said Isabel
Clark has always behaved herself in a peaceable and quiet Manner and that they do not conceive that her [245] remaining in
the Country will in any wise prove dangerous or detrimental to
the Freedom and Independance of this and the United States—

It is therefore resolved that a Permit be made out for the
said Isabel Clark to remain at her Habitation unmolested —

Adjourned —

Met Albany 10th October 1780

Present

John M. Beeckman ⎱   ⎰ Isaac D. Fonda
Mathew Visscher ⎰   ⎱ Samuel Stringer

Peter Smith of the Manor of Rensselaerwyck appeared before the Board and informed us that he had received in Payment from Melchert File three fifty Dollar Bills Continental Money which on being inspected were found counterfeit and it appearing probable to this Board that the said Counterfeit money is circulated through the State by some of the disaffected Inhabitants with a view of embarrassing the public Operations and it being highly necessary that an Enquiry should be made into the same therefore resolved in Consequence of the said Information that the said Peter Smith be bound in a Recognizance to appear at the next Supream Court to be held on the third Tuesday in October Instant to give Evidence with Respect to the said Counterfeit Bills —

Peter Smith of the East District of the Manor
of Rensselaerwyck Farmer in £100

Philip Coenradt having also received Counterfeit Bills from the said Melchert File —

Resolved that he also enter into a Recognizance [246] to appear at the next Supream Court to give Evidence against the said Melchert File —

Philip Coenradt of the East District of
Manor of Rensselaerwyck Farmer in. £100

Resolved in Consequence of the above information of Peter Smith and Philip Coenradt that Melchert File be ordered to attend this Board on Tuesday the 17th Day of October Instant —

The Board having received Information that Ryneir

Vischer of this City has received in Payment Counterfeit Continental Money and he having been sent for and appearing with the said Money and informed us he had received the same from Isacher Childs —

Isacher Childs being sent for and examined with Respect to the said Counterfeit Money says that he received the same from a certain Johnson —

Johnson being sent for and not being able to inform us where he received the same resolved that he be informed that this Board do insist on knowing where and from whom he received the same —

Application was made to this Board for a Permit to Mrs Edgar to go to Canada —

Resolved that Mrs Edgar be informed that this Board are not authorized to grant Permits for that purpose —

Adjourned —

Met Albany 11th October 1780 —

Present

John M. Beeckman ⎱ ⎰ Isaac D. Fonda
Mathew Visscher ⎰ ⎱

[247] Application was made to the Board by Major Reed for a Permit for Doctor George Smith to go With his Family to Canada —

Resolved that Major Reed be informed that this Board are not vested with a power to grant Permits of that nature but that we have no Objections to Dr Smith's going provided he can obtain his Excellency the Governor's Permission —[1]

---

[1] The Albany board advised Dr. Smith or Smyth, in a letter of this date that it had no objection to his obtaining a pass to Canada, provided it was allowed by Colonel W. Malcolm, commanding the northern department, and Malcolm actually gave the pass on the 13th The minutes of October 17 and 18 show that the board vitiated this pass and put Smith under a recognizance and bail, limiting him " to remain within the Limits of his dwelling

1780
Oct. 11. A Petition signed by Wilhelmas Van Antwerp Esqr Justice of the peace and a number of other well affected Inhabitants of Nistageune was laid before the Board, setting forth that Margaret McCulpin in Consequence of her Husband's having gone off to the Enemy has been ordered to depart this State or remove to such Parts of it as are in the Power of the Enemy and praying (on Account of the unexceptionable Character of the said Margaret McCulpin) that she may be permitted to remain at he[r] Habitation unmolested —

Resolved in Consequence of the above Petition that a Permit be granted to the said Margaret McCulpin for the purpose above mentioned —

Abraham Hoogteling at present in Confinement was ordered to be brought before the Board and examined & then recommitted —

Adjourned —

1780
Oct. 14.

Met Albany 14th October 1780 —
Present

John M. Beeckman }
Isaac D. Fonda } { Samuel Stringer

John Kluck having been confined for being disaffected to the American cause and deemed dangerous to the [248] safety of the safety[1] [state] was brought before the Board and we judging his Confinement to have been sufficiently long and he offering good Bail for his future good Conduct —

House and Yard and not to depart the same ". On October 26, Smith appealed to Governor Clinton, stated his plight and averred that the change of base must have been inspired by some private enemy of his in the board.— *George Clinton Papers*, nos. 3263, 3311, archives of New York State Library.
[1] Error in the original manuscript.

Therefore resolved that he be liberated from Confinement on his entering into Recognizance for his good Behaviour doing his duty and appearing before any three of the Commissioners for Conspiracies when called upon during the Continuance of the present war with Great Britain —

1780
Oct. 14.

John Kluck of the Manor of Rensselaerwyck
Potter in.............................. £100
John Horn of the same place Butcher his
Bail in.............................. £100

Cap! John Decker Robison having been ordered to deliver up John Smith to this Board agreeable to the Tenor of his Recognizance appeared with the said John Smith resolved that as the said Smith is indicted for a Robbery committed at Frederick Berringer's that he be committed in order that he may be tried —

Adjourned —

Met Albany 15th October 1780

1780
Oct. 15.

Present

John M. Beeckman } { Isaac D. Fonda
Mathew Visscher }

Whereas this Board has received Information that Col! Malcolm the Commanding Officer in this place has granted Permission to Dr. George Smith with his Family and Mrs Edgar to go to Canada and the present time being adjudged very improper by this Board to permit the said persons to go on account of the Enemy's being on the Frontiers —

It is therefore resolved that it be recommended to [249] Col¹ Malcolm to detain the said Doctor Smith and Mrs Edgar untill their going can be no way Prejudicial —

Adjourned —

Met Albany 16ᵗʰ October 1780

Present

John M. Beeckman }   { Samuel Stringer
Mathew Visscher   }   { Isaac D. Fonda —

Resolved that Susannah Parie, John Barney and Nancy Thompson who this Board has been informed are able to prove several charges alledged against Angus M̄c Donald and Dr Thomas Thompson be severally cited to appear before us forthwith that they may be examined —

John Van Valkenburgh who lately left the Enemy at New York and who is at present an Kinderhook being able to give some very material information respecting sundry inhabitants of this County now with the Enemy whereby the Grand Jury will be able to proceed against them agreeable to the Confiscation Law it is therefore resolved that he be cited to appear at the next Supream Court to be held on the third Tuesday in October instant —

Christian Smith of the East District of the Manor of Rensselaerwyck being able to prove that John Smith was concerned in the Robbery committed on Frederick Berringer it is therefore resolved that he be cited also to appear at the next Supream Court —

The Board having received information from Catharine Burlingham that Alexander Keerklaer of New Scotland has harboured and concealed Joseph Bettis an Emissary from the [250] Enemy resolved in Consequence of the said Information that the said Alexander Kerklaer be ordered forthwith to appear before us to answer the above charge —

Adjourned —

Met Albany 17th October 1780.
Present

John M. Beeckman }   { Mathew Visscher
Samuel Stringer   }   { Isaac D. Fonda

A Letter from Doctor George Smith was laid before the Board wherein he informs us that he has thought proper to remove from this place to Fort Edward and the said Doctor Smith having received express orders from this Board on no pretence to leave the City —[1]

It is therefore resolved that a warrant be made out directed to John Tillman Junr for the Apprehension of the said Dr Smith and his son Terence Smith —

Israel Smith of Brattleborough in the County of Cumberland laid before the Board a Letter from Col.^l Eleazer Patterson directed to his Excellency Governor Clinton by whom the said Letter was referred to this Board which Letter is in the words following (to wit) (See letter on File)

It appearing from the Contents of the above Letter and also from the Information of the said Israel Smith that Timothy Church, Comfort Joy and Jonathan Mills Church have held a Correspondence and kept up an Intercourse with a certain Oliver Church now an Officer in the British Army —

It is therefore resolved that a warrant be made out for the immediate apprehension of the said Timothy [251] Church, Comfort Joy and Jonathan Mills Church and that the said warrant be inclosed in a Letter to Col.^l Paterson —

Resolved also that a citation be made out to Lieutenant Joathan Church to appear before the Board forthwith in order that he may be examined as to the above —

Adjourned —

[1] Cf. the note under October 11th

Met Albany 18th October 1780

Present

John M. Beeckman ⎱　　⎰ Mathew Visscher
Samuel Stringer ⎰　　⎱ Isaac D. Fonda

Col! Henry K. Van Rensselaer appeared before the Board and informed that Nicholas Williams of the Eas[t] District of the Manor of Rensselaerwyck has lately entertained in his house his son who was on his way from New York to Canada as an Express —

Resolved in Consequence of the above Information that a warrant be made out for the Apprehension of the said Nicholas Williams and that Col! Rensselaer be requested to procure a person to serve the same —

There being the greatest reason to suspect from Dr Smith's present conduct that he is endeavoring to mislead the minds of weak and ignorant People it is therefore resolved that he be sent for —

Doctor Smith appearing and being examined resolved in order to prevent such Conduct in future that he enter into Recognizance to remain within the Limits of his dwelling House and Yard and not depart the same and that he do not hold any Correspondence either by word or Deed upon [252] Political Matters with any Person or Persons inimical to the American cause which may tend to the Prejudice of this or the United States of America, and appear before any three of the Commissioners for Conspiracies when called upon that he shall remain under these Restrictions during the continuance of the present war with Great Britain unless sooner discharged —

George Smith of the City of Albany Physician
in £300
Thomas Reed of the same place Gentleman
his Bail in........................... £300

Adjourned

Met Albany 19ᵗʰ October 1780
Present

John M. Beeckman ⎱   ⎰ Mathew Visscher
Samuel Stringer   ⎰   ⎱ Isaac D. Fonda

The Board having received information that the Reverend
Samuel Swertfeger does frequently go to the Hellebergh under
a Pretence of preaching the Gospel but in fact to inculcate
Doctrines tending to disaffect the minds of well disposed
Persons and he being at present in this City it is therefore
resolved that he be sent for —

The said Samuel Swertfeger appearing it is resolved that
he enter into Recognizance with a sufficient surety for his
good behaviour and appearing before any three of the Commissioners for Conspiracies when thereunto required & that
he do not depart the Limits of the District in which he at
present resides unless it be to preach the Gospel to the
different Congregations in whose Employ he at present is
and that he do not mislead the minds of his Heerors by inculcating Principles inconsistant with the Freedom and
Independ- [253] ance of this and the United States —

Samuel Swertfeger of the East District of
    the Manor of Rensselaerwyck Clerk...... £100
William Zoble of the City of Albany Tobaco-
    nist his Bail in £100

A Letter from Major Dickison at Stillwater dated the
18ᵗʰ Instant was laid before the Board wherein he informs
us that he has apprehended and sends to us under Guard a
certain Person who calls himself John Mᶜ Mullin who he suspects to be a spy from the Enemy, and the said John Mᶜ-
Mullin being brought before the Board and examined thereupon resolved that he be committed and that a Mittimus be
made out for him —

1780
Oct. 19.

The above mentioned John M.ͨ Mullin having in the Course of his Examination mentioned the Names of several Persons at whose houses he was secreted and harboured on his way into the Country and among others Patrick Ryan of the Green Island in the Manor of Rensselaerwyck therefore resolved that a warrant be made out for the immediate apprehension of the said Patrick Ryan.

Resolved that a Letter be wrote to General Schuyler at Saragtoga informing him of the Purport of M.ͨ Mullins Examination —

Adjourned —

1780
Oct. 20.

Met Albany 20ᵗʰ October 1780
Present

John M. Beeckman ⎱ ⎰ Mathew Visscher
Samuel Stringer   ⎰ ⎱ Isaac D. Fonda

Patrick Ryan for whose apprehension a warrant [254] was Yesterday made out was brought before the Board on being examined he denies having seen John M.ͨ Mullen at his house —

Whereupon ordered that the said John M.ͨ Mullen be brought before us —

The said John M.ͨ Mullen being interrogated as to the charge by him alledged against the said Patrick Ryan confesses that the said Patrick Ryan was not at Home during the time he was in his house whereupon resolved that the said Patrick Ryan be discharged and that the said M.ͨ Mullen be recommitted —

The Board having received information that a certain James Ayres at present in this City is endeavouring at this Time to dissuade Persons who are on their way to repel the Incursions of the Enemy to throw down their Arms which dangerous and distructive Principles having a Tendency to subvert the Constitution of the State and the said James Ayres being adjudged in the Opinion of this Board dangerous to the safety and wellfare of the State

Therefore resolved that he be apprehended forthwith and confined —

Adjourned —

Met Albany 21st October 1780

Present

John M. Beeckman } { Isaac D. Fonda
Samuel Stringer   }

The Board having received information that there is at present in this City a certain Person whose conduct and Conversation renders him very suspicious therefore [255] resolved that Jacob Kidney the Door Keeper be ordered to bring the said Person forthwith before the Board.

Jacob Kidney having agreeable to order apprehended the above mentioned person and brought him before us On being examined he says that his Names [*sic*] is James Small and that he is resident in Cambridge District resolved that he be confined untill he prod.ices a Certificate of his Character —

Thomas Bourn a Deserter from Burgoyne's Army and William Allen of New Concord in Kings District having been apprehended as appearing to be of Suspicious Characters and being examined and giving a satisfactory Account of themselves therefore resolved that they be discharged —

Received a Letter from Peter Cantine Esqr wherein he informs us that he sends under Guard Hendrick Blunt, Hendrick Bonistel, and Petrus Bonistel who are Persons that are disaffected to the American Cause and whose going at large at this time may be dangerous to the State resolved in consequence of the above Letter that they be severally confined and that a Mittimus be made out for them —

Adjourned —

Met Albany 22nd October 1780 —

Present

John M. Beeckman } { Jeremiah Van Rensselaer
Samuel Stringer } { Isaac D. Fonda
Mathew Visscher }

A Letter from the Honorable Major General [256] Schuyler was laid before the Board wherein he informs us that he sends under Guard Hans Peter Snyder and James Brisben Inhabitants of Saragtoga District for Harbouring concealing and forwarding into the Country Spy's sent from the Enemy, and also James Van Driesen who has come from the Enemy in the Character of a Spy. resolved that they be severally committed and that a Mittimus for that purpose be made out —

Thomas Griffiths and Robert Reynolds two of Sir John Johnson's party were brought before the Board on being Examined they say they are Deserters from the Enemy resolved that they be detained untill the Board are better satisfied as to their Characters —

Adjourned --

Met Albany 23^{d} October 1780

Present

John M. Beeckman } { Samuel Stringer
Mathew Visscher }

A Letter from the Reverend Valentine Rathburn respecting a Number of Persons from New Lebanon at present confined in Goal was laid before the Board which Letter is in the words following (to wit) (see Letter on file) resolved that the Consideration thereof be postponed till a future day —

Thomas Griffiths and Robert Reynolds who were Yesterday examined were again brought before the Board and examined, their Examination's are in the words following (to wit) (see Examinations on file)

James Van Driesen was Also brought before the [257] Board and examined, his Examination is in the words following (to wit) (see Examination on file)

Hans Peter Snyder was also brought before the Board and examined and then ordered to be recommitted

Adjourned —

Met Albany 24th October 1780

Present

John M. Beeckman } { Isaac D. Fonda
Samuel Stringer }

A Negro Man having been sent to Goal by General Schuyler who was apprehended on his way to the Enemy was this day at the request of his Master brought before the Board and being examined says he was persuaded to go off by a certain Man Whose name is Shepherd who is one of the people called Shaking Quakers —

Resolved that the said Negro Man be discharged —

Capt Jacob Van Aernam appeared before the Board and informed us that he had apprehended at the Hellebergh a certain Jacob Schell formerly an Inhabitant of that place but at present a Soldier in Sir John Johnson's Regiment and the said Jacob Schell being examined says that he received Directions from Sir John at the time he left him to inform the inhabitants of the Country that those who did not take up Arms would not be molested in their Persons or Property by the Kings Troops — resolved that he be committed and that a Mittimus be made out for him

Adjourned —

[258]   Met Albany 25ᵗʰ October 1780
Present

John M. Beeckman } { Isaac D. Fonda
Samuel Stringer

At the request of Col! Paine the Board having met proceeded to the Examination of John Mc Mullen his Examination is in the following words (to wit) (see his Examination on File) ordered that he be recommitted —

Jacob Schell and James Van Driesen were also brought before the Board and examined and ordered to be recommitted —

Adjourned —

Met Albany 27ᵗʰ October 1780
Present

John M. Beeckman } { Samuel Stringer
Jeremiah Van Rensselaer } { Isaac D. Fonda

Christian Frihart belonging to Sir John Johnson's Party was brought before the Board and being examined says as follows (to wit) (see Examination on file)

Benjamin Benton also belonging to Sir John's Corps having been taken Prisoner and brought before the Board was also examined his examination is in the words following (to wit) (see Examination on File) —

Adjourned —

Met Albany 28:th October 1780

Present

John M. Beeckman ⎱   ⎰ Isaac D. Fonda
Mathew Visscher ⎰   ⎱

[259] Zepheniah Batchelor Esq.r appeared before the Board with Peter Jost an Inhabitant of Johnstown in Tryon County who he informed us had gone to Sir John at the Destruction of Caughnawaga and the said Peter Jost being examined denies the above Charge and Offers to swear that he was taken a Prisoner and says he is able to prove the same by several creditable Persons and it appearing to us from sundry Circumstances that what has been alledged by the said Peter Jost is true

Therefore resolved that he be discharged —

Major Newkerk of Tryon County appeared before the Board and informed us that among the Prisoners who are ordered down to Fishkill there is a certain [blank] who has always behaved himself as a peaceable subject of this State & has been reputed a Friend to the American Cause that he was last spring taken Prisoner by the Enemy and joined Sir John for no other Purpose than that he might have an Oppertunity of making his Escape, resolved therefore that Col.l Malcolm be requested to detain him —

Adjourned

Met Albany 29.th October 1780

Present

John M. Beeckman ⎱   ⎰ Samuel Stringer
Mathew Visscher ⎰   ⎱

A Letter was laid before the Board from the Hon.ble Major General Schuyler wherein he informs us that he sends to us under Guard two Prisoners named William Vrooman and Henry Tinkey — That the said William Vrooman has aided comforted and assisted a certain James Van [260] Driesen a spy from the Enemy and that the said Henry Tinkey has harboured and assisted John Mc Mullen also a spy from the Enemy —

Resolved that they be severally committed and that a Mittimus be made out for them —

In the above mentioned Letter of General Schuyler mention is also made of a Number of Tory woemen who are at present at Saragtoga and who are desirous of going to Canada resolved that his Excellency the Governor be informed of the same by one of the Members of this Board and that the necessity of their departure be pointed to him —

Adjourned

Met Albany 30th October 1780

Present

| John M. Beeckman | | | Isaac D. Fonda |
| Jeremiah Van Rensselaer | | | Samuel Stringer |

A Letter from Col^l Macolm dated at Schenectady was laid before the Board wherein he informs that he sends to us under Guard two prisoners named Isaac Aerse and Adam Hoofer who were of Sir John Johnson's Party at the time of his destroying the Settlement of Schohary — resolved that they be Examined —

The said Isaac Aerse and Adam Hoofer being examined say as follows — (See their Examination on file) — ordered that they be confined and that a Mittimus be made out for them —

Capt Blackley appeared before the Board and informed us that agreeable to a warrant from this Board [261] (transmitted to Col^l Patterson on the 17th Instant) he had apprehended Capt Timothy Church and Jonathan Mills Church resolved that they be [brought] before [the] Board and severally Examined —

Capt Timothy Church and Jonathan Mills Church being examined say as follows (see their Examinations on File) —

Lieu^t Jonathan Church who was cited to appear this Day before us as a Witness against the said Timothy Church & Jonathan Mills Church appeared and was examined (see his Examination on file) —

Resolved on Consideration of the above Examinations that Jonathan Mills Church be discharged and that Timothy Church be discharged on entering into a Recognizance for his Appearance before any three of the Commissioners for Conspiracies when called upon and for his good Behaviour and doing his duty during the continuance of the present war with Great Britain —

> Timothy Church of Brattleborough in the
> County of Cumberland Farmer in........ £300
> Benjamin Butterfield of the same place
> Farmer his Bail in.................... £200

Adjourned —

Met Albany 31st October 1780—
Present

John M. Beeckman
Jeremiah Van Rensselaer } { Samuel Stringer

Resolved that David Fairchilds be liberated from his present Confinement on entering into a Recognizance for his good Behaviour doing his duty and appearing before any three of the Commissioners for Conspiracies when thereunto required [262] during the continuance of the present war with Great Britain —

David Fairchilds of Ballstown in the County
of Albany Farmer in................... £100
Mathew Fairchilds of the same place Taylor
his Bail in............................ £100

John Leslie a Deserter from Sir John Johnson's Party appeared before us and being examined and requesting Permission to go to his Excellency the Governor resolved that he have the same granted him —

Adjourned

Met Albany 6th November 1780

Present

John M. Beeckman
Jeremiah Van Rensselaer } { Isaac D. Fonda

Hugh Mc Manus of Tryon County Constable appeared before the Board with Albert Van Der Werken as a Prisoner which said Van Der Werken he informs us he had apprehended by order of Zepheniah Batchelor Esqr and some of the other Justices of Tryon County and the said Albert Van Der Werken being examined says that he last Spring went off to Canada with Robert Snell that afterwards repenting of what he had done he returned with an Intention of throwing himself upon the Mercy of the Country —

Resolved that the said Albert Van Der Werken be ordered to attend this Board to Morrow Morning and that he be informed in the mean time his case will be taken into Consideration —

William Hoofer being brought before the Board [263] was examined and then ordered to be recommitted —

Zepheniah Batchelor Esqr laid before the Board a return of a Number of woemen whose Husbands are gone off to the Enemy and who he has warned agreeable to the Act of the Legislature of this State for the Removal of the Families

of Persons who have gone over to and joined the Enemy
Ordered that the said return be filed —

A Letter from the Commissioners for Conspiracies at
Poughkeepsie dated the 3ᵈ Instant was laid before the Board
wherein the[y] inform us that they send to us a certain
William Laird an Inhabitant of Tryon County who says he
was taken Prisoner last spring by the Enemy and that he has
in Sir John's late Expedition made his escape from them
resolved that he be ordered to attend this Board to Morrow
Morning —

A Letter from Doctor George Smith[1] was laid before the
Board wherein he sets forth the distressed Situation of his
Family by means of his being confined to his house and the
same being taken into Consideration resolved that he enter
into a Recognizance to remain within the Limits of this City
untill this Board shall think proper to discharge him from
these Restrictions and that he shall not hold Correspondence
upon Political Matters during that Time which may in any
manner be prejudicial to the United States —

George Smith of the City of Albany, Phy-
sician in £500
Thomas Reed of the same Place Esqʳ his
Bail in. £500

Adjourned

[264] Met Albany 7ᵗʰ November 1780

Present

John M. Beeckman } { Isaac D. Fonda
Jeremiah Van Rensselaer }

Albert Van Der Werken who was Yesterday before the
Board and was ordered to attend again this day appeared

¹ See note under date of October 11th.

agreeable to order and prayed that Peter Sietz and Mʳ Cannon who have been Prisoners in Canada and were lately exchanged might be examined and the said Persons being Examined say while they were in Canada they saw Albert Van Der Werken there and that he acted as a Bar Keeper in a Tavern and they could not learn that he had taken up Arms in the Enemies service —

Resolved in Consequence of the above information that the said Albert Van Der Werken be permitted to go at large on entering into a Recognizance for his good Behaviour doing his duty and appearing before any three of the Commissioners for Conspiracies when called upon during the continuance of the present war with Great Britain —

Albert Van Der Werken of Johns Town in
Tryon County Farmer in.............. £200
Jacob Van Der Werken of the Sant Vlacte in
the County of Tryon Farmer his Bail.... £200

Johan Jost Warner having been bound for his Appearance at the Supream Court held in this City on the third Tuesday in October last and there having been no Grand Jury in that time —

Therefore resolved that the said Johan Jost Warner enter [265] into Recognizance of anew for his Appearance at the next Supream Court to be held at the City Hall in this City on the third Tuesday in January next and not depart the Court without Leave —

Johan Jost Warner of Schohary Farmer in.. £100

Resolved that the said Johan Jost Warner also enter into a Recognizance for the appearance of his wife Margaret Warner at the next Supream Court —

Johan Jost Warner Bail for his wife Margaret
Warner in............................. £50

William Laird appearing agreeable to the Order of Yesterday resolved that he enter into Recognizance for his Appearance before Zepheniah Batchelor Esqr of Tryon County with a sufficient surety to enter into Recognizance for his good Behaviour doing his duty and appearing before any three of the Commissioners for Conspiracies when called upon during the Continuance of the present war with Great Britain —

    William Laird of Kingsborough in Tryon
       County Farmer in.................... £100
    Jacob Van Der Werken of the Sant Vlacte in
       Tryon County Farmer his Bail in....... £100

Adjourned —

          Met Albany 8th November 1780
Present

    John M. Beeckman   } {
                          Isaac D. Fonda
    Jeremiah Van Rensselaer } {

William Loucks appeared before the Board agreeable to our order and being examined says as follows (to wit) (see Examination on File)

Information having been received from M^{rs} [266] Campbell who lately was exchanged and came from Canada that John Docksteder of Tryon County did last Spring take into his House a wounded Soldier of Sir John Johnson's Party and that he did after the said Soldier was recovered for some time keep him in his House in woman's Cloath's untill he made his Escape to Canada — It is in Consequence thereof resolved that a warrant be made out for the said John Dockstader and transmitted to Zepheniah Batchelor Esqr to have the same served as soon as possible —

Adjourned —

Met Albany 9th November 1780 —
Present

John M. Beeckman
Jeremiah Van Rensselaer } { Isaac D. Fonda

Resolved that William Shanklin be liberated from Confinement on his entering into a Recognizance with a sufficient surety for his good Behaviour doing his duty and appearing before any three of the Commissioners for Conspiracies when thereunto required during the Continuance of the present war with Great Britain —

William Shanklin of the East District of the
Manor of Rensselaerwyck Labourer in... £100
Andrew Shanklin of the City of Albany Labourer Bail in........................ £100

Col! Anthony Van Bergen appeared before the Board and informed us that a Number of disaffected Persons have of late associated back of Cooksakie under a Pretence of Religious worship but that he is well persuaded from the Political Chara[c]ters of the said persons and other Circumstances [267] that such meetings are only held to Deliberate upon such Matters as may tend to injure the American Cause to prevent which in future

It is resolved that a warrant be made out and delivered to Col! Van Bergen for the Apprehension of the persons above described and that he be requested to have the same served as soon as possible —

Abraham Hooghteling was brought before us and examined on his Examination he says that a Number of persons have been lately enlisted by Jacob Halenbeeck at Niscuthaw and places adjacent and that their Intention is early in the spring to Join the Enemy which Examination is in the words following (to wit) (See Examination on file)

Adjourned —

Met Albany 10th November 1780
Present

John M. Beeckman	Isaac D Fonda
Jeremiah Van Rensselaer	Samuel Stringer
Mathew Visscher	

The Board taking into Consideration the Examination of Abraham Hooghteling who was examined Yesterday Resolved in Consequence thereof that the Honble Brigadier Gen! Ten Broeck be requested to order a party of the Cooksakie Militia now in this City to go and apprehend all such Persons as are mentioned in the Examination of the said Abraham Hooghteling —

General Ten Broeck having appointed Lieu! Rykert Van Den Bergh with a Party of Col! Van Bergens Regiment to go and apprehend the said Persons — Resolved that Instructions be made for him which Instructions are in the words following (to wit) (See instructions on File)

[268] It appearing also from Hoogteling's Examination that a Number of Persons in Livingston's Manor are concerned in the Enlistment mentioned in the said Examination therefore resolved that General Ten Broeck be also requested to detach a Party of that Quarter for the Apprehension of all such Persons and that Instructions be made out to the Officer who is to command the said party which Instructions are in the following words (to wit) (see Copy Instructions on File)

The Board having received information that John Waltymier who frequently passes thro the Country as an Express from the enemy crosses Hudsons River at Hendrick Claws who lives near the Kinderhook Landing an[d] that said Claw harbours Waltymier   It is therefore resolved that a Letter be wrote to Col! Abraham Van Alstyne requesting him to have the said Hendrick Clauw apprehended and brought before us —

Lieu. Rykert Van Den Bergh having in Consequence of our warrant apprehended Jacob Halenbeeck Jun. and he being brought before the Board and examined resolved that he be committed and that a Mittimus be made out for him —

Resolved that General Ten Broeck be requested to detach a Party of Col. Van Ness's Regiment to go to Coyemans and there to take Charge of and bring to Goal such Prisoners as may be delivered over to him by Lieu. Van Den Bergh —

Alexander Bryant of the Half Moon [269] was brought before us by Col. Schoonhoven in order that he might be examined as to sundry disaffected Persons and the said Bryant being examined his Examination is as follows (to wit) (see Examination on File)

Adjourned —

Met Albany 11.th November 1780
          Present

Jeremiah Van Rensselaer ⎞   ⎧ Samuel Stringer
Mathew Visscher   ⎠   ⎨ Isaac D. Fonda

Abraham Hoogteling was ordered to be brought before the Board & being again Examined ordered that he be recommitted —

Cap. Cornelius Hogeboom appeared before the Board and informed that he had agreeable to the Directions received from us proceeded to Coyemans where he had received of Lieu. Van Den Bergh the following persons as Prisoners (to wit) John Witbeeck, Nicholas Huyck, Johannis Huyck Jun., Peter Huyck, David Van Dyck, William Hoogteling,

Johannis Witbeeck, Henry Huyck, Joachim Collyer, John Schram, John Ver Plank, Peter Finehout, and William Plato — resolved that they be severally committed and that a Mittimus be made out for them —

William Plato one of the persons above mentioned was ordered to be brought before us for Examination on being Examined he says as follows (to wit) (See his Examination on File) —

It appearing from the Examination of James Van Driesen that Archibald Mc.Neal and Ezekiel Ensign of [270] Saragtoga Jo[t]ham Bemus of Stillwater and some others have carried on a Correspondence with the Enemy and have aided comforted and assisted Parties going to and coming from the enemy It is resolved in Consequence of the said Information that a warrant be made out for the immediate apprehension of the said Persons and that the same be forthwith transmitted to General Schuyler now at Saragtoga —

Adjourned —

Met Albany 12th November 1780

Present

Jeremiah Van Rensselaer } { Samuel Stringer
Mathew Visscher   } { Isaac D. Fonda

Lieu.^t Van Den Bergh appeared before the Board and informed us that he had agreeable to our warrant apprehended John Coenly, Lowrence Deal and Beriah Kelly and they being severally produced and Examined resolved that they be committed and that a Mittimus be made out directed to the Goaler to take them into his Custody and detain them until discharged by an order of this Board —

Adjourned

Met Albany 13th November 1780 —
Present

Jeremiah Van Rensselaer ⎱   ⎰ Isaac D. Fonda
Samuel Stringer   ⎰   ⎱

Captain Bleecker of Col! Gansevoort's Regiment appeared
before the Board and informed us that he had agreeable to
a warrant of this Board delivered to him by Gen! Schuyler
apprehended Archibald M?Neal, Ezekiel Ensign [271]
Jotham Bemus and Joseph Carr and they being severally
brought in & Examined resolved that they be committed and
that a Mittimus be made out to the Sheriff to take them into
his Custody and safely keep until discharged by this Board.

Lowrence Deal and John Coenly who were Yesterday
confined were ordered to be brought before the Board and
examined their Examinations are as follows (to wit) (see
Examination on file)   ordered that they be recommitted —

Adjourned —

Met Albany 14th November 1780
Present

Mathew Visscher   ⎱   ⎰ Samuel Stringer
Jeremiah Van Rensselaer ⎰   ⎱ Isaac D. Fonda

Peter Finehout was brought before the Board and examined his Examination is as follows (to wit) (see Examination
on File)

The Board having been informed that Hoogteling and
Lena Hoogteling residing at Aquatuck will be able to give
Information respecting the Persons apprehended in that
Quarter and who are at present in Confinement therefore
resolved that they be severally cited to appear before us to
Morrow Morning at 10 OClock —

Cap! Coenradt Klyne appeared before the Board &

informed that agreeable to an order of this Board he had apprehended Henry Smith Jun[r] , Henry Bonestel, James M[c]Coy, John Harvey, John Bunt, John Snoeck, Thomas Whiting, John Hoogteling and Henry Hoogteling and they being brought before the Board and examined ordered that they be committed and that [272] a Mittimus be made out for them —[1]

A Letter from Col[l] Peter Livingston was laid before the Board dated the 11th Instant wherein he informs us that he sends an Examination of Anna Proper respecting James M[c]Coy which Examination is as follows (to wit) (see Examination on File) —

A Letter from Col[l] Henry J. Van Rensselaer was laid before the Board dated 16th Instant respecting John Harvey who was lately apprehended and brought to Goal by Cap[t] Coenradt Klyne in which Letter he informs us that the said Harvey is a very dangerous Person ordered that the said Letter be filed —

Adjourned —

Met Albany 15th November 1780

Present

Mathew Visscher ⎱
Isaac D. Fonda ⎰   ⎰ Samuel Stringer

Resolved that William Lees be liberated from Confinement on entering into a Recognizance for his Appearance before any three of the Commissioners for Conspiracies when thereunto required doing his duty & be of the good Behaviour for and during the Continuance of the present war with Great Britain —

---

[1] Captain Cline, Kline or Klyne, was paid £9 „ 0 „ 2d. in " hard money " for this service. The original voucher is in *Revolutionary Manuscripts*, vol. 40, p. 162, State Comptroller's office.

William Lees of Nistageune in the County of
    Albany Blacksmith in................. £100
Jesse Fairchild of the City of Albany Black-
    smith his Bail in...................... £100

The Board having received information that [273] Joseph
Stalker of the East District of the Manor of Rensselaerwyck
is knowing to several Villianies committed by persons living
at New Scotland such as harbouring spies from the Enemy
&c: resolved that the said Joseph Stalker be cited to appear
before us on Friday next in Order to his being Examined
as to the above

Resolved that Johannis Huyck be liberated from Confinement on his entering into a recognizance for his good
Behaviour doing his duty and appearing before any three
of the Commissioners for Conspiracies when thereunto
required for and during the Continuance of the present war
with Great Britain —

Johannis Huyck of Hackatough in the County
    of Albany Labourer in................. £100
Gerrit Van Wie of the west District of the
    Manor of Rensselaerwyck Cordwainer his
    Bail in............................. £100

Resolved that Jacob Halenbeeck Jun: be liberated from
Confinement on his entering into a Recognizance for his
remaining within the Limits of the Dwelling house and
Yard of Samuel Pruyn situate within the third Ward of
this City until discharged from the said Restrictions by this
Board or any other three of the Commissioners for Conspiracies and for his good Behaviour during that Time —

Jacob Halenbeeck Jun: of Klinkenbergh in
    the County of Albany Farmer in........ £500
Jacob Halenbeeck of the same place Farmer
    his Bail in........................... £500

Resolved that James Whitacre be discharged from Confinement on entering into a Recognizance for his good
[274] Behaviour doing his duty and appearing before any
three of the Commissioners for Conspiracies when thereunto required for and during the Continuance of the present
War with Great Britain —

> James Whitacre of Nistageune in the County
> of Albany Labourer in................ £100
> Williams Lees of the same place Blacksmith
> his Bail in........................... £100

Adjourned —

Jeremiah Van Rensselaer } { John M. Beeckman
Samuel Stringer   } { Mathew Visscher

Resolved that John Hocknel be discharged from Confinement on his entering into a Recognizance for his good Behaviour, doing his duty and appearing before any three of the Commissioners for Conspiracies when thereunto required for
and during the Continuance of the present war with Great
Britain —

> John Hocknel of the West District of the
> Manor of Rensselaerwyck Farmer in..... £100
> Peter Scharp of the City of Albany Carpenter
> his Bail in........................... £100

Col! Abraham Van Alstyne having agreeable to a Request
of this Board of the 10th Instant caused Hendrick Clauw
to be apprehended and brought before us and the said Clauw
being examined and it appearing probable to this Board
from his Examination and other [275] Circumstances that
he is innocent of the Crime laid to his Charge but as the said
Hendrick Clauw is reputed a disaffected Person —

Therefore resolved that previous to his being discharged he enter into a Recognizance for his good Behaviour doing his duty and appearing before any three of the Commissioners for Conspiracies when thereunto required for and during the Continuance of the present war with Great Britain and for his procuring a good sufficient Bail on or before the 25ᵗʰ day of November Instant —

    Hendrick Clauw of the District of Kinder-
      hook in the County of Albany Carpenter in £100

James Van Driesen was brought before the Board & examined and ordered to be recommitted —

Resolved that Joseph Hawkins be liberated from Confinement on his entering into a Recognizance for his good Behaviour doing his duty and appearing before any three of the Commissioners for Conspiracies when thereunto required for and during the Continuance of the present war with Great Britain and for his remaining within the Limits of this City and not departing the same (unless it be to do Militia or other Military Duty) without the Consent and Approbation of this Board —

    Joseph Hawkins of Kingsbury in the County
      of Charlotte Yeoman in................. £100
    William Shepherd of the City of Albany
      Cutler his Bail in £100

Adjourned —

[276]   Met Albany 17ᵗʰ November 1780
Present

    John M. Beeckman   } { Samuel Stringer
    Jeremiah Van Rensselaer } { Mathew Visscher

Resolved that John Bont be discharged from Confinement on his entering into a Recognizance for his future good Behaviour doing his duty and appearing before any three of the Commissioners for Conspiracies when thereunto required for and during the Continuance of the present war with Great Britain.

John Bont of Claverack District Weaver in. . £100
John Decker Robison of the same place
Carpenter his Bail in.................... £50
Elisha Talmidge of the same place Blacksmith also his Bail in.................. £50

Resolved that Peter I. Miller be discharged from Confinement on his entering into a Recognizance for his future good Behaviour doing his duty and appearing before any three of the Commissioners for Conspiracies when thereunto required for and during the continuance of the present war with Great Britain.

Peter I. Miller of Claverack District Wheelwright in £100
John Decker Robison of the same place
Carpenter his Bail in................. £ 50
Elisha Talmidge of the same place Blacksmith also his Bail in.................. £ 50

Resolved that Joel Platt be discharged from Confinement on his entering into a Recognizance for his future [277] good Behaviour doing his duty and appearing before any three of the Commissioners for Conspiracies when thereunto required for and during the continuance of the Present war [with] Great Britain.

Joel Pratt of New Lebanon in the County of Albany Farmer in.................. £100
Ase Stower of the same place Farmer his
Bail in............................. £100

Resolved that Joseph Meacham be discharged from Confinement on his entering into a Recognizance for his future

1780
Nov. 17.

good Behaviour doing his duty and appearing before any
three of the Commissioners for Conspiracies when thereunto
required during the continuance of the present war with
Great Britain —

> Joseph Meacham of New Lebanon in the
> County of Albany Farmer in............ £100
> Isaac Garnsey of Half Moon District Farmer
> Bail in £100

Resolved that Hezekiah Hammond be discharged from
Confinement on his entering into a Recognizance for his
future good Behaviour doing his duty and appearing before
any three of the Commissioners for Conspiracies when
thereunto required during the continuance of the present
war with Great Britain

> Hezekiah Hammond of the State of Masse-
> chusets Bay Farmer in................. £100
> Isaac Garnsey of Half Moon District Farmer
> his Bail in.......................... £ 50
> Ase Stower of New Lebanon in the County
> of Albany Farmer also his his Bail in.... £ 50

Mrs Mills wife of Abel Mills appeared before the Board
agreeable to order and was examined her examination is as
follows (to wit) (see Examination on File) —

[278] A Letter from Samuel Ten Broeck Esqr of Livingston's Manor was laid before the Board by Harmanus Rose
Constable with an Examination respecting Thomas Mc Feal
who said Harmanus Rose informed us he had apprehended
and had in his Custody and the said Thomas Mc Feal being
Examined resolved that he be committed and that a Mittimus
be made out for him —

Johannis Shaver Esqr and Capt John Decker Robison
appeared before the Board and informed us that Peter Bean

is a dangerous and disaffected person and that he endeavours by his Conversation to intimidate weak & ignorant persons and that John Bartle is also a dangerous and disaffected person in Consequence of which Information

Resolved that Major Samuel Ten Broeck of Livingston's Manor be requested to have the said Peter Bean and John Bartle apprehended and forthwith sent to us.

Adjourned.

Met Albany 18th November 1780

Present

| John M. Beeckman | } | { | Mathew Visscher |
| Jeremiah Van Rensselaer | } | { | Samuel Stringer |

Resolved that Calvin Harlow be discharged from Confinement on his entering into a Recognizance for his future good Behaviour doing his duty and appearing before any three of the Commissioners for Conspiracies when thereunto required during the Continuance of the Present war with Great Britain —

Calvin Harlow of New Lebanon in the
County of Albany Farmer in............ £100
Joseph Meacham of the same place Farmer
his Bail in......................... £100

[279] Resolved that Hans Sneack be discharged from Confinement on his entering into a Recognizance for his future good Behaviour doing his duty and appearing before any three of the Commissioners for Conspiracies when thereunto required during the continuance of the present war with Great Britain.

Hans Sneack of Claverack District Farmer in. £100
John Decker Robison of the same place
Farmer his Bail in.................... £100

Resolved that John Harvey be discharged from Confinement on his entering into a recognizance for his good Behaviour doing his duty and appearing before any three of the Commissioners for Conspiracies when thereunto required during the continuance of the present war with Great Britain.

> John Harvey of Claverack District Farmer in £100
> Jacob F. Shaver of Livingstons Manor Esq.
> his Bail in £100

Resolved Beriah Kelly be discharged from Confinement on his entering into a Recognizance for his future good behaviour doing his duty and appearing before any three of the Commissioners for Conspiracies when thereunto required during the Continuance of the present war with Great Britain.

> Beriah Kelly of Norwich in the State of
> Connecticut in....................... £100
> Ezra Cleveland of the west District of the
> Manor of Rensselaerwyck Farmer his
> Bail in............................... £100

Adjourned.

[280]   Met Albany 20th November 1780
   Present

John M. Beeckman }   { Samuel Stringer
Mathew Visscher   }

Resolved That Thomas Ayres be discharged from confinement on his entering into a Recognizance for his future good behaviour doing his duty and appearing before any three of the Commissioners for Conspiracies when thereinto [sic] required during the continuance of the present war with Great Britain

Thomas Ayres of New Lebanon in the County

of Albany Labourer in................ £100
Peter Ayres of the same place Farmer his
Bail in £100

The Board having from sundry Circumstances the greatest reason to think that the Information of Abraham Hoogteling was entirely false and as several persons have been confined on account of the same therefore resolved that the said persons be discharged from Confinement, but as all of them have from the Commencement of the present Contest been disaffected to the American Cause it is ordered that previous to their discharge they severally enter into a Recognizance for their good Behaviour doing their duty and appearing before any three of the Commissioners for Conspiracies when thereunto required during the continuance of the present war with Great Britain.

Johannis I. Witbeeck of Niscuthaw Farmer in £100
Cornelius Van Der Zee of the same place
Farmer his Bail in.................... £100

Johannis L. Witbeeck of Acquatough in the
County of Albany Farmer in............. £100
[281] Isaac Witbeeck of Cooksakie Farmer
his Bail in........................... £100

Nicholas Huyck of Acquatough Farmer in.. £100
Cornelius Huyck of the west District of the
Manor of Rensselaerwyck Farmer his Bail
in.................................... £100

John Ver Plank of Hacketock Farmer in... £100
Cornelius Huyck of the west district of the
Manor of Rensselaerwyck Farmer his
Bail in............................... £100

Hendrick Huyck of the west District of the
Manor of Rensselaerwyck Farmer in.... £100
Hendrick Van Sante of Ni[s]cuthaw Farmer
his Bail in.......................... £100

David Van Dyck of Niscuthaw Farmer in.. £100
Eli Arnold of the City of Albany Cooper his
Bail in.............................. £100

Wouter Witbeeck of Manettenhook Farmer
in................................. £100
Peter W. Hilton of the City of Albany Cooper
his Bail in.......................... £100

Joachim Collier of Cooksakie Farmer in... £100
Isaac Witbeeck of the same place Farmer his
Bail in.............................. £100

Isaac Huyck of Hacketock Farmer in...... £100
Isaac Witbeck of Cooksakie Farmer his Bail
in.................................. £100
Cornelius Huyck of the west District of the
Manor of Rensselaerwyck Farmer his
Bail in.............................. £100

Resolved that Lowrence Deal, John Garret and John
Coenly severally enter into a recognizance for their future
good behaviour doing their duty and appearing before any
three of the Commissioners for Conspiracies when thereunto required during the Continuance of the present war
with Great Britain & also for their appearance at the next
Supreme Court of Judicature to be held for the State of New
York at the City Hall in this City on the third Tuesday in
January next (or wheresoever the [282] said Court shall

then be held in the State aforesaid) and not depart the
Court without Leave.

1780
Nov. 20.

Lowrance Deal of Cooksakie Farmer in £100
Cornelius Conine of the same place Farmer
his Bail in............................ £100

John Garret of Cooksakie District Farmer
in.. £100
Richard Bronck of the same place Esq.ʳ his
Bail in................................. £100

John Coenly of Cooksakie District Farmer
in.. £100
Cornelius Conine of the same place Farmer
his Bail in............................ £100

It being suggested to the Board that Simeon Garret who
lives upon the Farm formerly occupied by John Waltymier
has frequent Intercourse with the said Waltymier and
harbours him when on his way through the Country
resolved in Consequence of the said Information that the
said Simeon Garret be cited to appear before this Board
forthwith

Adjourned.

Met Albany 21ˢᵗ November 1780
Present

1780
Nov. 21.

John M. Beeckman ⎱ ⎰ Samuel Stringer
Jeremiah Van Rensselaer ⎰ ⎱

Dʳ George Smith appeared before the Board & informed
us that from an Expectation of going to Canada he has
disposed of all his Effects and that he is greatly reduced in
his Circumstances and finds it impossible to maintain his
family in this City and being desirous of removing to the

1780
Nov. 21. Farm at present occupied by John Jolley situate in the west
District of the Manor of Rensselaerwyck resolved that he
have Permission granted him for that Purpose on his entering into a Recognizance for his remaining within the Limits
of the said Farm and not [283] leaving the same without
Leave previously obtained for that purpose from this Board
and that he shall not during his residence at the said [farm]
correspond with or in any Manner whatsoever give any
Intelligence to the Enemies of this or the United States and
for his good Behaviour during the said time and for his
appearance when called upon.

    George Smith of the City of Albany Physi-
      cian in............................... £100
    Patrick Smith of the same place Merchant
      his Bail in........................... £100

    Resolved that William Bartow, Jacob Halenbeeck, Junr,
Peter Finehout, Ebenezer Stanton, Nathan Stanton, Arnold
Skoelfield, Peter Huyck, and William Hoogteling, be
severally discharged from Confinement on entering into
Recognizance for their good Behaviour doing their duty and
appearing before any three of the Commissioners for Conspiracies when called upon during the Continuance of the
present war with Great Britain —

    William Bartow of Cooksakie District La-
      bourer in............................ £100
    Myndert Van Schaick of the same place
      Farmer his Bail in.................... £100

    Jacob Halenbeeck Junr of Klinkenbergh
      Farmer in........................... £100
    Samuel Pruyn of the City of Albany Yeo-
      man his Bail in...................... £100

Peter Finehout of Acquatough Labourer in. . £100
Daniel G. Van Antwerp of the same place
Farmer his Bail in.................... £100

Ebenezer Stanton of Cooksakie District
Farmer in........................... £100
Daniel G. Van Antwerp of the same place
Farmer his Bail in.................... £100

Nathan Stanton of Cooksakie District Farmer
in.................................... £100
Daniel G. Van Antwerp of the same place
Farmer his Bail in.................... £100
[284] Arnold Skolfield of the west District of
the Manor of Rensselaerwyck in......... £100
Wilhelmas Row of the same place Farmer
his Bail in........................... £100

Peter Huyck of Auckquetuck Farmer in... £100
Michael Klink of the same place Farmer
his Bail in........................... £100

William Hoogteling of Niscuthaw Farmer in. £100
Michael Klink of Auckquetough Farmer his
Bail in.............................. £100
Resolved that Philip Philips be discharged on his entering
into a Recognizance for his good Behaviour doing his duty
and appearing before any three of the Commissioners for
Conspiracies when thereunto required during the continu-
ance of the present war with Great Britain
Philip Philips of the Eas[t] District of the
Manor of Rensselaerwyck Weaver in..... £100
Thomas Knowlton of the same plac[e] Farmer
his Bail in........................... £100
Adjourned.

Met Albany 22nd November 1780 —

Present

Jeremiah Van Rensselaer }   { Samuel Stringer
John M. Beeckman

A Certificate was laid before the Board signed by Col.!
Killian Van Rensselaer and sundry other Officers certifying
that the said John Low who is at present in Confinement has
ever evinced a warm Attachment to the American Cause and
has been ready on every Occasion to do his duty in the Militia

Resolved in Consequence of the same that the said [285]
John Low be discharged on entering into a Recognizance
for his good Behaviour doing his duty and appearing before
any three of the Commissioners for Conspiracies when
called upon during the Continuance of the present war with
Great Britain.

John Low of the East District of the Manor
of Rensselaerwyck Yeoman in.......... £100
Nicholas Low of the same place Gentleman
his Bail in............................ £100

Whereas James Bramley and Peter Livingstone of the
Hellebergh have been severally cited to appear before this
Board and refused and neglected to do the same it is there-
fore resolved that a warrant be made out directed to Cap.t
Jacob Van Aernam authorizing him to apprehend the said
James Bramley and Peter Livingstone and forthwith bring
them before us at the City Hall in this City —

Adjourned —

Met Albany 23^{d} November 1780 —

Present

John M. Beeckman   }   { Samuel Stringer
Jeremiah Van Rensselaer

1780
Nov. 23.

Resolved that Johannis Huyck be discharged from Confinement on his entering into a Recognizance for his future good Behaviour doing his duty and appearing before any three of [the] Commissioners for Conspiracies when thereunto required during the Continuance of the present war with Great Britain —

Johannis Huyck of Acquatough in the County
  of Albany Farmer in.................. £100
[286] Peter Van Wie of the West District of
  the Manor of Rensselaerwyck Farmer his
  Bail in............................. £100

Resolved that Andries Loucks be discharged from Confinement on Frederick Cranse entering into a Recognizance for the good Behaviour of the said Andries Loucks & for doing his duty and appearing before any three of the Commissioners for Conspiracies when thereunto required during the Continuance of the present war with Great Britain —

Frederick Cranse of the Hellebergh Farmer
  as Bail for Andries Loucks in.......... £100

Resolved that Johan Jost Warner be discharged on entering into a Recognizance for his future good Behaviour doing his duty and appearing before any three of the Commissioners for Conspiracies when thereunto required during the Continuance of the present war with Great Britain —

Johan Jost Warner of Schohary in the County
  of Albany Labourer in................ £100
Philippus Warner of the Bever Dam Farmer
  his Bail in........................... £100

Resolved that Nicholas Sea be discharged from Confinement on entering into a Recognizance for his future good Behaviour doing his duty and appearing before any three of the Commissioners for Conspiracies when thereunto

required during the Continuance of the present war with
Great Britain —

> Nicholas Sea of Schohary Farmer in....... £100
> Philippus Warner of the Bever Dam Farmer
>   his Bail in......................... £100

A Letter from the Commissioners for Conspiracies at
Poughkeepsie was laid before the Board wherein they [287]
inform that they send to us a certain John Davis of Tryon
County whom they have caused to be apprehended on suspicion of his having stolen two Horses —

Resolved that the said John Davis be committed until
an inquiry can be made into the Crime wherewith he stands
Charged —

Adjourned —

1780
Nov. 24.

Met Albany 24th November 1780 —

Present

> John M. Beeckman }   { Mathew Visscher
> Samuel Stringer }   { Isaac D. Fonda

John Bartle agreeable to an order of this Board of the 7th
Instant appeared and the crime as alledged against him
being read to him and he denying the same resolved that the
said John Bartle have Permission granted him to appear
again on the 4th day of December next and bring with him
such Evidences as he may think Proper to invalidate the
said Charge

Also Resolved that Capt Robison be informed of the
Proceedings respecting John Bartle and that he be requested
also to attend on that day —

Hugh Mc Manus appeared before the Board and informed
that agreeable to our order he had apprehended John

Docksteder and the said Docksteder being Examined and it appearing that he is not the person who it was intended Should be apprehended therefore resolved that he be discharged —

Resolved that Hendrick Bonistel be discharged from Confinement on his entering into a Recognizance for his good Behaviour doing his duty [288] and appearing before any three of the Commissioners for Conspiracies when thereunto required during the Continuance of the present war with Great Britain —

Hendrick Bonistel of Claverack District
Labourer in £100
John Blunt of the same place Farmer his
Bail in............................. £100

Adjourned —

Met Albany 25th November 1780
Present

John M. Beeckman ⎱ ⎰ Isaac D. Fonda
Samuel Stringer ⎰ ⎱

Simeon Garret appeared before the Board this day agreeable to our order and being Examined as to his Connection with John Waltymier he says as follows (see his Examination on file) —

Resolved that the said Simeon Garret be discharged on his entering into Recognizance for his good Behaviour doing his duty and appearing before any three of the Commissioners for Conspiracies when called upon during the Continuance of the present war with Great Britain and for his procuring a sufficient Bail by the 2nd day of December next —

Simeon Garret of Cooksakie District Farmer
in £100

1780
Nov. 25.   James Bramley having been apprehended by Cap.ᵗ Jacob
Van Aernam and brought before the Board resolved that he
be confined and that a Mittimus be made out to the Goaler
commanding him to detain and keep in close Confinement
the said James Bramley until discharged by an order of this
Board —

Adjourn[e]d

1780
Nov. 26.   [289]   Met Albany 26.ᵗʰ November 1780 —
Present

John M. Beeckman }   {
Samuel Stringer   }   { Jeremiah Van Rensselaer

James Hamilton appeared before the Board and informed
us that having agreeable to directions received from Captain
Jacob Van Aernam apprehended James Bramley and being
on his way to this City with said Bramley in order to bring
him before the Board, David Gibson did assault him the
said James Hamilton and endeavoured to rescue the said
Bramley —

Resolved in Consequence of the above Information that a
warrant be made out for the immediate apprehension of the
said David Gibson and that the said warrant be directed to
the said James Hamilton and that he be authorized in case
any Resistance should be made by the said Gibson or any
other Person to call to his assistance such a Number of Persons as he may think proper to carry the above warrant into
Execution —

Adjourned

1780
Nov. 27.   Met Albany 27.ᵗʰ November 1780
Present

Mathew Visscher }   { Isaac D. Fonda
John M. Beeckman }   { Samuel Stringer

James Bramley who was on the 25ᵗʰ Instant confined was brought before the Board and examined   ordered that he be recommitted —

David Gibson who was agreeable to a warrant issued Yesterday apprehended and confined was also brought before the Board and examined and it appearing from sundry Circum-[290]stances that the said David Gibson has been uniformly attached to the American Cause and has on every Occasion done his duty and a[c]knowledged his Error in attempting to rescue James Bramley therefore resolved that the said David Gibson be discharged and cautioned against such conduct in future —

The Board having received Information that Peter Waley of the Hellebergh is a disaffected Person and that he conceals himself in the woods to Escape doing Militia and other duty and he being at present at Home — resolved that a warrant be made out directed to Richard Hilton to apprehend the said Peter Waley and forthwith bring him before us —

Adjourned —

Met Albany 28ᵗʰ November 1780 —

Present

John M. Beeckman ⎱   ⎰ Samuel Stringer
Mathew Visscher   ⎰   ⎱

Richard Hilton appeared before the Board and informed us that agreeable to our warrant he had apprehended Peter Waley and he being brought before us and examined resolved that he be committed and that a Mittimus be made out for him —

John Ab: Pearson appeared before the Board for the Purpose of entering into a Recognizance as Bail for Simeon Garret resolved that he enter into the same for the good Behaviour of the said Simeon Garret and for his doing his duty and appearing before any three of the Commissioners for Conspiracies when thereunto required during the Continuance of the present war with Great Britain —

> [291]   John Ab. Pearson of Niscuthaw in the
> County of Albany Farmer as Bail for
> Simeon Garret in...................... £100

Adjourned —

Met Albany 29ᵗʰ November 1780 —

Present

| John M. Beeckman | | Isaac D. Fonda |
| Samuel Stringer | | Mathew Visscher |

Resolved that Thomas Purchase be discharged from Confinement on entering into a Recognizance for his good Behaviour doing his duty and appearing before any three of the Commissioners for Conspiracies when thereunto required during the Continuance of the present war with Great Britain —

> Thomas Purchase of New-town in the County
> of Albany Farmer in £100
> Jacob Ostrander of the same place Farmer
> his Bail in............................. £100

Anna Proper of Livingston's Manor having been directed by Col! Peter Livingston to appear before this Board to be examined with Respect to the Conduct of sundry disaffected persons of Livingston's Manor appeared and was Examined which Examination is as follows (to wit) (see Examination on File)

A Letter from Col! Peter Livingston respecting Anna Proper was laid before the Board and the same being read was ordered to be filed —

A Letter from Col! Henry J. Van Rensselaer dated the

16th Instant respecting John Harvey a Prisoner now in Confinement was laid before the Board and the same being [292] read was ordered to be filed —

A Letter from the Board of Commissioners for Conspiracies at Poughkeepsie dated the 24th Instant respecting Ann Standerren was also laid before the Board and the same being read was ordered to be filed —

Resolved that Jacob I. Truax be discharged from Confinement on entering into a Recognizance for his good Behaviour doing his duty and appearing before any three of the Commissioners for Conspiracies when thereunto required during the Continuance of the present war with Great Britain and also for his appearance at the next Supream Court of Judicature to be held for the State of New York at the City Hall in the City of Albany on the third Tuesday in January next (or wheresoever the said Court shall then be held in the State Aforesaid) and not depart the Court without Leave —

Jacob I. Truax of the City of Albany Innkeeper in £100
Isaac I. Truax of the County of Albany Innkeeper his Bail in £50
John W. Truax of D°. . . . D°. . . . D°. . . . in. . £50

Adjourned —

Met Albany 30th November 1780 —

Present

John M. Beeckman ⎱   ⎰ Isaac D. Fonda
Samuel Stringer ⎰   ⎱

The Board proceeded to the Consideration of the Charge alledged against Robert Caldwell whereupon it is resolved that he be discharged on his entering into a Recognizance

with a sufficient surety for his good Behaviour doing his
duty and appearing before any three of the Commissioners
[293] for Conspiracies when thereunto required during the
Continuance of the present war with Great Britain —

　　Robert Caldwell of Schacktikook in the
　　　County of Albany Weaver in............ £100
　　Robert Todd of the Half Moon District in
　　　the County of Albany Weaver his Bail in.. £ 50
　　Dirck Scouting of the same place Farmer
　　　also his Bail in....................... £50
Adjourned —

　　　　　　　Met Albany 2ⁿᵈ December 1780
　　　Present

　　　John M. Beeckman ⎞　⎧ Mathew Visscher
　　　Samuel Stringer　　⎠　⎩

A Letter from Ebenezer Russell Esqʳ dated White Creek
the 18th November last was laid before the Board wherein
he sets forth the distressed Situation of the Family of Samuel
Burns now a Prisoner confined in the Goal in this City and
requesting that the said Burns may be admitted to Bail if
is can be done consistently with the safety of the State
which Letter being read ordered that the same be filed and
that the Consideration thereof be postponed till a future Day —

A Letter from Major Richard Esselstyne of Claverack
was also laid before the Board wherein he requests that
Henry Hoogteling an Inhabitant of Claverack District may
be liberated from Confinement and offering to become
surety for the said Hoogteling which Letter being read
ordered that the same be filed and taken into Consideration
on Monday next —

Adjourned —

[294]   Met Albany 4ᵗʰ December 1780 —

Present

John M. Beeckman }   { Mathew Visscher
Samuel Stringer   }   {

It having been suggested to the Board that William Tyler is gone to Canada and has Joined the enemy and Amos Lucas having became [sic] surety for the Appearance of the said William Tyler when called upon resolved in Consequence of the said Information that an order be made out and sent to the said Amos Lucas forthwith to deliver him up to this Board or to pay the Recognizance Money —

The Board having been informed that from the Assertions of some Persons at present with the Enemy there is good Reason to suppose that William Laird at present residing at Johnstown who some time ago entered into a Recognizance before us to appear when called upon is at present enlisting Men for the service of the enemy with whom he intends to join them as soon as they make a descent into the Country — resolved in Consequence of the said Information that the said William Laird be cited to appear forthwith before this Board & that the Citation for the said Laird be inclosed in a Letter to Zepheniah Batchelar Esqᵣ and that he be requested to have the same served —

The Board then proceeded to the Consideration of the Letter of Major Esselstyne delivered to this Board on the 2ⁿᵈ Instant resolved in Consequence of the said Letter that Henry Hoogteling be discharged from Confinement on his entering into a Bond conditioned for his good Behaviour doing his duty and [295] appearing before any three of the Commissioners for Conspiracies when thereunto required

during the Continuance of the Present War with Great
Britain —

> Henry Hoogteling of Claverack in the County
> of Albany Farmer in................... £100

Resolved that the above mentioned Bond be transmitted
to Major Esselstyne in order that he may sign the same as
Surety for Henry Hoogteling.

Thomas Yarns was brought before the Board and examined and then ordered to be Recommitted —

Resolved upon the Application of William Lees, That Ann
Standerren (who was some time ago sent to Poughkeepsie
on Account of her Influence in bringing over Persons to the
Persuasion professed by the People called Shaking Quakers
the said Persuasion having a Tendency to alienate the
minds of the People from their Allegiance to the State by
inculcating an Opinion of the Unlawfulness of taking up
Arms in defence of the American Cause) and it appearing
that many of the Persons of the said Persuasion have been
reformed and that no further Evil is to be apprehended
from her Influence or Example therefore resolved that the
said Ann Standerren have Permission to return to Nistageune
on the said William Lees and James Whitakre entering into
a Bond conditioned for the said Ann Standerren's appearing
before any three of the Commissioners for Conspiracies
when thereunto required for her good Behaviour and not
saying or consenting to any Matters or Things inconsistant
with the Peace and safety of this and the United States

> William Lees of Nistageuna in the County of
> Albany   Blacksmith   as   Bail   for   Ann
> Standerren in........................ £100
> James Whitacre of the same place Yeoman
> also her Bail in....................... £100

[296]   Met Albany 5th December 1780

Present

John M. Beeckman }   { Isaac D. Fonda
Samuel Stringer   }

Nicholas Sea appearing before the Board requests that
Christian Weaver may be accepted as his Surety instead of
Philip Warner whereupon resolved that the said Christian
Weaver be accepted accordingly and that he enter into a
Recognizance for the good Behaviour of the said Nicholas
Sea and for his doing his Duty and appearing before any
three of the Commissioners for Conspiracies when called upon
during the Continuance of the present war with Great Britain

    Christian Weaver of Schohary in the County
    of Albany Farmer as Bail for Nicholas
    Sea in............................... £100

Adjourned —

            Met Albany 6th December 1780

John M. Beeckman }   { Samuel Stringer
Isaac D. Fonda   }   { Jeremiah Van Rensselaer

The Board conceiving it necessary that Jacob I. Truax
of this City should be prosecuted agreeable to Law for his
Conduct in adhering to the Enemy and as the Witnesses
against him who are John Cuppernull and John I. Vrooman
of Tryon County have neglected to attend the Supreme
Court altho they have been requested so to do —

    It is therefore resolved that a Letter be wrote to Zepheniah
Batchelar Esqr Justice of the Peace of the County of [297]
Tryon requesting him to cite the said John Cuppernull and
John I. Vrooman before him and take their Recognizance

1780
Dec. 6. for their Appearance at the next Supream Court to be held on the third Tuesday in January next to give Evidence against the said Jacob I. Truax

Resolved that a Letter be wrote to Col! Van Schonhoven of the Half Moon requesting him to order Alexander Bryant to appear before this Board for the Purpose of being examined as to sundry Transactions of the Disaffected in Half Moon District —

Adjourned —

1780
Dec. 7.

Met Albany 7<u>th</u> December 1780

Present

John M. Beeckman } { Isaac D. Fonda
Samuel Stringer

An Anonimous Letter directed to the Commissioners for Conspiracies was laid before the Board setting forth that John Cobham is a Dangerous Person and that his going to the Northward gives great Reason to suspect that he Conveys Intelligence to the Enemy resolved in Consequence of the above Letter that the said John Cobham be ordered on no Pretence whatever to leave this City unless he shall previously obtain Permission from this Board for that Purpose —

Resolved that Peter Werley be discharged from Confinement on entering into a Recognizance for his good Behaviour doing his duty and appearing before any three of the Commissioners for Conspiracies when thereunto required for and during the Continuance of the Present war with Great Britain

Peter Werley of the Hellebergh in the County
of Albany Farmer in.................... £100
[298] William Monk of the same Place
Farmer his Bail in.................... £100
Andries Ward of the same Place
Farmer also his Bail in................ £100

It appearing from the Examination of James Van Driesen that Archibald M:Neal of the Scotch Patent and his son Alec M:Neal have aided and assisted the Party (with which he the said Van Driesen was going to the Enemy) in making their Escape to Canada resolved in Consequence thereof that a warrant be made out for the immediate apprehension of the said Archibald M:Neil and Alec M: Neal and that the same be inclosed in a Letter to General Schuyler at Saragtoga and that he be requested to have it served —

Adjourned —

    Met Albany 11th December 1781 [*sic* for 1780] —
    Present

        John M. Beeckman } { Isaac D. Fonda
        Samuel Stringer }

John Hoogteling being brought before the Board and his Examination taken and it appearing that the Charges as alledged against the said John Hoogteling are not of sufficient weight to render his Confinement any longer necessary therefore resolved that he be discharged —

James Oynes being brought before the Board and his Examination taken   ordered that he be recommitted —

James Brisbin being also ordered to be brought before the Board was examined   ordered that he be Recommitted—

William Griffen being also brought before the Board was examined   ordered that he be recommitted —

Adjourned —

[299]   Met Albany 12th December 1780
    Present

        John M. Beeckman } { Mathew Visscher
        Samuel Stringer }

A Letter from Ebenezer Clark and Alexander M<u>c</u> Nit Esq<u>rs</u> two of the Commissioners for Conspiracies for the County of Charlotte dated New Perth 2<u>nd</u> Instant was laid before the Board setting forth that they inclose a Petition signed by sundry of the Inhabitants of Kingsbury in Favour of Thomas Yarns, William Griffin and William Bell who are at present in Confinement   resolved that the said Petition be taken into Consideration at some future Day —

A Letter from Dirck Swart Esq<u>r</u> directed to this Board and dated 12<u>th</u> November last was laid before us by M<u>r</u> Visscher wherein he informs us that a Petition has lately been set on Foot and signed by a Number of Persons in Favour of Jotham Bemus who is at Present confined in Goal and requesting when the said Petition is laid before the Board to be informed of it as he is desirous of disproving a Part at least of the said Petition ordered that the said Letter be filed.

A Letter from Lieutenant Col<u>l</u> Weisenfelt dated at Fort Schuyler inclosing a Copy of an Examination of an Indian who came from the enemy was laid before the Board and as the said Examination contains Information which should be communicated to General Clinton therefore resolved that M<u>r</u> Beeckman wait upon him with the same —

Adjourned —

[300]   Met Albany 13<u>th</u> December 1780
Present

John M. Beeckman ⎫   ⎧ Isaac D. Fonda
Samuel Stringer   ⎭   ⎩

The Board having taken into Consideration the Petition presented on the 12<u>th</u> Instant in Favour of William Griffen and others resolved in Consequence thereof that the said

William Griffen be liberated from Confinement on entering into a Recognizance for his good Behaviour doing his Duty and appearing before any three of the Commissioners for Conspiracies when thereunto required during the Continuance of the present war [with] Great Britain —

William Griffen of the County of Charlotte
Farmer in £100
William High of the same Place Farmer his
Bail in £100

Joseph Hawkins appeared before the Board and requested Permission to go to Charlotte County and remove from thence his Family and Effects and the same being agreed to by his Bail William Shepherd resolved that he have Permission granted him accordingly —

The Board being desirous of reexamining Alexander Bryant and he being ordered to appear and now attending agreeable to our Order   resolved that he be examined —

The said Alexander Bryant being examined and his Examination being reduced to writing is as follows (to wit) (see Examination on File) —

Adjourned —

[301]   Met Albany 14th December 1780
     Present

     John M. Beeckman ⎱   ⎰ Mathew Visscher
     Samuel Stringer   ⎰   ⎱

Resolved that James Bramley be discharged from Confinement on his entering into a Recognizance with a sufficient surety for his good Behaviour doing his Duty and appearing before any three of the Commissioners for Conspiracies when thereunto required during the Continuance of the Present war with Great Britain —

James Bramley of the Hellebergh in the
    County of Albany Innkeeper in......... £100
David Kittle of the same place Farmer his
    Bail in............................... £100

A Petition signed by a Number of the well affected Inhabitants of Saragtoga District was laid before the Board setting forth that Jotham Bemus of Stillwater since his liberation from Confinement has acted in every Respect as a friend to the American Cause that he has chearfully contributed all his Power towards supplying the Army and has in every Respect manifested a Disposition to support the Independance of the United States which said Petition being read ordered that the same be filed —

Ordered that the Secretary inform Dirck Swart Esqr that the above Petition was presented to this Board and requesting him as soon as possible to come down for the Purpose mentioned in his Letter of the 12th Instant —

Adjourned —

[302]   Met Albany 16th December 1780
Present

John M. Beeckman } { Jeremiah Van Rensselaer
Samuel Stringer

Resolved that William Vrooman be discharged from Confinement on entering into a Recognizance for his good Behaviour doing his duty and appearing before any three of the Commissioners for Conspiracies whenever thereunto required during the Continuance of the Present war with Great Britain —

William Vrooman of Saragtoga District
    Farmer in............................ £100

Jeremiah Van Rensselaer Esq.ʳ i[n]formed the Board that he had received of Gerard Bancker Esqʳ Treasurer of this State the sum of One hundred Dollars of the New Emission for the purpose of defraying the Necessary Expenditures of this Board —

Resolved that out of the above money the Secretary pay to Stephen Bell £10 „ 5 on Account

Adjourned

Met Albany 18th December 1780

Present

> John M. Beeckman } { Mathew Visscher
> Samuel Stringer }

Resolved that Henry Smith be discharged from Confinement on entering into a Recognizance for his good Behaviour doing his duty and appearing before any three of the Commissioners for Conspiracies whenever thereunto required during the Continuance of the present war with Great Britain

> [303]   Henry Smith of the Manor of Livingston Farmer in £100
> Teunis Smith of the same place Farmer his Bail in. £100

Adjourned —

Met Albany 21st December 1780

Present

> Samuel Stringer   } { Mathew Visscher
> John M. Beeckman }

A Letter from Major Rosekrans at Saragtoga was laid before the Board wherein he informs that he sends to us under Guard Archibald McNeal of the Scotch Patent who agreeable to our Request he had caused to be apprehended, and the said Archibald McNeal being brought before the Board & examined and it appearing from his Examination that he is guilty of the Crime wherewith he stands charged therefore resolved that he be committed and that a Mittimus be made out for him —

Adjourned —

Met Albany 22nd December 1780

Present

| John M. Beeckman | | Mathew Visscher |
| Samuel Stringer | | Jeremiah Van Rensselaer |

James Brisben requesting to be brought before the Board and being brought accordingly requested that he might be liberated from Confinement on his procuring sufficient Bail for his good Behaviour in future Resolved on Consideration of the above Request that he be informed that the Board will liberate him on his procuring a surety for his remaining within the Limits of the City of Albany until discharged by this Board —

[304] Joseph Carr also requesting to be liberated from Confinement resolved that he be informed that the Board will liberate him on his entering into a similar Recognizance with the above mentioned James Brisben —

Jotham Bemus at present in Confinement requesting of the Board to be admitted to the Liberty of the Goal resolved that it be granted him on his procuring a sufficient Bail for his remaining a true and faithfull Prisoner in the City Hall of the said City —

William McLaughlin of the City of Albany
Innkeeper as Bail for Jotham Bemus in.. £100

The Board being informed that John Cobham, John Stiles

and the Man living at a Place called the Half way House
in Jessup's Patent are concerned in forwarding Intelligence
to Canada resolved in Consequence of the said Information
that Col! Gansevoort be requested to have them apprehended
& forthwith sent to us —

A Letter from Col! Peter R. Livingston was laid before
the Board inclosing an examination of Jacob Kline of the
Manor of Livingston's from which Examination it appears
that Wilhelmas Turner, Coenradt Turner, and James Turner
being disaffected Persons and intending to create Confusion
and Disturbance so as to embarrass the Government of this
State have opposed the said Jacob Kline in collecting the
Taxes assessed on the Inhabitants of the District and are
daily by every means in their Power endeavouring to disturb
the Publick Peace ordered that the same be filed —

Adjourned —

[305]   Met Albany 23ᵈ December 1780 —
    Present
        John M. Beeckman }   { Mathew Visscher
        Samuel Stringer   }   { Jeremiah Van Rensselaer

A Letter from Lieuᵗ Col! Henry J. Van Rensselaer dated
at Claverack was laid before the Board in which Letter he
informs that Thomas Whiting at present in Confinement has
always sustained the Character of a harmless inoffensive
Man and that he does not conceive that his being liberated
from Confinement will any way endanger the Safety of the
State — which Letter being taken into Consideration

Thereupon resolved that the said Thomas Whiting be discharged on entering into a Recognizance for his good Behaviour doing his duty and appearing before any three of the
Commissioners for Conspiracies when thereunto required during the Continuance of the present war [with] Great Britain —

Thomas Whiting of Claverack District
Labourer in.......................... £50

A Letter from Major Esselstyne was laid before the Board wherein he informs that he has at present in his Possession the Arms and Ammunition belonging to those Persons who have been apprehended on the Information of Abraham Hoogteling & the said Information appearing to be altogether false therefore resolved that Major Esselstyne be ordered to deliver up the said Arms and Ammunition to the Persons respectively from whom they have been taken —

Resolved that a Letter be wrote to Brigadier General Rensselaer to request him to transmit to this Board a List of such Persons of his Brigade who have been Delinquent in doing Militia [306] Duty in order that such of them who have entered into Recognizance before this Board may be prosecuted upon the same

Resolved that Alexander M.ᶜKey be ordered to deliver up to this Board on or before the 8.ᵗʰ day of January next Hugh Rose, Alexander Carsan and Walter Trumble for whose appearance and good Behaviour he has become Surety —

Resolved that James Beatty be ordered to deliver up to this Board on or before the 8.ᵗʰ day of January next John Parks for whose Appearance before us when called upon he became Surety —

William M.ᶜLaughlin who Yesterday became surety for Jotham Bemus's remaining a true and faithfull Prisoner within the City Hall of this City appeared before the Board & informed that he was unwilling any longer to remain Bail for the said Jotham Bemus and John Horn of the Manor of Rensselaerwyck offering to become surety for the said Jotham Bemus resolved that the said John Horn accordingly enter into a Recognizance for the said Jotham Bemus's remaining a Prisoner within the City Hall in this City and for his good Behaviour during that Time —

John Horn of the Manor of Rensselaerwyck
Butcher as Bail for Jotham Bemus in.... £100

Jacob Truax of this City having forfeited his Recognizance appeared this day and paid the sum of Two hundred and forty four Dollars of the Money emitted pursuant to a Resolution of Congress of the 18th of March last Resolved that the same be delivered over into the Hands of the Secretary to be made use of in defraying the Expenditures of this Board —

[307] Resolved in Consequence of the application of Archibald M:Neil and Ezekiel Ensign that they be severally liberated from Confinement on entering into a Recognizance for their remaining within the following Limits (to wit) the House and Yard of Patrick Smith situate in the first ward of the City of Albany and that they do not hold any Correspondence either by word or deed upon Political matters with any Person or Persons which may in any Manner tend to be prejudicial to the Measures pursued or which may be pursued by the United States of America or either of them for the Maintainance of Liberty & Independance of the said United States and that they shall appear before any three of the Commissioners appointed for detecting and defeating all Conspiracies that may be formed in this State against the Liberties of America whenever they shall be thereunto required and that they shall remain under these Restrictions untill discharged or otherwise ordered —

Archibald M:.Niel of Saragtoga in the County
of Albany Merchant in................. £500
Robert M:.Clallen of the City of Albany
Merchant also his Bail in.............. £250
Thomas Shipboy of the same place Merchant
also his Bail in...................... £250

Ezekiel Ensign of Saragtoga Innkeeper in... £500
John Roff of the Manor of Rensselaerwyck
    Merchant his Bail in £250
James Caldwell of the City of Albany Mer-
    chant also his Bail in................ £250

Captain Cline of Livingston's Manor appearing before
[308] the Board informed us that agreeable to orders received from Col. Peter Livingston he had apprehended
Wilhelmas Turner, James Turner and Coenradt Turner
resolved that the Charges as alledged against them be
taken into Consideration until Monday Morning next and
that the said Wilhelmas Turner, James Turner and Coenradt Turner enter into a Recognizance each of them to
remain within the Limits of this City and to appear before
this Board on Monday the 25$\underline{th}$ day of December Instant at
ten of the Clock in the Forenoon and in the mean time to
be of the good Behaviour —

Wilhelmas Turner of Livingston's Manor
    Farmer in............................ £100
James Turner   of D°....D° in......... £100
Coenradt Turner of D°....D° in......... £100

Adjourned —

Met Albany 25$\underline{th}$ December 1780
Present

Samuel Stringer   }   { John M. Beeckman
Mathew Visscher }   { Jeremiah Van Rensselaer

Resolved that John Stalker be discharged from Confinement on entering into a Recognizance for his good Behaviour doing his duty and appearing before any three of the
Commissioners for Conspiracies when thereunto required during the Continuance of the present war with Great Britain —

John Stalker of Claverack District Labourer
in................................... £100
Ambrose Stalker of the same place Farmer
his Bail in............................ £100

The Board taking into Consideration the Charges as
alledged against Wilhelmas Turner, James Turner & Coenradt Turner and the[y] appearing this Day agreeable to the
[309] Tenor of the Recognizance entered into by them on
the 23ᵈ Instant resolved that they have Permission to return Home on their severally entering into a Recognizance
for their good Behaviour doing their Duty and appearing
before any three of the Commissioners for Conspiracies
when thereunto required during the Continuance of the
present war with Great Britain and also for their appearance at the next supreme Court of Judicature to be held
for the State of New York at the City Hall in this City on
the third Tuesday in January next (or wheresoever the said
Court shall then be held in the state aforesaid) and not to
depart the Court without Leave —

Wilhelmas Turner of the Manor of Living-
ston Farmer in....................... £100
Coenradt Cline of the same place Farmer his
Bail in £100

James Turner of the Manor of Livingston
Farmer in........................... £100
Coenradt Cline of the same place Farmer his
Bail in £100

Coenradt Turner of the Manor of Living-
ston Farmer in....................... £100
Coenradt Cline of the same place Farmer his
Bail in £100

1780
Dec. 25.

Resolved that a Letter be wrote to Peter Livingston Esqr to request him to bind over Johannis Van Deusen and Wheater Hicks to appear at the next Supreme Court as Witnesses against the aforementioned Turners and also that he bind over all such Persons as are able to prove the Charges alledged against them — And that he also be desired to have a certain John Moore who is at present at Livingston's Manor apprehend[ed] and forthwith sent to us —

The Board having received Information that Peter Bean of Livingston's Manor has lately declared himself as an Enemy to the American Cause and dissuaded Persons from [310] enlisting in the Continental Service and Richard Warn of the same place being a disaffected and dangerous Person —

Resolved therefore that a warrant be made out directed to Capt Coenradt Cline forthwith to apprehend and bring before us the said Peter Bean & Richard Warn —

Adjourned —

1780
Dec. 27.

Met Albany 27th December 1780
Present

John M. Beeckman }   { Samuel Stringer
Mathew Visscher   }   {

The Board being informed that Adam Killmer who is at present Confined in Goal is entirely destitute of Provisions and other Necessaries and not having it in his Power to procure any on Account of his Poverty —

It is therefore resolved that he be liberated from Confinement on entering into a Recognizance with a Sufficient Surety for his good Behaviour doing his duty and appearing before any three of the Commissioners for Conspiracies whenever thereunto required during the Continuance of the present war with Great Britain and also for his Appearance at the next Supream Court of Judicature to be held for the State of New York at the City Hall in this City on the third Tuesday in January next (or wheresoever the said Court shall then be held in the State aforesaid) and not to depart the Court without Leave —

Adam Killmer of Livingston's Manor in the
    County of Albany Blacksmith in........ £100
Gideon Wolcot of the same place Blacksmith
    his Bail in............................ £100

Adjourned —

[311]   Met Albany 28th December 1780
    Present

Jeremiah Van Rensselaer ⎱   ⎰ John M. Beeckman
Samuel Stringer   ⎰   ⎱ Mathew Visscher

James Brisben having made Application to the Board to be released from Confinement and his request being taken into Consideration thereupon resolved that the said James Brisben be liberated from Confinement on entering into a Recognizance for his good Behaviour and Appearance before any three of the Commissioners for Conspiracies when called upon and also for his remaining within the Limits of this City and not departing the same without Leave obtained for that Purpose from any three of the said Commissioners or unless it be to do Militia Duty —

James Brisben of Saragtoga District Farmer
    in.................................. £100
Peter Scharp of the City of Albany Carpenter
    his Bail in......................... £100

Adjourned —

Met Albany 29ᵗʰ December 1780

Present

John M. Beeckman
Samuel Stringer   Isaac D. Fonda
Mathew Visscher   Jeremiah Van Rensselaer

Joseph Carr of Stillwater having petitioned the Board to be released from Confinement and the Prayer of the said Petition being taken into Consideration resolved thereupon that he be discharged from Confinement on entering into a Recognizance for his good Behaviour and appearance before any three of the Commissioners for Conspiracies and for his remaining [312] within the Limits of the City of Albany and not departing the same unless he shall have leave previously obtained from any three of the said Commissioners or unless it be to do Militia duty —

Joseph Carr of Stillwater in the County of
Albany Farmer in...................... £100
Alexander Baldwin of the same place Farmer
his Bail in........................... £100

Resolved that Henry Tinkey be also discharged from Confinement on entering into a Recognizance for his good Behaviour and appearance before any three of the Commissioners for Conspiracies when thereunto required and also for his remaining within the Limits of this City and not departing the same without Leave previously obtained for that Purpose from any three of the said Commissioners or unless it be to do Militia Duty —

Henry Tinkey of the Scotch Patent in the
County of Charlotte Farmer in.......... £100
Albert Van Derwerken of Saragtoga in the
County of Albany his Bail in........... £100

On Application of Jotham Bemus resolved that he also
be liberated from Confinement on entering into a Recognizance conditioned for his good Behaviour appearing before any three of the Commissioners for Conspiracies when thereunto required and for his remaining within the Limits of the City of Albany and that Part of the Manor of Rensselaerwyck which lies to the South of the North end of Steenbergh and not further East and West in the last mentioned [313] Place than the River to the East and the Foot of the Hill to the West & not departing the said Limits and Bounds unless with Leave previously obtained for that Purpose from any three of the said Commissioners or when called upon to do Militia Duty —

> Jotham Bemus of Still Water in the County
>   of Albany Farmer in................... £100
> Reuben Wright of the same Place Farmer his
>   Bail in............................. £100
> Job Wright of the same place Farmer also his
>   Bail in............................. £100

Adjourned —

Met Albany 2nd January 1781 —

Present

> Jeremiah Van Rensselaer } { Samuel Stringer
> Mathew Visscher   }

A Letter from George White Esqr dated the 1st Instant was laid before the Board inclosing an Examination of Bernard Carpenter from which said Examination it appears that Abner Darling of Pitts Town is a dangerous and disaffected Person for which Reason the said George White Esqr having had him apprehended and sent to us, and that the said Abner Darling being brought before the Board and examined resolved that the said Abner Darling be permitted to return Home on entering into a Recognizance for his good Behaviour doing his duty and appearing before any three of the Commissioners for Conspiracies when thereunto required during the Continuance of the present war with Great Britain and remaining within the Limits of Pitts Town & not departing the same without Leave obtained from any three of the said Commissioners or unless it be to do Militia Duty —

Abner Darling of Pitts Town Farmer in...... £100
Moses James of King's District Farmer his Bail in............................... £100

[314] Resolved that George Hicks be discharged on entering into a Recognizance for his good Behaviour doing his Duty & appearing before any three of the Commissioners for Conspiracies whenever thereunto required during the Continuance of the present war with Great Britain and remaining within the Limits of King's District and not departing the same without leave obtained from any three of the said Commissioners or unless it be to do Militia duty —

George Hicks of New-town Farmer in....... £100
John Herrington of the East District of the Manor of Rensselaerwyck Farmer his Bail in................................. £50
Jabez Landers of the same Place also his Bail in................................. £50

A Petition of Archibald McNeal and Ezekiel Ensign was presented to the Board praying for Permission to go to their Families at Saragtoga resolved on taking the Prayer of the said Petition into Consideration that they be informed that the Board cannot grant their Request.

Adjourned

Met Albany 3ᵈ January 1781

Present

John M. Beeckman ⎱ ⎰ Isaac D. Fonda
Samuel Stringer ⎰ ⎱

A Letter from Alexander Webster and Ebenezer Clark Esqʳˢ of Charlotte County was laid before the Board in which they request that James Gillis who is at present in Confinement may be liberated on Bail as the said Gillis has always behaved himself in an Inoffensive Manner and the same being taken into Consideration Resolved that the Board cannot [315] at this Time liberate him —

Application being also made by Archibald McNeal of the Scotch Patent to be admitted to Bail resolved that he be informed that the Board cannot at this Time liberate him —

Samuel Stringer Esqʳ informed the Board that he had received information that Peter Ball of the Bever Dam is at present at and about his Home and that he is come into the Country for the Purpose of Enlisting Men for the Enemy resolved that it be recommended to the said Samuel Stringer to obtain the fullest Information he possibly can as to the above and that in the mean while the Board will devise Measures to have him apprehended —

Adjourned

Met Albany 5ᵗʰ January 1781

Present

John M. Beeckman ⎱ ⎰ Mathew Visscher
Samuel Stringer ⎰ ⎱

Application being made by Dʳ George Smith for Permission to come to this City for the purpose of setling his private Business and Patrick Smith his Bail agreeing to the same resolved that he have Permission granted him for the space of six Days, and the said Dʳ Smith requesting also Permission

to visit a Patient at Col! Gerrit Van Denbergh's resolved
also that Permission be granted him for that Purpose with the
Consent & approbation of his said Bail —

Robert Adems requesting Permission of the Board to go to
Johnstown for the Purpose of setling his Business and
Thomas Shipboy Bail for the said Robert Adems consenting
to the same resolved that the said Robert Adems have Per-
mission [316] granted him accordingly till the 17$\underline{th}$ day of
January Instant —

A Letter from Hugh Mitchell, Abraham Outhout and
Ryneir Mynderse Esq$\underline{rs}$ Commissioners for Conspiracies at
Schenectady dated the 2$\underline{nd}$ Instant was laid before the Board
wherein they inform us that Archibald M$\underline{c}$Kellop and William Rodgers who are under Recognizance to this Board
refuse to do any Militia Duty when called upon and are
adjudged by them to be dangerous Persons —

Resolved in Consequence of the above Letter that the said
Archibald M$\underline{c}$Kellop and William Rodgers be ordered forthwith to appear before this Board.

A Certificate signed by Richard Esselstyne and Lowrence
Fonda Esq$\underline{rs}$ two of the Justices of the Peace for the County
of Albany was laid before the Board in which they certify that
agreeable to the Act of the Legislature entitled "An Act for
the Removal of the Families of Persons who have Joined the
Enemy" they have warned the following Women to depart the
State or remove to such Parts of it as are in the Power of the
enemy within twenty days from the Time of the Notice given
to them — (to wit) Elsie Elizabeth Finkel, Margaret Finkle,
Margaret Seman, Catharine Seman, Maria Stever, Eva
Houser, Christina Benneway, Maria Reepenberger, Gertruy
Wear, Anna Charter, Sintie Coventry, Bata Scharp, Margaret Shufelt, Cornelia Gardineir, & Maria Herpst, and the
said Richard Esselstyne and Lowrence Fonda certifying that

the said Elsie Elizabeth Finkle, Margaret Finkle, Margaret Seman, Catharine Seman, Maria Stever Eva Houser and Christina Benneway have always behaved themselves in an unexceptionable Manner and that they do [317] not think their remaining at their Habitations will endanger the safety of the State ordered that the said Certificate be filed —

Adjourned —

Met Albany 8th January 1781
Present

John M. Beeckman } { Mathew Visscher
Samuel Stringer }

John Parks of the Breakabeen having been represented to this Board as a disaffected Person and it being deemed necessary on Account of his Residence on the Frontiers of this State that he should be laid under Restrictions and having ordered the said John Parks to appear for that Purpose and he appearing this day agreeable to our order resolved that he enter into a Recognizance for his good Behaviour doing his duty and appearing before any three of the Commissioners for Conspiracies when thereunto required during the Continuance or the Present war with Great Britain —

John Parks of the Breakabeen in the County
of Albany Farmer in.................. £100
James Beatty of the same place Farmer his
Bail in............................ £100

The Board being informed that there is at present in this City a certain Daniel McLoud who is possessed of a Pass signed by Philip Pell Esqr Commissary of Prisoners of this State under which Pass the said Daniel McLooed has during the whole of last Summer screened himself from Militia Duty resolved in Consequence of the said Information that Jacob

Kidney be ordered to bring the said Daniel M<u>c</u> Looed forthwith before the Board —

Jacob Kidney appearing with Daniel M<u>c</u>Looed agreeable to
order and the said Pass being produced and it appearing that
the same was given upwards of a Year ago therefore resolved
tat the [318] said Pass be taken from the said Daniel M<u>c</u>Looed
and delivered to the said Philip Pell Esq<u>r</u> and it appearing
necessary to this Board from the Principles professed by the
said Daniel M<u>c</u>Looed that he should be restricted in his Conduct therefore ordered that he appear before this Board on the
12<u>th</u> Instant with a good sufficient surety for his future good
Behaviour doing his duty and Appearance when called upon.

Adjourned

Met Albany 9<u>th</u> January 1781

Present

John M. Beeckman ⎫   ⎧ Mathew Visscher
Samuel Stringer   ⎭   ⎩

Walter Trumble of Corey's Bush having been represented
to this Board as a disaffected person and it being deemed
necessary on account of his Residence on the Frontiers that
he should be laid under Restrictions and having ordered the
said Walter Trumble to appear for that Purpose & he appearing this day agreeable to our order resolved that he
enter into a Recognizance for his good Behaviour doing his
duty and appearing before any three of the Commissioners
for Conspiracies when thereunto required during the Continuance of the present war with Great Britain —

Walter Trumble of Corey's Bush in the
County of Albany Farmer in. £100
Alexander M<u>c</u>Key of Jericho in the County
of Albany Weaver his Bail in £100

Adjourned —

[319]   Met Albany 10.th January 1781

Present

John M. Beeckman }   { Isaac D. Fonda
Samuel Stringer   }   {

Robert McClallen and Thomas Shipboy who some Time since became surety for Archibald McNeal appeared before the Board and requested that the said Archibald McNeal might have Permission to go to Saragtoga and likewise that Ezekiel Ensign might have a similar Indulgance

And we having considered the said Request and judging from the present Situation of affairs that their going Home at this Time may be attended with dangerous Consequences to the State therefore resolved that they be informed that their Request cannot be complied with.

It appearing to the Board from the Examination of Jotham Bemus that his wife Mrs Bemus is knowing to many enimical Transactions of Angus McDonald of Livingston's Manor resolved therefore that an order be made out and sent to Mrs Bemus to appear forthwith before this Board in order that she may be examined as to the above —

It being suggested to the Board that Abraham Vollwyder and Andries Tollhamer of Nistageune are dangerous & disaffected Persons who by their Conduct and Conversation daily give Offence to the Friends of the American Cause resolved therefore that the said Abraham Vollwider and Andries Tollhamer appear before the Board forthwith, with Each a sufficient surety to enter into Recognizance for their future good Behaviour & appearance before any three of the Commissioners for Conspiracies when called upon —

Adiourned —

[320]   Met Albany 12th January 1781

       Present

          John M. Beeckman $\Big\}$ $\Big\{$ Mathew Visscher
          Samuel Stringer

      Daniel Mc Loed appearing agreeable to an order of this Board with William Fuller as his Surety   resolved that he enter into a Recognizance for his good Behaviour doing his duty and appearing before any three of the Commissioners for Conspiracies when thereunto required during the Continuance of the present war with Great Britain —

      Daniel McLoed of the City of Albany La-
      bourer in.. .... £100
      William Fuller of the same place Joiner his
      Bail in £100

      On Application of Jotham Bemus for Permission to go to Stillwater to settle his Business (to which his Bails Job Wright and Reuben Wright consenting)   resolved that Permission be granted him accordingly and that he have Time given him for fourteen Days for that Purpose —

      Archibald McKellop having on the 5th Instant been cited to appear before the Board in Consequence of a Letter received from the Commissioners of Conspiracies at Schenectady and he appearing this day and being examined as to Information received respecting him and utterly denying the same and being willing to give Surety for his future good Conduct   resolved that he enter into Recognizance for his appearance before any three of the Commissioners for Conspiracies when thereunto required and for his doing his duty & being of the good Behaviour for and during the Continuance of the present war with Great Britain —

[321] Archibald M<u>c</u>Kellop of Schenectady

Farmer in £100

Charles Martin of the same Place Merchant

his Bail in £100

Adjourned —

Met Albany 16th January 1781

Present

John M. Beeckman }   { Mathew Visscher
Jeremiah Van Rensselaer }

Application being made to the Board for Permission for Archibald M<u>c</u>Neal and Ezekiel Ensign to go to Saragtoga for the Purpose of arranging their Family affairs and their Bails severally consenting thereto resolved that they have Permission granted them accordingly for fourteen Days from this Day at the Expiration of which Time they are again to repair to this Place —

Lourence Deal, John Garret and John Coenly appeared before the Board and requested to be discharged from that Part of their Recognizance requiring their Appearance at the next Supream Court and they engaging to make known to the Board whenever John Waltymier shall again come in that Part of the Country in which they reside and their Request being taken into Consideration resolved that they be discharged accordingly —

Adjourned —

Met Albany 17th January 1781

Present

John M. Beeckman }   { Isaac D. Fonda
Samuel Stringer }

Resolved that Hans Peter Snyder be discharged from
Confinement on entering into a Recognizance for his good
Behaviour doing his duty and appearing before any three
of the Com-[322]missioners for Conspiracies when thereunto
required during the Continuance of the present War with
Great Britain And to remain within the Limits of the
District of Livingston's Manor —

> Hans Peter Snyder of Saragtoga Farmer in. . £100
> Jacob Powers of Livingston's Manor Farmer
> his Bail in............................ £100

Peter Bean of Livingston's Manor having been apprehended on the Information of Johannis Shaver Esq: for
drinking the King's Health and for dissuading Persons from
entering into the nine Month's Service, was brought before
the Board resolved that he enter into Recognizance 'for his
good Behaviour doing his duty and appearing before any
three of the Commissioners for Conspiracies when thereunto required during the Continuance of the present War
with Great Britain — And also for his appearance at the
next Supream Court of Judicature to be held for the State
of New York at the City Hall in the City of Albany on the
third Tuesday in January Instant (or wheresoever the said
Court shall then be held in the State aforesaid) to answer
unto all such Matters and Things as shall be then and there
exhibited against him And not to depart the Court without
Leave

> Peter Bean of Livingston's Manor Farmer in £100
> Coenradt Cline of the same place Farmer his
> Bail in £100

Resolved that the Secretary pay to Cap: Coenradt Cline

the sum of £9 „ 0 „ 2 on account of Services Performed in apprehending and bringing to Goal John Snoeck Henry Hoogteling and others —[1]

Adjourned —

[323]   Met Albany 18ᵗʰ January 1781 —

Present

John M. Beeckman ⎱ ⎰ Mathew Visscher
Isaac D. Fonda   ⎰ ⎱

Joseph Carr who was by Recognizance bound to remain within the Limits of this City appeared before the Board and requested Permission to go to Stillwater to see his Family And his Bail Alexander Baldwin consenting thereto resolved that he have Permission granted him accordingly for fourteen Days —

Henry Tinkey being also bound by Recognizance to remain within the Limits of this City appeared before the Board & requested to Go to his Family at the Scotch Patent and his Bail Albert Van Der Werken consenting to the same resolved that he have leave granted him accordingly for Fourteen Days —

A Petition signed by Elbert Willet Thomas Hun and a Number of other respectable and well affected Inhabitants of this City was laid before the Board setting forth that Jane Moffit whose Husband is at present with the Enemy has been warned agreeable to an Act of the Legislature of this State for the Removal of the Families of Persons who have joined the Enemy been warned to depart the State or remove to such Parts of it as are at present in the Power of the Enemy, that notwithstanding the Political Sentiments

[1] The original voucher is in *Revolutionary Manuscripts*, vol. 40, p. 162, State Comptroller's office.

of her Husband the said Jane Moffit has always been esteemed a Friend to the American Cause and that they do not conceive that her remaining within the State will tend in any Manner whatsoever to the Prejudice of the Freedom or Independance of this or the United States and the said Petition being [324] taken into Consideration resolved that in Consequence thereof that a Permit be granted to the said Jane Moffit to remain at her Habitation —

Adjourned —

Met Albany 20th January 1781

Present

John M. Beeckman } { Samuel Stringer
Mathew Visscher   }

Elsie Elizabeth Finkle, Margaret Finkle, Margaret Seman, Catharine Seman, Maria Stever, Eva Houser and Christina Benneyway whose Husbands are at present with the enemy having been warned by Richard Esselstyne and Lourence Fonda Esq^{rs} to depart the State or remove to such Parts of it as are in the Power of the Enemy agreeable to an Act of the Legislature of this State entitled "An Act for the Removal of the Families of Persons who have joined the Enemy" and the said Justices having recommended the said women above named as Persons of inoffensive Characters who they do not in any Manner conceive dangerous to the Safety of the State and the said above mentioned Women having petitioned this Board for Permits to remain at their Habitations resolved in Consequence of the Recommendation of the said Justices that Permits be granted them accordingly —

It being represented to the Board by the Goaler that James Gillis at present confined in Goal is very Ill and that a Continuance of his Confinement may endanger his Life therefore

resolved that he be permitted to go to the House of the Widow 1781
Jan. 20.
M:Neal in this City and their remain until he is recovered
of his [325] Indisposition on Neal Shaw's entering into a
Recognizance that the said James Gillis during his Continuance at the House of the said M:s M:Neil shall be of the
good Behaviour —

    Neal Shaw of the Manor of Rensselaerwyck
    Innkeeper Bail for James Gillis in......... £100

James Brisben who was by Recognizance bound to remain
within the Limits of this City appeared before the Board and
requested Permission to go to Saragtoga to see his Family
and his Bail Peter Sharp consenting thereto resolved that he
have Permission granted him accordingly until the 15th day
of February next

Archibald M:Neil of the Scotch Patent having p[e]titioned
the Board to be released from Confinement and the prayer of
the said Petition being taken into Consideration resolved thereupon that he be discharged on entering into a Recognizance
for his good Behaviour and appearance before any three of the
Commissioners for Conspiracies & for his remaining within the
Limits of the City of Albany and not departing the same
unless he shall have leave previously obtained from any three
of the said Commissioners or unless it be to do Militia Duty—

    Archibald M:Neil of the Scotch Patent in the
    County of Charlotte Farmer in........ £100
    Evans Umphrey of Tomhenick in the County
    of Albany Farmer his Bail in.......... £100
Adjourned —

        Met Albany 26th January 1781   1781
Jan. 26.
Present

    John M. Beeckman   Samuel Stringer
    Mathew Visscher   Reyneir Mynderse

[326] Resolved that Gilbert Miller be discharged from Confinement on entering into a Recognizance for his good Behaviour doing his duty and appearing before any three of the Commissioners for Conspiracies when thereunto required during the Continuance of the Present War with Great Britain —

Gilbert Miller of Ballstown Farmer in....... £100
Joseph Bettis of the same place Farmer his
Bail in............................. £100

Resolved that William Bettis be discharged from Confinement on entering into a Recognizance for his good Behaviour doing his duty and appearing before any three of the Commissioners for Conspiracies when thereunto required during the Continuance of the present war with Great Britain —

William Bettis of Ballstown Farmer in....... £100
Teunis Van Vleek of the same place Farmer
his Bail in £100

Resolved that Samuel Burns be discharged from Confinement on his entering into a Recognizance for his good Behaviour doing his duty and appearing before any three of the Commissioners for Conspiracies when thereunto required during the Continuance of the present war with Great Britain —

Samuel Burns of New-town Farmer in....... £100
William Bradshaw of Half Moon District
Farmer his Bail in.................... £50
John Flinn of the same place Farmer also his
Bail in £50

John Murray having been ordered to appear before this Board to enter into Recognizance of a new appearing this

Day agreeable to the said Order resolved that he be bound for his good Behaviour doing his Duty and appearing before any three of the Commissioners for Conspiracies when thereunto [327] required during the Continuance of the present war with Great Britain —

1781
Jan. 26.

John Murray of Breakabeen Farmer in..... £100
Hugh Alexander of the Manor of Rensselaerwyck Blacksmith his Bail in............. £100

Adjourned —

Met Albany 27th January 1781
Present

1781
Jan. 27.

Samuel Stringer   } { Isaac D. Fonda
John M. Beeckman } { Mathew Visscher

Angus M:Donald of Livingston's Manor petitioned the Board to be released from Confinement resolved that he be informed that he cannot as yet be liberated —

Application was made to the Board by James Gillis for Permission to go to the place of his abode at the Scotch Patent for the Purpose of removing his Family and Effects in the Interior Parts of the Country and his Bail consenting to the same resolved that he have Permission granted him accordingly and that he remove by the first Day of March next —

William Hutton petitioned the Board to be released from Confinement on Bail and as the said William Hutton has been a long Time in Confinement therefore resolved that he be informed that the Board will liberate him provided he can procure a sufficient surety for his future good Behaviour and appearance when called upon —

Adjourned —

[328]   Met Albany 29ᵗʰ January 1781

     Present

     John M. Beeckman ⎱   ⎰ Isaac D. Fonda
     Mathew Visscher   ⎰   ⎱ Samuel Stringer

Hannah Bemus wife of Jotham Bemus having been ordered to appear before the Board appeared this day agreeable to the said order and being interrogated as to Angus Mᶜ-Donald of Livingston's Manor carrying on an Intercourse with the Enemy and harbouring British Officers who were passing through the Country as Expresses and she refusing to answer to the same and there being great Reason to suppose that she is acquainted with the above Circumstances —

Therefore resolved that she be committed until she gives Satisfactory Answers to the same and that a Mittimus be made out for her —

Henry Wiesner Esqʳ laid before the Board a Petition of Joshua H. Smith at present confined to the Goal of Orange County by the Commissioners for Conspiracies at Pougkeepsie which Petition is in the following words (to wit) (see Petition on File) —

Resolved that Mʳ Wiesner be informed that this Board will not interfere with the Business of the Commissioners for Conspiracies above mentioned —

Resolved that William Hutton be discharged from Confinement on entering into a Recognizance for his good Behaviour & appearing before any three of the Commissioners for Conspiracies when thereunto required during the Con-
[329] tinuance of the present war with Great Britain —

     William Hutton of Lansingburgh Cord-
     wainer in £100
     John Watt of New Scotland in the County
     of Albany Farmer his Bail in............ £100

Adjourned

Met Albany 30th January 1781

Present

John M. Beeckman } { Samuel Stringer
Isaac D. Fonda

Application was made to the Board by Archibald McNeil to go to the place of his Abode at the Scotch Patent for the purpose of removing his Family and effects in the Interior Parts of the Country and his Bail consenting to the same resolved that he have Permission granted him accordingly & that he remove by the first day of March next

Adjourned

Met Albany 31st January 1781

Present

John M. Beeckman } { Mathew Visscher
Isaac D. Fonda   { Samuel Stringer

Resolved that Garrit Van Der Pool be discharged from Confinement on entering into a Recognizance for his good Behaviour & appearing before any three of the Commissioners for Conspiracies when thereunto required [during] the Continuance of the Present war with Great Britain —

Garrit Van Der Pool of the East District of
   the Manor of Rensselaerwyck Farmer in... £100
William Seaton of the same place Farmer his
   Bail in £100

Adjourned —

[330]   Met Albany 1st February 1781

Present

John M. Beeckman } { Mathew Visscher
Isaac D. Fonda

It appearing to the Board that Peter Ten Broeck is Exchanged and under Parole to go to New York — Ordered that the Bond of the said Peter Ten Broeck and Wessel Ten Broeck his Bail be given up to John Ten Broeck of the Great Imboght Brother to the said Peter Ten Bro[e]ck —

Adjourned

Met Albany 2nd February 1781

Present

Isaac D. Fonda } { Samuel Stringer
John M. Beeckman }

Archibald Campbell having been ordered to appear before this Board to enter into Recognizance of anew & he appearing this Day agreeable to the said order resolved that he be bound for his good Behaviour doing his duty & appearing before any three of the Commissioners for Conspiracies when thereunto required during the Continuance of the present war with Great Britain —

Archibald Campbell of the District of Cambridge in the County of Albany Farmer in. £100
William Reed of New Perth in Charlotte County Miller his Bail in.............. £100

Adjourned

[331] Met Albany 3^{d} February 1781 —

Present

John M. Beeckman   } { Isaac D. Fonda
Jeremiah Van Rensselaer } { Mathew Visscher

Resolved that Angus McDonald be discharged from Confinement on entering into a Recognizance for his good Behaviour doing his duty and appearing before any three of the Commissioners for Conspiracies when thereunto required during the Continuance of the present war with Great Britain —

Angus McDonald of Livingston's Manor
Farmer in......................... £150
Abraham Vossburgh of Claverack Farmer his
Bail in.............................. £150

Adjourned —

Met Albany 5th February 1781 —
Present

John M. Beeckman ⎱ ⎰ Isaac D. Fonda
Samuel Stringer ⎰ ⎱

Resolved that Thomas Yarns be discharged from Confinement on entering into a Recognizance for his good Behaviour doing his duty and appearing before any three of the Commissioners for Conspiracies when thereunto required during the Continuance of the present war with Great Britain

Thomas Yarns of Kingsbury in Charlotte
County Farmer in.................... £100
Rowland Perry of Palmertown in the County
of Albany Farmer his Bail in.......... £100

As the above mentioned Thomas Yarns live[s] upon the Frontiers and has it in his Power to aid and Comfort the Enemy resolved that he be ordered to remove into the Interior Parts of this State by the first day of May next —

Adjourned —

[332]   Met Albany 6th February 1781
Present

John M. Beeckman ⎱ ⎰ Isaac D. Fonda
Samuel Stringer ⎰ ⎱

1781
Feb. 6.

Melchart Van Deusen Esqr of Tryon County appeared before the Board and informed us that he has received Information that a certain Albert Van Der Werken is able to prove that Major Jellis Fonda was knowing to Robert Snell who lived with the said Jellis Fonda going to the Enemy last spring

Resolved in Consequence of the above Information that Albert Van Der Werken be cited to appear immediately before this Board in order to his being examined as to the same —

Adjourned —

1781
Feb. 7.

Met Albany 7th February 1781

Present

John M. Beeckman } { Isaac D. Fonda
Samuel Stringer }

Albert Van Der Werken appeared agreeable to the Order of Yesterday and was examined as to the Information against Major Jellis Fonda, on his Examination he says that he was informed by Robert Snell that Major Fonda was privy to his going off but does not from his own Knowledge [know] whether it be true —

The said Albert Van Der Werken also says that a certain Peter Boon of Tryon County is able to give some very material Information respecting sundry disaffected Persons [333] of that Place resolved that the said Peter Boon be ordered immediately to attend this Board in order that he may be examined as to the same —

The Board received Information that William Laird who came from the Enemy under a Pretence of his deserting from them is come with an Intention of enlisting Men for the Service of the enemy   It is therefore resolved that James

Crosset and Benjamin Crosset who are Bail for the Appearance of the said William Laird be ordered forthwith to deliver him up to this Board —

Adjourned —

Met Albany 8th February 1781

Present

John M. Beeckman ⎱ ⎰ Samuel Stringer
Isaac D. Fonda ⎰   ⎱

Resolved that James McKoy (a Deserter from the British
Army at present in Confinement on a Complaint of Disaffection) be discharged from Confinement on his entering
into a Recognizance for his good Behaviour and appearing
before any three of the Commissioners for Conspiracies
when thereunto required during the Continuance of the
present war with Great Britain

James McKoy of Livingston's Manor Tay-
    lor in £100
Christopher Hagedorn of the same place
    Farmer his Bail in.................... £100

Adjourned —

Met Albany 9th February 1781

Present

Isaac D. Fonda ⎱ ⎰ Samuel Stringer
John M. Beeckman ⎰   ⎱

[334] Col! Abraham Veeder appeared before the Board
and informed us that he had received Information that a certain Coenradt Coon has been lately sworn for the King in the
House of Thomas Bebee by an Emissary from the Enemy —

Resolved that the said Thomas Bebee be cited forthwith to
appear before this Board to give Information as to the above

Adjourned —

Met Albany 13th February 1781

Present

Samuel Stringer
John M. Beeckman } { Isaac D. Fonda

It appearing to the Board from the Information of Walter Quackenbush that Harmen Haver of Livingstons Manor did lately in Conversation with Garret Quackenbush call him the said Walter Quackenbush and the said Garret Quackenbush damned Rebels and the said Harmen Haver sustains the Character of a disaffected Person therefore resolved that a warrant be made out to bring the said Harmen Haver forthwith before this Board —

Thomas Bebee who was on the 9th Instant cited to appear before the Board appeared and being Examined as to the Information given by Col! Veeder confesses that Coenradt Coon was sworn for the King at his House but that it was contrary to his inclination and that he would have opposed the same if he had had it in his Power and it appearing that Col! Veeder received the Information [335] from the said Thomas Bebee and that the said Bebee is well affected to the American Cause therefore resolved that he be discharged

Adjourned —

Met Albany 15th February 1781

Present

John M. Beeckman }
Mathew Visscher } { Isaac D. Fonda

Ezekiel Ensign made application to the Board for Permission to go to his place of abode at Saragtoga and his request being taken into Consideration resolved that the same be granted on his taking an Oath that he will not dire[c]tly or indirectly give aid or Comfort or Intelligence

to the Enemies of the United States of America and that he
will make known to the Commissioners for Conspiracies all
treasonable actings & doings attempted against the same
whenever it shall come to his knowledge during the Continuance of the present War with Great Britain — And the
said Ezekiel Ensign having taken the said Oath resolved
with the Consent of his Bail that he have Leave to remain
at his place of abode at Saragtoga —

1781
Feb. 15.

Archibald McNeil made application to go & see his
Family at Saragtoga ordered with consent of his Bail that
he have leave granted him until Monday next —

William Robins having been ordered to appear before
this Board to enter into Recognizance of anew and he appearing this day agreeable to the said order   resolved that
[336] he be bound for his good Behaviour doing his Duty
and appearing before any three of the Commissioners for
Conspiracies when thereunto required during the Continuance of the present War with Great Britain —

William Robins of the Township of Argyle
in the County of Charlotte Farmer in.... £100
Edward Savage of White Creek in the County
of Charlotte Esqʳ his Bail in............ £100

Adjourned —

Met Albany 16ᵗʰ February 1781
Present

1781
Feb. 16.

John M. Beeckman ⎫   ⎰ Samuel Stringer
Isaac D. Fonda   ⎭   ⎱

George Tellford having been ordered to appear before
this Board to enter into Recognizance of anew and appearing
this Day agreeable to the said Order   resolved that he be
bound for his good Behaviour doing his duty and appearing
before any three of the Commissioners for Conspiracies

when thereunto required during the Continuance of the
present war with Great Britain

> George Tellford of the District of Cambridge
>   in the County of Albany Farmer in........ £100
> Moses Martin of White Creek in the County
>   of Charlotte Esq.ʳ his Bail in £100

William Blake having been ordered to appear before this
Board to enter into Recognizance of anew appearing this
day agreeable to the said Order resolved that he be bound
for his good Behaviour doing his duty and appearing before
[337] any three of the Commissioners for Conspiracies when
thereunto required during the Continuance of the Present War
with Great Britain

> William Blake of the District of Cambridge in
>   the County of Albany Farmer in £100
> Moses Martin of White Creek in the County
>   of Charlotte Esq.ʳ his Bail in............ £100

Adjourned

Met Albany 17ᵗʰ February 1781
          Present

          John M. Beeckman ⎫   ⎧ Samuel Stringer
          Isaac D. Fonda   ⎭   ⎩

Resolved that Thomas M?Feal be discharged from Confinement on entering into a Recognizance for his good Behaviour doing his Duty & appearing before any three of the
Commissioners for Conspiracies when thereunto required during the Continuance of the present war with Great Britain

> Thomas M?Feal of Livingston's Manor La-
>   bourer in £100
> Abraham Bloodgood of the City of Albany
>   Innkeeper his Bail in................. £100

Adjourned —

Met Albany 19th February 1781

Present

John M. Beeckman ⎱   ⎰ Samuel Stringer
Isaac D. Fonda   ⎰   ⎱

Resolved that William Bell be discharged from Confinement on entering into a Recognizance for his good Behaviour doing his duty and appearing before any thre[e] of the [338] Commissioners for Conspiracies when thereunto required during the Continuance of the present war with Great Britain —

William Bell of Fort Edward in the County
of Albany Farmer in £100
Duncan Shaw of Charlotte County Farmer
his Bail in......................... £100

As the above mentioned William Bell lives upon the Frontiers and has it in his Power to aid and Comfort the Enemy resolved that he be ordered to remove into the Interior Parts of this State by the first Day of April next —

Adjourned —

Met Albany 20th February 1781

Present

John M. Beeckman ⎱   ⎰ Isaac D. Fonda
Samuel Stringer   ⎰   ⎱

An Affidavit of Zachariah Holsapple taken before Samuel Ten Broeck Esqr of Livingston's Manor was laid before the Board whereby it appears that Teunis Smith of Livingston's has lately harboured and concealed two British Officers who were enlisting Men for the Enemies Service   resolved in Consequence of the said Affidavit that a warrant be made out for the apprehension of the said Teunis Smith and that

634   State of New York

1781
Feb. 20.

Citations be sent to Simon Rockefeller & Johannis Miller who were knowing to the said Officers being at the House of the said Teunis Smith and that the said warrant and Citations be sent to the said Samuel Ten Broeck Esq! for the purpose of having them served —

Adjourned —

1781
Feb. 21.

[339]   Met Albany 21st February 1781.

Present

Mathew Visscher ⎱   ⎰ Isaac D. Fonda
Samuel Stringer ⎰   ⎱

William Bradshaw and John Flinn who did on the 26th day of January last become surety for Samuel Burns appeared before the Board and requested Permission to deliver up the said Samuel Burns in discharge of themselves, resolved that the said William Bradshaw and John Flinn be accordingly discharged and that the said Samuel Burns be committed and that a Mittimus be made out for him.

Adjourned —

1781
Feb. 22.

Met Albany 22nd February 1781

Present

Samuel Stringer ⎱   ⎰ Isaac D. Fonda
Mathew Visscher ⎰   ⎱

Joel Abbot informed the Board that a certain Jacob Timmerman has harboured and secreted Emissaries from the Enemy and has assisted Persons who were on their way to Canada and the Examination of the said Joel Abbot being taken as to the same is in the words following (to wit) (see Examination on File) resolved in Consequence of the said Examination that a warrant be made out for the said Jacob Timmerman.—

It also appearing to the Board from the said Examination of Joel Abbot that the wife of William Nelling Junr was privy to Timmerman secreting Persons from the enemy therefore resolved that a warrant be also made out to apprehend her.—

[340] Resolved that John Todd be discharged from Confinement on entering into a Recognizance for his good Behaviour doing his duty and appearing before any three of the Commissioners for Conspiracies when thereunto required during the Continuance of the present war with Great Britain.—

John Todd of White Creek in the County of
    Charlotte Carpenter in £100
Isaac Little of the same place Farmer his
    Bail in............................. £100
Robert Gitty of the same place Farmer also
    his Bail in......................... £100
Adjourned —

Met Albany 23^d February 1781
Present

Samuel Stringer } { Isaac D. Fonda
Mathew Visscher }

Resolved that John Wykoff be discharged from Confinement on entering into a Recognizance for his good Behaviour doing his duty and appearing before any three of the Commissioners for Conspiracies when thereunto required during the Continuance of the present war with Great Britain

John Wykoff of Nistageuna Labourer in £100
David Maxwell of Ballstown Farmer his
    Bail in............................. £100

Zachariah Holsapple whose Examination taken before

1781
Feb. 23.

Samuel Ten Broeck Esq.ʳ was laid before the Board on the 21ˢᵗ Instant was brought before us and being Examined and his Examination being reduced to writing is in the words following (to wit) (see Examination on File)

Adjourned.—

1781
Feb. 27.

[341]   Met Albany 27ᵗʰ February 1781

Present

John M. Beeckman }   { Isaac D. Fonda
Samuel Stringer   }   {

His Excellency Governor Clinton having requested by Letter that James Van Driesen may be liberated from Confinement and the Board taking the said Request into Consideration do thereupon resolve that the said James Van Driesen be accordingly discharged.—

Lieut.ᵗ Col.ᴵ Henry K. Van Rensselaer appeared before the Board and informed that there has lately been a Meeting of a Number of disaffected Persons in the East District of the Manor of Rensselaerwyck at the House of James Lister at which Meeting was publicly read by Jabez Spencer a Proclimation of Sir Henry Clinton Commander in cheif of the British Forces in America which Conduct being in open Violation of the Laws of this State and destructive of the Peace and good Government of the same and having a Tendency to Alienate the Minds of Friends of the American Cause —

Therefore resolved that a warrant be made out for the immediate Apprehension of the said Jabez Spencer together with all such other disaffected Persons as were present at the said Meeting and that the said warrant be delivered to Cap.ᵗ Robert Woodward for the Purpose of having the same served.

Resolved that John May and John J. Van Valkenburgh who were present at the above mentioned Meeting be cited to appear before this Board to Morrow Morning in Order that they may be examined as to the same. 1781 Feb. 27.

Adjourned.

[342]   Met Albany 28th February 1781   1781 Feb. 28.
     Present

John M. Beeckman ⎱   ⎰ Mathew Visscher
Isaac D. Fonda ⎰   ⎱ Samuel Stringer

John May having been cited to appear before the Board this Day appeared agreeable to Order & being examined as to the Meeting at James Lister's at which Sir Henry Clinton's Proclamation was read he saith as follows (to wit) (see his Examination on File).—

In Consequence of the above Examination resolved that a warrant be made out directed to the said John May for the immediate Apprehension of Silas Wood and William Bruce, and that the said John May be directed to search the Houses of the said Silas Wood and William Bruce for treasonable Papers, and that he bring the Bodies with the said Papers forthwith before us.—

Alexander Cone having been apprehended by Capt Ichabod Turner for being concerned in dispersing Sir Henry Clinton's Proclamation and being brought before the Board and Examined resolved that he be committed and that a Mittimus be made out for him —

Adjourned.—

     Met Albany 1st March 1781. —   1781 Mar. 1.
     Present

John M. Beeckman ⎱   ⎰ Isaac D. Fonda
Samuel Stringer ⎰   ⎱

Application was made to the Board by James Gillis for Permission to go to his Place of Abode at the Scotch [343] Patent and his Bail Neal Shaw consenting to the same resolved that he have Permission accordingly until the first Day of April next.—

Application was also made to the Board by Archibald M?Neal for Permission to go to his Place of Abode at the Scotch Patent to which his surety Evans Humphrey consenting resolved that he have Permission accordingly until the first day of April next —

Major Jacob Schermerhorn appeared before the Board with Yutlope Chrencher & Hendrick Schermerhorn who he informed us are able to give Information concerning a Number of disaffected Inhabitants at Schodack and the said Yutlope Chrencher and Hendrick Schermerhorn being examined say as follows (to wit) (see their Examination on File) —

Resolved that in Consequence of the above Examinations of Yutlope Chrencher and Hendrick Schermerhorn that a warrant be made out directed to Cap! Nicholas Staats for the immediate Apprehension of Martin Egbertse and Johannis Kittle —

Adjourned —

Met Albany 2<u>nd</u> March 1781

Present

     John M. Beeckman } { Mathew Visscher
     Samuel Stringer   } { Isaac D. Fonda

Lieu! David Hustead appeared before the Board and informed that agreeable to our warrant he had apprehended John Cone and David Ni[c]hols for dispersing about the Country Sir Henry Clinton's Proclamation and that he had also apprehended James Lister, Thomas Hicks and Henry

[344] Filkens who were present at the reading of one of the 1781
Mar. 2. said Proclamations at the House of the said James Lister and they being severally brought before the Board and Examined resolved that John Cone and David Nichols be confined and that James Lister, Thomas Hicks, and Henry Filkins be ordered to appear before the Board to Morrow Morning —

Gersham Odell one of the Constable's of Hosick District appeared before the Board and informed that he had apprehended Jacob Timmerman against whom a warrant was issued by this Board upon the Information of Joel Abbot & the said Jacob Timmerman being brought before us and examined ordered that he be committed and that a Mittimus be made out for him —

A Letter from Abraham Fonda Esq.ᵣ and Col.ᴵ Abraham Wemple dated as Schenectady was laid before the Board wherein they inform that they send to us under Guard John Mekelmay, John Curry & George Scott who have harboured and secreted two Men who were on their way to the Enemy resolved that they be Confined and that a Mittimus be made out for them. —

Adjourned —

Met Albany 3.ᵈ March 1781   1781
Mar. 3.
    Present

    John M. Beeckman ⎱ ⎰ Mathew Visscher
    Samuel Stringer   ⎰ ⎱ Isaac D. Fonda

Resolved that Abraham Robison who is Surety for Andries Stoll be ordered forthwith to deliver up the said Andries Stoll.—

[345] Lieu.ᵗ David Hustead appearing before the Board was examined his Examination is as follows (to wit) (see Examination on File)

Capt Henry Dencker appearing before the Board agreeable to order was examined his Examination is as follows (to wit) (see Examination on File)

Capt Nicholas Staats appeared before the Board & informed that he had apprehended agreeable to our warrant John J. Van Valkenburgh, John Kittle, Jacobus Moll, Peter Wyngart, Andries Wessels, Martin Egbertse and Peter Van Valkenburgh and they being brought before us and examined resolved that Martin Egbertse Peter Wyngaert, Jacobus Moll, John Kittle and John J. Van Valkenburgh be committed and that a Mittimus be made out for them.—

It appearing to the Board from a Recommendation of sundry well affected Inhabitants that John J. Van Valkenburgh has during the present Contest behaved himself in a peaceable and inoffensive Manner yet as he is reputed to be disaffected to the American Cause therefore resolved that previous to his Discharge he enter into a Recognizance for his future good Behaviour doing his Duty and appearing before any three of the Commissioners for Conspiracies when thereunto required for and during the Continuance of the present War with Great Britain.—

John J. Van Valkenburgh of Schodack in the
County of Albany Farmer in............ £200

Andries Wessels apprehended by Capt Staats being recommended to the Board as a Peaceable Person yet as he is also [346] reputed to be disaffected to the American Cause therefore resolved that previous to his Discharge he enter into a Recognizance for his good Behaviour doing his Duty and appearing before any three of the Commissioners for Conspiracies when thereunto required during the Continuance of the present war with Great Britain —

Andries Wessels of Schodack in the County of
Albany Labourer in.................. £100

1781
Mar. 3.

Samuel Hill of the west District of the Manor of Rensselaerwyck having been present at James Lister's when Sir Henry Clinton's Proclamation was there read & being Examined and it appearing from the Recommendation of Capt Woodward that the said Samuel Hill has always behaved himself as a Zealous Friend to the American Cause therefore resolved that he be discharged

The above mentioned Samuel Hill mentioning to the Board his willingness to apprehend Jabez Spencer resolved that a warrant for that Purpose be made out and delivered to him. —

Thomas Hicks, James Lister, and Henry Filkins appearing before the Board agreeable to the Order of Yesterday were again examined and as it does not appear that they were concerned in or promoted the reading the Proclamation before mentioned but as they sustain the Characters of being disaffected to the American Cause therefore resolved that they procure Sureties for their future good Behaviour —

James Lister appearing with Israel Thomas as surety [347] resolved that he enter into Recognizance for his good Behaviour doing his Duty and appearing before any three of the Commissioners for Conspiracies when called upon during the Continuance of the present war with Great Britain —

James Lister of the East District of the
  Manor of Rensselaerwyck Farmer in £100
Israel Thomas of the same place Farmer his
  Bail in.............................. £100

Thomas Hicks and Henry Filkins being unable to procure Bail other than for their Appearance with sufficient sureties at some future day resolved that they severally enter into a Recognizance for their Appearance on Tuesday next with sufficient sureties to become bound with them for their future good Conduct and Appearance when called upon. —

1781
Mar. 3.

Thomas Hicks of the East District of the
Manor of Rensselaerwyck Farmer in..... £100
David Hustead of the same place Farmer his
Bail in............................... £100
Robert Woodward of the same place Farmer
also his Bail in....................... £100

Henry Filkins of the East District of the
Manor of Rensselaerwyck Farmer in.... £100
David Hustead of the same place Farmer his
Bail in............................... £100
Robert Woodward of the same place Farmer
also his Bail in....................... £100

Adjourned. —

1781
Mar. 5.

Met Albany 5ᵗʰ March 1781
Present

John M. Beeckman ⎱   ⎰ Isaac D. Fonda
Samuel Stringer ⎰   ⎱

Abraham Bloodgood appeared before the Board with
Thomas McFeal for whom he some Time since entered
[348] Recognizance and surrendered the said Thomas
McFeal resolved that the said Abraham Bloodgood be
accordingly discharged from the said Recognizance and
that the said Thomas McFeal stand committed till he procure
another sufficient surety —

John McFall appearing before the Board and offering to
become surety for the above mentioned Thomas McFeal
resolved that the said Thomas McFall be discharged on
entering into a Recognizance for his good Behaviour doing
his Duty and appearing before any three of the Commissioners for Conspiracies when thereunto required during the
Continuance of the present War with Great Britain. —

Thomas McFeal of the Manor of Livingston
in the County of Albany Labourer in..... £100
John McFall of the same place Farmer his
Bail in............................. £100

The Board having received Information that William
Laird is at Johnstown and that there is the greatest Reason
to think that he intends soon to go to Canada therefore
resolved that a warrant be made out and directed to any
Constable of Tryon County for the immediate Apprehension of the said William Laird. —

Thomas Hicks who was on the third Instant bound for
his Appearance before this Board with a sufficient surety
appeared resolved that he enter into a Recognizance for
his good Behaviour, doing his duty and appearing before
any three of the Commissioners for Conspiracies when
thereunto required during the Continuance of the present
war with Great Britain. —

Thomas Hicks of the East District of the
Manor of Rensselaerwyck Farmer in.... £100
[349] David Hustead of the same place Farmer
his Bail in........................... £100

Henry Filkins who was also on the third Instant bound
for his Appearance before this Board with a sufficient
surety appeared resolved that he enter into a Recognizance
for his good Behaviour doing his duty and appearing before
any three of the Commissioners for Conspiracies when
thereunto required during the Continuance of the present
war with Great Britain. —

Henry Filkins of the East District of the
Manor of Rensselaerwyck Farmer in.... £100
Abraham Filkins of the same place Farmer
his Bail in........................... £100

Teunis Smith of Livingston's Manor having by Virtue of a warrant from this Board been apprehended by Jacob Powers Constable was brought before the Board and being interrogated as to his harbouring two British Officers, he denied the same and it appearing from the Recommendation of his Officers that he has always behaved himself well and there being great Reason to think that the Charge as alledged against him by Zachariah Holsapple is untrue therefore resolved that he be discharged.—

Johannis Smith of Livingston's Manor being also examined on the Information of Zachariah Holsapple as to the Officers said to have been at the House of Teunis Smith above mentioned and it appearing that he is altogether unacquainted with the same therefore resolved that he be discharged.—

Bowles Arnold having been present at the Meeting at James Lister's where Sir Henry Clinton's Proclamation was read appeared agreeable to our order and being Examined as [350] to the same resolved that he be committed and that a Mittimus be made out for him.—

Lieu.^t Col^l Henry K. Van Rensselaer appeared before the Board and informed us that a few days since he issued his warrant agreeable to Law for the Apprehension of Andries Stoll and Harpert Witbeeck who had been fined by a Court Martial for Neglect of Militia Duty which Fine they refused to pay that the said Andries Stoll & Harpert Witbeeck had been apprehended by Serjeant Elijah Adams and that after being so apprehended a Number of disaffected Persons (to wit) Robert Mackesny, Samuel Mackesny, John Mackesny, Walter Mackesny, John Barham, Peter Kimmell, Lowrence Snyder, Jacob Fraligh, Sander Bulson, Christopher File, Jacob Kerncross, Coenradt Heydorn, John Melius, Abraham Van Aernam, Andries Colekamer & others did

forceably rescue the said Andries Stoll and Harpert Wit- 1781 Mar. 5.
beeck from the said Elijah Adams resolved in Consequence
of the above information that a warrant be made out for
the immediate apprehension of the said Persons above
mentioned & all others concerned in the said Rescue.—

Adjourned.

Met Albany 6th March 1781 1781 Mar. 6.
Present

John M. Beeckman } { Isaac D. Fonda
Samuel Stringer }

John Cone and David Nichols who ·a few days ago were
confined for dispersing Sir Henry Clinton's Proclamations
about the Country were brought before the Board and
severally examined resolved that they be recommitted.—

[351] Hezekiah Van Orden Esq.ʳ appeared before the
Board and requested that George Burk a Deserter from
the British Army might be discharged from Confinement
& that he the said Hezekiah Van Orden would take the said
George Burk in his Care resolved that he be discharged
accordingly.—

John Scott who was confined at the Request of Abraham Fonda Esq.ʳ and Col.ˡ Abraham Wemple for harbouring two Men who were on their way to the Enemy was
brought before the Board and examined resolved that he
be recommitted.—

Cap.ᵗ Robert Woodward appeared before the Board and
informed that Nicholas Miller, John Miller, and John J.
Miller were present at the Meeting at James Lister's where
a Proclamation of Sir Henry Clinton was read; & that the
said Nicholas Miller, John Miller and John J. Miller
appeared to be warmly engaged in promoting the reading the
said Proclamation wherefore it is resolved that a warrant be

1781
Mar. 6. made out directed to Capt Nicholas Staats for their immediate Apprehension

Adjourned. —

1781
Mar. 7.

Met Albany 7th March 1781

Present

John M. Beeckman
Samuel Stringer
Isaac D. Fonda

Mathew Visscher
Jeremiah Van Rensselaer

His Excellency Governor Clinton having in Consequence of the Information received by this Board from Lieu.^t Col.^l Henry K. Van Rensselaer on the 5th Instant ordered a Party of [352] Col.^l Cuyler's Regiment to apprehend all those who were concerned in rescueing Andries Stoll and Harpert Lansing from the Custody of Elijah Adams and they having apprehended a Number of disaffected Persons concerned in the said Rescue and the said Persons being by order of his Excellency the Governor brought before the Board and severally Examined their Names are as follows (to wit) Samuel Swertfeger, Melchert File, Jacob Weeger Junr, John Weeger, Christopher File, Christopher Shaver Robert Machesny, Walter Machesny, Abraham Roberts, John Smith, Harper Lansing, Coenradt Heydorn, Coenradt Colehamer, John Klint, Andries Stoll Samuel Machesny, Jacob Fraligh and Isaac Hop resolved that they be severally committed and that a Mittimus be made out for them.—

The Board having received Information that a certain Person supposed to be a spy from the Enemy has been at the House of Lieu.^t Cleveland and the said Cleveland being ordered to appear before us and he appearing on being examined says that he does not recollect having seen any such Person at his House resolved that it be recommended to him to be Extremely vigilant in learning the Characters of such Persons as he entertains in his House and from Time to Time give Information to this Board of all such Persons of whom he may be suspicious.—

William Rowke being apprehended and brought before the Board as a suspicious Person on being examined says that he is enlisted during the war for a class   resolved that he be delivered over to Lieu꜀ Snow.—

Adjourned.

[353]   Met Albany 8ᵗʰ March 1781

Present

> John M. Beeckman }   { Mathew Visscher
> Isaac D. Fonda   }   { Hugh Mitchell

The Board having received Information that at the house of Dirck Van Der Wilgen at the Hellebergh there has lately been a Meeting of a Number of disaffected Persons at which said Meeting among others were present Peter Seeger and Gerrit Seeger resolved in Consequence of the said Information that the Said Dirck Van Der Wilgen Gerrit Seeger and Peter Seeger be cited to appear before the Board to give Information as to the above Meeting —

John Curry, John Mekelmay and John Scott having made application to the Board to be liberated from Confinement on Bail and the same being taken into Consideration resolved that they be severally liberated accordingly on entering into Recognizance to appear within ten Days from the Date hereof with each of them a sufficient surety before the Commissioners for Conspiracies at Schenectady and that before the said Commissioners they severally enter into a Recognizance for their good Behaviour doing their duty and appearing before any three of the Commissioners for Conspiracies during the Continuance of the present war with Great Britain —

John Curry of Ballstown in the County of
Albany Farmer in £100

John Mekelmay of the same Place Farmer in. £100

John Scott of the same place Farmer in.... £100

Adjourned.—

[354]   Met Albany 9th March 1781 —

Present

John M. Beeckman ⎱   ⎰ Isaac D. Fonda
Samuel Stringer   ⎰   ⎱

Robert Simmons late a Capt in the Enemies Service being
at present in this City and it being conceived necessary that
he should be examined and he being sent for and appearing
was examined his Examination is as follows (to wit)
(see Examination on File)

Resolved that Melchert File be discharged from Confinement on entering into a Recognizance for his good Behaviour
doing his duty and appearing before any three of the Commissioners for Conspiracies when thereunto required during
the Continuance of the present war with Great Britain —

Melchert File of the East District of the
Manor of Rensselaerwyck Farmer in.... £100
Isaac Van Aernam of the City of Albany
Hatter his Bail in...................... £100

Resolved that Nicholas Miller be discharged from Confinement on entering into a Recognizance for his good
Behaviour doing his Duty and appearing before any three
of the Commissioners for Conspiracies when thereunto
required during the Continuance of the present war with
Great Britain

Nicholas Miller of the East District of the
Manor of Rensselaerwyck Innkeeper in.. £100
John Ja. Miller of the same place Taylor
his Bail in............................ £100

Resolved that John J. Miller be discharged from [355] confinement on entering into a Recognizance for his good Behaviour doing his duty and appearing before any three of the Commissioners for Conspiracies when thereunto required during the Continuance of the present war with Great Britain.—

John J. Miller of the East District in the
Manor of Rensselaerwyck Farmer in.... £100
Nicholas Staats of the same Place Farmer
his Bail in............................ £100

Resolved that John Andrew be discharged from confinement on entering into a Recognizance for his good Behaviour doing his duty and appearing before any three of the Commissioners for Conspiracies when thereunto required during the Continuance of the present war with Great Britain.—

John Andrew of New-town in the County
of Albany Labourer in £100
Coenradt Nestly of the same place Farmer
his Bail in £100

The Board being informed that Samuel Inglis of the west District of the Manor of Rensselaerwyck was present at the Reading of Sir Henry Clinton's Proclamation at the House of James Lister resolved in Consequence thereof that the said Samuel Inglis be cited to appear before this Board forthwith to answer to the same. —

Resolved that Lieut David Hustead and David Sprague be cited to appear forthwith before the Board in order that they may be examined as to the Meeting at James Lister's.—

Derick Van Der Welgen, Peter Seeger & Gerrit Seeger

having been cited to appear before the Board for the Purpose of being Examined respecting a Meeting of a Number of [356] disaffected Persons at the Hellebergh at which they were present and they appearing agreeable to the said order were severally examined and say as follows (to wit) (see their Examination on File)

Adjourned

Met Albany 10th March 1781 —
Present

John M. Beeckman   }   { Isaac D. Fonda
Jeremiah Van Rensselaer }   { Samuel Stringer

James Brisben appeared before the Board and requested Permission to go to his Place of Abode at Saragtoga and remain some time with his Family which Request of the said James Brisben being taken into Consideration resolved that he have Leave granted him accordingly until the first day of April next. —

Henry Tinkey also restricted by Recognizance to the Limits of this City appeared before the Board and requested to go to his Place of Abode at the Scotch Patent resolved on considering the same that he also have Leave granted until the first day of April Next. —

Resolved that Nicholas Muller enter into a Recognizance for his appearance at the next Supream Court of Judicature held for the State of New York at the City Hall in this City on the third Tuesday in April next (or wheresoever the said Court shall then be held in the State aforesaid) and not to depart the Court without Leave. —

Nicholas Muller of the East District of the
Manor of Rensselaerwyck Innkeeper in.. £100
[357] Jerone Van Valkenburgh of Schodack
Farmer his Bail in.................... £100

Resolved that John J. Miller enter into a Recognizance for his appearance at the next Supream Court of Judicature held for the State of New York at the City Hall in the City of Albany on the third Tuesday in April next (or wheresoever the said Court shall then be held in the State aforesaid) and not to depart the Court without Leave. —

John J. Miller of the East District of the
Manor of Rensselaerwyck Farmer in.... £100
Jerone Van Valkenburgh of Schodack Farm-
er his Bail in........................ £100

Samuel Swertfeger having been confined for being concerned in the late Meeting of the disaffected on the Hosick Road and it appearing that the charge is not well founded therefore resolved that he be discharged. —

Adjourned

Met Albany 12th March 1781
Present

John M. Beeckman ⎱ ⎰ Mathew Visscher
Samuel Stringer ⎰ ⎱ Isaac D. Fonda

Resolved that John Klint be discharged from Confinement on entering into a Recognizance for his good Behaviour doing his Duty and appearing before any three of the Commissioners for Conspiracies when thereunto required during the Continuance of the Present War with Great Britain —

John Klint of the East District of the Manor
of Rensselaerwyck Schoolmaster in...... £100
John Leonard of the west District of the
Manor of Rensselaerwyck Farmer his Bail
in................................... £100

[358] Resolved that Martin Egbertse be discharged from Confinement on entering into a Recognizance for his good

Behaviour doing his duty and appearing before any three of the Commissioners for Conspiracies when thereunto required during the Continuance of the Present war with Great Britain. —

Martin Egbertse of Schodack Innkeeper in.. £100
Jacob Schermerhorn of the same place
Farmer his Bail in................... £100

Resolved that John Jerone Van Valkenburgh be discharged from Confinement on entering into a Recognizance for his good Behaviour doing his duty and appearing before any three of the Commissioners for Conspiracies when thereunto required during the Continuance of the Present war with Great Britain. —

John Jerone Van Valkenburgh of Schodack
Farmer in........................... £400
Jacob Schermerhorn of the same place
Farmer his Bail in................... £400

Resolved that Bowles Arnold be discharged from Confinement on entering into a Recognizance for his good Behaviour doing his duty and appearing before any three of the Commissioners for Conspiracies when thereunto required during the Continuance of the present war with Great Britain. —

Bowles Arnold of the East District of the
Manor of Rensselaerwyck Farmer in.... £100
Reuben Rowley of the same place Farmer
his Bail in......................... £100

It appearing evident to this Board from the Examination of Jonas Odell that Augustus Jeram is a dangerous and disaffected Person and that his going at large unless under Restrictions may be attended with evil [359] Consequences

to the Safety of the State It is therefore resolved that a
warrant be made out directed to John May for the immediate
Apprehension of the said Augustus Jeram. —

Adjourned. —

1781
Mar. 12.

Met Albany 13th March 1781

Present

1781
Mar. 13.

John M. Beeckman ⎱ ⎧ Mathew Visscher
Isaac D. Fonda ⎰ ⎩ Samuel Stringer

Resolved that Seth Rowley be cited to appear forthwith
before the Board for the Purpose of being examined as to
sundry Persons concerned in distributing about the Country
Sir Henry Clinton's Proclamation. —

Henry Simpson of the west District of the Manor of
Rensselaerwyck appeared before the Board & informed us
that a few days ago Evert Jansen came to his House in a
Sleigh and had with him Joseph Bettis and that the said
Jansen & Bettis after remaining there sometime went
away together resolved in Consequence of the above Information that the said Evert Jansen be immediately apprehended and brought before us. —

Jacob Kidney appearing informed the Board that he had
agreeable to order apprehended Evert Jansen & the said
Evert Jansen being Examined and unwillingly [sic] to answer
candidly to the Questions proposed to him therefore resolved
that he be committed and that a Mittimus be made out for
him. —

Lieutenant Nicholas Bower appeared before the Board
and informed us that agreeable to the Directions of [360]
Samuel Ten Broeck Esqr he had brought up from Livingston's Manor a Prisoner who calls himself William
Hartley who the said Samuel Ten Broeck had caused to be
apprehended as a Suspicious Person and the said William

1781
Mar. 13.

Hartley being brought before the Board & examined resolved that he be committed and that a Mittimus be made out for him. —

Resolved that David Nichols be discharged from Confinement on entering into a Recognizance for his good Behaviour doing his duty and appearing before any three of the Commissioners for Conspiracies when thereunto required during the Continuance of the Present war with Great Britain. —

David Nichols of Stephen-town in the County
of Albany Farmer in................... £100
Ichabod Turner of the same place Farmer
his Bail in........................... £100

Resolved that Jacob Freligh be discharged from Confinement on entering into a Recognizance for his good Behaviour doing his duty and appearing before any three of the Commissioners for Conspiracies when thereunto required during the Continuance of the Present war with Great Britain. —

Jacob Freligh of the East District of the
Manor of Rensselaerwyck Labourer in... £100
Martin Freligh of the same place Farmer
his Bail in........................... £100

Adjourned —

1781
Mar. 14.

[361]   Met Albany 14th March 1781. —

Present

John M. Beeckman   Jeremiah Van Rensselaer
Isaac D. Fonda   Mathew Visscher
Samuel Stringer

It appearing from the Examination of Henry Simpson that Joseph Bettis has been harboured by One Thomas who lives in the west District of the Manor of Rensselaerwyck on a Farm formerly belonging to Abraham Boom resolved in Consequence of the same that a warrant be made out directed to Jacob Hilton forthwith to apprehend & bring before us the said Thomas. —

Jacobus Moll who was the other Day confined being brought before the Board and he acknowledging his Fault and promising to amend his Conduct in future therefore resolved that he be discharged from Confinement —

William Hartley who was Confined on Suspicion of his being a spy from the Enemy was brought before the Board and examined and then ordered to be recommitted. —

Resolved that Alamander Cone be discharged from Confinement on entering into a Recognizance for his good Behaviour doing his duty and appearing before any three of the Commissioners for Conspiracies when thereunto required during the Continuance of the present War with Great Britain. —

Alamander Cone of Stephen Town in the
County of Albany Joiner in............ £100
Ichabod Cone of the same place Farmer his
Bail in............................. £100

[362] His Excellency Governor Clinton having requested the Board to examine William Hartley in his Presence and his Excellency now attending for that Purpose the said William Hartley was brought before the Board and being Examined says as follows (to wit) (see Examination on File)

It appearing from the above Examination that Ryneir Vischer of this City is concerned with other disaffected Persons in endeavouring by enlisting Men for the enemy to subvert the Liberty and Independance of this State and as the said Ryneir Visher sustains the Character of disaffection therefore resolved that a warrant be made out and directed to Jacob Kidney for the immediate apprehension of the said Ryneir Vischer —

Adjourned —

1781
Mar. 15.

Met Albany 15th March 1781

Present

John M. Beeckman } { Isaac D. Fonda
Samuel Stringer }

Lieu^t Jacob Snyder of Schohary appeared before the Board and informed us that by order of Col^l Peter Vrooman he had apprehended Hendrick Kneiskern Junr and Jacob Saltsbergh who last Fall assisted Sir John Johnson in destroying Schohary and the said Hendrick Kneiskern Junr and Jacob Saltsbergh being examined resolved that they be committed and that a Mittimus be made out for them —

Resolved that the Examination of Lieu^t [363] Jacob Snyder with Respect to the Conduct of sundry disaffected Persons at the Bever Dam be taken which is in the words following (to wit) (see Examination on File)

Sander Bulson having been apprehended with those Persons concerned in the Rescue of Harpert Lansing and Andries Stoll and Lieu^t Col^l Henry Van Rensselaer having certified to the Board that the Conduct of the said Sander Bulson had always been inoffensive & that he has done his duty in the Militia therefore resolved that he be discharged from Confinement.—

Resolved that James Bruce of the East District of the Manor of Rensselaerwyck be cited forthwith to appear before this Board with a sufficient surety to enter into Recognizance of anew.—

Samuel Inglis having been present at the Meeting at

James Lister's at which was read a Proclamation of Sir Henry Clinton having been cited to appear before the Board appeared resolved that he enter into a Recognizance for his appearance At the Court of Oyer and Terminer at present held in the City Hall of this City then and there to answer such Matters as shall be alledged against him and not to depart the Court without Leave.—

    Samuel Inglis of the East District of the Manor of Rensselaerwyck Cooper in...... £100

Abraham Van Aernam who was apprehended for assisting in the Rescue of Lansing and Stoll requesting to be discharged from Confinement and his [364] Conduct notwithstanding his Political Principles having always been unexceptionable (expect[1] in the present Instance) therefore resolved that he be discharged.—

    Adjourned.—

           Met Albany 16th March 1781
Present

    John M. Beeckman } { Isaac D. Fonda
    Samuel Stringer

    William Hartley being again brought before the Board and examined says that Nathaniel Cotton of Cooksakie is concerned in enlisting Men for the Service of the enemy and that the said Cotton furnished him with a Pass to travel through the Country in order that he the said William Hartley might be able the better to carry on his Practices against the State.—

    Resolved in Consequence of the above Information that a warrant be made out directed to John Tillman Junr forthwith to apprehend & bring before us the said Nathaniel Cotton.—

[1] So in the original for " except."

Resolved that Johannis Kittle be discharged from Confinement on entering into Recognizance for his good Behaviour doing his duty and appearing before any three of the Commissioners for Conspiracies when thereunto required during the Continuance of the present war with Great Britain —

> Johannis Kittle of Schodack in the County
> of Albany Farmer in.................. £200
> Philip Schermerhorn of the same place Cord
> wainer his Bail in..................... £100
> [365] Jacob J. Van Valkenburgh of the same
> place Cordwainer also his Bail in........ £100

William Hartley having also informed the Board that Samuel Baker of the East District of the Manor of Rensselaerwyck has in his Possession Commissions from New York which he is to deliver to such Persons as are willing to enlist Men for the Service of the Enemy and that he has also with him Proclamations of Sir Henry Clinton which he disperses about the Country and Capt Nicholas Staats having been requested to apprehend the said Samuel Baker and bring him before the Board this day appear'd with him and the said Samuel Baker being examined   Resolved that he be committed and that a Mittimus be made out for him.—

It being suggested to the Board that Mrs Visscher (Mother of Ryneir Visher who was a few days ago confined) is on Account of the confinement of her said son reduced to a State of Indigence and want as she with her Family depend solely upon him for their Support.—

Resolved therefore that the said Ryneir Vischer be liberated from Confinement on entering into Recognizance for his good Behaviour doing his duty & appearing before any three of the Commissioners for Conspiracies when thereunto

required during the Continuance of the present war with
Great Britain.—

 Ryneir Vischer of the City of Albany Silver
  Smith in.............................. £100
 Teunis Visscher of the same place Yeoman
  his Bail in.......................... £100

Resolved that Peter Wyngaert be discharged from [366]
Confinement on entering into Recognizance for his good
Behaviour doing his duty and appearing before any three of
the Commissioners for Conspiracies when thereunto required
during the Continuance of the present war with Great
Britain —

 Peter Wyngaert of Schodack in the County
  of Albany Farmer in.................. £100
 Jacob J. Van Valkenburgh of D° Cord-
  wainer his Bail in..................... £ 50
 Philip Schermerhorn of D°.....D° also his
  Bail in............................... £ 50

Adjourned.—

   Met Albany 17th March 1781 —
  John M. Beeckman ⎱ ⎰ Mathew Visscher
  Isaac D. Fonda ⎰ ⎱ Samuel Stringer

 Jacob Saltsbergh of Schohary who was the other day
confined was brought before the Board for examination and
having been examined was ordered to be Recommitted —
 Resolved that Jacob Weeger Jun. be discharged from
Confinement on his entering into a Recognizance for his good
Behaviour doing his duty and appearing before any three of
the Commissioners for Conspiracies when thereunto required for and during the Continuance of the present war

with Great Britain and also for his Appearance at the next
Supream Court of Judicature to be held for the State of New
York at the City Hall in the City of Albany on the third
Tuesday in April next (or wheresoever the said Court shall
then be held [367] in the State aforesaid) to answer to such
Matters as shall be alledgèd against him and not depart
the Court without Leave.—

    Thomas Weeger Jun�r of the East District of
       the Manor of Rensselaerwyck Farmer in.. £100
    Thomas Weeger of Tomhenick in the County
       of Albany Farmer his Bail in £100

Resolved that John Cone be discharged from Confinement
on entering into a Recognizance for his good Behaviour
doing his duty and appearing before any three of the Com
missioners for Conspiracies when thereunto required during
the Continuance of the present war with Great Britain —

    John Cone of Stephen Town Farmer in.... £100
    Benjamin Sacket of the same place Farmer
       his Bail in £100

Resolved that Johannis Weeger be discharged from
Confinement on his entering into Recognizance for his good
Behaviour doing his duty and appearing before any three
of the Commissioners for Conspiracies when thereunto
required during the Continuance of the present war with
Great Britain.—

    Johannis Weeger of the East District of the
       Manor of Rensselaerwyck Farmer in.... £100
    Coenradt Heyner of the same place Farmer
       his Bail in £100

John May appeared before the Board with Jasper Crandel
and Stephen Wilcocks who he informed us he had appre-

hended by order of Daniel Hull Esq.ʳ Justice of the Peace &
the said John May at the same time laid before the Board
sundry Examinations taken by the said Daniel Hull respecting the [368] Conduct of the said Jasper Crandell and
Stephen Wilcocks which Examinations being read and it
appearing therefrom that the said Crandell and Wilcocks
are disaffected and dangerous Persons therefore resolved
that they be committed and a Mittimus made out for
them —

Adam Pabst heretofore bound by Recognizance being
ordered to appear before this Board with a sufficient surety
to enter Recognizance of a new appeared resolved that
he be bound for his good Behaviour doing his duty and
appearing before any three of the Commissioners for Conspiracies when thereunto required during the Continuance
of the present war with Great Britain.—

Adam Pabst of the Hellebergh in the County
    of Albany Farmer in.................. £100
Andries Ward Jun.ʳ of the same place Farmer
    his Bail in.......................... £100

Adjourned

          Met Albany 18ᵗʰ March 1781
Present
    John M. Beeckman ⎱ ⎰ Isaac D. Fonda
    Samuel Stringer ⎰ ⎱

Daniel Hewson who last Year went to Canada from this
City and joined the Enemy and who lately surrendered himself at Fort Schuyler being brought to his Excellency Governor Clinton and he referring the said Daniel Hewson to
this Board for Examination & the said Daniel Hewson
being examined says as follows (to wit) (see his Examination on File)

1781
Mar. 18.
Ordered that a Mittimus be made out for the said Daniel Hewson —

[369] Nathaniel Cotton having been apprehended by James Green by order of this Board upon the Information of William Hartley resolved that the said James Green attend with the said Nathaniel Cotton before this Board to Morrow Morning.—

Adjourned —

1781
Mar. 19.

Met Albany 19th March 1781

Present

John M. Beeckman }
Mathew Visscher }   { Isaac D. Fonda

Nathaniel Cotton who was Yesterday brought before the Board by James Green being again produced was examined as to the Charges alledged against him by William Hartley which he utterly denying and producing to this Board a Recommendation of his uniform Attachment to the American Cause signed by Leonard Bronck Esqr of Cooksakie in whose House the said Nathaniel Cotton has for two Years past resided resolved on Considering of the Above Recommendation that the said Nathaniel Cotton be discharged. —

Daniel Hewston who was Yesterday confined being brought before the Board was again examined ordered that he be recommitted. —

Adjourned

1781
Mar. 20.

Met Albany 20th March 1781

Present

John M. Beeckman }
Mathew Visscher }   { Isaac D. Fonda

Resolved that Hendrick Kittle be discharged from Confinement on entering into a Recognizance for his [370] appearance on the third Tuesday in April next at the Supream Court of Judicature to be held for the State of New York at the City Hall in this City (or wheresoever the said Court shall then be held in the State aforesaid) to answer to such Matters as shall then and there be alledged against him and not to depart the Court without Leave —

    Hendrick Kittle of the East District of the
        Manor of Rensselaerwyck Farmer in.... £100
    Jacob J. Van Valkenburgh of the same place
        Cordwainer his Bail in................ £100

    Resolved that Nicholas Shaver be discharged from Confinement on entering into a Recognizance for his good Behaviour doing his duty and appearing before any three of the Commissioners for Conspiracies when thereunto required during the Continuance of the Present war with Great Britain —

    Nicholas Shaver of the East District of the
        Manor of Rensselaerwyck Farmer in.... £100
    John Tillman of the City of Albany Innkeeper his Bail in..................... £ 50

    Resolved that Isaac Hops be discharged from Confinement on entering into a Recognizance for his Appearance at the next Supream Court of Judicature to be held for the State of New York at the City Hall in this City on the third Tuesday in April next (or wheresoever the said Court shall then be held in the State aforesaid) and not to depart the Court without Leave —

    Isaac Hops of the East District of the Manor
        of Rensselaerwyck Farmer in........... £100
    [371] Barent Heyner of the same place Farmer
        his Bail in £100

Adjourned —

Met Albany 21st March 1781

Present

John M. Beeckman ⎱   ⎰ Isaac D. Fonda
Samuel Stringer ⎰   ⎱

Resolved that Jacob Timmerman Alias Jacob Carpenter
be discharged from Confinement on entering into a Recognizance for his good Behaviour doing his duty and appearing before any three of the Commissioners for Conspiracies
when thereunto required during the Continuance of the
present war with Great Britain

Jacob Timmerman alias dictus Jacob Carpenter of Hoosick District in the County of
Albany Farmer in..................... £100
Abraham Bovee of the same place Farmer
his Bail in........................... £ 50
Johannis Daet Junr of the same place Farmer
also his Bail in .... £ 50

Adjourned —

Met Albany 22nd March 1781

Present

John M. Beeckman ⎱   ⎰ Samuel Stringer
Mathew Visscher ⎰   ⎱ Isaac D. Fonda

Daniel Hewston being again ordered to be brought before
the Board and being further examined ordered that he be
recommitted.—

Resolved that John Smith be discharged from [372] Confinement on entering into a Recognizance to appear at the
next Supream Court of Judicature to be held for the State
of New York at the City Hall in this City on the third
Tuesday in April next (or wheresoever the said Court shall
then be held in the State aforesaid) to answer to such Matters

as shall be alledged against him and not to depart the Court without Leave and in the Mean time be of the good Behaviour — 1781 Mar. 22.

John Smith of the East District of the Manor of Rensselaerwyck Farmer in........... £100
John Freer of the same place Weaver his Bail in................................ £100

William Hartley being ordered to be brought before the Board for further Examination was accordingly brought and examined ordered that he be recommitted —

It appearing from the Examination of William Hartley that John Van Deusen of Great Barrington living near Monument Mountain is possessed of Commissions and Proclamations which he has received from the Enemy at New York —

Resolved in Consequence of the said Information that a Letter be wrote to Timothy Edwards Esqr at Stockbridge requesting him to have the House of the said John Van Deusen searched which Letter is in the following words (to wit) (here take in Letter)

Adjourned

Met Albany 23^d March 1781 1781 Mar. 23.

Present

John M. Beeckman	Samuel Stringer
Isaac D. Fonda	Mathew Visscher

[373] Resolved that Abraham Roberts be discharged from Confinement on entering into a Recognizance for his appearance at the next Supream Court of Judicature to be held for the State of New York at the City Hall in this City on the third Tuesday in April next (or wheresoever the said Court shall then be held in the State aforesaid) to answer to such

Matters as shall be alledged against him and not to depart
the Court without Leave. —

> Abraham Roberts of the East District of the
>   Manor of Rensselaerwyck Farmer in.... £100
> William Van Den Bergh of the City of Albany
>   Labourer his Bail in................... £100
> Isaac Vosburgh of the west District of the
>   Manor of Rensselaerwyck Labourer also
>   his Bail in.......................... £100

Resolved that Coenradt Colehamer be discharged from
Confinement on Stephenus Colehamer and Paul Snyder's
entering into Recognizance for the Appearance of the said
Coenradt Colehamer at the next Supream Court of Judicature to be held for the State of New York at the City Hall in
this City on the third Tuesday in April next (or wheresoever
the said Court shall then be held in the State aforesaid) to
answer to such Matters as shall be alledged against him
and not to depart the Court without Leave —

> Stephenus Colehamer of the East District of
>   the Manor of Rensselaerwyck Farmer
>   Bail for Coenradt Colehamer in........ £100
> Paul Snyder of the same place Farmer also
>   his Bail in.......................... £100

[374] Resolved that Coenradt Heydorn be discharged
from Confinement on entering into Recognizance for his
Appearance at the next Supream Court of Judicature to be
held for the State of New York at the City Hall in this City
on the third Tuesday in April next (or wheresoever the said
Court shall then be held in the State aforesaid) to answer to
such Matters as shall be alledged against him and not to
depart the Court without Leave —

Coenradt Heydorn of the East District of the
    Manor of Rensselaerwyck Farmer in.... £100
Petrus Heydorn of the same place Farmer
    his Bail in........................... £100

Adjourned —

Met Albany 24<u>th</u> March 1781

Present

    John M. Beeckman } { Isaac D. Fonda
    Samuel Stringer   } {

Resolved that Stephen Wilcocks be discharged from Confinement on entering into a Recognizance for his good Behaviour doing his duty and appearing before any three of the Commissioners for Conspiracies when thereunto required during the Continuance of the present war with Great Britain.—

Stephen Wilcocks of Little Hosick in the
    County of Albany Farmer in........... £100
Ephraim Jackson of the same place Farmer
    his Bail in........................... £100

Resolved that Joseph Crandell be discharged from Confinement on entering into a Recognizance for his good Behaviour doing his duty and appearing before [375] any three of the Commissioners for Conspiracies when thereunto required during the Continuance of the present war with Great Britain. —

Jasper Crandell of Little Hosick in the
    County of Albany Farmer in........... £100
Thomas Crandell of the same place Farmer
    his Bail in...... .... £100

Resolved that Daniel Hewson Jun<u>r</u> be discharged from Confinement on entering into a Recognizance for his good Behaviour doing his duty and appearing before any three of the Commissioners for Conspiracies when thereunto required during the Continuance of the present war with Great Britain —

> Daniel Hewson Junr of the City of Albany
> Cordwainer in.......................... £100
> Casper Cogh of Stonearabia in Tryon County
> Farmer his Bail in.................... £ 50
> John Hoogkerk of Albany Taylor also his
> Bail in.............................. £ 50

Adjourned

Met Albany 26th March 1781

Present

> John M. Beeckman ⎰   ⎱ Isaac D. Fonda
> Samuel Stringer   ⎰   ⎱

A Certificate signed by John McKesson Esqr Clerk of the Supream Court was laid before the Board certifying that Christopher File (who was confined for being concerned in the Rescue of Harpert Lansing and Andries Stoll) has given sureties to the Court for his good Behaviour in future for twelve Kalander Months & as the said Christopher File stands Committed by Virtue of a Mittimus of this Board resolved that the said Mittimus be withdrawn and that the said Christopher File be discharged from Confinement —

[376] Resolved that Isaac Aarse be discharged from Confinement on Abraham Bloodgood of the City of Albany entering into a Recognizance for the said Isaac Aarse's being of the good Behaviour doing his duty and appearing before any three of the Commissioners for Conspiracies when thereunto required during the Continuance of the present war with Great Britain —

> Abraham Bloodgood of the City of Albany
> Innkeeper as Bail for Isaac Aarse in...... £100

Resolved that Andries Stoll be discharged from Confinement on his entering into a Recognizance for his Appearance
at the next Supream Court of Judicature to be held for the
State of New York at the City Hall in this City on the third
Tuesday in April next (or wheresoever the said Court shall
then be held in the State aforesaid) to answer to such Matters
as shall be alledged against him and not depart the Court
without Leave

> Andries Stoll of the East District of the
>   Manor of Rensselaerwyck Blacksmith in.. £100
> Henry Dencker of the same place Farmer
>   his Bail in.......................... £100

Adjourned

Met Albany 27th March 1781

Present

John M. Beeckman } { Isaac D. Fonda
Samuel Stringer   } { [Stewart Dean]

A Letter from the Honble Brigadier General James
Clinton was laid before the Board wherein he informs us
that there is at present in Goal a Prisoner of war named
John Palmer to whose liberation from Confinement he has
no [377] Objection provided the said John Palmer procure
Bail to this Board for his appearance before any three of the
Commissioners for Conspiracies when called upon until
exchanged or otherwise discharged from his Recognizance
and Volkert A. Douw being willing to become surety for the
said John Palmer resolved that he accordingly enter into
Recognizance for the appearance of the said John Palmer
as above mentioned —

> Volkert A. Douw of the City of Albany as
>   Bail for John Palmer in........... £100

A Certificate signed by Robert Harper Esqr Clerk of the

Council of Appointment was laid before the Board whereby it appears that Stewart Dean Esq.ʳ was on the 26ᵗʰ day of March Instant appointed by the Honᵇˡᵉ the Council of Appointment a Commissioner for Conspiracies for this County in the Stead of Mathew Visscher and Jeremiah Van Rensselaer Esqʳˢ who have resigned in Consequence of which said Certificate the said Stewart Dean took the Oath of Office as prescribed in and by an Act of the Legislature of this State entitled " An Act for appointing Commissioners for Conspiracies and declaring their Powers " and took his Seat at the Board accordingly —

Capᵗ Ichabod Turner appeared before the Board and informed us that he had apprehended Seth Rowley an Inhabitant of Stephen Town for having been present at the Meeting at James Lister's and for being one of the Chief Promoters in having Sir Henry Clinton's Proclamation read at the said Meeting resolved in Consequence of the said Meeting that the said Seth Rowley be confined and that a Mittimus be made out for him —

Adjourned.—

[378]   Met Albany 28ᵗʰ March 1781
Present

John M. Beeckman } { Isaac D. Fonda
Stewart Dean   } {

John Cobham having been ordered by this Board not to leave this City without our Permission and appearing this Day before us requested the Liberty of going to Fort Miller for the Purpose of settling his private Business resolved in Consequence of the said Application that a Permit be granted him accordingly —

Colᴸ Veeder appeared before the Board and informed us

that Philip Cough of the Hellebergh lately went down the Country under a Pretence of going to Philadelphia but that it appears from many concurring Circumstances that he has been at New York and that the said Philip Cough took with him from the Hellebergh a woman whose Husband is gone off to the Enemy and who is supposed to be at New York resolved in Consequence of the said Information that the said Philip Cough be cited forthwith to appear before this Board to answer to the above Charge.—

Nicholas Cluet having been cited to appear before the Board appearing was examined as to the Conduct of some disaffected Persons living on the Nistageune Road —

A Letter from Jacob Ford Esqr of Kings District was laid before the Board inclosing sundry Examinations respecting the Conduct of Ambrose Vincent, John Mandigo and Stokes Potter which Letter and examinations are in the words following (to wit) (See Letter and Examinations on File)

[379] resolved that the Consideration of the above Letter and Examinations be postponed untill to Morrow.—

Adjourned

Met Albany 29th March 1781
Present

| John M. Beeckman | | Isaac D. Fonda |
| Samuel Stringer | | Stewart Dean |

Resolved that Harpert Lansing be discharged from Confinement on entering into a Recognizance for his Appearance at the next Supream Court of Judicature to be held for the State of New York at the City Hall in the City of Albany on the third Tuesday in April next (or wheresoever the said Court shall then be held in the State aforesaid) to answer to such Matters as shall be alledged against him and not to depart the Court without Leave.—

1781
Mar. 29. Harpert Lansing of the East District of the
Manor of Rensselaerwyck Farmer in £100
Jacob Vischer of Cooksborough in the
County of Albany Farmer his Bail in £100

The Board taking into Consideration the Letter and Examinations Yesterday received from Jacob Ford Esq.ʳ do resolve on Consideration thereof that a warrant be made out for the Apprehension of Ambrose Vincent, John Mandigo and Stokes Potter —

Resolved that the above warrant be transmitted to the said Jacob Ford and that a Letter be wrote requesting him to have the same served as soon as possible and that he bind over the Witnesses against the said Ambrose Vincent, John Mandigo [380] and Stokes Potter to appear at the next Supream Court —

Adjourned —

1781
Mar. 30.   Met Albany 30ᵗʰ March 1781
Present

| John M. Beeckman | Stewart Dean |
| Isaac D. Fonda | Samuel Stringer |

Philip Cough who was on the 28ᵗʰ Instant cited to appear before this Board appearing was examined and it appearing from his Examination that the Charges as alledged against him by Col.ˡ Veeder are groundless therefore resolved that he be discharged —

Peter Livingston of the Hellebergh having forfeited the Recognizance by him entered into before this Board therefore resolved that he be cited to appear with all Convenient speed to show cause why the same should not be prosecuted —

The Recognizance of Philip Empey, Johannis Staring,

Nicholas Ault, Peter Fikes and Adam Shaver having become forfeited to the State by their going to and Joining the enemy resolved therefore that the Secretary to this Board make out the said Recognizance in order that the Bails may be prosecuted on the same by the Attorney General —

Adjourned —

1781
Mar. 30.

Met Albany 31st March 1781

Present

1781
Mar. 31.

John M. Beeckman } { Isaac D. Fonda
Samuel Stringer } { Stewart Dean

Resolved that Seth Rowley be discharged from [381] Confinement on entering into a Recognizance for his appearance at the next Supream Court of Judicature to be held for the State of New York at the City Hall in the City of Albany on the third Tuesday in April next (or wheresoever the said Court shall then be held in the State aforesaid) to answer to such Matters as shall be alledged against him and not to depart the Court without Leave —

Seth Rowley of Stephen Town in the County
of Albany Farmer in £100
Amos Miner of the same place Farmer his
Bail in £100

The Board having received Information from Capt John Van Wie that the two sons of Hezekiah Schoenmaker are mising and that there is Reason to suspect they are gone to the Enemy in order to determine which it is resolved that a Citation be made out for the said Hezekiah Schoenmaker to appear before this Board forthwith in order that he may be examined as to the same —

Adjourned —

Met Albany 2nd April 1781

Present

John M. Beeckman } { Stewart Dean
Samuel Stringer

Archibald McNeil of the Scotch Patent appeared before the Board and informed us that agreeable to the Tenor of his Recognizance he appeared to wait the further Order of this Board — resolved that the said Archibald McNeil remove with his Family into the interior Part of this State by the 1st day of May next and that he be informed [382] that unless he complies with this order his Recognizance will be prosecuted —

Neal Shaw appeared before the Board and laid before us a Letter from James Gillis for whom he is surety in which Letter the said Gillis prays that his non Appearance on this day may not be construed as a Forfe[i]ture of his Recognizance as he is unable to come on Account of his being indisposed —

Resolved that the same James Gillis be also ordered by the first day of May next to remove with his Family into the Interior parts of this State —

Henry Tinkey appeared before the Board and laid before us a Request of his Bail that he might be indulged with Permission to remain some time longer at home —

Resolved that the said Henry Tinkey by the first day of May next also remove his Effects and Family into the Interior Parts of this State —

Adjourned

Met Albany 3^d April 1781

Present

John M. Beeckman } { Samuel Stringer
Isaac D. Fonda   { Stewart Dean

The Board having received Information that D<u>r</u> George Smith is at present in this City and as he has received no Permission from this Board for that Purpose therefore resolved that Jacob Kidney the Door Keeper be ordered to bring the said D<u>r</u> Smith forthwith before us. —

1781
Apr. 3.

[383] D<u>r</u> Smith being brought before the Board says in Justification of his Conduct that he was ordered to Town by Gen<u>l</u> Clinton for the Purpose of preparing himself to go to Canada in order to his being exchanged and the same being deemed Satisfactory resolved that he be discharged and Permission be granted him to remain in Town for eight days to settle his Business —

Adjourned —

Met Albany 5<u>th</u> April 1781

1781
Apr. 5.

Present

John M. Beeckman) (Samuel Stringer
Isaac D. Fonda   ) (Stewart Dean

Resolved that John Hodkison be discharged from Confinement on entering into a Recognizance for his good Behaviour and appearing before any three of the Commisioners for Conspiracies when thereunto required and remaining within the Limits of the City of Albany until exchanged or otherwise discharged by this Board —

John Hodkison of the City of Albany Labourer in........................... £100
Rykert Bovee of Maple Town in the County of Albany Farmer his Bail in.......... £100

Captain Benjamin Du Bois appeared before the Board and informed the Board that Samuel Van Buskerk, Luke Dewitt and the wife of Johan Jurie Fought are dangerous and disaffected Persons whose going at Large may be dangerous to the State. —

Resolved in Consequence of the above Information that a warrant be made out for them and That Cap: Du Bois be requested to have the same served —

[384] James Brisben who was by Recognizance bound to remain within the Limits of this City appeared before the Board and requested Permission to go to Saragtoga to see his Family and his Bail Peter Sharp consenting thereto resolved that he have Permission granted him accordingly untill the first day of May next —

Adjourned —

Met Albany 6ᵗʰ April 1781

Present

Samuel Stringer } { Isaac D. Fonda
Stewart Dean }

John Kerner appeared before the Board and informed us that Frederick Shaver of the East District & the Manor of Rensselaerwyck by his Conduct & Conversation daily gives Offence to the well affected Subjects of the State —

Wherefore resolved that a warrant be made out for the Apprehension of the said Frederick Shaver and that the said warrant be directed to the said John Kerner in order that he may serve the same —

A Letter from his Excellency Governor Clinton to the Honorable Brigadier General James Clinton was laid before the Board by Samuel Stringer Esq: wherein the Governor in-informs that he has received Information that there are a number of Persons who last Fall came from the Enemy at the Hellebergh and Places Adjacent and recommending it to General Clinton to detach Parties from Kats Kill, Cooksakie, Schohary and from this place for the purpose [385] of apprehending all such persons resolved in Consequence

of the said Letter that the Honble Brigadier Genl Gansevoort
be sent for in order to consult wtih him as to the Steps necessary to be taken in carrying the above plan into Execution—

Adjourned

Met Albany 7th April 1781

Present

| John M. Beeckman | Samuel Stringer |
| Isaac D. Fonda | Stewart Dean |

Frederick Shaver having been apprehended was brought
before the Board and being examined and it appearing to
us necessary that the said Frederick Shaver be laid under
a Recognizance therefore resolved that previous to his Discharge he enter into a Recognizance for his good Behaviour
and appearing before any three of the Commissioners for
Conspiracies when thereunto required —

Frederick Shaver of the East District of Rens-
selaerwyck Farmer in.................. £100
John Kerner of the same place Farmer his
Bail in............................. £100

Resolved agreeable to the plan Yesterday adopted by
General Gansevoort that a Letter be wrote to Major Schermerhorn requesting him with a Party of Men to go to Coyemans in order to apprehend such as are endeavouring to
escape to the East side of the River —

Adjourned

Met Albany 10th April 1781

Present

| John M. Beeckman | Stewart Dean |
| Isaac D. Fonda | |

[386] William Dewitt appeared before the Board &
brought before us a certain person who he had apprehended

on Suspicion of his being a spy from the Enemy who being
examined says his Name is Abel Bacon and he being unable
to give a Satisfactory Account of himself therefore resolved
that he be confined and that the Goaler be directed to keep
him in Custody untill he shall be discharged by an order
of this Board —

Adjourned —

Met Albany 11ᵗʰ April 1781
            Present

                John M. Beeckman ⎫   ⎧ Stewart Dean
                Isaac D. Fonda   ⎭   ⎩

Mᵣ Fonda informed the Board that he had received Information that Philip Lansing who last Spring joined the
Enemy is come from Canada and is supposed to be on his
way to New York with dispatches. —

Resolved that it be recommended to Mᵣ Fonda to obtain
the fullest Information of this Matter and endeavour if
possible to have the said Philip Lansing apprehended —

A Letter from Captain Ichabod Turner was laid before
the Board informing us that Seth Rowley who was by us
bound for his Appearance at the next Supream Court has
inlisted in the nine months Service and recommending it to
us to discharge the said Seth Rowley from that Part of his
Recognizance requiring his Appearance at Court and we
having considered the Contents of the said Letter do resolve
that the said Seth Rowley be discharged accordingly —

[387] Joseph Hawkins appeared before the Board and
requested from us Permission to go and look for a Farm
on which he might remove his Family resolved that he have
leave granted him accordingly. —

Adjourned. —

Met Albany 12<u>th</u> April 1781

Present

John M. Beeckman } { Isaac D. Fonda
Samuel Stringer   } { Stewart Dean

Robert Kenneday appeared before the Board and laid before us a Letter from Col! Anthony Van Bergen wherein he informs us that he sends to us under Guard a person who he has had apprehended on Suspicion and the said person being brought before us and examined says his Name is Jonathan OBrian and that he is a deserter from Col!. James Livingston's Regiment resolved that he be confined and that Col!. Livingston be informed thereof. —

The Board having received Information that Hezekiah Schoenmaker and Henry Schoenmaker have left there places of abode some time ago in order to avoid doing Militia Duty and paying their Rates and are now Secreted about Cooksakie resolved in Consequence of the said Information that a warrant be made out & directed to Robert Kenneday of Cooksakie to apprehend the said Hezekiah Schoenmaker and Henry Schoenmaker and forthwith bring them before us at the City Hall in this City. —

Adjourned —

[388]   Met Albany 13<u>th</u> April 1781

Present

John M. Beeckman } { Samuel Stringer
Isaac D. Fonda   } { Stewart Dean

Brigadier General James Clinton laid before the Board a letter received by him from Teunis Van Wagenen at Cats Kill dated 12<u>th</u> Instant in which he informs him that agreeable to his Directions he had proceeded to the Westward with a Party of Men and has apprehended Jurry Hoofman,

1781
Apr. 13.

Frederick Lobus, Frederick Schraader and Johannis Vrobert who say they were taken prisoners at the Surrender of Burgoyne, John Carrigill and James Davidson Deserters from the Continental Army and Peter Laraway and Luke Dewitt Inhabitants of this County and they being severally brought before us and examined resolved that they be committed except John Carrigill who producing a Furlough from Capt Jansen of Col.^{l} Van Schaick's Regiment was discharged   ordered that a Mittimus be made out for them—

Samuel Stringer Esqr laid before the Board an Extract of a Letter from the Honorable Major General Heath setting forth that two Men have lately left New York with Dispatches for Canada and containing a Description of their Persons and Dress.—

Resolved in Consequence of the same that Letters be wrote to Col.^{l} Abraham Wempell at Schenectady, Major Ezekiel Taylor at Stillwater and to the Commanding Officer at Saragtoga informing them of the same and requesting them to use every possible Means to apprehend those Persons. —

[389] Abel Bacon who was on the 10th Instant confined on Suspicion of his being a spy from the Enemy was brought before the Board and it appearing to us from sundry Circumstances that the said Bacon is no other than one of those infatuated People denominated Shaking Quakers and that he was on his way to Nistageune therefore resolved that the said Abel Bacon be discharged and be ordered not to frequent those parts in future on any Pretence whatever unless he is furnished with proper Credentials of his attachment to the American Cause. —

Adjourned.—

1781
Apr. 14.

Met Albany 14th April 1781

Present

John M. Beeckman   }   { Samuel Stringer
Isaac D. Fonda   }   { Stewart Dean

The Board having received Information that there is at present in Town a person who passes by the Name of Henry Thiell who is endeavouring to depreciate the Money emitted agreeable to a Resolution of Congress of the 18th day of March 1780 by exchanging three pounds of the said Money for one Pound in Specie and it appearing from other Circumstances and also from the Examinations of John Lansing Junr Esqr, John H. Wendell Esqr and James Dennison that the said Henry Thiell is a Suspicious person therefore resolved that he be sent for and examined —

1781 Apr. 14.

The above mentioned Henry Thiell appearing & being examined says he is lately from Philadelphia and that he came to this place to settle his private Business —

Resolved on Considering the above that the said Henry [390] Thiell enter into a Recognizance to appear before any three of the Commissioners for Conspiracies when called upon and that he do not depart beyond the Limits of this City without Leave previously obtained from this Board —

> Henry Thiell of Philadelphia in the State
> of Pensylvania Blacksmith in............ £500
> Hugh Dennison of the City of Albany Inn-
> holder his Bail in..................... £500

Adjourned —

Met Albany 15th April 1781
Present

1781 Apr. 15.

> John M. Beeckman ⎱   ⎰ Stewart Dean
> Isaac D. Fonda   ⎰   ⎱ Samuel Stringer

Lieu^t Col^l Barent Staats appeared before the Board and informed us that there is at present at the House of James Watson living on the Road to Coyemans a Person who appears very Suspicious who has been there four or five days that he supposes the said person is a Spy from the Enemy—

1781
Apr. 15.

Resolved in Consequence of the said Information that Lieu.ᵗ Coenrad Gansevoort be requested to take three or four Men of Col.! Cuyler's Regiment and endeavour to apprehend the said Person

Adjourned —

1781
Apr. 16.

Met Albany 16ᵗʰ April 1781 —
[Present]

John M. Beeckman ⎱   ⎰ Isaac D. Fonda
Samuel Stringer   ⎰   ⎱ Stewart Dean

Lieu.ᵗ Gansevoort who at the Request of this Board went with a Party of Men to apprehend the Person Yesterday described by Col.! Staats appearing informed us that having [391] last Night apprehended the said Person and brought him to Town for the Purpose of confining him the said Person had made his Escape —

Resolved thereupon that a Letter be wrote to Cap.ᵗ Van Wie to request him With a Party of his Company to endeavour if possible to apprehend him —

A Letter from Zepheniah Batchelor Esq.ʳ was laid before the Board dated the 14ᵗʰ Instant wherein he informs us that William Laird and D.ʳ Tice are still in the Neighbourhood of Johnstown and recommending it to have them apprehended and we having good Reason to think that they intend to go and join the Enemy this Spring resolved therefore that a Warrant be made out for the Apprehension of the said William Laird and D.ʳ Tice & that the same be forwarded to the said Zepheniah Batchelor in order that it may be served —

Mathew Visscher Esq.ʳ laid before the Board a Letter from William Whiting Esq.ʳ dated at Great Barrington the 5ᵗʰ Instant which is in the words following (to wit) (see Letter on File)

Adjourned —

Met Albany 17th April 1781 —

Present

John M. Beeckman } { Stewart Dean
Samuel Stringer   } { Isaac D. Fonda

Major Reed laid before the Board a Letter from the Honorable Brigadier General James Clinton wherein the General requests that Dr George Smith may have Liberty to remove with his Family and Effects to the New City and that he be under the same Restrictions he is now under until he is exchanged resolved that the same be taken into Consideration —

[392] Serjeant Soal appeared before the Board & informed us that he had apprehended Thomas Gleason the Person who Yesterday made his Escape from Lieu^t Gansevoort and the said Thomas Gleason being brought in and examined resolved that he be confined and that a Mittimus be made out for him —

It appearing from the Examination of the above mentioned Gleason and from sundry other Circumstances that James Watson who was confined for harbouring the said Gleason was no way concerned or privy to any Part of the Conduct of the said Gleason but as the said James Watson has always sustained the Character of a disaffected Person therefore resolved that previous to his Discharge he enter into Recognizance for his good Behaviour doing his duty and appearing before any three of the Commissioners for Conspiracies when thereunto required for and during the Continuance of the present war with Great Britain —

James Watson of the west District of the
   Manor of Rensselaerwyck Innkeeper in... £100
Volkert A. Douw of the City of Albany Gentle-
   man his Bail in...................... £100

Adjourned —

Met Albany 18th April 1781

Present

John M. Beeckman ⎱   ⎰ Samuel Stringer
Isaac D. Fonda   ⎰   ⎱ Stewart Dean

Two Affidavits of Carrel Nier and Jacob Nier taken before the said Johannis Van Deusen Esq: were laid before the Board which Affidavits set forth that they the said Carrel Neir and Jacob Neir having apprehended Harmen [393] Haver by virtue of a warrant from this Board and being on their way With him to Albany that Hendrick Platner and Jacob Platner of Claverack did advise the said Harmen Haver to make his Escape and that they called the said Haver out of the House in order the better to enable him to do it resolved in Consequence of the said Affidavits that an Order be made out to the said Hendrick and Jacob Platner forthwith to deliver up to this Board the said Harmen Haver—

Resolved that Hendrick Knieskern be discharged from Confinement on entering into Recognizance for his good Behaviour doing his duty and appearing before any three of the Commissioners for Conspiracies when called upon for and during the Continuance of the present war with Great Britain

Hendrick   Knieskern   of   Schohary   in   the
    County of Albany Farmer in. £100
William Knieskern of the same place Farmer
    his Bail in. £100

A Letter from Johannis Van Dusen and Lowrence Fonda Esqrs Justices of the Peace dated at Claverack the 15th Instant was laid before the Board wherein they inform us that they send to us the Examinations of several disaffected Persons and two Men as Prisoners named Teunis Reipenbergh and Jacob M. Hoogteling who they suspect have been concerned in the Robbery committed on Cap⁺ Casparus Conyne resolved that the said Teunis Reipenbergh & Jacob M. Hoogteling be confined and that a Mittimus be made out for them —

Resolved that James Watson Jun⁺ be discharged from Confinement on entering into a Recognizance for his good Behaviour doing his duty and appearing before any three of the [394] Commissioners for Conspiracies when called upon during the Continuance of the present war with Great Britain —

> James Watson Jun⁺ of the West District of
>   the Manor of Rensselaerwyck Labourer in. £100
> Barent I. Staats of the same place Esq⁺
>   his Bail in......................... £100

Adjourned

                Met Albany 19ᵗʰ April 1781 —
     Present

          John M. Beeckman ⎫   ⎰ Samuel Stringer
          Isaac D. Fonda   ⎭   ⎱ Stewart Dean

Jacob Saltsbergh who last Fall came with Sir John Johnson and was at the destruction of Schohary was brought before the Board and Examined his examination is as follows (to wit) (see Examination on File) ordered that he be recommitted —

Samuel Stringer Esq⁺ laid before the Board an Examination of George Boarck taken by Hezekiah Van Orden Esq⁺ from which it appears that Abraham Person Jun⁺ and Abraham Dewit intend to go off and join the Enemy whenever a fit Oppertunity shall present resolved in Consequence of the same that a Letter be wrote to Lieu⁺ Teunis Van Wagenon at Cats Kill to request him to have the said Abraham Person Jun⁺ and Abraham DeWit apprehended and forthwith sent to us —

Information having been received that a certain John Cole is lately come from New York and is at present in the East Camp resolved in Consequence of the said Information that a Letter be wrote to Cap:ᵗ Tiel Rockefeller requesting him [395] to apprehend the said John Cole and forthwith bring him before us

Resolved that a Letter be wrote to William Whiting Esq:ʳ at Great Barrington inclosing a Description of a certain William Scott who frequently goes to New York and returns with false Continental Money and requesting him to have the said William Scot apprehended which Letter is in the words following (to wit) (see Copy Letter on File) —

Adjourned

Met Albany 20ᵗʰ April 1781

Present

John M. Beeckman ⎱ ⎰ Isaac D. Fonda
Samuel Stringer   ⎰ ⎱ Stewart Dean

Benjamin Randell and Stephen Randell appeared before the Board and informed us that Jacob Best of Hosick has harboured and secreted in his House John Ruyter formerly an Inhabitant of Hosick who at the Time he was so secreted by the said Jacob Best was a Captain in the British Service which Charge they say can be plainly and Satisfactorily proved by Peter Crandell and Hugh Baily —

And the said Benjamin Randell and Stephen Randell further inform that John Babcock Joseph Allport and Dennis Dun are disaffected Persons and that they have drank the Kings Health and that Jacob Lantman also is a dangerous and disaffected Person who in the Year 1777 when General Burgoyne came down did assist in murdering some men who had been driving Cattle to General Gates's Army and that Stephen Card has advised many Persons to

accept of Sir Henry Clinton's Proclamations telling them it
contained Offers of [396] Peace and that it would be the last Time that any would be made and that Elisha Runnels & Thomas Stephens were present when the said Stephen Card made use of those Expressions —

Resolved in Consequence of the above Information that a Warrant be made out for the immediate apprehension of the said John Babcock, Dennis Dun, Stephen Card and Jacob Lantman and that the same be directed to Jacob Kidney Constable —

Thomas Gleason who was the other day committed to Goal requested to be brought before the Board in order to give some Information respecting William Hartley & he being brought in and Examined says that a certain Man of the Name of Butler has brought a Letter to the said Hartley & that the said Hartley was to write an answer which said Butler was to call for — Ordered that the said Thomas Gleason be recommitted —

Adjourned —

Met Albany 21st April 1781

Present

| John M. Beeckman | Samuel Stringer |
| Isaac D. Fonda | Stewart Dean |

Jacob Kidney appeared before the Board & informed us that he had apprehended Jacob Lantman, John Babcock, Dennis Dun and Stephen Card and they being severally examined and denying the Charge alledged against them and offering to disprove the same resolved therefore that they be severally bound by Recognizance to appear before any three of the Commissioners for Conspiracies [397] at the City Hall in this [City] on Wednesday next and that in the mean Time they be of the good Behaviour —

1781
Apr. 21.

Jacob Lantman of Hosick in the County of Albany Farmer in £100
Michael Lantman of the same place Farmer his Bail in £100

John Babcock of Hosick in the County of Albany Farmer in £100
Michael Lantman of the same place Farmer his Bail in £100

Dennis Dun of Hosick in the County of Albany Farmer in £100
Johannis Duet of the same place Farmer his Bail in £100

Stephen Card of Hosick in the County of Albany Farmer in £100
Daniel Kyneir of the same place Farmer his Bail in £100

Resolved in Consequence of the Information Yesterday given by Benjamin Randell and Stephen Randell that a warrant be made out for the Apprehension of Jacob Best and Joseph Allport of Hosick District and that the same be delivered to the said Benjamin Randell in Order to have it served —

Samuel Stringer Esq[r] informed the Board that he had advanced to Peter Seeger Eight New Emission Dollars for the Purpose of apprehending Joseph Bettis ordered that he be credited for the same —[1]

Resolved that Peter Crandell, Hugh Baily, John Ryley, Oliver Bartley, Elisha Reynolds, Thomas Stephens, and

[1] Included in Stringer's sworn statement, October 21, 1784, in *Revolutionary Manuscripts*, vol. 40, p. 160, State Comptroller's office.

Samuel Shaw be cited to appear before this Board on Wednesday next in order to support the Charges before us exhibited
by Benjamin Randell and Stephen Randell against the said
Jacob Lantman, John Babcock, Dennis Dun, Stephen
Card, Jacob Best and Joseph Allport —

Thomas Butler of Hosick District having been [398]
apprehended on the Information Yesterday given to this
Board by Thomas Gleason and being Examined as to the
same positively denies the Charge but as there is great
Reason to imagin from the Character of disaffection hitherto
sustained by the said Thomas Butler that what has been
alledged against him is true therefore resolved that he be
confined and that a Mittimus be made out for him —

Harmen Haver who the Board were on the 18th Instant
Informed had made his Escape from the Guard who had
apprehended him appeared this day and surrendered himself up to us and produced Certificates of several of the
Officers of the Regiment to which he belongs of his having
behaved himself as a peaceable and quiet Inhabitant &
that he has ever done his duty as a good Subject of the
State   resolved in Consequence of the said Recommendations that the said Harmen Haver be discharged until the
further order of this Board —

Adjourned —

Met Albany 23d April 1781 —
Present

John M. Beeckman ⎱   ⎰ Samuel Stringer
Isaac D. Fonda   ⎰   ⎱ Stewart Dean

Capt Benjamin Du Bois appeared before the Board and
informed us that he had agreeable to our warrant apprehended Luke De Wit and the said Luke De Wit being pro-

duced and examined acknowledges that he drank King George's Health

Resolved that he be Confined and that a Mittimus be made out for him —

[399] A Number of Germans who belonged to Genl: Burgoyne's Army having been apprehended on account of their Inimical Conduct and Conversation & being brought before the Board and examined resolved that they be committed until the further Order of this Board —

Adjourned

Met Albany 25th April 1781

Present

John M. Beeckman   Isaac D. Fonda
Samuel Stringer   Stewart Dean

The German Prisoners who were examined on the 23^d: Instant being again Brought before the Board & it appearing that some of them are Deserters and that others are Prisoners of War resolved therefore that it be recommended to the Honorable Brigadier General James Clinton that he discharge such of the said Germans as are Deserters and that he discharge also such of the said Prisoners of War as are recommended by Persons who are well Attached to the American Cause —

Adjourned —

Met Albany 26th April 1781 —

Present

John M. Beeckman   Isaac D. Fonda
Samuel Stringer   Stewart Dean

Peter Crandell appeared before the Board agreeable to our order of the 21st Instant and being examined under oath says that Jacob Lantman last Summer when ordered out

with a Party of Militia to apprehend some Persons [400]
who were come from Canada said that he would not go
after such Persons and that he did not look upon them as
Enemies. Resolved In Consequence of the said Examination, that the said Jacob Lantman, be bound by Recognizance, for his good Behaviour, doing his duty, and appearing before any three of the Commissioners for Conspiracies, when called upon during the Continuance of the
present war with Great Britain —

Jacob Lantman of Hosick in the Cou[n]ty of
    Albany Farmer in £100
Michael Lantman of the same place Farmer
    his Bail in............................ £100

Capt Joshua Babcock appeared before the Board and
informed us that agreeable to our warrant he had apprehended Jacob Best and the said Jacob Best being brought
before us and examined and it appearing from his Examination that the charge alledged against him is well founded
therefore resolved that the said Jacob Best enter into a
Recognizance for his good behaviour and appearing before
any three of the Commissioners for Conspiracies when
thereunto required during the Continuance of the present
war with Great Britain and also for his appearance at the
Supream Court of Judicature now held at the City Hall in
this City to answer to such Matters as shall then and there
be alledged against him and not depart the Court without
Leave —

Jacob Best of Little Hosick in the County of
    Albany Farmer in..................... £100
Isaac Vosburgh of the west district of the
    Manor of Rensselaerwyck Brick Maker his
    Bail in............................... £100

[401] John Babcock appeared before the Board & being examined as to the Charge alledged against him of drinking the King's Health utterly denied the same and requested that Jacob Best might be examined under Oath as to the Truth of his Assertions and the said Jacob Best being Examined says that he was present when John Allport drank the king's Health in Babcock's presence and that the said John Babcock instead of joining with the said Allport reprimanded him for doing it   resolved that the said John Babcock attend at this Board to Morrow Morning —

Capt John Ryley having been ordered to appear before this Board to give Information respecting John Babcock & others appeared and being examined says that last New Years day he was at the House of the said Babcock and that the said Babcock together with Dennis Dun, Jacob Best, and John Allport did in his Hearing drink the king's Health   resolved that the said John Ryley be directed to attend the Grand Jury in Order to give them the above Information —

Thomas Butler who was the other day confined on the Information of Thomas Gleason was brought before the Board and nothing further appearing against him therefore resolved that he be discharged on entering into a Recognizance with sufficient Sureties for his good Behaviour doing his duty and appearing before any three of the Commissioners for Conspiracies when thereunto required for and during the Continuance of the present war with Great Britain —

Thomas Butler of Hosick in the County of
  Albany Innkeeper in.................. £100
Joshua Babcock of the same place Cord-
  wainer his Bail in.................... £100
John Randell of the same place Farmer also
  his Bail in........................... £100

[402] Stephen Card appeared before the Board and laid
before us sundry Certificates of his Attachment to the American Cause   Resolved in Consequence of the said Certificates that the said Stephen Card be discharged.

Adjourned

Met Albany 27th April 1781 —
Present

John M. Beeckman } { Isaac D. Fonda
Samuel Stringer } { Stewart Dean

John Babcock appeared before the Board agreeable to our order of Yesterday   resolved that the said John Babcock enter into a Recognizance for his Appearance at the Supream Court of Judicature at present held in the City Hall of this City then and there to answer to such Matters as shall be alledged against him and not to depart the Court without leave —

John Babcock of Hosick in the County of
Albany Innkeeper in.................... £100
Joshua Babcock of the same place Cord-
wainer his Bail in...................... £100

Dennis Dun also appearing agreeable to our order resolved that he enter into a Recognizance for his Appearance at the Supream Court of Judicature at present   held at the City Hall in this City to answer to such Matters a[s] shall be then and there alledged against him and not to depart the Court without Leave —

Dennis Dun of Hosick in the County of
Albany Farmer in...................... £100
Michael Lantman of the same place Farmer
his Bail in............................. £100

The Board having received Information that John Andrew of Newtown has this Morning acknowledged [403]

himself a King's Man   resolved in consequence of the said
Information that the said John Andrew be forthwith apprehended by Jacob Kidney and brought before us —

Thomas Butler who was Yesterday liberated from Confinement appeared before the Board and produced two
Certificates the one signed by the Selectmen and several
Militia Officers of the Township of Worthington in the
County of Hampshire in the Commonwealth of Massa-
chuset's Bay setting forth that the said Thomas Butler has
from the Commencement of the present Contest behaved
himself as a Zealous and firm Friend to the American
Cause, the other signed by several Militia Officers & other
well affected Inhabitants of the District of Hosick and the
same being read and taken into Consideration   resolved in
Consequence thereof that the said Thomas Butler be and
he is hereby discharged from the Recognizance entered into
by him before this Board on the 26ᵗʰ Instant —

Jacob Kidney appeared with John Andrew whom agreeable to our order he had apprehended resolved that the said
John Andrew be committed and that a Mittimus be made
out for him —

Samuel Stringer Esqʳ informed the Board that he has
received Information that Simeon Smith of Pits Town Innkeeper entertains disaffected Persons; drink's King George's
health and speaks disrespectfully of the Authority of this
State. resolved in Consequence of the said Information that a
warrant be made out directed to Lieutenant Jonathan Brown
forthwith to apprehend and bring before us the said Simeon
Smith —

Resolved that a Citation be sent to Jonathan Brown [404]
William McCoy and Mary Sawyer to appear before the
Board forthwith to prove the Charges above alledged against
the said Simeon Smith.

Lieu.^t Jacob Platner and Hendrick Platner appeared before the Board and being questioned as to their advising Harmen Haver to make his Escape from the Guard who had him in Custody the said John Platner acknowledges he did Advise Harmen Haver to go home and obtain a Certificate from his Officers of his Conduct and then deliver himself up to the Commissioners at Albany and the said Jacob Platner having always sustained an Irreproachable Character and Hendrick Platner appearing no way concerned in the affair therefore resolved that the said Jacob Platner and Hendrick Platner be discharged

1781
Apr. 27.

Adjourned

Met Albany 30.th April 1781 —

Present

1781
Apr. 30.

John M. Beeckman } { Stewart Dean
Samuel Stringer }

Berijah Tyler appeared before the Board and produced a Letter signed by Stephen Salisbury and William Dawes dated at Worcester in the State of Massachusetts Bay on the 25 Instant setting forth that Thomas Glason who was by Our order apprehended and confined is of an infamous Character and that he has lately enlisted for three Years to serve in the Continental Army ordered that the same be filed —

Resolved in Consequence of the above Letter that an Order be sent to James Watson to deliver up to Berijah Tyler the Horse of the said Thomas Gleason by us Committed to his Care [405] on the said Tyler's paying the Charges accrued in keeping said Horse —

Resolved that Jacob Saltsbergh be discharged from Confinement on his entering into a Recognizance for his good Behaviour doing his duty and appearing before any three of the Commissioners for Conspiracies when thereunto required during the Continuance of the present war with Great Britain —

Jacob Saltsbergh of the Bever Dam in the
County of Albany Farmer in............ £100
Jacob Cuyler of the City of Albany Mer-
chant his Bail in..................... £100

Whereas there are several Families remaining settled on the North side of Hudsons River in and about Jessup's Patent, who are all disaffected; and this Board conceiving it highly improper they should be let to remain there —

Have resolved, that it is necessary, for the Safety of those Frontiers, that all the said Families be ordered forthwith to remove from thence with all their Effects down into the Interior parts of the Country, without delay; and that all Boats, Canoes, or other Conveniences, for the purpose of Crossing the River, and which can be found on either side of the same, be destroyed, and that all the Males of 16 Years old and upwards, be ordered to appear before this Board on or before the 20th day of May next at their peril —

And whereas this Board has received Information that there are a Number of Tory Women (whose Husbands have joined the Enemy) residing, and going from parts below to reside, above Saragtoga which this Board from Manifest Reasons disapprove of; therefore Resolved, that the said Women be all brought down below Saragtoga and ordered there to Remain as they will answer they [sic] Contrary at their Peril; until they shall receive [406] further Instructions from this Board or from some other proper Authority —

Resolved that Brigadier General Clinton be requested by this Board, to issue an Order to the Officer commanding at Saragtoga to have the above necessary Resolves executed; and that a List of all such Persons as may be removed and brought down as aforesaid be handed to this Board, with any

Information that may be collected and thought worthy of their Attention towards the wellfare of the State —

Adjourned —

Met Albany 1ˢͭ May 1781 —

Present

John M. Beeckman } { Samuel Stringer
Isaac D. Fonda   } { Stewart Dean

A Letter from the Commissioners for Conspiracies dated at Schenectady the 26ᵗʰ April last was laid before the Board which Letter is in the words following (to wit) (See Letter on File) —

Andries Cogh, Andries Wolters, George Pattshold and Johan Hendrick Zachariah Bause, German Prisoners of war having been apprehended by order of General Clinton and confined and the General being of Opinion that they may be serviceable to the Country should they be admitted to Bail resolved therefore that they be bound in Recognizance with sufficient sureties for their good Behaviour and appearance before any three of the Commissioners for Conspiracies when thereunto required during the Continuance of the present war with Great Britain —

[407] Andries Cogh of the Hellebergh in the
County of Albany in.................. £100
Jacob Zimmer of the same place Farmer his
Bail in £100

Andries Walters late of the Hellebergh in..... £100
Jacob Zimmer of the same place Farmer his
Bail in £100

George Paatshold late of the Hellebergh in. . £100
Jacob Zimmer of the same place Farmer his
Bail in £100

Johan Hendrick Zachariah Bause late of
the Hellebergh in £100
Johannis Casselman of the Bever Dam
Farmer his Bail in £100

Adjourned —

Met Albany 2nd May 1781
Present

| John M. Beeckman | Samuel Stringer |
| Isaac D. Fonda | Stewart Dean |

General Clinton having recommended it to the Board to
discharge Christian Hartwick a German Prisoner of war on
Bail resolved in Consequence of the said Recommendation
that the said Christian Hartwick be discharged on his entering
into a Recognizance for his good Behaviour and appearing
before any three of the Commissioners for Conspiracies when
thereunto required during the Continuance of the present war
with Great Britain —

Christian Hartwick late of the Hellebergh
Farmer in............................ £100
Peter Cook of the City of Albany Merchant
his Bail in £100

Mrs Welsh whose Husband is at present with the Enemy
appeared before the Board and requested a Permit to go to
Canada resolved that the Secretary to this Board certify to
General Clinton that we have no Objection to Mrs Welsh's
going with the first Flag to her Husband —

Hugh McManus Constable of Tryon County [408] appeared
before the Board and informed us that agreeable to our war-
rant he had apprehended Dr John Tice and the said Dr Tice
being produced and examined resolved that the said Hugh
McManus take him again into his Charge and have him
ready to produce to this Board when called upon —

Luke DeWit was brought before the Board and examined
Ordered that he be recommitted —

General Clinton having certified to this Board his Desire that William Giffert a German Prisoner of war should be admitted to Bail resolved that he be bound for his good Behaviour and appearance before any three of the Commissioners for Conspiracies for and during the Continuance of the present war with Great Britain —

William Giffert late of the Hellebergh
  Farmer in............................ £100
John Tillman Sen.ʳ of the Manor of Rens-
  selaerwyck Innkeeper his Bail in £100

Peter Larawa being brought before the Board and examined ordered that he be recommitted —

Dᵣ John Tice being again brought before the Board and examined on Consideration of the Charge alledged against the said Dᵣ Tice resolved that he enter into Recognizance with Sufficient surety for his remaining within the Limits of this City and appearing before any three of the Commissioners for Conspiracies when called upon until discharged from the said Recognizance by the said Commissioners —

John Tice of the State of Pensylvania Prac-
  ti[ci]oner of Physick in................. £100
John Tillman of the Manor of Rensselaerwyck Innkeeper his Bail in............. £100

[409]   Met Albany 3ᵈ May 1781
    Present

    John M. Beeckman ⎱   ⎰ Samuel Stringer
    Isaac D. Fonda   ⎰   ⎱ Stewart Dean

The Board having received Information that Joseph Bettis keeps at present at the Hellebergh and other places

**1781
May 3.** in that Neighbourhood and is collecting a party of Men to
go off to the Enemy —

Resolved in Consequence of the said Information that
Application be made to General [James Clinton] for a Party
of the Levies and to General Gansevoort for a Party of
Militia to go and apprehend the said Joseph Bettis with his
Party and also resolved that Abraham Outhout Esqʳ one of
the Commissioners for Conspiracies residing at Schenectady
at present in Town be sent for and made Acquainted with the
above Information and that he be also informed that this
Board conceive it necessary that a Party of Men should be
sent from Schenectady for the purpose of falling upon the
Rear of those Settlements —

Information being exhibited to this Board that a certain
John Wasbrook is at present on the East side of the River
that he is a Stranger and of a suspicious Character therefore
resolved that a Warrant be made out directed to Jacob Van
Alstyne authorizing him forthwith to apprehend and bring
before us the said John Wasbrook —

A Letter from Teunis Van Wagenen dated Cats Kill the
2ⁿᵈ Instant was laid before the Board informing that he sends
to us under Guard a certain Samuel Davidson who he had
caused to be apprehended as a dangerous Person and the said
Davidson being produced and Examined and it ap- [410]
pearing from his Examination that he is a Deserter from the
Line of the Pensylvania Army therefore resolved that he be
sent to General Clinton to be disposed as he may think proper —

Adjourned —

**1781
May 4.**

Met Albany 4ᵗʰ May 1781 —
Present

John M. Beeckman ⎱　⎰ Samuel Stringer
Isaac D. Fonda 　⎰　⎱ Stewart Dean

Resolved in Consequence of the plan Yesterday concluded upon for the Apprehension of Joseph Bettis with his Party that a Letter be wrote to Col! Anthony Van Bergen at Cooksakie to detach a Party of Men to Peesink for the purpose of scouring the woods in that Quarter in Order that if Bettis should endeavour to make his Escape that way that he may be apprehended —

1781
May 4.

James Watson Jun! who on the 18th day of April last entered into a Recognizance before this Board appeared before us this day and informed us that he intends to go and reside at Springfield in the State of Massachusetts Bay for the Purpose of lear[n]ing the Tanners Trade and requested to be discharged from his said Recognizance and the said Application being taken into Consideration resolved thereupon that the said James Watson Jun! be and he is hereby discharged from the said Recognizance —

Lieu! Jonathan Brown appeared before the Board and informed us that agreeable to our warrant he had apprehended Simeon Smith and that he had also agreeable to our Directions summoned William McCoy as an Evidence against the said Simeon Smith ordered that the said William McCoy be examined —

[411] William McCoy being Examined under Oath saith as follows (to wit) (see Examination on File) —

Simeon Smith being brought before the Board and the Charges above alledged against him being read to him and he possitively denying the same and offering to prove himself Innocent of the Crime alledged against him wherefore resolved that the said Simeon Smith have Permission to return Home on his entering into Recognizance for his good Behaviour doing his duty and appearing before any three of the Commissioners for Conspiracies when thereunto required during the Continuance of the present war with Great Britain and also for his appearing at the next Supream Court of Judicature to be held for the State of New York at the City Hall in this City on the last Tuesday in July next (or wheresoever the said Court shall then be held in the State aforesaid) to answer to such Matters as shall then and there be alledged against him and not to depart the Court without Leave —

 Simeon Smith of Pitts Town in the County
  of Albany Innkeeper in £100
 Archibald Campbell of the City of Albany
  Merchant his Bail in £100

 Jonathan Brown and Seth Stalker being severally called before the Board and Examined as to the Political Conduct of Simeon Smith their Examinations are as follows (to wit) (see Examinations on File) —

 Mathew Visscher Esq⸗ appeared before the Board and informed us that he had received Information that a Number of Negroes at Nistageune and the Bought intend shortly to go off to Canada with Joseph Bettis resolved in Consequence of the said Information that a Letter be wrote to Captain Hendrick Ostram to have the following Negroes apprehended (to wit) Jack the Negro Man of [412] Wilhelmas Van Antwerp Esq⸗, Pomp the Negroe of Naning Vischer, Jack the Negroe of Bastian Cregier, and Jack the Negroe [of] Martinus Cregier, and that he keep them separately and bring them before us at the City Hall in this City —

 Resolved also that a Letter be wrote to Captain Levinus Lansing to apprehend and bring before us the Negroe of Cornelius Van Den Bergh named Sans, and the Negro of Johannis Lansing named Tom and they also be brought down separately —

 A Party of Levies and of the Militia being now ready for the Purpose of executing the Plan for Apprehending Joseph

Bettis with his Party resolved that Instructions be made out for the Officer commanding the said Party which Instructions are in the following words (to wit) (see Draft Instructions on File) —

A Letter from Major Popham Aid De Camp to Brigadier General James Clinton was laid before the Board setting forth that the General is willing that Hazelton Spencer should be liberated from Confinement and have the Liberty of the Town and be subject to such Restrictions as this Board may think proper resolved that the Subject of the above Letter be taken into Consideration untill to Morrow Morning —

Adjourned —

Met Albany 5th May 1781 —

Present

John M. Beeckman } { Stewart Dean
Isaac D. Fonda   } { Samuel Stringer

The Board having taken into Consideration the Letter Yesterday received from Major Popham respecting Hazelton Spencer and Conceiving that there can be no Impropriety in [413] liberating the said Hazelton Spencer from Confinement therefore resolved that he be liberated accordingly on entering into a Bond with a sufficient surety for his remaining within the following Limits in the City of Albany, (to wit) to the North to the Bridge at General Ten Broeck's to the west to the Fort and to the south to the House at present occupied by Thomas Lansing and for his not holding any Correspondence by word or deed upon Political Matters with any Person or Persons who hold Principles Inimical to the Measures pursued by the Congress of the United States of America and that he shall appear before the Commissioners for Conspiracies or either of them when required —

Hazelton Spencer in...................... £500
Abraham Ja: Lansing of the East District of
the Manor of Rensselaerwyck Farmer his
Bail in £500

Capt Hendrick Ostrom appeared before the Board and informed that agreeable to our Request he had apprehended the Negroes mentioned in our Letter of Yesterday and the said Negroes being severally brought before the Board and Examined and confessing their Intention of going off with Joseph Bettis and Jack the Negroe of Wilhelmas Van Antwerp and Pomp the Negroe of Naning Visscher appearing to be principally concerned in the above Schem[e] therefore resolved that they be committed and that a Mittimus be made out for them —

Henry Simpson appeared before the Board and informed that the Party of Men who Yesterday went in Search of Joseph Bettis had apprehended a Certain Daniel Sherwood and that he had become Surety to the Officer commanding the said Party to deliver up the said Sherwood to this Board and that the said Daniel [414] Sherwood being Examined and producing Vouchers of his having been enlisted last Summer in the Nine Months Service and of his Attachment to the American Cause therefore resolved that he be discharged —

Harmanus Cuyler of Cooksakie laid before the Board a Letter from Teunis Van Wagenon dated Cats Kill 4.th Instant wherein he informs us that he sends to us Wessel Van Dyck as a Prisoner on Account of his being concerned in carrying Off David Abeel and his son and that he will send up the Proof against him as soon as possible which Letter being read ordered that the same be filed —

Resolved in Consequence of the above Letter that the said Wessel Van Dyck be confined and that a Mittimus be made out for him —

Adjourned —

Met Albany 7th May 1781 —
Present

| John M. Beeckman | Samuel Stringer |
| Isaac D. Fonda | Stewart Dean |

A Letter from Capt Cornelius J. Jansen dated at Saragtoga the 6th Instant was laid before the Board setting forth that one of his Scouts had apprehended at Jessup's Patent a certain Stephen Fairchilds and the said Fairchilds being Examined and not being able to give a satisfactory Account of himself resolved that he be committed and that a Mittimus be made out for him —

A Letter was also laid before the Board from Teunis Van Wagenen dated at Catts Kill the 6th Instant wherein [415] he informs us that he sends to us under Guard Abraham Dewitt and Abraham Person Junr who have been apprehended agreeable to a warrant issued by this Board and that he also sends John Person who is a dangerous and disaffected Person resolved that they be severally examined & that a Mittimus be made out for them —

Pomp the Negro Man of Naning Vischer being at the Request of his Master again brought before the Board and Examined and it appearing that he is possessed of no other Information than what he has already mentioned therefore resolved that at the Request of his said Master that he be discharged —

Adjourned —

Met Albany 8th May 1781 —
Present

| John M. Beeckman | Samuel Stringer |
| Isaac D. Fonda | Stewart Dean — |

Jack the Negro Man of Wilhelmas Van Antwerp being again brought before the Board was examined and it appear-

ing that his former Examination contains all the Information
which he is able to give and he offering to give Information of
Joseph Bettis or any other Person that may in future ask him
to go to Canada resolved therefore that he be discharged
from Confinement —

Peter Larawa was brought before the Board for the Purpose of being examined and the said Larawa appearing unwilling to give a Candid Confession with Respect to the
Conduct of the disaffected Inhabitants at Peesink therefore
resolved that he be recommitted

Adjourned —

[416]   Met Albany 9th May 1781 —

Present

John M. Beeckman ⎱   ⎰ Samuel Stringer
Isaac D. Fonda   ⎰   ⎱ Stewart Dean

Information was exhibited to the Board that a certain
David Waters an Inhabitant of this City has offered to Exchange the Money lately emitted by the Authority of Congress for Hard Money at the Rate of three for one and it
appearing highly probable that the said David Waters does
it with no other View than to depreciate the Money as he
has been always esteemed a disaffected Person   it is therefore
resolved that a warrant be made out directed to Jacob Kidney forthwith to apprehend and bring before us the said
David Waters resolved also that John Shepherd and Henry
Hart be cited forthwith to appear before this Board to prove
the Charges as above alledged against the said Waters —

Jacob Kidney appeared and informed that agreeable to
our Order he had apprehended David Waters and the said
Waters being produced and acknowledging the same and at
the same Time confessing also that he did say that if the

Commissioners should confine him for his Conduct that he would after being released go to the Enemy at New York resolved therefore that he be confined and that a Mittimus be made out for him —

John Shepherd and Henry Hart appearing and being severally examined say as follows (to wit) (see their Examinations on File)

The Board being also informed by William Dewit that M: Fomfried the French Merchant has also asked more in New Money for his Tea than the Current Exchange resolved that he be sent for to answer the above —

[417] M: Fomfried appearing and being made acquainted with the above Charge and he positively denying the same resolved that he be discharged and cautioned against depreciating the New Money at his Peril —

Adjourned —

Met Albany 12th May 1781 —
Present

John M. Beeckman }   { Samuel Stringer
Isaac D. Fonda   }   {

Hugh M:Manus Constable for Tryon County appeared before the Board and informed us that agreeable to a warrant issued by this Board for William Laird he had apprehended the said Laird & the said Laird being Examined and it appearing from his own Examination and also from a Letter to this Board from Zepheniah Batchelor Esq: that the said William Laird in [sic] enlisted in the Nine Month's Service and he offering faithfully to do his duty in future resolved therefore that the same be taken into Consideration untill this Afternoon —

The Board being informed that there is at present in

Town a certain Isaac Larawa an Inhabitant of the Hellebergh who may if examined give some Material Information respecting several Persons in that Quarter it is therefore resolved that Jacob Kidney be ordered to have the said
Isaac Larawa before the Board this Afternoon —

Lieutenant Seth Perry appeared before the Board and
informed us that he had apprehended a Man on Suspicion
and the said Person being produced and Examined says
that his Name is Christian Smith that he is a Soldier in
the Continental Army [418] in Col! Van Schaick's Regiment that he deserted about two Month's ago at Livingston's
Manor to which he was advised by a certain Smith an Inhabitant of that place that whilst at Livingston's Manor he
was advised by Jurie Wheeler to go to New York and then
enlist in the Enemies Service and the said Examination
being committed to writing ordered that the said Christian
Smith be delivered over to Major John Graham —

The Board having taken in Consideration the Case of
William Laird resolved that he be discharged with paying
to the Constable the Costs accrued by his Apprehension —

Jacob Kidney agreeable to order attending with Isaac
Larawa and the said Larawa being examined resolved that
he be discharged —

A Certificate signed by sundry of the well affected Inhabitants of Arlington in the County of Charlotte was laid before the Board from which it appears that Stephen Fairchilds who was the other day taken at Jessup's Patent and
sent down by Cap! Jansen has from the Commencement of
the present Contest been esteemed a Friend to the American
Cause   resolved in Consequence of the said Certificate that
the said Stephen Fairchilds be discharged on entering into
a Recognizance for his future good Behaviour doing his
duty and appearing before any three of the Commissioners

for Conspiracies when called upon during the Continuance
of the present war with Great Britain —

Stephen Fairchilds of Arlington in the County
  of Charlotte Farmer in.................. £100
Joseph Hall of the City of Albany Silversmith
  his Bail in........................... £100

It appearing from sundry Circumstances [419] that
George Sittamon of the Hellebergh is a disaffected Person
and that he entertains Persons who to screen themselves
from Justice are lurking in the Country it is therefore Resolved that an Order be sent to the said George Sittamon
forthwith to appear before this Board with a good sufficient
Bail to enter into Recognizance for his good Behaviour and
appearance when called upon and that the same be delivered
him by Isaac Larawa —

Adjourned —

Met Albany 14.th May 1781 —

Present

John M. Beeckman ⎱   ⎰ Samuel Stringer
Isaac D. Fonda   ⎰   ⎱ Stewart Dean

A Recommendation in Favor of Marcy French wife of
Charity French who is at present with the Enemy signed
by Isaac Sawyer, Benjamin Hicks, and other Zealous Friends
to the American Cause was laid before the Board setting
forth that the said Mar[c]y French has by John J^s Bleecker
Esqr been warned agreeable to the Directions of an "Act
entitled "An Act for the Removal of the Families of Persons who have joined the Enemy" to depart this State or
remove to such parts of it as are in the Power of the Enemy
and recommending the said Marcy French as a person of
an unexceptional Character and that they do not think that

her remaining at her present Habitation will not in any way injure the Liberties and Independance of this and the United States resolved in Consequence of the said Recommendation that a Permit be granted to the said Marcy French for the Purpose above Mentioned —

[420] David King having been apprehend[ed] as a Person of a Suspicious Character was brought before the Board and examined and it appearing that he is a Deserter from Col. Van Schaick's Regiment of Continental Forces resolved thereupon that he be delivered over to Major John Graham —

Adjourned —

Met Albany 15th May 1781 —
         Present

         John M. Beeckman ⎱   ⎰ Samuel Stringer
         Isaac D. Fonda   ⎰   ⎱ Stewart Dean

Information having been given to this Board that there are at present in the East District of the Manor of Rensselarwyck two German Prisoners of war named Andries Hernockle, and Christopher Whiting who daily by their Conduct and Conversation give Offence to the Friends of the American Cause therefore resolved that a Letter be wrote to Capt Jacob De Forest requesting him forthwith to apprehend and bring before us the said Andries Hernockle & Christopher Whiting —

Francis Utt formerly an Inhabitant of Tryon County appeared before the Board agreeable to our Order and being examined as to the Character and Conduct of Dr John Tice says that Tice last Fall informed him that Sir John would come down and advised the said Francis Utt to take Protection under him and at the same Time also informed him that he knew a great Deal but could not divulge it because he was sworn — Resolved in Consequence of the 1781 May 15. said Information that the said John Tice be committed and that a Letter be wrote to Major Graham to request him [421] when he goes down with the Prisoners of war to West Point to take with him also the said Tice and from thence send him by the first Party that goes to Philadelphia to his Family and caution him not again to be Seen in this State during the present Contest.

William Wederwax having been apprehended & confined on Suspicion of his being concerned in the Robberies lately Committed at Claverack and it appearing that the Suspicion was ill founded and he being a Continental Soldier belonging to Coll: Van Schaick's Reg.t therefore Resolved that he be delivered over to Major Graham —

Peter Davis having been confined for stealing two Publick Horses and having taken a Bounty from a Class and therewith paid for the Horses resolved that he also be delivered over to Major Graham —

Thomas Orton and Gideon Orton appeared before the Board and informed that they had agreeable to the Resolutions of this Board been removed with their Families from Jessups Patent and that being hurried away they had been obliged to leave great Part of their Effects behind and requested Permission for themselves and the other Persons whose Families were removed to go and fetch the Remainder of their Effects resolved that they have Permission granted them accordingly and that in ten days they all of them appear before this Board —

On Application of John Hodkison resolved that he have Permission granted him to go and work at Tunnicliff's Farm with Anthony Waine and that he every Evening make his Appearance before one of the Members of this Board

Adjourned —

[422]   Met Albany 16th May 1781 —

Present

John M. Beeckman ⎱   ⎰ Isaac D. Fonda
Stewart Dean   ⎰   ⎱ Samuel Stringer

Resolved that Constant King be liberated from Confinement on entering into Recognizance for his good Behaviour doing his duty and appearing before any three of the Commissioners for Conspiracies when thereunto required during the Continuance of the present war with Great Britain and also for his appearing at the next Supream Court of Judicature to be held for the State of New York at the City Hall in the City of Albany on the last Tuesday in July next (or wheresoever the said Court shall then be held in the State aforesaid) and not to depart the Court without Leave —

Constant King of White Creek in the County
of Albany Cordwainer in............... £100
John Fisher of Cambridge in the County
aforesaid Millwright in................ £100

Archibald McNeal appearing before the Board agreeable to our Order and he requesting Permission to remain on his Farm in the Scotch Patent and the said Request being taken into Consideration   Resolved thereupon that if the said Archibald McNeal take the Oath of Allegiance to this State that Permission will be granted him Accordingly —

The Board having tendered the Oath of Allegiance to Archibald McNeal and he refusing to take the same and declaring at the same Time his Intention of Not taking up Arms in Defence of the American Cause therefore resolved that he be confined & that a Mittimus be made out for him —

[423]   Duncan McArthur also of the Scotch Patent being questioned as to his Political Principles and declaring his Intention of not taking up Arms in defence of the Country and

acknowledging at the same time that he was sworn for the King when Burgoyne came down therefore resolved that he also be confined and that a Mittimus be made out for him —

Lieu! Col! Henry K. Van Rensselaer appeared before the Board and informed us that Thomas Blewer who is at present under a Recognizance to this Board has refused to do his duty and has made use of Expressions which Evidently denotes his disaffection to the American Cause it is therefore Resolved that he be ordered to attend this Board on Saturday the 19th day of May Instant —

Adjourned —

Met Albany 17th May 1781 —
Present

John M. Beeckman	Samuel Stringer
Isaac D. Fonda	Stewart Dean

On Application of John T. Fisher resolved that Abraham Person Junior be liberated from Confinement on his entering into a Recognizance with the said John T. Vischer his Surety for his Remaining within the Limits of the City of Albany and not departing the same Unless he previously obtains Permission from this Board and that he be of the good Behaviour until discharged by this Board —

Abraham Person Jun! of the Groote Imboght
    District in the County of Albany Farmer in. £100
John T. Fischer of the City of Albany Yeo-
    man his Bail in...................... £100

Resolved that Major Graham who takes with [424] him to west point a Number of Continental Prisoners be requested also to take with him Thomas Gleason and deliver him to some Officer of the Line of the Troops of the Massachu[set]ts Bay —

Adjourned —

Met Albany 18th May 1781 —

Present

John M. Beeckman } { Isaac D. Fonda
Samuel Stringer   }

Resolved that Samuel Baker be liberated from Confinement on entering into a Recognizance for his good Behaviour
doing his duty and appearing before any three of the Commissioners for Conspiracies when thereunto required for and during the Continuance of the present War with Great Britain —

Samuel Baker of the East District of the
   Manor of Rensselaerwyck Weaver in...... £100
Henry K. Van Rensselaer of the same place
   Esq⁺ his Bail in...................... £100

The Board being informed that William Jackson of New
Scotland and his wife are able to give some very material
Information respecting sundry Transactions in that Quarter
it is therefore resolved that the said William Jackson and
his wife be ordered forthwith to attend this Board —

Adjourned

Met Albany 22nd May 1781 —

Present

John M. Beeckman } { Stewart Dean
Samuel Stringer   } { Isaac D. Fonda

William Jackson of New Scotland having been cited [425]
together with his wife to appear before the Board appeared
and the said Mrs Jackson being Examined under Oath says
that she was informed by a man on the Road near Slingerlandt's Mill that there was a Party of the Militia coming to
New Scotland that the Man was an utter Stranger to her
having never seen him before ordered that she appear again
before the Board this Afternoon —

It appearing from the Description given by Mrs Jackson of the Man who met her on the Road and who informed her of the Militia coming to New Scotland that the said Person is a Servant Man at present in the Service of Major Reed therefore Resolved that Jacob Kidney be ordered to bring the said Person forthwith before the Board —

James Parke a Prisoner of War at present in Confinement made Application to the Board to be released from Confinement in Order that he may have it in his Power to provide for the Subsistanance [sic] of a wife and four helpless Children who are destitute of the Common Necessaries of Life and the said Request being taken into Consideration resolved thereupon that the said James Parke be released accordingly on William McLoughlins entering into a Recognizance for his remaining within the Limits of the City of Albany and surrendering himself every evening a Prisoner to the Goaler of the City and County for the Time being and also for his appearing before any three of the Commissioners for Conspiracies when thereunto required and for his good Behaviour during that Time —

William McLoughlin of the City of Albany
Innkeeper as Bail for James Parke in.... [   ]

George Scharp of the East District of the Manor of Rensse[426] laerwyck appeared before the Board and informed us that at the Request of Capt Jacob De Forest he had taken into his Charge Christopher Witting and that he has him here ready to produce to the Board.—

The said Christopher Witting being produced and examined as to the Charge alledged against him which he utterly denying and it appearing however necessary that he should be laid under Restrictions therefore resolved that he be bound by Recognizance for his good Behaviour doing his duty and appearing before any three of the Commissioners for

Conspiracies when thereunto required during the Continuance of the present war with Great Britain —

> Christopher Witting of the East District of
> the Manor of Rensselaerwyck School Master in £100
> George Scharp of the same place Farmer his
> Bail in £100

Jacob Kidney appearing with Major Ried's Servant Man who being Examined says the Evening on which it was supposed he gave Intelligence of the Militia going to New Scotland he was by Major Ried sent to Town which he offering to swear resolved therefore that he be discharged —

> Adjourned —

Met Albany 24th May 1781 —
       Present

       John M. Beeckman }   { Stewart Dean
       Samuel Stringer

Andries Hernockle appeared before the Board and informed us that being apprized of the orders sent by us to Capt Jacob De Forest to apprehend him he had voluntarily come to surrender himself to us and the said Andries Hernockle being made [427] acquainted with the Crime alledged against him denied the same The Board however Conceiving it necessary that the said Hernockle should be laid under Restrictions — Therefore resolved that the said Andries Hernockle enter into Recognizance with a sufficient surety for his good Behaviour doing his duty and appearing before any three of the Commissioners for Conspiracies when thereunto required for and during the Continuance of the present War with Great Britain —

Andries Hernockle of the East District of
the Manor of Rensselaerwyck Farmer in.. £100
Johan George Warner of the same Farmer his
Bail in.............................. £100

Adjourned —

Met Albany 25th May 1781 —
Present

Samuel Stringer } { John M. Beeckman
Isaac D. Fonda }

Lambert Starnbergh, Hendrick Haynes Jun⁓, Dirck Miller, and John Schuyler having been apprehended and sent to us as Prisoners in Consequence of the Information exhibited against them by Rachel Youngs, Jacob Knieskern and Christina Enders and being severally Examined as to the Charges alledged against them — resolved that the same be taken into Consideration until to Morrow and that the said Lambert Starnbergh, Hendrick Haynes Jun⁓ Dirck Miller & John Schuyler enter into a Recognizance for their Appearance before this Board to Morrow at ten of the Clock in the Fore-noon and that they be of the good Behaviour during that Time

Lambert Starnbergh of Schoharie Labourer
in............................... £100
Archibald Campbell of the City of Albany
Merchant his Bail in................ £100
[428] Hendrick Haynes Jun⁓ of Thurlough
Labourer in £100
Hendrick Haynes Sen⁓ of the same place
Farmer his Bail in.................. £100

Dirck Miller of Duanesburgh Farmer in.... £100
Archibald Campbell of the City of Albany
Merchant his Bail in................ £100

John Schuyler of Schoharie Farmer in...... £100
Peter Man Jun.ᵣ of the same place Farmer
   his Bail in......................... £100
Adjourned —

        Met Albany 26ᵗʰ May 1781 —
Present

    John M. Beeckman ⎰ ⎰ Samuel Stringer
    Isaac D. Fonda ⎱ ⎱ Stewart Dean

The Board having resumed the Consideration of the
Charges alledged against Lambert Starnbergh, Hendrick
Haynes Jun.ᵣ, Dirck Miller, and John Schuyler and judging the same not of sufficient weight to justify their Imprisonment but at the same Time conceiving it necessary
that they should be bound by Recognizance for their future
good Conduct therefore resolved that they be severally
bound accordingly for their good Behaviour doing their
duty and appearing before any three of the Commissioners
for Conspiracies whenever thereunto required during the
Continuance of the present War with Great Britain —

   John Schuyler of Schohary Farmer in..... £100
   Peter Man of the same place Farmer his Bail
    in................................ £100

   Dirck Miller of Duanesburgh Farmer in... £100
   Nicholas Starnbergh of Schohary Farmer his
    Bail in............................ £100

   Lambert Starnbergh of Schohary Farmer in. £100
   Nicholas Starnbergh of the same place Farmer
    his Bail in......................... £100

Resolved also that the said Lambert Starnbergh and [429]
Dirck Miller take the following Oath (to wit) "That they

will behave as true and faithful Subjects of the State of New York and endeavor to support it as a True and Independant State, and that they will make known to this Board of Commissioners for detecting all Conspiracies that may be formed in this State any Plots or any thing that may come to their knowledge that is inimical or unfriendly to this or any of the United States of America or the aiding, or assisting, or the Secreting, harbouring, or Comforting any of their Enemies by any one or any of the disaffected who may be going off to them" —

Resolved that as Hendrick Haynes Jun.ᵗ is already under Recognizance for his good Conduct and appearance when called upon that he therefore be discharged —

The Board being informed that the Conduct of Duncan M.ᶜArthur notwithstanding his Character as a disaffected Person has always been enexceptionable therefore resolved that he be discharged from Confinement and permitted to go and reside at his former place of abode in the Township of Argyle in Charlotte County —

Resolved that Archibald M.ᶜNeal be discharged from Confinement on his Entering into Recognizance with a sufficient surety for his remaining within the Limits of the City of Albany and appearing before this Board on Monday next —

Archibald M.ᶜNeal of the Township of Argyle
in the County of Charlotte Farmer in.... £100
Evens Umphrey of Schatikook District
Farmer his Bail in.................... £100

Resolved that Wessel Van Dyck be discharged on entering into a Recognizance for his future good Behaviour doing his duty and appearing before any three of the Commissioners for Conspiracies when thereunto required during the Continuance of the present War with Great Britain —

[430] Wessel Van Dyck of Cater's Kill in the
County of Albany Farmer in............ £100
David Van Dyck of Niscuthaw in the County
aforesaid Farmer his Bail in............. £100

Resolved that Abraham Person Jun.ʳ be discharged from Confinement on entering into a Recognizance for his future good Behaviour doing his duty and appearing before any three of the Commissioners for Conspiracies when thereunto required during the Continuance of the present war with Great Britain —

Abraham Person Jun.ʳ of the Great Imbought
Farmer in............................. £100
John T. Visscher of the City of Albany Yeo-
man his Bail in...................... £100

Adjourned —

Met Albany 28.ᵗʰ May 1781 —
Present

John M. Beeckman ⎱ ⎰ Stewart Dean
Samuel Stringer ⎰ ⎱

Whereas this Board from sundry concurring Circumstances has great reason to think that Doctor George Smith and his son Terence Smith are Persons whose going at large at this Time may prove detrimental to the Safety of the State therefore resolved that Jacob Kidney be ordered to apprehend the said George Smith and Terence Smith and bring them forthwith before us —

Resolved that Abraham Dewit be discharged from Confinement on Zachariah Snyder of the Great Imboght District entering into Recognizance for the good Behaviour of the said Abraham De Witt for his doing his duty and appearing before any three of the Commissioners for Con-

spiracies when thereunto required during the Continuance
[431] of the present War with Great Britain —

    Zachariah Snyder of the Great Imboght Dis-
    trict in the County of Albany Farmer as
    Bail for Abraham De Witt in........... £100

William Swain of the County of Charlotte having entered into Bond for his appearance before this Board appeared and being Examined confesses that he did entertain in his House a certain Samuel Wallace who told him
that he intended to go to the Enemy and that he did at
another time also entertain in his House two Men who said
they were going to the Enemy resolved that the said
William Swain be confined and that a Mittimus be made
out for him —

Jacob Kidney appeared before the Board and informed
us that he has apprehended Terence Smith but that Doctor
Smith was not to be found whereupon resolved that the
said Terence Smith be confined and that a Mittimus be
made out for him —

As those Persons who were removed from Jessup's Patent
and who had our Permission to return and bring from
thence the Remainder of their Effects within ten day's
which is now past and as none of the said Persons have
yet made their Appearance before us agreeable to order
therefore resolved that a Letter be wrote to Col! Cornelius
Van Dyck requesting him forthwith to send down to us all
the said Persons —

Archibald M:Neal appearing before the Board agreeable
to the Recognizance entered into by him last Saturday and
having considered the Case of the said Archibald M:Neal
Resolved thereupon that he enter into a Recognizance with
a sufficient surety for his good Behaviour and remaining
[432] within the following Limits (to wit) to the North as far

1781
May 28.
as the Patroon's Mill's in the Manor of Rensselaerwyck and to the East and South and West the Limits of the City of Albany —

 Archibald M<u>c</u>Neal of the Scotch Patent in
  the County of Albany Farmer in........ £100
 Evans Umphrey of Schatikoke in the Cou[n]ty
  of Albany Farmer his Bail in.......... £100

Resolved that David Waters be discharged from Confinement on Martin G. Van Bergan's and Myndert Rooseboom's entering into a Recognizance for the good Behaviour of the said David Waters for his doing his duty and appearing before any three of the Commissioners for Conspiracies when thereunto required during the Continuance of the present War with Great Britain —

 Martin G. Van Bergan of the City of Albany
  Yeoman as Bail for David Waters in.... £100
 Myndert Rooseboom of the same place
  Merchant also his Bail in.............. £100

Adjourned —

1781
May 29.
    Met Albany 29th May 1781 —
  Present

   John M. Beeckman ⎱ ⎰ Stewart Dean
   Samuel Stringer ⎰ ⎱

A Letter from Robert Harper Esq<u>r</u> one of the Commissioners for Conspiracies at Poughkeepsie dated 25th Instant was laid before the Board wherein he informs us that he incloses two Letters the one from Brigadier General Waterbury dated at Stanford the 8<u>th</u> Instant to the Commissioners at Westchester County the other from the
[433] said Commissioners dated at Cortlandt's Manor the 17<u>th</u>

Instant to the Commissioners for Conspiracies at Pough- keepsie from which Letters it appears that Jeremiah Smith and Henry Skinkle have been apprehended at Stanford on Suspicion of their having been to New York and sent to the said Commissioners at Poughkeepsie who as they are Inhabitants of this County have by a Recognizance conditioned in the sum of One thousand Pounds with George Smith of Claverack as their Surety bound them for their Personal Appearance before this Board on this day and the said Jeremiah Smith and Henry Skinkle appearing this Day agreeable to the Tenor of the said Recognizance and being severally examined and it appearing evident from their Examinations that they have been to New York to the Enemy therefore resolved that they be committed and that a Mittimus be made out for them —

The Examinations of the said Jeremiah Smith and Henry Skinkle being reduced to Writing are as follows (to wit) (see Examination on File)

Adjourned —

Met Albany 30<u>th</u> May 1781 —

Present

| John M. Beeckman | Samuel Stringer |
| Isaac D. Fonda | Stewart Dean |

Information being Given to the Board that one of the sons of Rykert Radliff is gone off to the Enemy resolved in Consequence of the said Information that the said Rykert Radliff (who entered into Recognizance for the Personal Appear-[434] ance of his two sons John Radliff and Arent Radliff forthwith) deliver them up to this Board —

Mr Warner of King's District appeared before this Board and informed us that at the Request of Col- Whiting he waited upon us in Order to inform the Board that a Number of the People called Shaking Quakers had lately purchased Arms & Ammunition which was supposed to be done by them with a View to assist the Enemy should they come into the Country resolved in Consequence of the said Information that a Letter be wrote to Col.<u>l</u> Whiting requesting him to collect every Piece of Evidence concerning the above Transactions and such Persons against whom he can Obtain Proof to send us together with the Evidence against each particular Person—

The Honorable Brigadier General Clinton having suggested to the Board the necessity of having the disaffected Inhabitants residing at Ballstown removed from thence with their Families and Effects — resolved thereupon that a Letter be wrote to the Commissioners for Conspiracies at Schenectady requesting them as soon as possible to have all the Disaffected of Ballstown removed to the Interior Parts of this Country —

There being an absolute Necessity that the Families of those Persons who have gone off to the Enemy should be removed within the Enemies Lines and the Legislature having at their last Sitting passed a Law for their Removal which said Law has not as yet been published therefore resolved that a Letter be wrote to the Secretary of State requesting him by the first Conveyance to send to us a certified Copy of the said Act—

Resolved that Lukas Dewitt be discharged from [435] Confinement on entering into a Recognizance for his good Behaviour doing his Duty and appearing before any three of the Commissioners for Conspiracies when thereunto required during the Continuance of the Present War with Great Britain and America —

Lukas Dewitt of the Great Imbought Farmer in.............................. £100

Jacobus Perse of the same place Farmer his Bail in.............................. £100

Resolved that John C. Person be discharged from Confinement on entering into a Recognizance for his good Behaviour doing his duty and appearing before any three of the
Commissioners for Conspiracies when thereunto required
during the Continuance of the present War between Great
Britain and America —

> John C. Person of the Great Imbought Dis-
> trict Farmer in........................ £100
> Jacob Van Olinda of the Manor of Rens-
> selaerwyck Farmer his Bail in.......... £100

Resolved that Peter Larawa be discharged from Confinement on entering into a Recognizance for his good Behaviour
doing his duty and appearing before any three of the Commissioners for Conspiracies when thereunto required during
the Continuance of the present War with Great Britain —

> Peter Larawa of Ulster County Farmer...in. £100
> Peter West of the same place Farmer his Bail in. £100

Resolved that Lukas DeWitt Junr be discharged from
Confinement on entering into a Recognizance for his good
Behaviour doing his duty and appearing before any three
of the Commissioners for Conspiracies when thereunto
required during the Continuance of the present war with
Great Britain And also for his appearance at the next
Court of General [436] Sessions of the Peace to be held for
the City and County of Albany at the City Hall in said
City on the first Tuesday in June next to answer unto all
such Matters and things as [s]hall be then and there alledged
against him and not to depart the said Court without Leave —

> Lukas Dewitt Junr of Coocksakie District
> Farmer in........................... £100
> Zachariah Snyder of Great Imbought District
> Farmer his Bail in................... £100

1781
May 30.
Resolved that Teunis Reipenbergh be discharged from Confinement on entering into a Recognizance for his good Behaviour doing his duty and appearing before any three of the Commissioners for Conspiracies when thereunto required during the Continuance of the present War with Great Britain —

> Teunis Reipenbergh of Livingston's Manor
> Farmer in............................ £300
> Hendrick Reipenbergh of the same place
> Farmer his Bail in..................... £300

Stephen Bell appeared before the Board and informed us that in his way from Hosick to this place he met Dʳ Smith, Abraham Ja: Lansing, Levines Lansing, Thomas Lambson and some other Persons and that Dʳ Smith requested him in a particular Manner to avoid mentioning that he had seen him at that Place and it appearing probable that the said Dʳ Smith will pass through Bennington on his way to Canada Therefore Resolved that a Letter be wrote to Joseph Fay Esqʳ at Bennington requesting him to have the said Dʳ Smith apprehended if possible which Letter is in the following words (to wit) (see Copy Letter on File)

Ordered that the said Letter be dispatched to Bennington by Express —

[437] Samuel Stringer Esqʳ advanced to the Express Eight Dollars of the New Emission to defray his Expences on the Road —¹

Adjourned —

1781
May 31.
Met Albany 31ˢᵗ May 1781 —

Present

| John M. Beeckman | Samuel Stringer |
| Isaac D. Fonda | Stewart Dean |

¹ Included in Stringer's sworn statement, October 21, 1784, in *Revolutionary Manuscripts*, vol. 40, p. 160, State Comptroller's office.

James Brisben appeared before the Board and laid before us a Certificate signed by Capt Hezekiah Dunham and a Number of Persons Friends to the American Cause certifying that the said James Brisben has since the surrender of General Burgoyne behaved himself well in every Respect and that they are willing that he should be permitted to remain at his Place of Abode at Saragtoga, and Peter Scharp who is Bail for the said James Brisben agreeing to the same and the said Certificate being taken into Consideration resolved thereupon that Permission be granted him accordingly

Information being given to the Board that Robert Fullerton of Nistageune did converse with Philip Ryley Junr on the very day when said Ryley went off to the Enemy and there being great Reason to suspect that the said Robert Fullerton was privy to the said Ryley's going off and to his Intention of taking off with him two young Men by the Name of Devoe —

It is therefore resolved that Jacob Kidney be ordered to bring the said Robert Fullerton forthwith before the Board —

Jacob Kidney appearing informed that he had Robert Fullerton ready to produce to the Board and the said Fullerton [438] being called in and Examined under Oath confesses that he did converse with Philip Ryley the day he went off but did not know of his Intention whereupon resolved that the said Robert Fullerton be discharged —

Barney Cadogan of Schohary one of the Persons complained of in the Affidavit's laid before this Board by William Dietz Esqr appeared before the Board and laid before us sundry Recommendations from the Officers of the Militia Regiment commanded by Col.^l Peter Vrooman which said Recommendations being taken into Consideration thereupon resolved that they [sic] said Barney Cadogan be discharged —

Resolved that a Letter be wrote to Col! Vrooman to inform him that Hendrick Hoff and another Person from the Enemy have lately been seen at the Hellebergh and to request him to detach a Party to apprehend them —

Adjourned —

Met Albany 1st June 1781 —

Present

| John M. Beeckman | Isaac D. Fonda |
| Samuel Stringer | Stewart Dean |

Rykert Radliff who was ordered to deliver up to this Board his two sons John Radliff and Arent Radliff appeared and informed us that his sons are not gone off to the Enemy and as a proof of the same requested that Lieu! Moses Hudson might be Examined on that subject and it appearing by the Information of the said Lieu! Hudson that the said John Radliff and Arent Radliff are at present at Home therefore resolved that the said Rykert Radliff be discharged —

[439] The Honorable Brigadier General James Clinton having thought proper on the Application of this Board to detain in this City a Party of the Levies to be under the Direction of this Board and Ensign Philip Herwig being appointed to take the Charge and command of the said Men resolved that Instructions be made out for the said Ensign Herwig which Instructions are as follows (to wit) (see Copy Instructions on File) —

A Letter from Joseph Fay Esq! of this day's date in Answer to the Letter sent him by Express on the 30th of May last was laid before the Board wherein he Informs that Dr Smith is at Bennington where he has surrendered himself as a Prisoner which Letter is as follows (to wit) (see Letter on File) —

Resolved that a Letter be wrote to Joseph Fay Esq.ʳ in answer to the above Letter which is in the words following (to wit) (see draught Letter on File) —

Adjourned —

Met Albany 2ⁿᵈ June 1781 —

Present

| John M. Beeckman ⎱ | ⎰ Samuel Stringer |
| Isaac D. Fonda ⎰ | ⎱ Stewart Dean |

A Letter from Col.ˡ Anthony Van Bergen of Cooksakie of this day's Date was laid before the Board wherein he informs that he sends to us a Man who he has caused to be apprehended who calls himself John Walker and the said John Walker being brought before the Board and Examined and not being able to give a Satisfactory Account of himself therefore resolved that he be committed and that a Mittimus be made out for him —

[440] William Dewitt appeared before the Board and informed us that being on his way from Philadelphia to this Place he was this day on the Kinderhook Road about eight Miles from this City taken a Prisoner by Hans Walltimyer who after detaining him some Time and asking him a Number of Questions gave him his Liberty Resolved that the above Information be immediately communicated to General Clinton and General Gansevoort in order that some Plan may be fallen upon to apprehend the said Waltimyer —

Adjourned —

Met Albany 3ᵈ June 1781 —

Present

| John M. Beeckman ⎱ | ⎰ Samuel Stringer |
| Isaac D. Fonda ⎰ | ⎱ Stewart Dean |

1781
June 3.
Philip Herwig having been ordered with his Party of Men to apprehend Abraham Ja: Lansing, Levines Lansing & Thomas Lambson who were charged with conveying away Doctor George Smith and having apprehended the said Persons agreeable to order and they being brought before the Board and Examined and it appearing from their Examinations that their Meeting with D: Smith was merely Accidental and that they were no way concerned in his Escape therefore resolved that they be discharged —

Resolved that Ensign Herwig with his Party of Men go to Cap: Woodward's on the Kinderhook Road and their remain untill they are joined by William Dewit who will direct them to the Place where he [441] was made prisoner by Waltimyer who they will endeavour to apprehend —

Adjourned—

1781
June 4.
Met Albany 4th June 1781 —

Present

John M. Beeckman ⎱   ⎰ Samuel Stringer
Isaac D. Fonda   ⎰   ⎱ Stewart Dean

Col! Killian Van Rensselaer appeared before the Board and informed us that he has received undoubted Information that Walltimyer is yet on the East side of the River and that he thinks he may be apprehended in Case proper Exertions be made for that Purpose — Resolved that it be recommended to Col: Rensselaer to order the Militia at Schodack to keep a guard along the shore at that Place to prevent Waltimyer's crossing the River —

The Reverend Samuel Swertfeger appeared before the Board and requested Permission to go to Dutchess County for the Purpose of looking for a Place to remove his Family to; which request being taken into Consideration — Resolved that he have Permission Accordingly —

Simeon Garret appeared before the Board & informed that he has this morning been taken Prisoner by Hans Waltimyer who after detaining him some Time in the woods discharged him —

Resolved in Consequence of the above Information that General Schuyler and General Gansevoort be sent for to consult him on the most Effectual way to have the said Walltimyer apprehended —

Adjourned —

[442]   Met Albany 5ᵗʰ June 1781 —

Present

John M. Beeckman }   { Isaac D. Fonda
Samuel Stringer   }   { Stewart Dean

Adam Beam of the New City having been cited to appear before this Board for having conveyed D⁗ Smith in a Waggon to Bennington and appearing this day agreeable to order and being examined and it appearing from his Examination that he was altogether unacquainted with D⁗ Smith's Character and Situation therefore resolved that he be discharged —

It appearing to this Board from the Examination of Simeon Garret that Walltimyer has slept several Nights in the Barn of John Ver Plank of Coyeman's Patent and there being reason to suppose that the Information respecting the said John Ver Planck is true from his Character of Disaffection and the said John Ver Planck being at present in this place — Therefore resolved that Jacob Kidney be ordered to bring him forthwith before the Board —

Jacob Kidney appearing with John Ver Planck and he being Examined with Respect to Walltimyer's sleeping in his Barn and he being ready to swear that he never knew of said

1781
June 5.

Walltimyer being there which Assertion being deemed satisfactory to the Board therefore resolved that he be discharged —

Adjourned

1781
June 6.

[443]   Met Albany 6th June 1781 —

Present

John M. Beeckman ⎱   ⎰ Stewart Dean
Samuel Stringer   ⎰   ⎱ Isaac D. Fonda

Jeremiah Smith and Hendrick Skinkle who were some Time ago committed being brought before the Board were again Examined and being unwilling to make answers to the Questions proposed to them therefore resolved that they be recommitted —

It appearing to this Board that Peter Huyck has forfeited the Recognizance by him entered into before this Board ordered therefore that the Secretary make out the said Recognizance and transmit the same to the Attorney General in Order to its being prosecuted —

Nathaniel Cotton of Cooksakie being a material Witness against William Hartley who was some Time since confined as a spy from the Enemy and as the said William Hartley is to receive his Tryal by a Court Martial therefore Resolved that the said Nathaniel Cotton be cited to appear forthwith before this Board —

John Walker who was on the 2nd Instant apprehended on Suspicion by order of Col! Van Bergen was brought before the Board and being Examined says that he is a Continental Soldier belonging to the Massachusets Line and that he has deserted from West Point resolved that the said John Walker be delivered over to Col! Van Schaick whose Regiment is now on their way to West Point —

A Letter from Joseph Fay Esq᙮ dated at Bennington on the 3ᵈ Instant was laid before the Board which Letter is in the following words (to wit) (see Letter on File) —

Adjourned —

1781 June 6.

[444] Met Albany 9ᵗʰ June 1781 —

1781 June 9.

Present

John M. Beeckman } { Samuel Stringer
Isaac D. Fonda   } { Stewart Dean

William Parker, John Wait, Isabel Parker, Jane Wait, and James Parker Inhabitants of Tryon County having been apprehended for harbouring and supplying Parties from the Enemy with Provisions and being brought before the Board and it appearing from their Examinations that they have received Letters from the enemy therefore resolved that William Parker and John Wait be committed and that Isabel Parker, Jane Wait and James Parker have Permission to return to their Places of Abode to fetch from thence their Families and Effects —

Resolved that a Mittimus be m[a]de out for William Parker and John Wait —

Adjourned —

Met Albany 13ᵗʰ June 1781

1781 June 13.

Present

John M. Beeckman } { Isaac D. Fonda
Samuel Stringer   }

Hugh Mitchell and Abraham Outhout Esqʳˢ Commissioners for Conspiracies from Schenectady informed the Board that there are a Number of Persons at the Hellebergh who have harboured Walltimyer and Bettis and that there is a Necessity at this Time of removing from thence such Persons and the other disaffected Inhabitants in that Quarter and this Board being convinced of the Necessity of such a [445] measure especially as the Enemy are daily expected upon the Frontiers —

Therefore Resolved that it be recommended to the said Hugh Mitchell and Abraham Outhout to send a Party of men from Schenectady to apprehend some of those who are most notoriously disaffected in that Quarter and this Board will also send a Party that way to apprehend Joseph Bettis who is reported is still there —

Resolved that Col! Anthony Van Bergen be requested to send a party of his Regiment to Peesink and places Adjacent to apprehend all suspected Persons in that Quarter —

The Board having received Information from Col! Van Bergen that Robert Tripp being looked upon as a dangerous Person therefore Resolved that a warrant be made out for him and delivered to Col! Van Bergen to have the same served —

The Board having received Information that a certain Scott who is at present at New York has a Quantity of Wheat stored at Moore's at Kat's Kill and as the same ought to be seized for the use of the Publick therefore resolved that a Letter be wrote to Hezekiah Van Orden Esq! requesting him to make Enquiry concerning the said Wheat and have the same seized for the Public Use agreeable to Law which Letter is in the words following (to wit) (see Copy Letter on File)

A Letter from Teunis Van Wagenen dated at Kat's Kill dated the 26ᵗʰ Ultimo was laid before the Board which Letter is in the following words (to wit) (see Letter on File) —

Adjourned —

[446]   Met Albany 14th June 1781 —

Present

John M. Beeckman ⎱   ⎰ Samuel Stringer
Isaac D. Fonda   ⎰   ⎱

As there are a Number of disaffected Persons in the Regiment at present commanded by Major Ezekiel Taylor some of whom as they live upon the Frontiers it is necessary should be removed therefore resolved that Major Taylor be requested to furnish this Board as soon as possible with a List of his Regiment together with the Political Character of Each Man—

Capt John Grote appeared before the Board with Edward McGurkey who he informed us he had apprehended for endeavouring to enlist him the said John Grote for the Service of the King of Great Britain And producing a Guinea delivered him by the said Edward McGurkey as a Bounty and the said McGurkey being Examined confessing that he has taken an Oath to be true to the King resolved that he be confined and that a Mittimus be made out for him —

It being represented to the Board that Robert Bohannah of Nistageune is a dangerous and disaffected Person and there being Reason to suspect that he harbours persons from the Enemy It is therefore resolved that a warrant be made out directed to Philip Herwig to apprehend the said Robert Bohannah and that Nicholas Van Vranken of Nistageune be requested to assist the said Philip Herwig in the Execution of the above Warrant —

Adjourned —

[447]   Met Albany 15th June 1781 —

Present

John M. Beeckman ⎱   ⎰ Isaac D. Fonda
Samuel Stringer   ⎰   ⎱

June 15.   Capt John Grote appearing before the Board for the
  1781   Purpose of being Examined with Respect to Edward
M.ͨGurkey was examined accordingly and his Examination is
in the words following (to wit) (see Examination on File) —
    John Oliver, Jacob Daniels, Francis Winne and Eli
Arnold having been present at the Time that Edward
M.ͨGurkey attempted to Enlist John Grote and having been
Ordered to appear before the Board to be Examined concerning the same and attending for that Purpose were severally
examined and their examinations are as follows (to wit)
(see Examination on File) —

    Adjourned —

  1781   Met Albany 16th June 1781 —
June 16.
            Present

            John M. Beeckman ⎞   ⎛
            Samuel Stringer   ⎠   ⎝ Isaac D. Fonda

    Robert Bohannah for whose Apprehension a warrant was
on the 14th Instant made out being brought before the Board
by Philip Herwig and the Charges as alledged against him
being read to him, he utterly denied the same and as a proff
of his Innocence offered to take up and bring before this
Board all Persons who he finds travelling through that
Part of the Country where he resides and the Board being of
Opinion that by discharging the said Robert Bohannah they
may receive such Information from him respecting [448] Joe
Bettis and others as may enable the Board to have them
apprehended therefore resolved that he be discharged —
    Robert Brisben of Saragtoga having entered into Recogni-
zance before this Board and having since gone off to Canada
and joined the Enemy and Jonathan Pettit his Bail being
called upon to pay the Recognizance Money and appearing

for that Purpose resolved that the same amounting to 237 Dollars of the Money Emitted pursuant to a Resolution of the 18<u>th</u> of March be received and delivered over into the Hands of the Secretary to this Board —

Resolved that the List received from Major Ezekiel Taylor of the Regiment under his Command be transmitted to the Commissioners for Conspiracies at Schenectady —

Adjourned —

Met Albany 18<u>th</u> June 1781 —
Present

John M. Beeckman
Isaac D. Fonda   Samuel Stringer

The Honorable Brigadier General James Clinton having requested the Board to take the Examinations of William Empie and Randell Hewit who were taken Prisoners by a Party of Oneyda Indians near Crown Point and they being brought before the Board and examined say as follows (to wit) (see their Examinations on File) —

Resolved that they be recommitted —

Adjourned —

[449]   Met Albany 19<u>th</u> June 1781 —
Present

John M. Beeckman
Isaac D. Fonda   Samuel Stringer

The Board having taken into Consideration the Complaint exhibited to us by a Number of the approved Friends to the American Cause residing at the Hellebergh and places adjoining and being of Opinion from the frequent Parties from the enemy who are harboured in that Quarter by the

1781 June 19. disaffected; that such as are reputed dangerous Persons should be removed from that part of the Country and the Board having been furnished with List's of the names of the Persons belonging to the Companies of Capt Van Aernam, Capt Luke, Capt Grote, and Capt Slingerlandt and with the character of Each particular Person.

Resolved that the said List's be delivered to the Officer commanding the Party detached by General Clinton at the request of this Board to carry the above into Execution.

Isaac Sheldon Constable appeared before the Board & informed that he had apprehended two Persons at Stephen Town who appeared to be of suspicious Characters and the said Persons being brought in and Examined say their Names are John Cane and Jesse Adams and not giving a satisfactory Account of themselves resolved that they be committed and that a Mittimus be made out for them.

Coll Van Bergen having at the Request of this Board caused Robert Trip to be apprehended for harbouring Walltimyer and the said Robert Trip being brought before the Board and Examined his Examination is in the words following (to wit) (see Examinations on File) —

Adjourned —

1781 June 21. [450] Met Albany 21st June 1781 —

Present

John M. Beeckman, Samuel Stringer } { Isaac D. Fonda

William Epie who was on the 18th Instant committed was ordered to be brought before the Board and being again Examined his Examination is in the following words (to wit) (see Examination on File)

Randell Hewitt who was also on the 18th Instant committed

was ordered to be brought before the Board & being Ex- 1781 June 21.
amined his examination is in words following (to wit) (see
his Examination on File)

Adjourned.

Met Albany 26<u>th</u> June 1781 —   1781 June 26.

Present

 John M. Beeckman } { Isaac D. Fonda
 Samuel Stringer

Jacob Barger appeared before the Board and informed
us that he had apprehended a certain John Anderson who
appears to him to be of a suspicious Character and the said
John Anderson being brought in and Examined and not
giving a satisfactory account of himself therefore resolved
that he be committed and that a mittimus be made out for
Him —

Adjourned —

Met Albany 28<u>th</u> June 1781 —   1781 June 28.

Present

 John M. Beeckman } { Isaac D. Fonda
 Samuel Stringer   { Stewart Dean

Ephraim Hopping appeared before the Board and [451]
informs that he is lately deserted from Canada where he
has been some Time as a Prisoner and produced a Pass of
Thomas Chittendon Esqr to come to this Place and he being
desirous of going to his Excellency Governor Clinton at
Poughkeepsie resolved that a pass for that purpose be given
him —

Peter Seeger having been ordered to appear before the
Board appeared and was Examined —

Major John Graham having with a Party of Men been

1781
June 28. detached to the Hellebergh in order to apprehend Joe Bettis and other Emissaries from the enemy in that Quarter and having apprehended Jellis Legrange for harbouring the said Bettis and having also apprehended a certain John Low on suspicion and the said Jellis Legrange and John Low being Examined resolved as nothing appears against the said John Low that he be discharged and that Jellis Legrange be committed and that a Mittimus be made out for him —

Cornelius Van Sice being ordered to appear before the Board and being Examined says that the above mentioned Jellis Legrange brought him to Joe Bettis to Enlist which Examination is as follows (see Examination on File) —

Adjourned —

1781
June 29.

Met Albany 29th June 1781 —

Present

| John M. Beeckman | Isaac D. Fonda |
| Samuel Stringer | Stewart Dean |

The Examination's of John Bardine and Ebenezer French taken by William Schuyler, William Harper and David McMaster Esq^{rs} Justices of the Peace for the County of Tryon [452] were laid before the Board and it appearing from the said Examinations that Isaac Lawson who the said Justices have caused to be apprehended and sent to us is a Dangerous and disaffected Person therefore resolved that he be committed and that a Mittimus be made out for him —

Adjourned —

1781
June 30.

Met Albany 30th June 1781 —

Present

| John M. Beeckman | Isaac D. Fonda |
| Samuel Stringer | |

Resolved that Robert Trip be discharged from Confinement on entering into a Recognizance for his good Behaviour doing his duty and appearing before any three of the Commissioners for Conspiracies when thereunto required during the Continuance of the present war with Great Britain and also for his appearance at the next supream Court of Judicature to be held for the State of New York on the last Tuesday in July next at the City Hall in the City of Albany (or whosoever the said Court shall then be held in the State aforesaid) then and there to answer unto such things as shall be there alledged against him and not depart the Court without Leave — 1781 June 30.

> Robert Trip of Acquatough in the County
> of Albany Farmer in.................. £100
> Gideon Trip of King's District in the County
> aforesaid Farmer his Bail in.......... £100

Adjourned —

[453] Met Albany 31st June [sic for July 1] 1781 — 1781 July 1.

Present

> John M. Beeckman
> Samuel Stringer } { Isaac D. Fonda

Simon Relea, Daniel Relea, David Relea, George Sidnam, John Van Alstyne, Teunis Van Alstyne, Roeliff Seeger, and Evert Johnson having been apprehended by Major Graham for harbouring Joseph Bettis and other Emissaries from the Enemy and they being brought before the Board and Examined and the Charges against them appearing to be well founded therefore resolved that they be committed and that a Mittimus be made out for them —

Adjourned —

                    Met Albany 5th July 1781 —
            Present

            John M. Beeckman }   { Samuel Stringer
            Isaac D. Fonda   }

A Letter from Hugh Mitchell Esqr one of the Commissioners for Conspiracies at Schenectady was laid before the Board setting forth that Petrus Wermer who is at present in Confinement has by the Commissioners at Schenectady been bound by Recognizance for his good Behaviour doing his duty and appearance when called upon and Requesting that the said Petrus Wermer may be liberated unless some material Charges can be alledged against him and the s^d request being taken into Consideration and as no perticular Charges have yet been alledged against him the said Petrus Wermer therefore resolved that he be discharged —

    Adjourned —

[454]   Met Albany 6th 1781 —
            Present

            John M. Beeckman }   { Isaac D. Fonda
            Samuel Stringer }

Peter Van Slyck residing near Cooksakie appearing before the Board informs us that a Party of Robbers headed by a certain Joseph Smith (formerly a servant of Walltimyer) did on the first Instant enter his House and steel a Number of Articles of him and that in attempting to make his Escape they fired at him and wounded him in the Arm and that they took Prisoner at his House Peter Clauw who has since made his Escape from them and is this day come to Town and the said Peter Clauw appearing before the Board & being examined says as follows (to wit) (see his examination on File)
    Adjourned —

Met Albany 7th July 1781 —

Present

John M. Beeckman } { Samuel Stringer
Isaac D. Fonda   }

Col! Veeder appeared before the Board and requested
the liberation of Coenradt Coen from Confinement as the
said Coenradt Coen has always discovered a Willingness to
do his duty when required and the said request being taken
into Consideration resolved in Consequence thereof that the
said Coenradt Coen be discharged from Confinement and
cautioned against associating with disaffected Persons in
Future —

[455] Resolved that Peter Relea be discharged from Confinement on entering into a Recognizance for his good
Behaviour doing his duty and appearing before any three
of the Commissioners for Conspiracies when thereunto
required during the Continuance of the present war with
Great Britain —

Peter Relea of the west District of the Manor
of Rensselaerwyck Farmer in £100
Martin Sybert of the same place Farmer his
Bail in £100

Adjourned —

Met Albany 8th July 1781 —

Present

John M. Beeckman } { Samuel Stringer
Isaac D. Fonda   }

John Loe appeared before the Board and requested
Permission to go and reside at Christian Sant's at the Bever
Dam resolved that Permission be granted him accordingly
on the said Christian Sant's entering into a Recognizance

for the good Behaviour of the said John Loe and for his doing his duty and appearing before any three of the Commissioners for Conspiracies when thereunto required during the Continuance of the present War with Great Britain —

> Christian Sant of the Bever Dam in the
> County of Albany Farmer as Bail for
> John Loe in......................... £100

The Honorable Brigadier General James Clinton having signified to this Board his Approbation of Randell Hewit a Prisoner of war being liberated from Confinement upon giving Security to this Board to appear when called upon resolved therefore that he be liberated accordingly on Ephraim Hewit his Father [456] entering into a Recognizance for his remaining within the Limits of the Farm at present in Possession of the said Ephraim Hewit at Keyaderoseras and appearing before any three of the Commissioners for Conspiracies when called upon and for his good Behaviour until he shall be Exchanged or otherwise di[s]posed of —

> Ephraim Hewit of Keyaderoseras Patent in
> the County of Albany Farmer Bail for
> Randell Hewit in..................... £100

A Letter from Col. Van Bergen dated at Cooksakie the 4th Instant was laid before the Board inclosing the Examinations of Teunis Hoogteling, Peter Finehout, William Davis, and Israel Kelsey concerning the Robbery committed at Peter Van Slyck's which Letter and Examinations are as follows (to wit) (see Examinations & Letter on File) —

It appearing to this Board from the Examination of Peter Clauw that the Party who robbed Van Sluyck stopped at the House of Adrian Bradt at Niscuthaw and that Joe

Smith one of the said Party conversed for some time in private with the said Adrian Bradt and as the said Adrian Bradt has not given any Information concer[n]ing the said Party therefore resolved that he be ordered to appear before this Board to Morrow Morning —

Adjourned —

Met Albany 10th July 1781 —

Present

John M. Beeckman ⎱   ⎰ Isaac D. Fonda
Samuel Stringer ⎰   ⎱

It appearing from the Examination of Peter [457] Clauw that Adrian Bradt Junr (son of Adrian Bradt) was at Home when the party who robbed Peter Van Slyck was at his Father's House and that he conversed with them and the said Adrian Bradt Junr having been apprehended by Jacob Kidney and brought before the Board and being examined as to the same resolved that he enter into a Recognizance for his good Behaviour doing his duty and appearing before any three of the Commissioners for Conspiracies when thereunto required during the Continuance of the present war with Great Britain.

Andrian Bradt Junr of Niscuthaw in the
    County of Albany Farmer in £100
Peter S. Seeger of the same place Farmer his
    Bail in £100

Adrian Bradt having been cited to appear before the Board appeared and was Examined and the said Adrian Bradt appearing to be much indisposed and as his being confined at this Time may endanger his Life therefore resolved that he enter into Recognizance with sufficient sureties for his remaining within the Limits of this City untill discharged by this Board and for his good Behaviour in the mean Time —

> Adrian Bradt of Niscuthaw in the County of
> Albany Farmer in....................... £100
> James Van Zandt of the City of Albany Car-
> penter his Bail in....................... £100
> John Van Nist of the Normans Kill in the
> County of Albany Farmer also his Bail in. £100

Frederick Miller (son in Law of Adrian Bradt) having been cited to appear before the Board and being examined with Respect to the Party who robbed Van Slyck and who were at the said Adrian Bradt's and it appearing that he had no Conver- [458] sation with the said Party, yet on Account of his Connection with the said Adrian Bradt, It is resolved that he enter into a Recognizance for his good Behaviour and appearing before any three of the Commissioners for Conspiracies when thereunto required until discharged by this Board.

> Frederick Miller of Niscuthaw in the County
> of Albany Cordwainer in............... £100
> John N. Smith of the same place Wheel-
> wright his Bail in....................... £100

Lieut David Hustead Appeared before the Board with Lucius Palmer, Gideon Palmer, Isaac Palmer, Simon Chesley and Comfort Marks who he had apprehended on account of their intending to go to Canada & they being severally examined resolved that they be confined —

Adjourned —

Met Albany 11th July 1781 —

Present

John M. Beeckman }   { Isaac D. Fonda
Samuel Stringer   }

Lucius Palmer, Gideon Palmer, Isaac Palmer, Simon
Chesley and Comfort Marks who were Yesterday confined
being again brought before the Board and Examined as to
their Intention of going to the Enemy at Canada — Resolved
on Account of the youth and Inexperience of the said Lucius
Palmer, George Palmer, Isaac Palmer, Simon Chesley and
Comfort Marks and their Candid Acknowledgement's that
they be discharged on their taking the following Oath, (to
wit) —

I do swear upon the holy Evangelists of Almighty god
that I will be true to the State of New York and [459] will
Conduct myself as a good and faithful subject of the said
State ought to do; that and I will not aid, comfort, council
with, or Assist in any way whatever any of the Enemies of
the said State of New York or the United States of America
and that I will immediately make known any Plots that may
be intended against any of the said United States and
discover that may come to my knowledge any of their
Enemies whenever I [k]now there are any lurking about
in the Country to any Officer or to the Board of Commissioners — So help me God —

Adjourned —

        Met Albany 16th July 1781 —
Present

    John M. Beeckman ⎱ ⎰ Isaac D. Fonda
    Samuel Stringer ⎰ ⎱

Jacobus Van Sante appearing before the Board requested
to deliver up in Discharge of himself Adrian Bradt. resolved
that the said Jacobus Van Sante be discharged from the
Recognizance by him entered into for the said Adrian Bradt
and that the said Adrian Bradt be confined and a Mittimus
be made out for him —

1781
July 16.
Elizabeth Burrows having been Ordered to appear before the Board and appearing and being examined as to Joe Smith and his Party and she positively denying her having seen the said Smith or any of his Party resolved that she be discharged —

Gerrit Seeger having also been cited to appear before the Board and appearing and being Examined his Examination is as follows (to wit) (see Examination on File) —

Adjourned —

1781
July 19.
[460]   Met Albany 19th July 1781 —

Present

John M. Beeckman }   { Samuel Stringer
Isaac D. Fonda   }   {

Adrian Bradt Junr, Evert Sixbey, Jacobus Van Valkenburgh, Alexander Conning and Ann Conning his wife and Richard Kerknaer having been apprehended for harbouring and supplying with Provisions the Party who robbed Peter Van Slyck and being brought before the Board and severally examined resolved that they be committed and that a Mittimus be made out for them —

Adjourned —

1781
July 20.
Met Albany 20th July 1781 —

Present

John M. Beeckman }   { Samuel Stringer
Isaac D. Fonda   }   {

Lucas Taylor being charged with being privy to the harbouring of the Party who robbed Van Slyck being brought before the Board and Examined resolved that he enter into a Recognizance for his good Behaviour doing his duty and appearing before any three of the Commissioners for Conspiracies during the Continuance of the present war with

1781
July 20.

Great Britain and for his Appearance at the next Supream Court of Judicature to be held for the State of New York at the City Hall in this City on the last Tuesday in July Instant (or wheresoever the said Court shall then be held in the State aforesaid) to answer to such Matters as shall be alledged against him and not to depart the Court without Leave—

> Lucas Taylor of the West District of the
> Manor of Rensselaerwyck in. £100
> [461] Gerrit Van Wie of the same place
> Farmer his Bail in. £100

Staats Bradt who was also charged with being privy to the harbouring Joe Smith and the rest of the Party who robbed Peter Van Slyck being brought before the Board resolved that he enter into a Recognizance for his good Behaviour doing his duty and appearing before any three of the Commissioners for Conspiracies during the Continuance of the present war with Great Britain and for his Appearance at the next Supream Court of Judicature to be held for the State of New York at the City Hall in this City on the last Tuesday in July next (or wheresoever the said Court shall then be held in the State aforesaid) to answer to such Matters as shall be alledged against him and not to depart the Court without Leave —

> Staats Bradt of the West District of the
> Manor of Rensselaerwyck Farmer in. . . . £100
> Gerrit Van Wie of the same place Farmer
> his Bail in. £100

Jacob France of Thurlough, charged by William Summer with having assisted in the destruction of Currey Town being brought before the Board and Examined resolved that he be committed and that a Mittimus be made out for him —

Adjourned

Met Albany 21ˢᵗ July 1781 —

Present

John M. Beeckman ⎫ ⎧ Samuel Stringer
Isaac D. Fonda   ⎭ ⎩

Resolved that a letter be wrote to Hugh Mitchell Esqʳ
at Schenectady requesting him to take Cornelius Van
Sice's Recognizance for his appearance at the next supream
Court and transmit the same to this Board —

[462] A Letter from Zepheniah Batchelder Esqʳ Justice of
the Peace of Tryon County was laid before the Board wherein
he informs that John Cuppernul who formerly resided at
Stonearabia is removed to Schohary, and the said John Cuppernul being a material Witness against Jacob J. Truax —

Resolved in Consequence of the said Letter that a Letter
be wrote to Peter Vrooman Esqʳ at Schohary requesting him
to take the said John Cuppernull's Recognizance for his
appearance at the next supream Court and transmit the same
to this Board to be handed to the Court —

Evert Jansen being committed on a charge of having
harboured Joseph Bettis was brought before the Board and
Examined   Ordered that he be recommitted —

Adjourned —

Met Albany 23ᵈ July 1781 —

[Present]

John M. Beeckman ⎫ ⎧ Samuel Stringer
Isaac D. Fonda   ⎭ ⎩

Jacob France of Thurlough who was committed on the
20ᵗʰ Instant being brought before the Board and Examined
saith as follows (to wit) (see Examination on File) —
Ordered that he be recommitted —

Adjourned —

Met Albany 24th July 1781 —

Present

John M. Beeckman ⎫ ⎧ Isaac D. Fonda
Samuel Stringer ⎭ ⎩

William summer of Thurlough having been sent to
Goal by Col! Willet on Account of his having assisted the
[463] Enemy in the Destruction of Currey Town being
brought before the Board and Examined saith as follows
(see Examination on File) — Ordered that he be recommitted —

Adjourned —

Met Albany 25th July 1781 —

Present

John M. Beeckman ⎫ ⎧ Samuel Stringer
Isaac D. Fonda ⎭ ⎩

Resolved that Anne Conning be liberated from Confinement on James Jolley's entering into a Recognizance for her
Appearance at the next Supream Court of Judicature to be
held for the State of New York at the City Hall in the City
of Albany on the last Tuesday in July Instant (or wheresoever the said Court shall then be held in the State aforesaid)
to answer to such Matters as shall be alledged against her
and not to depart the Court without leave —

James Jolly of the West District of the Manor
    of Rensselaerwyck Farmer as Bail for
    Anne Conning in £100

Henry Haines, Coenradt Brown, Frederick Merkle,
Michael Merkle, Christian Merkle, Mathias Merkle, Ann
Frets, Henry Haines Junr, Christopher Redick, Henry
Frandts, Coenradt Hopper, Jacobus Hopper, George Walker,
John Summer, Christian Minor, Michael Frederick, Johannis

1781
July 25.

Coenradt, Christian Ottman, Jacob Haines, David Coffman, and George Cross having been apprehended by order of Col⁻ Willett on the Charge alledged against him [them] by William Summer of their having Assisted the Enemy in the Destruction of Currey Town and they being sent down to this Board resolved that they be confined and that a Mittimus be made out for them —

[464] It appearing from the Examination of William Summer that William Petrie Esqᵉ of Tryon County will be wanted as a witness at the ensuing Supream Court against the above mentioned Persons from Thurlough therefore resolved that a Letter be wrote to him requesting his Attendance at that Time —

Resolved that a Letter be also wrote to David Lewis requesting his attendance at the next Supream Court as a witness against the above mentioned from Thurlough —

Adjourned —

1781
July 26.

Met Albany 26ᵗʰ July 1781 —
Present

John M. Beeckman ⎱ ⎰ Isaac D. Fonda
Samuel Stringer ⎰ ⎱

Haze[l]ton Spencer who was some time ago with the approbation of General Clinton liberated from Confinement and restricted to the Limits of this City appeared before the Board and laid before us a further Approbation of General Clinton to permit the said Hazelton Spencer to go and reside at the New City and the same having been taken into Consideration and Abraham Jacob Lansing who is surety for the said Hazelton Spencer consenting to the same therefore resolved that the said Hazelton Spencer have leave accordingly and that he be ordered to make his appearance before this

Board once every Week during the time he remains at the New City as aforesaid.

William Somer being brought before the Board was again Examined and ordered to be recommitted

Adjourned —

[465]   Met Albany 27th July 1781 —

Present

John M. Beeckman ⎱ ⎰ Isaac D. Fonda
Samuel Stringer   ⎰ ⎱

Christina Hooper formerly of Thurlough in Tryon County having been cited to appear before the Board and she appearing this day agreeable to the said Order and being Examined as to the Thurlough Inhabitants saith as follows (to wit) (see Examination on File) —

Coenradt Brown, Christian Ottman, and Jacob Haines Junr being brought before the Board were Examined and Ordered to be recommitted —

Adjourned —

Met Albany 28th July 1781 —
Present

John M. Beeckman ⎱ ⎰ Isaac D. Fonda
Samuel Stringer   ⎰ ⎱

A Letter from Hugh Mitchell Esqr dated 27th Instant was laid before the Board informing that he sends down under Guard John Ward who was apprehended near Ballstown and was supposed to be on his way to Canada —

And the said John Ward being brought before the Board and examined and it appearing that he is a Deserter from the Enemy and has hitherto conducted himself well therefore resolved that he be discharged —

1781
July 28.
Archibald MᶜNeal appeared before the Board and requested Permission to go to his Place of abode at the Scotch Patent to which his Bail Evans Umphrey consenting resolved that he [466] have Permission accordingly until the first day of September next —

Adjourned —

1781
July 30.
Met Albany 30ᵗʰ July 1781 —

Present

John M. Beeckman ⎫ ⎧ Samuel Stringer
Isaac D. Fonda   ⎭ ⎩

A Letter from Flores Bancker Esqʳ dated 29ᵗʰ Instant was laid before the Board setting forth that a Number of disaffected Persons have lately been removed from the Western Frontiers to the East side of the River who he has great Reason to beleive from sundry Circumstances are meditating some Scheme against the wellfare of the State and requesting directions what steps it will be necessary to take with the above Persons —

And the subject of the above Letter being taken into Consideration — Resolved that it be recommended to the said Flores Bancker to make every possible discovery with Respect to the above Matter and transmit the same without delay to this Board —

It appearing from the Examination of William Summer that Christopher France formerly an Inhabitant of Thurlough who at present resides at Nistageune was in the Year 1778 on his way to join Genˡ Sᵗ Ledger when he had invested Fort Schuyler and that he last Fall also went to Schohary to assist Sir John Johnson in the destruction of Schohary resolved therefore that a warrant be made [467] out directed to Jacob Kidney to apprehend the said Christopher France and forthwith bring him before the Board —

The Board having received Information that Arthur Hewit of Pits Town is able to give some very material Information respecting Simeon Smith therefore resolved that the said Arthur Hewit be cited to appear before this Board in Order that he may be examined as to the Conduct of the said Simeon Smith —

Jellis Legrange requesting to be brought before the Board informed us that Joseph Bettis with some others are lately come from Canada and that there is a Prospect in case a Party of Men should be sent out that the said Bettis might be apprehended —

Resolved that in Consequence of the said Information that application be immediately made for a Party of Continental Troops to go in search of the said Joseph Bettis and that the said Party be directed to go to the House of the said Jellis Legrange and one Flager where they will strictly search for them —

Adjourned —

Met Albany 31st July 1781

Present

John M. Beeckman ⎱ ⎰ Isaac D. Fonda
Samuel Stringer ⎰ ⎱

Jellis Legrange again requesting to be brought before the Board & being brought accordingly says that Hans Waltymier is lately also come from Canada that he has brought Dispatches for some Persons in this City and that he Yesterday was in Town with them [468] resolved that it be recommended to the said Jellis Legrange to make what further discoveries he is able and that this Board will in that Case use their Influence with the Supream Court to procure his liberation from Confinement —

Christian Legrange appeared before the Board and in-

1781
July 31. formed that Joe Bettis has this day been at his House and that the said Bettis informed the said Christian Legrange's wife that he is this night to be at the House of one Fagler whose son went to Canada some Time since with the said Joe Bettis in Consequence of which Information resolved that the Honorable Brigadier Gen! James Clinton be requested to order out a Party of Col! Cortlandt's Regiment to apprehend the said Joe Bettis

Adjourned —

1781
Aug. 2. Met Albany 2ⁿᵈ August 1781 —

Present

John M. Beeckman } { Isaac D. Fonda
Samuel Stringer

Resolved that Hendrick Haines of Thurlough be discharged from Confinement on entering into a Recognizance for his good Behaviour and appearance before any three of the Commissioners for Conspiracies when thereunto required during the Continuance of the present War with Great Britain —

Hendrick Haines of Thurlough in the County
of Tryon Farmer in.................... £100
John Roff of the City of Albany Merchant
his Bail in........................... £100

Adjourned —

1781
Aug. 4. [469] Met Albany 4ᵗʰ August 1781 —

Present

John M. Beeckman } { Isaac D. Fonda
Samuel Stringer

Resolved that Rykert Kerknaer be discharged from Confinement on entering into a Recognizance for his good Behaviour doing his duty and appearing before any three of the Commissioners for Conspiracies when thereunto required during the Continuance of the present War with Great Britain —

Rykert Kernaer of the West District of the
Manor of Rensselaerwyck Farmer in..... £100
Francis Rosseau of the same Place Farmer
his Bail in........................... £100

Resolved that Michael Bruce enter into a Recognizance for his good Behaviour doing his duty and appearing before any three of the Commissioners for Conspiracies when thereunto required during the Continuance of the present War with Great Britain —

Michael Bruce of the West District of the
Manor of Rensselaerwyck Farmer in.... £100
Joshua Bloore of the City of Albany Merchant his Bail in...................... £100

Adjourned

Met Albany 6th August 1781 —
Present

John M. Beeckman ⎱ ⎰ Samuel Stringer
Isaac D. Fonda ⎰   ⎱

Edward McGurkey confined on the Complaint of Capt John Groote for endeavoring to enlist the said John Groot[e] [470] for the service of the enemy was brought before the Board and as no Indictment has been found against him — Therefore resolved that he be discharged from Confinement—

Adjourned

Met Albany 7th August 1781
Present

John M. Beeckman ⎱ ⎰ Samuel Stringer
Isaac D. Fonda ⎰   ⎱

Resolved that Jacobus Van Valkenburgh be discharged
from Confinement on entering into a Recognizance for his
good Behaviour doing his duty and appearing before any
three of the Commissioners for Conspiracies when thereunto
required during the Continuance of the present War with
Great Britain —

> Jacobus Van Valkenburgh of the West Dis-
> trict of the Manor of Rensselaerwyck
> Farmer in............................ £100
> John Oliver of the same place Farmer his
> Bail in.............................. £100

Christian Merkle of Thurlough at present in Confinement
being very Ill and as a Continuance in his present Situation
may endanger his Life — Therefore resolved that he have
Permission to go to the House of Christian Earing in this
City untill he is recovered of his Indisposition —

Adjourned —

            Met Albany 8th August 1781 —
     Present

     John M. Beeckman   Isaac D. Fonda
     Samuel Stringer   Stewart Dean

An Attempt having last Night been made by [471] Hans
Waltimier with a Party of Men to carry off General Schuyler
and it appearing probable that he will endeavour to Escape
by the way of the Nistageune Road —

It is therefore Resolved that a Letter be wrote to Col.
Philip Schuyler requesting him to detach Capt Levinis
Lansing's Company to go to the Wothoyct[1] and there remain
until to Morrow Morning and that he dispose of the Re-

---

[1] Evidently written corruptly for Uytkyck, a hill on the old road to
Niskayuna; also written at times as Kyck-uyt, and in English as Outlook.

mainder of his Men in such a Way as he may judge best to intercept the said Waltimier and his Party —

Resolved also that a Letter be wrote to Col! John H. Beeckman at Schodack to order out a Party of his Regiment to Guard the shore from the Kinderhook Dock to Schodack in Case Waltimier may Attempt to Cross the River

It being represented to the Board that James Dunneway of this City has been sworn by a Party of Men in the Woods — Resolved in Consequence of the said Information that the said James Dunneway be sent for and Examined —

James Dunneway appearing and being Examined says that a few days ago he was in the Woods about five or Six Miles from Town where he was taken Prisoner by three Men who swore him to Secrecy and that he has not since that Time seen them again ordered that he be discharged —

Jellis Legrange at present in Confinement having informed the Board that Waltimier has been in Town with Letters from Canada and that he has received his Information from William Empie & Terence [472] Smith who are also in Confinement wherefore resolved that the said William Empie and Terence Smith be brought before the Board and examined as to the same —

William Empie and Terence Smith being examined refuse to give any satisfactory Answers to the Questions proposed to them therefore resolved that they be recommitted —

Adjourned —

Met Albany 9th August 1781

Present

John M. Beeckman ⎱ ⎰ Isaac D. Fonda
Samuel Stringer ⎰ ⎱ Stewart Dean

It appearing to this Board highly probable from sundry Circumstances that Major Reed (who at present lives in the House formerly occupied by John Tunnicliff) was privy to the Attempt made by Hans Waltimier to take General Schuyler and as it is suspected that the said Major Read carries on a Correspondence with several Persons in Canada — It is therefore resolved that application be made to General Clinton for a Party of Men to go and apprehend him and that M.ʳ Fonda one of the Members of this Board go with the said Party for the Purpose of searching his House for treasonable Papers —

The Board having great Reason to think that Hans Waltimier who a few days ago was in Town with Letters from Canada has been at the House of Ivy Chambers in this City and it being the Opinion of this Board that by searching the House of the said Ivy Chambers [473] Papers might be found which have come from Canada therefore resolved that M.ʳ Stringer & M.ʳ Dean go to the House of the said Ivy Chambers and make search for such Papers —

It appearing to this Board from the Information received by Isaac D. Fonda Esq.ʳ One of the Members of this Board that two Young Men living on the Nistageune Road have joined Walitmier's Party and assisted in attempting to take General Schuyler therefore resolved that a Warrant be made out for their immediate apprehension —

Adjourned —

Met Albany 10.ᵗʰ Aug.ᵗ 1781 —
Present

John M. Beeckman } { Samuel Stringer
Isaac D. Fonda }

James Milligan having come to this place from Saragtoga, and General Schuyler intimating to this Board that the said James Milligan is come with a bad design and requesting to have him examined and he being apprehended and brought before this Board and being examined and not answering satisfactorily to the Questions proposed to him and there being Reasons to suspect that he is a Spy therefore resolved that he be committed and that a Mittimus be made out for him —

Adjourned —

Met Albany 11th August 1781 —

Present

| John M. Beeckman | | Samuel Stringer |
| Isaac D. Fonda | | |

It being suggested to the Board that Michael Merkle at present in Confinement is sick and that a [474] Continuance in his present Confinement may endanger his life therefore resolved that he be liberated on his entering into a Recognizance with a sufficient surety for his remaining within the House and Yard of Christian Earing situate in the third Ward of this City until he is recovered of his Sickness and in the mean Time be of the good Behaviour and appear before any three of the Commissioners for Conspiracies when thereunto required —

Michael Merkle of Thurlough in the County
of Tryon Farmer in................... £100
Christian Earing of the City of Albany Merchant his Bail in...................... £100

Lieu^t John Leonard appeared before the Board and informed there has been a Party of armed Men at his House last Night who came with an Intention to carry him off and that they have much abused his Wife and there being a Prospect of apprehending them in Case a Party of Men could be procured to go with the said Lieu^t Leonard there-

fore resolved that application be made for a Party of Men
to Gen! Clinton to endeavour to [a]pprehend the said Persons —

Adjourned —

Met Albany 12ᵗʰ August 1781 —
        Present
            John M. Beeckman ⎫   ⎰ Isaac D. Fonda
            Samuel Stringer ⎭   ⎱

Lieu! John Leonard who Yesterday went [475] out with
a Party [of] Men having apprehended Thomas Brown for
harbouring Joseph Bettis and the said Thomas Brown
being brought before the Board and examined resolved that
he be committed and that a Mittimus be made out for him

Adjourned —

Met Albany 13ᵗʰ August 1781 —
        Present
            John M. Beeckman ⎫   ⎰ Isaac D. Fonda
            Samuel Stringer ⎭   ⎱ Stewart Dean

A Letter from Col! M꞉Instrey the Commanding officer at
Saragtoga was laid before the Board wherein he informs that
he sends down to us under Guard a certain Moses Harris
Jun! who he has caused to be apprehended on suspicion of
his purchasing Provisions for the supply of the Enemy and
he being brought before the Board and examined and we
being of Opinion that the said Harris is not a Person of so
dangerous a Character as represented by Col! M꞉Instrey
therefore resolved that he be discharged on his procuring
Bail for his future good Behaviour —

An Indian Woman living with M꞉ˢ Gibbon's in this City
having reported that she saw in the Woods a dead Man who

appeared to be murdered and his Worship the Mayor[1] of this City having gone out to View the Dead Body and not being able to find the same and we being of Opinion that M<u>rs</u> Gibbons her Mistress whose Husband is gone off to the Enemy has caused the said Indian Woman to raise the said report with a [476] View to draw the Mayor out of the City in order to his being carried off by Persons prepared for that Purpose therefore resolved that the said Indian Woman be apprehended and that the said M<u>rs</u> Gibbons be ordered immediately to appear before this Board —

The above mentioned Indian Woman being apprehended and examined acknowledges that there was a Party of Men in the Woods who told her to go to the Mayor and inform him that there was a Man murdered in the Woods resolved that she be committed —

M<u>rs</u> Gibbons appearing and being examined denies that she knew any Thing of the Report propogated by her Wench resolved that she be discharged for the present an[d] ordered to attend again to Morrow Morning —

M<u>rs</u> Haywood being also supposed to be concerned in the above Scheme to have the Mayor taken Prisoner being sent for and examined and she denying the charge ordered that she attend again to Morrow Morning —

Adjourned —

Met Albany 14<u>th</u> August 1781 —

Present

John M. Beeckman }   { Samuel Stringer
Stewart Dean   }   { Isaac D. Fonda

A Letter from Hugh Mitchell and Abraham Outhout Esq<u>rs</u> Commissioners for Conspi- [477] racies at Schenectady was

---

[1] Abraham Ten Broeck was mayor of Albany at this time. He had been appointed by Governor Clinton in April, 1779.

1781
Aug. 14. laid before the Board wherein they inform that they send down to us Daniel Taylor a Person notoriously disaffected to the American Cause who is a Brother in Law of Joseph Bettis and has known of the said Bettis being in the Country without giving any Information concerning the same and the said Daniel Taylor being Examined resolved that he be committed and that a Mittimus be made out for him —

Frederick Crants appearing before the Board informed us that he would become Bail for Christian Merkle and Michael Merkle who were liberated from Confinement on Account of their being Sick resolved that Christian Earing be discharged from the Recognizance by him entered into for the said Michael Merkle and Christian Merkle and that the said Frederick Crants accordingly enter into a Recognizance for the said Christian Merkle and Michael Merkle remaining within the Limits of his the said Frederick Crants's Farm and that the said Christian Merkle & Michael Merkle will surrender themselves as Prisoners to this Board when they shall have recovered their Health and for their good Behaviour during that Time —

> Frederick Crants of the West District of the
> Manor of Rensselaerwyck Farmer as Bail
> for Christian Merkle and Michael Merkle
> in.................................... £100

Adjourned —

1781
Aug. 16.   [478]   Met Albany 16th August 1781 —

Present

| John M. Beeckman | Isaac D. Fonda |
| Samuel Stringer | Stewart Dean |

Capt Holtham Dunham & Lieu^t Benonie Grant having had Conferences in the Woods with David Jones and other

Persons from Canada and having been detected in the same and to avoid Punishment made their Escape with a[n] Intention to go to Canada and having been apprehended and sent down by Col<u>l</u>. M<u>c</u>Kinstrey in order to be confined and the said Holtham Dunham being brought before the Board and examined says as follows (to wit) (see Examination on File)

Resolved that a Mittimus be made out for them and that the examination of Benoni Grant be postponed until to Morrow Morning —

Adjourned —

Met Albany 17<u>th</u> August 1781 —
Present

John M. Beeckman ⎱   ⎰ Isaac D. Fonda
Samuel Stringer   ⎰   ⎱ Stewart Dean

Benonie Grant who was Yesterday committed to Goal being brought before the Board was Examined his Examination is as follows (to wit) (see Examination on File)

Resolved that Copies of the Examination's of Holtham Dunham and Benoni Grant be made out and transmitted to his Excellency Governor Clinton —

[479] It appearing highly probable to this Board from the Information of Cap<u>ts</u> Gerrit Groesbeeck & William Hunn that Thomas Reed who at present resides on the Farm of John Tunnicliff near this City knew of the Party that attempted to take General Schuyler Prisoner being in the Woods and was acquainted with their Intentions and the said Thomas Reed from his Intimacy and Connections with D<u>r</u> George Smith and other disaffected Persons to the American Cause giving great Reason to this Board to suspect that he is concerned in a Scheme prejudicial to the Publick good —

1781 Aug. 17.   Therefore resolved that a Warrant be made out directed to Jacob Kidney to apprehend and bring before us said Thomas Reed —

Adjourned —

1781 Aug. 18.   Met Albany 18ᵗʰ August 1781 —
Present

John M. Beeckman } { Isaac D. Fonda
Samuel Stringer } { Stewart Dean

Thomas Reed having been apprehended by Jacob Kidney agreeable to the Warrant of this Board and being examined resolved that he be committed and that a Mittimus be made out for him —

Capᵗ Robert Woodward appeared before the Board and informed us that he had apprehended a Man who calls himself Benoni Robins Forrister who he suspects to be a British Officer passing through the Country as a Spy and the said Benoni Robins Forrister being examined and not being possessed of any Vouchers relative [480] to his Attachment to the American Cause and being unable to give a satisfactory account of himself therefore resolved that he be committed until he shall produce a Certificate of his Character and ordered that a Mittimus be made out for him —

Adjourned —

1781 Aug. 21.   Met Albany 21ˢᵗ August 1781 —
Present

John M. Beeckman } { Isaac D. Fonda
Samuel Stringer } { Stewart Dean

It appearing from the Examination of Capᵗ Holtham Dunham and Benoni Grant that a certain Rodgers who lives at Fiddle Town near Saragtoga has supplied David

Jones with his Party who had come from Canada and were
secreted in the Woods for the Purpose of taking Major
McKinstrey the Commanding Officer at Saragtoga Prisoner
therefore resolved that a Letter be wrote to Major McKinstrey
requesting him to have the said Rogers apprehended and
sent down to this Board as soon as possible —

Lieut Moses Hudson appeared before the Board and
informed us that a Young Man of the Name of Fagler who
was last Year seduced by Joe Bettis to go to Canada has
returned and has sent in word that he is desirous of surrendering himself up provided he is not confined — Resolved that Lieut Hudson be informed that if the said
Fagler [give] himself up to this Board and will make a full
and [481] ample Confession of such Matters as he is acquainted with that in such Case the said Fagler will be
discharged on giving surety for his future good Conduct —

Adjourned —

Met Albany 22th August 1781 —
Present

John M. Beeckmann } { Samuel Stringer
Isaac D. Fonda }

The Board being informed that James Clay is returned
from Canada and that he lurks about the House of Henry
Haywood his Father in Law on Jan Fonda's Land in the
Vicinity of this City and Lieut Jacob Winney having offered
to apprehend the said James Clay therefore resolved that
a Warrant be made out directed to Lieut Winney & that
he be thereby authorized to search the House of the said
Henry Haywood and all other suspicious Houses in that
Neighbourhood —

Resolved that Moses Harris Jun: be discharged from
Confinement on entering into a Recognizance for his good

Behaviour doing his Duty and appearing before any three of the Commissioners for Conspiracies when thereunto required during the Continuance of the present War with Great Britain —

Moses Harris Jun.ʳ late of Dutchess County
    Labourer in.......................... £100
Dirck Swart of Stillwater in the County of
    Albany Esq.ʳ his Bail in................ £100

Cap.ᵗ William Hun having been requested to appear before the Board to be examined with Respect [482] to Thomas Reed at present in Confinement appeared his examination being taken is in the words following (to wit) (see Examination on File)

Adjourned —

Met Albany 23.ᵈ Aug.ᵗ 1781 —
    Present

    John M. Beeckman ⎱ ⎰ Stewart Dean
    Isaac D. Fonda ⎰ ⎱

A Letter was laid before the Board by Edward Chin Esq.ʳ from Thomas Reed setting forth that his wife has been brought to Bed and that she is exceedingly Ill and requesting to be released from Confinement for a few Days which application being seconded by the said Edward Chin resolved that for the Reason above assigned the said Thomas Reed be liberated on entering into a Recognizance to appear on Monday the 27.ᵗʰ Day of August Instant at the City Hall in this City before any three of the Commissioners for Conspiracies and for his good Behaviour in the mean Time —

Thomas Reed of the West District of the
    Manor of Rensselaerwyck Yeoman in... £500

Philip Van Rensselaer of the City of Albany Esq.r his Bail in .... £250 1781 Aug. 23.
Edward Chin of the same place Esq.r also his Bail in.......................... £250
Adjourned —

[483] Met Albany 24th August 1781 — 1781 Aug. 24.
Present

John M Beeckman	Isaac D. Fonda
Samuel Stringer	

The Board having received Information that among those Persons who took John Js Bleecker Esqr and who are at present Prisoners at Bennington there are some who are Inhabitants of this State and as Justice demands that they should be punished agreeable to Law —

Therefore resolved that a Letter be wrote to his Excellency Thomas Chittendon Esqr at Arlington requesting him to cause the said Persons to be delivered over to the Civil Authority of this State which Letter is in the Words following (to wit) (see Copy Letter on File)

Adjourned

Met Albany 25th August 1781 — 1781 Aug. 25.
Present

John M. Beeckman	Isaac D. Fonda
Samuel Stringer	Stewart Dean

Daniel Taylor being at his own request brought before the Board was examined and ordered to be recommitted

The Board having received Information that Archibald McNeal who by his Recognizance was restricted to the Limits of this City has exceeded the Bounds prescribed to him in the said Recognizance therefore resolved that his

Bails Thomas Shipboy and Robert McClallen be ordered forthwith to deliver up to this Board [484] the said Archibald McNeal —

Adjourned —

Met Albany 27th August 1781 —

Present

| John M. Beeckman | Samuel Stringer |
| Isaac D. Fonda | Stewart Dean |

Thomas Reed appeared before the Board agreeable to the Tenor of the Recognizance entered into by him on the 23.^d Instant and requested of the Board Permission to remain with his Family some Days longer on Account of the Illness of his wife resolved on taking the same into Consideration that Permission be granted him accordingly on his entering into a Recognizance to appear on Monday the 3.^d day of September next at the City Hall before any three of the Commissioners for Conspiracies to be of good Behaviour during that time & not to aid, Comfort, Assist, Entertain, harbour or hold any Correspondence either by word or deed upon Political Matters with any Person or Persons inimical to the Liberties of Independance of this or the United States of America and that he do not depart the Limits & Bounds of the Farm he at present resides on untill he comes to make his Appearance as aforesaid —

Thomas Reed of the West District of the
Manor of Rensselaerwyck Gentleman in. . £500
Leonard Gansevoort of the City of Albany
Esqr his Bail in £250
Cornelius Cuyler of the same place Esqr
also his Bail in. £250

[485] Resolved that Adrian Bradt Junr be discharged

from Confinement on entering into a Recognizance for his good Behaviour doing his duty and appearing before any three of the Commissioners for Conspiracies when thereunto required during the Continuance of the present War with Great Britain —

Adrian Bradt Jun.r of the West District of
  the Manor of Rensselaerwyck Farmer in. £100
John Devoe of the same Place Farmer his
  Bail in........................... £100

Resolved that Henry Haines Jun.r be discharged from Confinement on Henry Haines entering into a Recognizance for the good Behaviour of the said Henry Haines Jun.r for doing his duty and appearing before any three of the said Commissioners for Conspiracies when thereunto required during the continuance of the Present War with Great Britain —

Henry Haines late of Thurlough in Tryon
  County Farmer as Bail for his son Henry
  Haines Jun.r in..................... £400

Resolved that John Sommer be discharged from Confinement on Jacob Lawyer entering into a Recognizance for the good Behaviour of the said John Sommer & for his doing his Duty & appearing before any three of the Commissioners for Conspiracies when thereunto required during the Continuance of the Present War with Great Britain —

Jacob Lawyer of the City of Albany on Recognizance as Bail for John Sommer in... £200

Archibald Mc.Neal being brought before the [486] Board by his Bail agreeable to the order of this Board of the 25th Instant and being interrogated as to his exceeding the Bounds prescribed by his Recognizance and it appearing to have been done ignorantly and with no bad design therefore resolved that he be discharged —

A Letter from Hugh Mitchell Esq.ʳ dated at Schenectady
the 14ᵗʰ Instant inclosing a Copy of an Examination of
Daniel Taylor now in Confinement was laid before the
Board which Letter and Examination are in the following
words (to wit) (see Letter and Examination on File)

Adjourned

Met Albany 28ᵗʰ August 1781 —
Present

John M. Beeckman ⎱   ⎰ Samuel Stringer
Isaac D. Fonda   ⎰   ⎱ Stewart Dean

Resolved that Christian Miner be discharged from Confinement on entering into a Recognizance for his good
Behaviour doing his Duty and appearing before any three
of the Commissioners for Conspiracies when thereunto
required during the Continuance of the Present War with
Great Britain —

Christian Miner of New Rhraebeeck in
Tryon County Farmer in.............. £100
Jacob Bleecker Junʳ of the City of Albany
his Bail in......................... £100

Resolved that Frederick Merkle be discharged [487] from
Confinement on entering into a Recognizance for his good
Behaviour doing his duty and appearing before any three
of the Commissioners for Conspiracies when thereunto
required during the Continuance of the present War with
Great Britain

Frederick Merkle late of Thurlough in the
County of Tryon Farmer in........... £100
Stephen Frederick of the West District in
the Manor of Rensselaerwyck Farmer his
Bail in............................. £100

Resolved that William Baker who is surety for James Bruce be ordered forthwith to deliver up the said James Bruce as the Board are of Opinion that he ought to be bound in a New Recognizance —

Adjourned

Met Albany 29th August 1781 — •
Present

John M. Beeckman ⎱   ⎰ Samuel Stringer
Isaac D. Fonda ⎰   ⎱ Stewart Dean

Resolved that Earnest Fretz be discharged from Confinement on entering into a Recognizance for his good Behaviour doing his duty and appearing before any three of the Commissioners of Conspiracies when thereunto required during the Continuance of the present War with Great Britain —

Earnest Fretz late of Thurlough in the County
of Tryon Farmer in.................... £100
Christopher Roff of the West District of the
Manor of Rensselaerwyck Farmer in..... £100

[488] Frederick Crans who was surety for Christopher Merkle until he should be recovered of his Illness appeared before the Board and surrendered the said Christian Merkle and as Frederick Merkle is willing to become Bail for the said Christian Merkle and as there are no material Charges against him therefore resolved that he be discharged on the said Frederick Merkle's entering into a Recognizance for the good Behaviour of the said Christian Merkle for doing his duty and appearing before any three of the Commissioners for Conspiracies when thereunto required during the Continuance of the present War with Great Britain.

Frederick Merkle late of Thurlough in the
County of Tryon Farmer as Bail for Christian Merkle in........................ £100

1781
Aug. 29.

The Board having received Information from which they are induced to think that the Persons living on a Place formerly in the Possession of [blank] Cumming at Kat's Kill are endeavouring by every Means to injure the American Cause and as their Situation is such that they have it in their Power to afford Assistance to Parties coming from the Enemy therefore resolved that a Letter be wrote to Col⸢ Du Bois at Kat's Kill requesting him to cause them to be removed as soon as possible —

Adjourned —

1781
Aug. 30.

Met Albany 30ᵗʰ August 1781 —

Present

John M. Beeckman } { Stewart Dean
Isaac D. Fonda   } { Samuel Stringer

Resolved that Coonradt Brown be discharged [489] from Confinement on entering into a Recognizance for his good Behaviour doing his duty and appearing before any three of the Commissioners for Conspiracies for and during the Continuance of the present War with Great Britain —

Coenradt Brown of Thurlough in Tryon
County Farmer in...................... £100
Johannis Rykert of Schoharie in the County
of Albany Farmer his Bail in........... £100

Adjourned.[1]

¹ The extant minutes end here abruptly. On August 30, 1781, the Albany commissioners wrote to Governor Clinton about certain exchanges of prisoners, to which he wrote a reply on September 7th. Other correspondence between this board and the governor is extant, of a date later than the existing minutes. For examples, see *George Clinton Papers*, nos. 3948, 3976, 3986, 3987, 4005, 4010, 4023, 4024, in archives of New York State Library.

APPENDIXES

APPENDIX I

LAWS OF NEW YORK RELATING TO THE COMMISSIONERS FOR CONSPIRA- CIES AND THEIR POWERS

An Act appointing Commissioners for detecting and defeating Conspiracies, and declaring their Powers. Passed the 5th of February, 1778.[1]

WHEREAS the late Convention did appoint a Board of Commissioners, for the Purpose of enquiring into, detecting and defeating all Conspiracies, which might be formed in this State, against the Liberties of *America*.

And whereas, by Reason of the present Invasion of this State, and of the Disaffection of sundry of the Inhabitants of the same, it will be expedient to continue the said Board; which Experience hath shewn to be of great Use and Impor- tance. To the End therefore, that the State and the Peace of the same, may be effectually guarded and secured, against the wicked Machinations and Designs of the Foreign and Domestic Foes thereof.

Be it enacted by the People of the State of New-York, *represented in Senate and Assembly, and it is hereby enacted by the Authority of the same,* That the Governor, Lieutenant Governor, or President of the Senate, who, for the Time being, shall administer the Government of this State, be, and he hereby is authorised and empowered, from Time to Time, to appoint, by Commission, by and with the Advice

[1] First session (1777–8), chap. 3.— *Laws of New York;* Poughkeepsie: John Holt, 1782, pp. 6–7.

and Consent of the Council of Appointment, so many Persons, not exceeding ten, as he shall think proper, to be Commissioners for the Purposes aforesaid. And that the said Commissioners, or any three of them, be, and they hereby are authorised and empowered, to do and perform the several Acts, Matters and Things herein after mentioned, viz. That the said Commissioners, or any three of them, shall be, and they hereby are authorised and empowered, to send for Persons and Papers, and administer Oaths; and to apprehend and confine, or cause to be apprehended and confined, in such Manner, and under such Restrictions and Limitations, as to them shall appear necessary, for the public Safety, all Persons, whose going at large, shall, in the Judgment of the said Commissioners, or any three of them, appear dangerous to the Safety of this State. To take Bonds and Recognizances, from Time to Time, to the People of this State, for the good Behaviour, safe Custody, or Appearance of such of the said Persons, and of all others, now confined for the like Cause, as they may think proper, in such Sums, and upon such Conditions, as unto them shall appear expedient; and the said Bonds and Recognizances, if forfeited, to prosecute or to cancel and release, upon such Terms and Conditions; and to discharge from Confinement, any of the said Persons absolutely, and without any Terms or Conditions, as they may think proper. *And also*, from Time to Time, to make such Provision, for the safe Custody, and comfortable Subsistance of all Persons, who may from Time to Time be so confined as aforesaid, in such Manner as they may think proper. *Provided always*, That by Reason or Colour of any Thing herein contained, the said Commissioners, or any of them, shall not be empowered to inflict any corporal Punishment, upon any or either of the said Persons confined as aforesaid.

II. *And be it further enacted by the Authority aforesaid,* That no Judge or Magistrate, shall bail any of the Persons, who may be confined by Authority of the said Commissioners; and that no Court shall deliver any of the Gaols, within this State, of any Person or Persons, so confined as aforesaid, unless such Persons, shall have been indicted, and tried for the Offence or Offences, for which he or she, shall have been respectively committed.

III. *And be it further enacted by the Authority aforesaid,* That each and every of the said Commissioners, before they shall respectively take upon them, the Exercise of the said Office, do, before one or more of the said Commissioners, who are hereby empowered to administer the same, take the following Oath, *viz.*

" I, A.B. one of the Commissioners, according to the Form and Effect of an Act, entitled, An Act for appointing Commissioners for detecting and defeating Conspiracies, and declaring their Power, appointed, do, in the Presence of Almighty God, most solemnly promise and swear, that I will, to the best of my Knowledge and Ability, faithfully execute and perform, for the Benefit and Advantage of the People of the State of *New-York*, all and singular the Powers and Authorities, by Force and Virtue of the said Act, unto me given. So help me God.["]

IV. And for as much as the Execution of the said several Trusts, Duties and Powers, will be attended with considerable Expence; *Be it further enacted by the Authority aforesaid,* That the said Commissioners, be, and they hereby are, authorised and empowered, from Time to Time, to draw from the public Treasury of this State, all and every such Sum and Sums of Money, as they shall think proper. *Provided always,* That the said Commissioners, shall render a just and true Account of the Expenditure of the several Sums of

Money by them so drawn as aforesaid; and that the said
several Sums, shall not, in the Whole, exceed the sum of
Five Thousand Pounds.

V. *And it be further enacted by the Authority aforesaid,*
That the said Commissioners shall keep regular Minutes of all
their Proceedings, in Order that the same may be submitted,
if required, to the Consideration of the Senate or Assembly, or
to such Person or Persons, as shall be, for that Purpose
appointed; and that each and every of the said Commissioners do receive, for every Day, in which he shall be actually
employed in the Business aforesaid, the Sum of Twenty Shillings, for his Trouble and Expence, in attending upon the same.

VI. *And be it further enacted by the Authority aforesaid,*
That this Act shall continue in Force, until the first Day of
November, in the Year of our Lord One Thousand Seven
Hundred and Seventy-Eight, and no longer.

---

*An Act to enable the Person administering the Government of
this State for the Time being, to remove certain disaffected
and dangerous Persons and Families.* Passed the 1st of
April, 1778.[1]

WHEREAS divers disaffected and dangerous Persons
and Families, reside at or near the several Posts
and Passes within this State; and there is great Reason to
believe, that they communicate Intelligence to the Enemy;

I. *Be it therefore enacted by the People of the State of
New-York, represented in Senate and Assembly, and it is
hereby enacted by [t]he Authority of the same,*   That it shall
and may be lawful, to and for the Person administering the

---

[1] First session (1777-8), chap. 27.— *Laws of New York:* Poughkeepsie:
John Holt, 1782, pp. 25-26.

This act is printed as collateral to and explanatory of procedure relative to inimical persons.

Government of this State for the Time being, from Time to Time, as Occasion may require, and whenever he shall judge it necessary, for the public Safety, to cause all such dangerous disaffected Persons and Families, as now are, or hereafter shall happen to be resident at or near any Post, Pass or Encampment, within this State, to be removed to such other Place or Places within the same, as he shall deem expedient.

II. *And whereas* the Removal of the Persons or Families aforesaid, may prove very prejudicial to them; *It is further enacted by the Authority aforesaid,* That the Person administering the Government of this State, for the Time being, shall certify the Names of such Persons so removed, and a Description of the Houses and Farms, from which they shall be removed respectively, to the Commissioners of Sequestration of the County, to which such Persons shall be removed; who are hereby required to put them in Possession, on moderate Rents, of such sequestered Farms or Houses, in the said County as may be then, or thereafter vacant; having Respect to the Value of the Farms or Houses, from which such Persons may have been removed; *Provided, nevertheless,* That no Person or Persons, that shall be removed by Virtue of this Act, shall, by such Removal, gain a Settlement in the District he, she or they may be removed to; so as to charge such District with their Maintenance.

An Act for increasing the Number of Commissioners, for detecting and defeating Conspiracies within this State. Passed the 3d of *April,* 1778.[1]

WHEREAS by an Act, entitled, *"An Act appointing Commissioners for detecting and defeating Conspiracies, and declaring their Powers,"* made and passed by

1 First session (1777–8), chap. 31. —*Laws of New York:* Poughkeepsie: John Holt, 1782, pp. 30–31.

the Legislature of this State, the fifth Day of *February* last past; it is enacted, that the Governor, Lieutenant-Governor, or President of the Senate, who for the Time being, shall administer the Government of this State, be, and he is thereby authorised and empowered, from Time to Time, to appoint by Commission, by and with the Advice and Consent of the Council of Appointment, so many Persons, not exceeding ten, as he shall think proper, to be Commissioners for the Purposes therein mentioned; *And further*, That the said Commissioners, or any three of them shall be, and thereby are empowered and authorised to do and perform the several Acts, Matters and Things, therein after mentioned: For increasing the Number of the said Commissioners,

I. *Be it therefore enacted by the People of the State of New-York, represented in Senate and Assembly, and it is hereby enacted by the Authority of the same,* That the Person administering the Government of this State, for the Time being, be, and he is hereby farther authorised and empowered from Time to Time, to appoint in the Manner in and by the said Act mentioned, any farther or greater Number of Commissioners, not exceeding twenty, to be Commissioners, with the like Trust Powers and Authorities, and under the same Restrictions, Qualifications, Provisoes, Pay and Continuance, as are mentioned in the said in part recited Act.

II. *And it is further enacted by the Authority aforesaid,* That the said Commissioners, or any three of them, shall be, and they are hereby authorised and empowered, to do and perform the several Acts, Matters and Things, mentioned in the said in part recited Act: Any Thing in the said Act contained, to the Contrary thereof, in any Wise notwithstanding.

Provided always, That as many Quorums of three of the said Commissioners, as the whole Number of thirty will admit of, shall and may exercise the Powers and Authorities, so reposed in them as aforesaid, at one and the same Time; any Thing in this or the above recited Law, to the Contrary hereof, in any Wise notwithstanding.

An Act more effectually to prevent the Mischiefs, arising from the Influence and Example of Persons of equivocal and suspected Characters, in this State. Passed the 30th of *June,* 1778.[1]

WHEREAS certain of the Inhabitants of this State, have, during the Course of the present cruel War, waged by the King and Parliament of *Great-Britain,* against the People of these States, affected to maintain a Neutrality, which there is Reason to suspect was in many Instances, dictated by a Poverty of Spirit, and an undue Attachment to Property. *And whereas* divers of the said Persons, some of whom, advocated the *American* Cause till it became serious, have notwithstanding the Forebearance of their Countrymen, and contrary to the Faith pledged by their Paroles, ungratefully and insidiously from Time to Time, by artful Misrepresentations, and a subtle Dissemination of Doctrines, Fears and Apprehensions false in themselves, and injurious to the *American* Cause, seduced certain weak minded Persons from the Duties they owed their Country: *And whereas* the welfare of this State, loudly demands that some decisive Measures be taken with Respect to the said Persons; and it being repugnant to Justice as well as good Policy, that Men should be permitted to shelter themselves under a Government, which they not only refused to assist in rearing, but which, some of them daily endeavor to undermine and subvert; *And whereas,* such few of the said Persons, as may have been

[1] First session (1777–8), chap. 47.— *Laws of New York:* Poughkeepsie: John Holt, 1782, pp. 43–44.

led to take a neutral Part by conscientious Doubts and Scruples, have had more than sufficient Time to consider and determine the same;

I. *Be it enacted by the People of the State of* New-York, *represented in Senate and Assembly, and it is hereby enacted by the Authority of the same,* That the Commissioners appointed for inquiring into, detecting and defeating all Conspiracies, which may be formed in this State, against the Liberties of *America;* or any three of them be, and they hereby are authorised and strictly charged and required, to cause all such Persons, of neutral and equivocal Characters in this State, whom they shall think have influence sufficient to do Mischief in it, to come before them, and to administer to the said persons respectively, the following Oath, or if of the People called Quakers, Affirmation, *viz.*

"I, A.B. do solemnly, and without any mental Reservation or Equivocation whatever, swear and call God to Witness; or if of the People called Quakers, affirm, that I do believe and acknowledge, the State of *New-York,* to be of Right, a Free and Independent State. And that no Authority or Power, can of Right, be exercised in or over the said State, but what is, or shall be granted by or derived from the People thereof. *And further,* That as a good Subject of the said Free and Independent State of *New York,* I will to the best of my Knowledge and Ability, faithfully do my Duty; and as I shall keep or disregard this Oath. So help and deal with me Almighty God."

II. *And be it further enacted by the Authority aforesaid,* That if on the said Oath or Affirmation, being so tendered, the said Person or Persons shall refuse to take the same, the said Commissioners do forthwith remove the said Person or Persons so refusing, to any Place within the Enemy's Lines, and by Writing under their Hands and Seals, certify the Names of such Person or Persons, to the Secretary of this State, who is hereby required to Record and File the said Certificates.

III. *And be it further enacted by the Authority aforesaid*, That if any of the said Neutrals, shall abscond or absent himself with an apparent View to avoid the Force of this Act, the said Commissioners shall by Notice, published in one or more of the News-Papers of this State, demand of the said Person or Persons, so absconding or absenting, to appear before them, at such Place in this State, and at such Time, not exceeding twenty one Days from the Time of such Publication, as they shall assign. *And further*, That Default in such Appearance, shall be adjudged to amount to and is hereby declared to be a Refusal to take the said Oath or Affirmation.

IV. *And be it further enacted by the Authority aforesaid*, That if any of the Persons removed to Places within the Enemy's Lines by the said Commissioners, in pursuance of this Act, or who having as aforesaid, absconded or absented, shall not on Notice as aforesaid appear before the said Commissioners, and take the Oath or Affirmation aforesaid, shall thereafter be found in any Part of this State; such Person or Persons so found, shall on Conviction thereof, be adjudged guilty of Misprison of Treason.

And to the End, That this State may be in some Measure compensated for the Injuries it has sustained, by the evil Example or Practices of the said Neutrals, and that others may be detered on similar Occasions, from acting a Part so unmanly and ignominious;

V. *Be it further enacted by the Authority aforesaid*, That all Lands held in this State, on the twenty-sixth Day of *June* Instant, in Fee Simple or Fee Tail, or which may hereafter be acquired by, or devised, granted, or descend to any of the Persons who shall refuse to take the aforesaid Oath or Affirmation, when called upon by the said Commissioners, shall forever thereafter, be charged with double Taxes, in whosoever Hands the said Lands may hereafter be.

VI. *And be it further enacted by the Authority aforesaid,* That the said Commissioners, previous to the Removal of the said several Persons within the Enemy's Lines, shall from Time to Time, notify the Person administering the Government of this State for the Time being, of the several Persons so to be removed, who is hereby authorised to detain and confine, such of the said persons as he shall think proper, for the Purpose of exchanging them for any of the Subjects of this State, in the Power of the Enemy.

VII. *And be it further enacted by the Authority aforesaid,* That the Person administering the Government of this State for the Time being, be, and he is hereby required to do his best Endeavours, that this Act be fully and speedily carried into Execution, and all Magistrates, Sheriffs and Constables, are required to be aiding therein.

An Act for continuing the Powers of the Commissioners, for detecting and defeating Conspiracies. Passed the 29th of October, 1778.[1]

WHEREAS the Act of the Legislature of this State, for appointing Commissioners for detecting and defeating Conspiracies, and declaring their Powers; and the Act for increasing the Number of Commissioners for detecting and defeating Conspiracies, within this State, will expire on the first Day of *November* next;

Be it therefore enacted by the People of the State of New-York, *represented in Senate and Assembly, and it is hereby*

[1] Second session (1778-9), chap. 3.— *Laws of New York:* Poughkeepsie: John Holt, 1782, pp. 44-45.

enacted by the Authority of the same, That the said two several Acts, and the Powers and Authorities by them or either of them, granted to the said Commissioners, or[1] any, and every three of them, and a Power to the said Commissioners, or any three of them, to remove within the Enemy's Lines, all such Persons who in pursuance of the *"Act more effectually to prevent the Mischiefs arising from the Influence and Example of Persons, of equivocal and suspected Characters in this State,"* have already appeared before the said Commissioners, or any three of them, and have not taken the Oath in the said Act contained; shall be and are hereby continued until twenty Days after the next Meeting of the Legislature, and a Quorum of both Houses shall be convened to proceed on Business. And the Treasurer of this State, shall be, and he is hereby authorised and required to pay to the said Commissioners, or any three of them, such farther Sum or Sums, as they shall from Time to Time require, to defray the Expence of the Business committed to them, so as the Amount of such farther Sum or Sums, shall not in the whole, exceed the Sum of Three Thousand Pounds.

An Act to amend an Act, entitled, An Act more effectually to prevent the Mischiefs arising from the Influence and Example of Persons of equivocal and suspected Characters in this State, and for continuing the Powers of the Commissioners for detecting and defeating Conspiracies. Passed the 17th of *February*, 1779.[2]

WHEREAS by the Terms of the said Law, the Commissioners therein mentioned, are required on Re-

---

[1] Misprinted " ur " in Holt's edition.
[2] Second session (1778–9), chap. 10.— *Laws of New York:* Poughkeepsie : John Holt, 1782, p. 49.

fusal of any Person or Persons, to take the Oath or Affirmation therein prescribed, forthwith to remove the said Person or Persons so refusing, to any Place within the Enemy's Lines;

And whereas sound Policy and common Charity require, that every Person so refusing, should be admitted to take the said Oath or Affirmation, if he or she shall, notwithstanding such Refusal, voluntarily offer to take the same, before the Commencement of his or her actual Removal;

I. *Be it therefore enacted by the People of the State of New-York, represented in Senate and Assembly, and it is hereby enacted by the Authority of the same,* That every Person who has already refused, or shall hereafter refuse to take the said Oath or Affirmation, and shall, before the actual Commencement of his or her Removal as aforesaid, voluntarily offer to take the said Oath or Affirmation, before any three of the said Commissioners, shall be admitted to take the same, and on taking thereof, shall be, and hereby is declared to be fully and wholly absolved from the Penalties of the said Law, such former Refusal, or any Thing in the said Law, to the Contrary in any Wise notwithstanding. *Provided always,* That nothing herein contained, shall extend or apply to the Cases of those who by Virtue of the said Law, now are or shall hereafter be detained and confined, by the Person administering the Government of this State for the Time being, for the Purpose of Exchanging them for any of the Subjects of this State, in the Power of the Enemy.

II. *And be it further enacted by the Authority aforesaid,* That all and singular the Powers and Authorities, vested in the said Commissioners, are hereby continued until twenty Days after the next Meeting of the Legislature, and a Quorum of both Houses shall be convened on Business, in like Manner as the same are continued in and by an Act, entitled, *"An Act for continuing the Powers of the Commissioners for detecting and defeating Conspiracies,"* passed the 29th Day of *October* last: And the Treasurer of this State shall be, and he is hereby authorised and required, to pay to the said Commissioners, or any three of them, such further Sum or Sums, as they shall from Time to Time require, to defray the Expence of the Business committed to them, so as the Amount of such further Sum or Sums, shall not in the Whole, exceed the Sum of Three Thousand Pounds.

An Act for reviving the Powers of the Commissioners for detecting and defeating Conspiracies, and for other Purposes therein mentioned. Passed the 1st of *October*, 1779.[1]

WHEREAS the Act of the Legislature of this State, entitled, *"An Act for appointing Commissioners, for detecting and defeating Conspiracies, and declaring their Powers;"* and the Act entitled, *"An Act for increasing the Number of Commissioners for detecting and defeating Conspiracies, within this State,"* did expire in twenty Days after the present Meeting of the Legislature, and a Quorum of both Houses convened to proceed on Business;

I. *Be it enacted by the People of the State of* New-York, *represented in Senate and Assembly, and it is hereby enacted by the Authority of the same,* That the said two Acts, and the Powers and Authorities by them or either of them granted, to the said Commissioners, or any and every three of them, shall be and are hereby revived, and shall continue and be in full Force until twenty Days after the first Day of the next Meeting of a Quorum of the Legislature, and

[1] Third session (1779-80), chap. 7.— *Laws of New York:* Poughkeepsie: John Holt, 1782, p. 76.

the Treasurer of this State is hereby authorised and required, out of such Monies as may be in the Treasury, to pay to the said Commissioners, or any three of them, such further Sum or Sums, as they shall from Time to Time require, to defray the Expence of the Business committed to them, so as the Amount of such Sum or Sums, shall not in the whole, exceed the sum of Four Thousand Pounds.

And whereas the said Commissioners, or some Quorum or Quorums of them, may have done and performed divers Acts, Matters and Things, in and respecting their several and respective Offices and Places, since the Expiration of the said Laws, and by Reason thereof, the Legality and Validity of the said Acts, Matters and Things, may be drawn into Question;

II. *Be it therefore enacted by the Authority aforesaid,* That all and singular the said Acts, Matters and Things, shall be as good, valid and effectual in the Law, to all Intents, Constructions and Purposes whatsoever, as if the said Laws had not expired by their own respective Limitations, but had been in full Force and Effect, at and immediately before the passing of this Law; any Thing in the said Laws or either of them to the Contrary hereof, in any Wise notwithstanding.

And whereas in and by the said two recited Acts, no Provision is made to enable the Council of Appointment, from Time to Time, to remove any one or more of the said Commissioners, and appoint other or others in his or their Stead,

III. *Be it enacted by the Authority aforesaid,* That the said Power and Authority of Removal and Appointment, is and are hereby fully vested in the said Council, to be exercised by them, from Time to Time, in their Discretion, to all Intents, Constructions and Purposes in the Law whatsoever.

An Act to authorise any two Justices of the Peace, to enlarge Persons who shall desert from the Enemy, and for other Purposes therein mentioned. Passed *March* 13th, 1780.[1]

I. *BE* it enacted by [the] *People of the State of* New-York, *represented in Senate and Assembly, and it is hereby enacted by the Authority of the same,* That whenever any Person, who shall have come from within the Lines of the Enemy, shall be confined in the common Gaol of any County within this State; it shall and may be lawful, for any two Justices of the Peace of such County, to enlarge the Person so confined, upon his or her entering into Recognizance to the People of this State, either with or without Surety; and in such Sum or Sums as the said Justices, in their Discretion, shall deem proper: The Condition of which Recognizance shall be, that he or she will appear at the next Court of Oyer and Terminer and General Gaol Delivery, to be held in and for such County; or that he or she shall reside at the Place, and within the Bounds within this State, to be assigned by the said two Justices; or that he or she shall be of good Behaviour, during the present War. And the said Justices may in their Discretion, insert one or more of the foregoing Conditions in such Recognizance. *Provided,* That such Justices shall not, by Virtue of this Act, enlarge any Person who shall be in Custody, by Virtue of a Warrant under the Hand and Seal of any Judge of the Supreme Court; nor any Person whose going at large will, in the Opinion of such Justices, be dangerous to the State. *And provided also,* That nothing in this Act contained, shall be construed to excuse any Person, so enlarged on Recognizance, from doing Duty in the Militia of this State; nor shall his Absence from the Place assigned by such Justices, for his Residence while on

[1] Third session (1779–80), chap. 58.— *Laws of New York:* Poughkeepsie: John Holt, 1782, p. 127.

Command in the Militia, be deemed a Breach of such Recognizance.

II. *And be it further enacted by the Authority aforesaid,* That whenever any Person shall desert from the Army of the Enemy, or come over from within their Lines, and shall voluntarily surrender himself or herself to a Justice of the Peace, it shall and may be lawful for such Justice to call to his Assistance one other Justice of the same County, and to bind the Person so surrendering himself or herself, in Recognizance, and deal with him in all Respects as is before directed for Persons in actual Custody; which Recognizance shall be subject to the Provisoes mentioned in the preceding Clause. *Provided,* That nothing in this Act contained, shall be construed to prevent any Person from being apprehended and dealt with according to Law, for any Offence committed after such Person shall have left the Enemy's Lines.

Whereas the several Laws, relating to the Commissioners for enquiring into, detecting and defeating all Conspiracies which may be formed in this State, against the liberties of *America,* are now expired;

And whereas there are several Persons now confined by Order of the said Commissioners, and several Persons are bound by Recognizance, taken before the said Commissioners: To the End therefore, that Provision may be made in the Premises;

III. *Be it further enacted by the Authority aforesaid,* That it shall be lawful for any three Persons who were such Commissioners, in their Discretion, to discharge the several Persons so in actual Confinement, without Bail, or upon the said Persons respectively entering into Recognizance, with or without Surety, for their respective Appearance at any Court of Oyer and Terminer and General Gaol Delivery, to be held in and for any County within this State; and to discharge any Recognizances heretofore taken before the said Commissioners, except such Recognizances as may have been taken for the Appearance of any Person or Persons, at any Court of Oyer and Terminer and General Gaol Delivery; and that the Powers of the said Commissioners shall be revived, and hereby are continued for the several Purposes aforesaid accordingly.

IV. *And be it further enacted by the Authority aforesaid,* That this Act shall continue in Force, until thirty Days after the rising of the Legislature, at their next Meeting.

An Act to revive the Laws appointing Commissioners for detecting and defeating Conspiracies. Passed *June* 14th, 1780.[1]

WHEREAS the Act *"for appointing Commissioners for detecting and defeating Conspiracies, and declaring their Powers,"* passed the fifth Day of *February,* 1778; and the Act *"for increasing the Number of Commissioners for detecting and defeating Conspiracies within this State,"* passed the third Day of *April,* 1778, are expired;

And whereas there is great Reason to apprehend that Emissaries from the Enemy are lurking in different Parts of the State, and that the disaffected Inhabitants are conspiring against the public Peace and Safety: By Reason whereof, it hath become necessary to revive the Powers of the said Commissioners;

Be it therefore enacted by the People of the State of New-York, *represented in Senate and Assembly, and it is hereby*

[1] Third session (1779–80), chap. 62.— *Laws of New York:* Poughkeepsie: John Holt, 1782, p. 131.

enacted by the Authority of the same, That the said two Acts and the Powers and Authorities by them or either of them granted to the Commissioners appointed or to be appointed by Virtue of the said Acts, or any and every three of them shall be, and are hereby revived, and shall continue and be in full Force during the Continuance of the present War with *Great-Britain.* That each Commissioner shall be allowed for each Day he shall be actually employed in the Execution of the said Office, the Sum of Fourteen Shillings of the Money to be issued, agreeable to the Resolutions of Congress, of the eighteenth Day of *March* last; and that the Treasurer of this State shall, out of any Monies which may be in the Treasury, advance to the said Commissioners, or any three of them, such Sum or Sums, as they shall from Time to Time require, to defray the Expence of the Business hereby committed to them, not exceeding in the Whole, the Sum of Two Thousand Pounds of like Money aforesaid.

An Act for the Removal of the Families of Persons who have joined the Enemy. Passed the 1st of *July,* 1780.[1]

WHEREAS many and great Mischiefs do arise, by permitting the Families of Persons who have joined the Enemy, to remain at their respective Habitations, inasmuch as such Persons frequently come out in a private Manner, to gain Intelligence and commit Robberies, Thefts and Murders, upon the good People of this State, and are concealed and comforted by their respective Families;

I. *Be it therefore enacted by the People of the State of New-York, represented in Senate and Assembly, and it is*

[1] Third session (1779-80), chap. 76.— *Laws of New York:* Poughkeepsie: John Holt, 1782, pp. 143-144.

hereby enacted by the Authority of the same, That the Justices
of the Peace, resident in each Ward, Town, Manor, Precinct
and District, within this State, shall notify the Wives of all
such Persons, as aforesaid, that they depart this State within
twenty Days after such Notice, or repair to such Parts of it as
are within the Power of the Enemy; and at their Discretion
to take with them all or any of their Children, not above the
Age of twelve Years: That for the Want of a Justice of the
Peace in any Ward, Town, Manor, Precinct or District, the
Supervisor, and for Want of a Supervisor, the Commissioners for detecting and defeating Conspiracies, shall cause
such Notice to be given, as aforesaid.

II. *And be it further enacted by the Authority aforesaid*,
That in Case any of the Persons aforesaid, shall, after the Space
of twenty Days after such Notice, be found in any Part of this
State; they shall and are hereby declared to be out of the
Protection of the Laws of this State; and shall be liable
to be proceeded against as Enemies of this and the United
States:

Provided nevertheless, That this Law shall not extend to
affect such of the said Persons as shall procure Permits to
remain at their respective Habitations, from under the Hands
and Seals of any three of the Commissioners for detecting and
defeating Conspiracies, within this State.

III. *And be it further enacted by the Authority aforesaid*,
That the several Justices of the Peace, or Supervisor as aforesaid, shall, immediately after Notice shall be given to the
several Persons aforesaid, to depart this State, give Information to some one Board of Commissioners as aforesaid,
of all such Persons as aforesaid, together with the Characters
of the said Persons respectively; and the said Commissioners
are hereby authorised to give Permits as aforesaid, to any of
the said Persons, which they may esteem of good Character,

and not dangerous to the Liberties and Independence of this, and the United States.

An Act to accommodate the Inhabitants of the Frontiers with Habitations, and for other Purposes therein mentioned. Passed March 22d, 1781.[1]

I. *BE it enacted by the People of the State of New-York, represented in Senate and Assembly, and it is hereby enacted by the Authority of the same,* That it shall be lawful to and for the Person administering the Government of this State for the Time being, or such Person or Persons as he shall authorise for the Purpose, in their Discretion, and by Licence under their Hands respectively, upon an Application on Behalf of any Number of Families, not less than three, to permit the said several Families on whose Behalf such Application shall be made, to possess and occupy to and for their Use, such unoccupied Houses, Farms, Lands or Tenements, lying on the Frontiers of, this State, as the Person or Persons granting such Licence, shall appoint and deem most convenient, for the Purpose of accommodating the Families on whose Behalf such Application shall be made; and that the said several Families shall, by Virtue of such Licence, be authorised to take Possession of, occupy, and improve such Houses, Farms, Lands or Tenements, as shall be specified in the said Licence; and that it shall in like Manner, be lawful for the Person administering the Government for the Time being, or such other Person as shall grant any such Licence, whenever they shall respectively deem the Necessity which induced the Granting thereof to cease, to revoke any or every such Licence; and

[1] Fourth session (1780–81), chap. 35.— *Laws of New York:* Poughkeepsie: John Holt, 1782, pp. 180–181.

that each and every Person, in whose favour such Licence
shall be granted, who shall not within twenty Days after such
Revocation, remove from the said Houses, Farms, Lands
or Tenements, which he or she was so permitted to possess,
occupy and improve, shall be deemed as Trespassers from
the Beginning, and as such, shall be liable to an Action, at
the Suit of the Person in whose Possession such Houses,
or Farms, Lands or Tenements were, before the granting
such Licence, his or her Heirs and Assigns; and that each
and every Person in whose Favour such Licence shall be
granted, who shall hold over, after the Revocation of such
Licence, shall and may be proceeded against upon the
Statutes of forcible Entry and Detainer, by the Person in
Possession of such Houses, Farms, Lands or Tenements,
immediately before the granting of such Licence, his or her
Heirs or Assigns: *And further* That it shall be lawful for
the Person administering the Government, to cause any
Houses or other Buildings, on the Frontiers of this State,
to be fortified, and to be taken and held as Posts or Fort-
resses, for such Time and in such Manner, as he shall deem
necessary and expedient.

Provided always, that nothing herein contained shall be
construed to prevent the Person so in Possession, before
the granting of the Licence, from possessing, occupying and
improving an equal and proportional Part of such Houses,
Farms, Lands or Tenements, with the several Families in
whose Favour such Licence shall be granted: *And provided also*, That if any Person in whose favour such Licence
shall be granted, shall commit any unnecessary Waste or
Destruction in such Houses, Farms, Lands or Tenements,
they shall severally and respectively, with respect to such
Waste, be deemed as Trespassers, and as such shall be subject to an Action, at the Suit of the Person so in Possession

as aforesaid, immediately before the granting of the Licence, his or her Heirs or Assigns.

And whereas certain disaffected Subjects, who reside on the Frontiers of this State, privately maintain, comfort, and aid the Enemy, in their Incursions on the said Frontiers, and the public Safety requires that they should be compelled to remove from their respective Habitations, to the interior Parts of the State;

II. *Be it therefore further enacted by the Authority aforesaid*, That it shall and may be lawful, to and for the Person administering the Government of this State for the Time being, or the Brigadier, or commanding Officer of the Brigade of Militia; or where the Militia is not formed into a Brigade, a Majority of the Field-Officers of the Regiment within which such disaffected Persons shall reside, to cause all such Persons and Families, as he or they shall deem dangerous and disaffected, and as now are, or hereafter shall be resident and inhabiting on the said Frontiers, to be removed from their respective Habitations, to the interior Parts of the State.

And whereas it may be necessary to remove or destroy the Stock, Grain, or Forage, in many Parts of the Frontiers, in order to prevent the same from falling into the Hands of, or from being applied to the Comfort and Subsistence of the Enemy;

III. *Be it therefore further enacted by the Authority aforesaid*, That it shall be lawful for the Person administering the Government for the Time being, from Time to Time, in his Discretion, to order and direct all or any Part of the Stock, Grain, or Forage, at any Place or Places on the Frontiers, to be removed to such other Places as he shall direct; and in Case such Stock, Grain or Forage, cannot conveniently be removed, or if the Person possessing the same, shall refuse to remove such Stock, Grain or Forage, then to order and direct the same to be destroyed.

IV. *And be it further enacted by the Authority aforesaid,* That it shall be lawful for the Commissioners for defeating and detecting Conspiracies, and each of them, or such other Person or Persons as shall be authorised for the Purpose by the Person administering the Government, for to notify the Wives of all Persons who have voluntarily gone over to and joined, or shall hereafter voluntarily go over to and join the Enemy, to depart this State in like Manner as the Justices of the Peace and Supervisors, in the respective Wards, Towns, Manors, Districts or Precincts, are authorised in and by the Act, entitled, *"An Act for the Removal of the Families of Persons who have joined the Enemy."* And further, That it shall be lawful for the said Commissioners, and each of them, and each of the said several Persons so to be authorised as aforesaid, to take and sell all the Goods and Chattels in the Possession of the Wives of Persons who have voluntarily gone over to and joined, or shall hereafter go over to and join the Enemy, and to apply the Monies arising therefrom, to defraying the Expence of removing such Wives, and such of their respective Children as are not above twelve Years of Age, within the Lines of the Enemy — And that the said Commissioners and other Persons, who shall take and sell any such Goods and Chattels as aforesaid, shall account for the Expenditure of the said Monies with the Auditor-General of this State.

An Act to repeal an Act, entitled, "An Act to revive the Laws appointing Commissioners for detecting and defeating Conspiracies, and to give certain Powers to Magistrates and Courts, in Cases therein mentioned. Passed 27th March, 1783.[1]

I. *B*E *it enacted by the People of the State of* New-York, *represented in Senate and Assembly, and it is hereby enacted by the Authority of the same,* That the Act, entitled, *"An Act to revive the Laws appointing Commissioners for detecting and defeating Conspiracies,"* shall be, and the same is hereby repealed[.]

' II. *And be it further enacted by the Authority aforesaid,* That the Commissioners aforesaid shall, forthwith after the passing of this Act, deliver the Recognizances by them taken, and not forfeited, to the Clerk of the Court of General Sessions of the Peace of the County in which the same were taken; and the Person or Persons bound by such Recognizances, shall be subject to the Directions of, and be compelled to appear before the said Sessions, in like Manner as they were respectively required by Law to subject themselves to the Direction of, and were compellable to appear by the said Recognizances before such Commissioners, and such Recognizances shall to all Intents and Purposes have the like Effect, and be estreated or discharged in the same Manner as if the same had been entered into before such Court of Sessions,

III. *And be it further enacted by the Authority aforesaid,* That the said Commissioners shall, as soon as may be, deliver all such Recognizances, as may have become forfeited to the People of this State, to the Clerk of the Su-

[1] Sixth session (1782–83), chap. 51.— *Laws of New York:* Poughkeepsie: John Holt, 1783, pp. 298–299.

preme Court; to the End that Prosecutions may be instituted for Recovery of the same.

IV. *And be it further enacted by the Authority aforesaid,* That the said Commissioners shall exhibit their Accounts to the Auditor, on or before the first Monday of August next, that the same may be ascertained and settled; and it is hereby made the Duty of the Auditor to report to the Legislature, at their next Meeting after the said first Monday in August, the Amount of such Accounts respectively.

V. *And be it further enacted by the Authority aforesaid,* That the said Commissioners shall, on or before the first Day of May next, make Return to a Justice of the Peace of the County in which such Commissioners reside, of the Names of the Persons by them committed, and the Causes of such Committment, that the said Justice may take Order thereon in due Form of Law — That no Person committed by the said Commissioners, shall be discharged before the first day of May next.

VI. *And be it further enacted by the Authority aforesaid,* That it shall and may be lawful, to and for any Justice of the Peace within this State, to cause to be arrested and brought before him, any Person who shall come within his Jurisdiction, out of any Place in the Power of the Enemy, and to require sufficient Security for the Appearance of the Offender at the next Court of General Sessions of the Peace to be held for the County where such Offender shall be apprehended; and for his good Behaviour in the mean Time; and for the Want of such Security, to commit such Offender to the common Gaol, there to remain until he shall find such Security, or until the next General Sessions of the Peace where the Recognizance or Mittimus, as the Case may be, shall be returned, and which Recognizance or Mittimus shall respectively set forth, that the Offender, bound

over or committed, had without lawful Authority come
within the Jurisdiction of such Justice, out of a Place within
the Power of the Enemy; and thereupon it shall and may
be lawful, to and for the Court of General Sessions of the
Peace to commit such Offender to the common Gaol, there
to remain until the then next Court of Oyer and Terminer
and General Gaol Delivery in the County, to answer unto
all such Matters and Things as shall then and there be objected against such Offender (unless he shall be sooner
thence discharged by due Course of Law) or the said Court
of General Sessions of the Peace may take Surety according to their Discretion, for the Appearance of the Offender at
such Court of Oyer and Terminer and General Gaol Delivery, as aforesaid, then and there to answer in Manner
aforesaid; or the said Court of General Sessions of the
Peace may take Surety only for the good Behaviour of the
Offender, or may permit him to go at large without Surety,
as the said Court in their Discretion shall judge fit:

Provided always, That nothing in this Act contained, shall
be construed in any Wise to restrain the Supreme Court of
Judicature of this State, or any of the Justices of the said
Court, from dealing with such Offender according to the
Law, for any Crime of which such Offender may be accused
or indicted before the said Court, or with which such
Offender may be charged before any Justice of the said
Court.

Certified Pay-Bill of Leonard Gansevoort, Jr. as Secretary to the
Albany Board, 1778-1783

(One-half reduced)

APPENDIX II

FINANCIAL ACCOUNTS.

———

This appendix is devoted to transcripts of the financial accounts of the entire body of commissioners for detecting and defeating conspiracies. It is the result of a careful page for page examination of manuscript records of the State Auditor and State Treasurer, now in the archives of the New York State Library. The *Audited Accounts* are by far the most important, because they are engrossed entries copied from the statements, bills or receipts which received approval from the State Auditor, and preserve full data. The *Day Book* and *Accounts* of the State Treasurer give the record of actual payment, but in much briefer form. Liquidation of these claims was not completed during the period of the war— hence the examination had to be prosecuted through subsequent years. Taken together, these records are believed to show, substantially, a complete account of the expenses of the commissioners in the seven counties in which they operated as a State body. It has not been deemed of value to print the co-ordinate bookkeeping records of these two State officers, from ledgers and journals. A conspectus of extant records follows:

STATE AUDITOR.

Audited Accounts, A and B, two folio volumes.

Book "A" contains the audits from May 22, 1782 to March 17, 1786. Book "B" contains those from March 18, 1786 to October 31, 1794. The dates are dates of audit of claims which begin as early as May, 1775.

Journal, two folio volumes.

Vol. 1: June 17, 1775 to December, 1785.

Vol. 2: January, 1786 to January, 1794.

STATE TREASURER

Day Book, folio.—Vol. 2: April 1, 1778 to September 20, 1784.

Accounts, three composite folio volumes.

Vol. 1: May 31, 1775 to December 31, 1780.

Vol. 2: January 4, 1781 to December 31, 1785.

Vol. 3: January 3, 1786 to January 10, 1797.

Journal, two folio volumes.

Vol. 1: May 31, 1775 to October 2, 1782.

Vol. 2: September 18, 1778 to September 20, 1784.

Ledger (bound with "Auditor's Journal") covers from May 31, 1775 to December 31, 1782.

The original receipts or other vouchers, mounted in a ponderous volume, are in the office of the State Comptroller, in *Revolutionary Manuscripts,* vol. 40. They are somewhat in a disarranged state, and many of them have suffered material mutilation by being cut down. By this unjustifiable process many indorsements and voucher numbers, relative to entries in the volumes of *Audited Accounts,* have been lost, whilst others are destroyed by the process of mounting them.

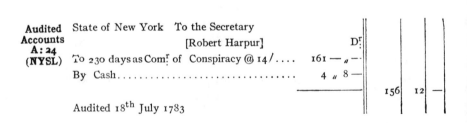

Audited
Accounts
A: 24
(NYSL)

State of New York   To the Secretary
                [Robert Harpur]   D.ͬ

To 230 days as Com.ͬ of Conspiracy @ 14/....   161 — „ —

By Cash.............................   4 „ 8 —

                                         156   12   —

Audited 18ᵗʰ July 1783

Audited Accounts A : 24 (NYSL)	The State of New York D^r in Acco^t with Henry Williams as Commissioner for defeating Conspiracies —			
	For my Services for the days on which I was actually employ'd as Commissioner for defeating & detecting Conspiracies between 6th Septr 1780 & 1st Jany 1783 being 247 days at 14/ allow'd by Act 14th June 1780			
	247 days @ 14/	172 „ 18 —		
	1783 Jany 14. 8th Feby 20th & 26th March 4 days @ 14/	2 „ 16 —		
			175	14 —
	Audited 18th July 1783			

Audited Accounts A : 24 (NYSL)	State of New York to Gilbert Livingston D^r			
	To my Services for the days on which I was actually employ'd a$_s$ Com^r for detecting & defeating Conspiracies between 23^d Augt 1780 & the 6th day of Jany 1783 being 237 days @ 14/ ۶ day	165 „ 18 —		
	Credit			
	1780			
	Decr 2 By Cash rece'd	2 „ 16 —		
			163	2 —
	Audited 18th July 1783			

Audited Accounts A : 29-30 (NYSL)	State of New York to Brinton Paine, Joseph McCracken, Peiatiah Fitch Senr & Alex^r McNutt Commissioners for detecting & defeating Conspiracies D^r			
	1781, April 12. Brinton Paine, Two Days attending & One Days travel at 14/ ۶ day	2 „ 2 —		
	Joseph McCracken Two Days ditto	1 „ 8 „ —		
	Alex^r McNutt....Two Days ditto	1 „ 8 „ —		
	May 22. Brinton Paine, Jo^s McCracken & Alex^r McNutt One Day each & Paine One day travel	2 „ 16 „ —		

Augt 29. The same Two days each, except ⎫
Brinton Paine One Day only...... @ 14/ ⎭   3 ‖ 10 —

Septr 6. The same......The same..........   3 ‖ 10 —

To an Express from White Creek to Saratoga..   10 —

8. To....ditto.........................   10 —

10. To....ditto to Little White Creek.......   10 —

16. To sending Two Expresses to Benning- ⎫
ton from White Creek & there waiting One ⎬
Day extraordinary.................... ⎭   3 ‖ — ‖ —

1782, May 8, 9, 10. McCracken, McNutt &
Fitch 3 days each......................   6 ‖ 6 ‖ —

17. The same One Day each..............   2 ‖ 2 ‖ —

1783, Feby 28. Fitch & McNutt, One Day each   1 ‖ 8 ‖ —

To a Clerk 12 Days @ 14/..............   8 ‖ 8 ‖ —

Decr 31. McCracken, McNutt & Fitch 1 day
each....................................   2 ‖ 2 ‖ —

To Sundries paid for Expence of Prisoners..   1 ‖ 18 ‖ —

To Money paid to Persons for private intel- ⎫
ligence............................ ⎭   5 ‖ — ‖ —

                            46 | 8 | —

Audited 4th Feby 1784

State of New York to Ebenezer Purdy, Israel
Honeywell, Joseph Strang, Nathan Rockwell & Philip Leek for incidental Expences
& services done as Com^{rs} of Conspiracies in
West Chester County   D^r

1781, Jany. To Cash paid Expences of a Guard   Continental
to carry Peter Ferris to Poughkeepsie Goal..£125 ‖ 12 ‖ —

Febr^y. To d^o to carry 3 dangerous Persons ⎫
to Poughkeepsie Goal................. ⎭   120 ‖ — ‖ —

March. To d^o to carry a dangerous Man to d^o..   32 ‖ — ‖ —

April. To d^o p^d for carrying Abraham Whit- ⎫
more a disaffected Man to ditto........ ⎭   80 ‖ — ‖ —

May. To d^o paid a Guard of 3 Men to carry ⎫
Smith & Skenkly to Goal.............. ⎭   256 ‖ — ‖ —

                    Continental   £613 ‖ 12 ‖ —

Exchange at 40 for 1 is Specie............	15 ͵ 6 ͵ 9				

June. To Cash p^d a Guard for their Expence to carry sundry dangerous Persons to Poughkeepsie Goal................... 8 ͵ 8 ͵ —

To d° p^d Jesse Brush Expence of Guard to attend the Commiss^rs during the time of their sitting......................... 2 ͵ 12 ͵ —

To d° One Quire of Paper.................. 3 ͵ —

To d° Andrew Brown to go below the Lines after a dangerous Person.............. 3 ͵ 4 ͵ —

To John Drake for the Expence of a Guard to take Care of Prisoners.............. 3 ͵ 6 ͵ 6

To Cash for Expense of a Man to go to Poughkeepsie to the Governor............... 1 ͵ 12 ͵ —

34 ͵ 12 ͵ 3

To 55 days Wages for Eben^r Purdy at 14/...... 38 ͵ 10 ͵ —

51....d°....Israel Honeywell........... 35 ͵ 14 ͵ —

16....d°....Joseph Strang............. 11 ͵ 4 ͵ —

27....d°....Nathan Rockwell.......... 23 ͵ 18 ͵ —

5....d°....Philip Leak............... 3 ͵ 10 ͵ —

147 ͵ 8 ͵ 3

C^r

1784, Jany 29. By Cash reced of Treasurer by Ebenezer Purdy....................... 20 ͵ — ͵ —

127 | 8 | 3

Audited March 19th 1784 —

State of New York to Alex^r Webster Eben^r Clark, Alex^r McNutt & John McClung Commiss^rs of Conspiracy in the County of Charlotte for incidental Expences & Services   D^r

1778, May 2. To Cash p^d Continental J. Doty ℔ Vouch^r   £3 ͵ 4 ͵ — ͵ ͵   1 ͵ 7 ͵ 9¾

30. To d°....Josh^a Conkey. 3 ͵ 4 ͵ — ͵ ͵   1 ͵ 6 ͵ 1¼

June 7. To d°....Beach.... 1 ͵ 12 ͵ — ͵ ͵   12 — ¾

Augt 5. To....d° p^d Alex^r
Inmitt [*sic*].............. 9 ″ 12 ″ — } .. 3 ″ 5 ″ 6
To....d° Eben^r Clark..... 1 ″ 4 ″ —

18. To d° p^d Reuben Turner — 16 —
21. To d° ....Gershom } .. — 19 ″ 5½
Woodward.............. 2 ″ 16 ″ —

Septr 1. To d° p^d Robert
Armstrong.............. 5 ″ 1 ″ — } .. 1 ″ 9 ″ 9
2. To d°....William Lyll.. — 18 —

Decr 2 To d° p^d Robert Gilly — 12 —
To d° .... d° & Wilson.... 3 ″ 4 ″ — } .. 1 ″ 7 ″ 1¼
To d° Alex^r Simpson..... 4 ″ 16 ″ —

1779, Jany 5. To d° p^d John
Armstrong.............. — 16 —
8. To d° James Henderson 2 ″ 8 ″ 6 } .. — 12 ″ 11¼
9. To d° John Hursdon..... — 8 —
To d° Alex^r Turner...... 1 ″ 4 —

April 21. To d° p^d John
Hunsdon............... 7 ″ 18 ″ 2 — 13 ″ 8
July 16. To d° p^d Edward
Savage................ 4 ″ 16 ″ 6 — 6 ″ 2¼
To d° p^d Robert Stewart in hard Money..... 6 ″ 12 ″ —
To 101 days Service as Com^r by Alex^r Web-
ster on the first Act passed 5th Feb^y
1778 @ 20/ Cont! is 12/6 Specie; all } 63 ″ ? ″ 6
before the 27th March 1783 when the
Act was repeald...................
To 90 days service by Ebenezer Clark @ 12/6 56 ″ 5 —
To 132 days d° by Alex^r McNutt..12/6...... 82 ″ 10 —
To 138 days....d°....by John McClung 12/6 86 ″ 5 —

306 ″ 15 ″ 1

C^r

1778, June 3. By cash from Matthew Fisher[1]
at 265 Cont! to 100 hard.................. 150 18 10¼

155 | 16 | 2¾

Audited April 13th 1784

[1] The correct form of the name is the Dutch equivalent Visscher.

Audited Accounts A : 108 (NYSL)	State of New York to Andrew Rynex D^r To attending the Commissioners of Conspiracy as Constable in the District of Schenectady in the Year 1781 Nine Days at 6/ ℔ day Audited 12th October 1784	2	14	—
Audited Accounts A : 108 (NYSL)	State of New York to Reynier Mynderse Dr For attending as Commissioner of Conspiracy in the Years 1780, 1781 & 1782....Eighty Days at 14/ ℔ day Audited 12th October 1784	56	—	—
Audited Accounts A : 108 (NYSL)	State of New York to Hugh Mitchell Dr For attending as Commissioner of Conspiracy in the Years 1780, 1781 & 1782....Ninety Five Days @ 14/ Audited 12th October 1784	66	10	—
Audited Accounts A : 112 (NYSL)	State of New York to Abraham Oothout Dr For attending as Commissioner of Conspiracy in the Years 1780, 1781 & 1782....86 days @ 14/ ℔ day	60	4	—
	To Necessaries provided for a Party of Men under the Command of Major Wemple as ℔ Bill......	1	18	—
		£62	2	—
	Audited October 18th 1784			

The State of New York in Account Current whit [*sic*] the Commissioners for detecting and defeating Conspiracies.[1]

	Vouchers for money paid D^r			
Audited Accounts A : 147 (NYSL)	N.° 1 Isaiah Butler............................	£10	—	—
	„ 2 Rutger Bleecker........................	20	—	—
	„ 3 Justicia van Hoesen[2]................	7	—	—
	„ 4 Commissioners of Charlotte County..............	400	—	—
	„ 5 Jonathan Beacraft..................	7	—	—

[1] The original statement in the handwriting of Leonard Gansevoort, Jr., is in *Revolutionary MSS.*, vol. 40, p. 159, in the office of the State Comptroller, and is more accurate as to names. Serious errors are here pointed out in annotations.

[2] Justice Van Hoesen.

			£		
Audited	N.º	6 Peter Bont...................................	£3	4	—
Accounts	"	7 Burger Blauw[1]..............................	3	4	—
A : 147	"	8 Jacob Wiltse................................	4	—	—
(NYSL)	"	9 Joseph Gilford..............................	17	2	4
	"	10 Jacob van Valkenburgh......................	12	16	—
	"	11 Isaac Shelden..............................	5	10	—
	"	12 Cornelius C Muller.........................	4	7	—
	"	13 Cloude van Deusen..........................	4	—	—
	"	14 Richard Bronck............................	3	4	—
	"	15 Cornelius van Deusen.......................	—	16	—
	"	16 Leonard Gansevoort Junior..................	16	1	4
	"	17 Cornelius Humfrey..........................	14	—	8
	"	19 Christopher Hawk..........................	—	16	—
	"	18 Cornelius Humfrey..........................	6	2	—
	"	20 John Smith................................	40	—	—
	"	21 Leonard Gansevoort Junior..................	4	—	—
	"	22 Wilhelmus Haines..........................	1	4	—
	"	23 Isaac A. Fonda.............................	21	4	—
	"	24 John Seton................................	5	—	—
	"	25 Cornelius Humfrey..........................	7	2	8
	"	26 John Smith................................	6	7	8
	"	27 Mathew Aerson.............................	8	17	4
	"	28 John Ryley................................	460	18	4
	"	29 John Sloss................................	—	16	—
	"	30 James Knowles............................	4	16	—
	"	31 Cornelius Groesbeeck.......................	4	2	—
	"	32 Samuel Lauden[2]...........................	2	8	—
	"	33 Cornelius Humfrey..........................	4	—	—
	"	34 Daniel Kettle.............................	3	—	—
	"	35 Christopher Hawk..........................	3	4	—
	"	36 Clyne and Robinson[3]......................	26	8	—
	"	37 Jacob Klyne[4].............................	11	—	—
	"	38 John Ryley................................	7	16	—
	"	39 Samuel Shaw..............................	5	16	—
	"	40 John Vischer..............................	34	16	—

[1] Burger Clauw.
[2] Samuel Loudon, the printer.
[3] Robison.
[4] Kline.

			£		
Audited Accounts A : 147 (NYSL)	N°	41 Samuel Loadman............................	£5	15	6
	"	42 Stephen Bell................................	16	17	4
	"	43 Isaac Bogert................................	27	6	—
	"	44 David van Rensselaer......................	15	14	8
	"	45 Peter Gunsalis..............................	92	15	6
	"	46 Cornelius C: vanden Bergh................	63	13	6
	"	47 John Lansing Junior.......................	20	—	—
	"	48 Leonard Gansevoord Junior...............	18	—	—
	"	49 Ab^m Lansing & Ab^m vanden Berg.........	98	5	—
	"	50 Alexander Anderson........................	8	—	—
	"	51 Isaac Goes..................................	5	—	—
	"	52 Stephen Bell................................	24	12	—
	"	53 John H: Beeckman..........................	19	16	—
	"	54 Cornelius Humfrey..........................	42	—	—
	"	55 Hugh Mitchell..............................	43	—	—
	"	56 Myndert Wemple[1].........................	4	—	—
	"	57 Robert Smith...............................	1	4	—
	"	58 Wessel van Schaick.........................	26	—	—
	"	59 Volkert Dawson.............................	13	17	4
	"	60 Stephen Bell................................	25	4	—
	"	61 John Smith.................................	20	—	—
	"	62 Jeremiah van Rensselaar...................	6	8	—
	"	63 Col: Porters[2].............................	36	—	—
	"	64 Cornelius C: Miller........................	34	2	—
	"	65 Stephen Viele...............................	16	—	—
	"	66 Christopher P: Yates.......................	166	4	—
	"	67 Stephen Bell................................	47	16	—
	"	68 Denis M: Carty.............................	4	16	—
	"	69 William Colbrath[3].........................	20	—	—
	"	70 Peter Magee................................	27	10	8
	"	71 Jonathan Sever.............................	2	—	—
	"	72 Philip Conine...............................	100	—	—
	"	73 Stephen Hoyt[4].............................	25	—	—
	"	74 Samuel T: ten Broeck[5].....................	10	2	8

[1] Myndert A. Wemple.
[2] Porter.
[3] Colbreath.
[4] Hoit or Hayt.
[5] Samuel I. Ten Broeck

			£		
N?:	75	Edward Archer	£22	10	—
"	76	Mathew Vischer	4	—	—
"	77	David Gibson	28	14	—
"	78	Cloude van Deusen & Peter Bont	7	8	—
"	79	Commissioners of Charlotte county	100	—	—
"	80	Hugh McAdam	32	—	—
"	81	John C Lansing[1]	217	17	3
"	82	Jeremiah Fonda	8	—	—
"	83	William Harrison	28	5	4
"	84	John Mc Coy	11	15	—
"	85	John Ja Beeckman	24	10	—
"	86	Henry Shaver	80	—	—
"	87	Bethuel Washburn	197	—	—
"	88	Cornelius Cuyler	92	11	4
"	89	Jesse Fairchilds[2]	222	16	—
"	90	Ezra Buel	8	—	—
"	91	Bethuel Washburn	128	12	—
"	92	Jacob Slingerland[3]	28	12	—
"	93	Peter Seeger	20	—	—
"	94	Jeremiah van Rensselaar	15	12	—
"	95	John 5 Lansing	202	8	10
"	96	Petrus Wynkoop	100	—	—
"	97	Bethuel Washburn	371	2	—
"	98	Bethuel Washburn	67	12	—
"	99	Richard Yselstyn[4]	7	11	4
"	100	Bethuel Washburn	41	17	—
"	101	Bethuel Waschburn	58	4	—
"	102	Isaac D: Fonda	74	3	—
"	103	John Fonda Junior	74	—	—
"	104	Thomas Ismay	91	19	6
"	105	Daniel Dickinson[5]	46	16	—
"	106	Leonard Gansevoort Junior	144	—	—
"	107	Amaziach Winchester[6]	96	16	—
"	108	Jacob Gaul	50	—	—
"	109	Bethuel Waschburn[7]	25	4	—
"	110	Mathew Vischer	210	—	—

[1] John 5 Lansing.
[2] Fairchild.
[3] Slingerlandt.
[4] Esselstyne.
[5] Dickison.
[6] Amaziah Winchester
[7] Washburn.

Audited Accounts A : 147 (NYSL)			
N.º 111 Jesse Fairchilds[1]	£765	12	—
„ 112 Stephen Bell	80	—	—
„ 113 Jacob Kidney	80	—	—
„ 114 Jacob Kidney	60	—	—
„ 115 Leonard Gansevoort Junior	292	8	—
Continental	£6506	16	1

1778	Money received C.ʳ			
28 April	To cash received from G: Bancker Esq.ʳ Treasurer of the State of New York	£1000	—	—
12 August	To cash from dito	1000	—	—
1779				
15 Jann	To ditto „ d.º in Sundry Payments	1000	—	—
31 May	To ditto ditto	1500	—	—
21 Oct:	To ditto ditto	2000	—	—
	Balance due commiss.ʳˢ carried to Specie account	6	16	1
	Continental	£6506	16	

J: V: Rensselaar ⎫
Math: Visscher   ⎬ late Commiss.ʳˢ
John M· Beeckman ⎭

D.ʳ

To Ball p.ʳ contra bro.ᵗ forward £6. 16. 1 reduced in Specie is	£—	3	4
N.º 111 To a Ballance on an Account of Jesse Fairchild	3	12	9
„ 112 To „ ditto „ „ d.º „ Stephen Bell	72	—	—
„ 54 To „ ditto „ „ d.º „ Cornelius Humfrey	20	19	6
„ 16 To an Acc: of James M.ᶜMaster	6	5	—
„ 1 To am.ᵗ of Stephen Bell's acct ℔ Voucher	30	—	—
„ 2 To d.º „ Jesse Hainhild[2]	81	17	10
" 3 To d.º Jacob Kidney	70	10	—
" 4 To d.º Robert Hassin[3]	2	—	—
„ 5 To d.º Peter Bronk	4	2	4
„ 6 To Robbert Kennedy	6	—	—
„ 7 To John D: Clute	—	8	—
„ 8 Coenraad Klyne	9	—	2

[1] Fairchild.
[2] The auditor's record is incorrect, as the name should be Fairchild.
[3] Harper.

				£	s	d
Audited Accounts A : 147 (NYSL)	N°.	9	John Fortfuydt.........................	£16	16	—
	"	10	Thomas Cole...........................	5	4	—
	"	11	Robert Kennedy........................	8	—	—
	"	12	Jac: Caldwell	12	—	—
	"	13	Stuwart Deane[1].......................	86	2	—
	"	14	John Vissher..........................	1	6	6
	"	15	David Gibson..........................	5	4	—
	"	17	Goose van Schaick.....................	14	16	—
	"	18	David Fonda...........................	1	17	8
	"	20	Am.t of Isaac D Fondas acct as Commissioner.....	467	19	6
	"	21	do " S: Stringer d.º d.º	283	6	—
	"	22	d.º " John M: Beeckman d.º	499	7	—
	"	23	d.º " Mathew Vissher[2] d.º	284	15	6
	"	19	Isaac D: Fonda........................	—	18	7
	"	24	Am.t of Jerem: Van Rensselaar acct as Commiss.r...	138	9	6
	"	25	" " L: Gansevoort Junior as Clerk............	534	12	6
	"	26	d.º to diff.t people.........................	23	5	4
				£2690	19	

	Cr:		£	s	d
1780					
16 Dec:	By cash from the Treasury..................		£41	—	—
1781					
17 Sept.	" d.º " d.º		160	—	—
19 Nov.	" d.º " d.º ....:.............		76	—	—
1782					
16 Jann	" d.º " d.º		73	14	—
11 Maart	" d.º " d.º		350	—	—
Received from forfeited Recognizances from T: Truax[3].....			80	—	—
" " " " " P. Trimhout[4]..			—	15	6
" " " " " P: Empie[5].....			12	—	—
" " " " " I. Collayer[6]....			20	—	—
Balances due the Commissioners......................			1868	9	6
			2690	19	—

[1] Stewart Dean.
[2] Visscher.
[3] Jacob Truax.
[4] Peter Finehout.
[5] Philip Empie.
[6] Isaac Collayer.

Audited Accounts A : 147 (NYSL)

	D.ʳ			
To Ball. pʳ Contra	1868	9	6
To amᵗ of Petrus Wynkoops acc.......................	60	—	—
" dᵒ Hugh Mitchel...............................	21	1	6
	1949	11	—
Balance due the Commissioners........................	1949	11	—

Audited 19 November 1784.

Audited Accounts A : 208 (NYSL)

State of New York D.ʳ to Joseph Gasharie Cornˢ. E. Wynkoop & Cornˢ. Schoonmaker Commissioners of Conspiracies

To Joseph Gasharie as ℔ Accoᵗ Nᵒ 1.	10 „ 6 „ —		
To Cornˢ. E. Wynkoop ℔ dᵒ 2.	9 „ 2 „ —		
To Cornˢ Schoonmaker ℔ dᵒ 3.	9 „ 16 „ —		
1781			
July 31 To Cash pᵈ Capᵗ Bogardus as ℔ Recᵗ.	6 „ — „ —		
1782			
Febʸ 8 To Cash pᵈ Cornˢ Bicker.. ℔ ditto..	3 „ 12 „ —		
26 To dᵒ paid Martin Snyder.. ℔ ditto..	3 „ 15 „ —		
June 8 To dᵒ paid Augustus Jay.. ℔ ditto..	2 „ 8 „ —		
	44 „ 19 „ —		
1781			
Decʳ By Cash rece'd of the Treasurer	40 „ — „ —	4	19	—

Audited 11ᵗʰ April 1785 —

Audited Accounts A : 208 (NYSL)

State of New York to Egbert Benson   D.ʳ

To my Service as a Commissioner for Conspi-cies from the 5ᵗʰ Febʸ 1778 to the time of my resigning the said Office 400 Days @ 20/ ℔ day pursuant to the Act of the Legislature of 5ᵗʰ Febʸ 1778...................	£400 „ — „ —		
Deduct for depreciation at 160 for 100 is equal to 12 / 6 ℔ day............... }	150 „ — „ —	250	—	—

Audited 11ᵗʰ April 1785 —

Audited Accounts A : 210 (NYSL)   State of New York to Robert Harpur   D.^r

For my Services as a Commissioner for Conspiracies from 13th July 1778 to 4th Jany 1780 pursuant to the Act of the Legislature of 5th Feby 1778 — 370 days @ 20/ .... 370 „ — „ —

Deduct for Depreciation at 160 for 100 .... 138 „ 15 „ —   231 | 5 | —

Audited 12th April 1785 —

Audited Accounts A : 213 (NYSL)   State of New York D.^r to Cornelius E. Wynkoop

For 50 days Service as a Commissioner for detecting and defeating Conspiracies from the 17th April 1778 to 26th Augt 1780 at Poughkeepsie...... @ 20 / ℔ day .... 50 „ — „ —

For 3 days service as ditto at Kingston @ 20/.   3 „ — „ —

53 „ — „ —

Deduct Depreciation at 160 for 100 .... 19 „ 17 „ 6   33 | 2 | 6

Audited 14th April 1785 —

Audited Accounts A : 213 (NYSL)   State of New York D.^r to Cornelius Schoonmaker

To 60 Days Service from 4th July 1778 to 15th Septr 1779 as a Commissioner of Conspiracies @ 20/ ℔ day .... 60 „ — „ —

To 39 Days ditto from 6th Septr 1780 to 26th March 1783 as above @ 14/ ℔ day ...... } 27 „ 6 „ —

87 „ 6 „ —

C.^r

By Depreciation deducted on £60 at 160 for 100 .... 22 „ 10 „ —   64 | 16 | —

Audited 14th April 1785 —

Audited Accounts A : 215 (NYSL)	State of New York D^r to Israel Thompson Esqr late one of the Commiss^{rs} of Conspiracies For 22 days Attendance (as Commissioner by Virtue of an Act of the Legislature passed 5th Feby 1778) between the 9th April & 25th June 1778 @ 20/......................	22 „ — „ —		
	To 3 days travelling to & from Pougkepsie @ 20/..............................	3 „ — „ —		
		25 „ — „ —		
	By Depreciation on £25 — „ — @ 160 for 100.	9 „ 7 „ 6	15 12 6	
	Audited 19th April 1785 —			

Audited Accounts A : 216 (NYSL)	State of New York D^r to Com^{rs} of Conspiracies To Teunis Tappen Secretary to the Commiss^{rs} for Amo^t of his Acco^t of incidental Charges and his Pay as Secretary to the Board...	500 „ 2 „ 8		

C^r

1779

March 11 By Cash return'd by Isaac Bloom for One Barrel Pork spoil'd — purchas'd for the Use of the Prisoners £18 „ — „ — Cont^l reduc'd to Specie at 1000 for 100...   1 „ 16 —

Octob^r By Cash rece'd from Sundry Tory Prisoners to defray their Expences Viz^t

William Tud.....	21 „ 12 „ 9	
William Ealigh...	2 „ 8 „ —	
William Brown...	2 „ 8 „ —	1 „ 17 „ 3
Nicholas Stickle..	5 „ 18 „ —	
William Wood....	2 „ 15 „ 4	
Simon Low......	2 „ 16 „ —	

Cont^l Curr^y 37 „ 18 „ 1
£37 „ 18 „ 1 Cont^l reduced to Specie @ 2032 for 100..........   3 „ 13 „ 3   496 9 5
Audited 19th April 1785

State of New York D^r to Com^{rs} of Conspiracies
for Dutchess County by Virtue of an Act of
the Legislature passed 5th Feb^{ry} 1778 —

To Zephaniah Platt, between 6th April 1778 &
1st Jany 1780 — 90 days @ 20/ ℔ day ⎫
£90 — „ — reduc'd at 160 for 100....... ⎭   56 „ 5 „ —

To Thomas Moffat between 10th June 1778 & ⎫
27th of same Month 15 days @ 20/...... ⎬   9 „ 7 „ 6
£15 — „ — reduc'd at 160 for 100...... ⎭

To Joseph Strang between 22^d June 1778 & ⎫
1st April 1779 — 13 days @ 20/.......... ⎬   8 „ 2 „ 6
£13 — „ — reduc'd at 160 for 100....... ⎭

To Peter Cantine Junr between 15th Nov^r ⎫
1779 & 20th of same Month — 6 days @ 20/ ⎬   3 „ 15 „ —   77 10 —
£6 — „ — reduc'd at 160 for 100........ ⎭

Audited 19th April 1785

State of New York D^r to Joseph Strang One of
the Commissioners for detecting & defeating
Conspiracies in Dutchess County

	Days
To my Services as Commiss^r from 19th March to May 5th 1777 both days included.........	15
To ditto from 23^d June to 4th July 1778......	7
To ditto from 13th Augt to 4th Septr 1778....	18
To ditto 14th & 15th Septr 1778 looking about to carry some Persons to be sent off........	2
To my Services as Commiss^r 1st & 2^d Octr 1778 attending the Commiss^{rs} at Pougkepsie & preparing to send Persons off......	2
To ditto from 1st to 10th Novr 1778 notifying such Persons as were directed to go within the Enemies Lines & sending them off.................................	4½
	48½ days

48½ days @ 20 ℔ day reduc'd at 160 100.....   30 „ 6 „ 3

Audited Accounts A : 284-5 (NYSL)

1778
Sept.ʳ 4 To Cash paid John Haynes
for 16 days riding in Service
of Commissioners   26 „ — „ —

To ditto p.ᵈ Samuel Lyon for noti-
fying Evidences & other Ser-   3 „ — „ —
vices

To ditto paid for Paper & Quills..   1 „ 1 „ 4

                                        30 „ 1 „ 4
£30 „ 1 „ 4 reduc'd at 400 for 100 is Specie.....   7 „ 10 „ 4

                                                    37 „ 16 „ 7

C.ʳ

1785
April 19 By an Acco.ᵗ audited this day for.....   8 „ 2 „ 6   29 14 1

Audited 19ᵗʰ October 1785 —

Audited Accounts A : 316 (NYSL)

State of New York D.ʳ to Ebenezer Purdy
as One of the Commiss.ʳˢ for detecting
Conspiracies
To Cash paid for hire of Guards & their
Expences while in Service........................   18 4 —
Audited 25ᵗʰ February 1786

Audited Accounts B : 44 (NYSL)

State of New York to Charles R. Webster
1783   Dr.
April 14   To inserting in the New York
Gazetteer an Act entitled an Act to repeal
an Act entitled An Act to revive the Laws
appointing Commissioners for detecting &
defeating Conspiracies & to give certain
powers to Magistrates & Courts therein
mention'd passed the 27ᵗʰ March 1783 making
in the said paper 4½ squares at 8/ ℔ square............   1 16 —
Audited 25ᵗʰ August 1786

Audited Accounts B : 127 (NYSL)	State of New York to Josiah Ingersol D^r To Certain services performed for the State at the Request of Zephaniah Platt and Egbert Benson late Commissioners for Conspiracies &c in transporting Certain quantities of Beef and having the same Smooked to prevent it from Spoiling in the year 1779......................................		2	0	0

Sworn to by Egbert Benson
Aud 22 Novr 1787

Audited Accounts B : 190 (NYSL)	The Commissioners for Conspiracies &c
	              To Robert Hoffman D^r
	              C^r				

	To 3 Barrell of Superfine Flour 1 3 0 each at 30/ ℔ hundred		7	17	6
	To 3 Barril @ 2/6 each			7	6
			£ 8	5	—

Sworn to by Stephen Hendrickson and
   Robert Hoffman
Audited June 30th 1789.

STATE TREASURER

Day Book, Vol.2 — April, 1778 to September, 1784

(Archives of New York State Library)

	£	s	d
April 28th 1778 Jeremiah V: Rensselaer, Isaac D. Fonda &c the Commiss^{rs} of Conspiracy in Albany appointed by virtue of the late Law. D^r To Cash............................1933........	1000	—	—
July 1st 1778 Sundry Accounts D^r To Cash vizt Zephaniah Platt &c the Commissioners of Conspiracy at Poughkepsie last app^d ....2002........	1500	—	—

	£	s	d
July 12 1778			
Jeremiah V Renselaer &ᶜ the Comm.ʳˢ of			
Conspiracy at Albany Dʳ to Cash.........2037........	1000	—	—
August 28.th 1778			
Zephaniah Platt &ᶜ Commissioners of Con-			
spiracy Dʳ To Cash.....................2038........	500	—	—
September 25.th 1778			
Sundry Accounts Dʳ To Cash viz.ᵗ			
Zepheniah Platt &ᶜ Comm.ʳˢ of Conspiracy.....2067........	500	—	—
November 8, 1778			
Sundry Accounts Dʳ To Cash viz.ᵗ			
Zephaniah Platt &ᶜ Commissioners of			
Consp.ʸ in part of the £3000 Credit			
by a Law passed the [blank].............2084	500	—	—
January 1.ˢᵗ 1779			
Sundry Accounts Dʳ To Cash viz.ᵗ			
Zephaniah Platt &ᶜ the Comm.ʳˢ of			
Consp.ʸ at Poughkepsie................2098	2000	—	—
January 1.ˢᵗ 1779			
Sundry Accounts Dʳ To Cash viz.ᵗ			
Egbert Benson &ᶜ Com.ʳˢ Conspiracy.......2104	4021	17	6
January 15.th 1779			
Jeremiah V Rensselaer &ᶜ The Albany Com.ʳˢ			
Conspiracy Dʳ			
To Rooseboom Bancker & White for so much			
J MᶜKesson received from them &			
paid you...........................£500 „ — „ —			
To Leonard Gansevoort Treasurer of the			
Co. of Albany for my Draft on			
L Gansevoort....................... 500 „ — „ —	1000	---	—
for the above two Sums See their Order &			
J MᶜKessons Receipt			
May 31.ˢᵗ 1779			
Jeremiah V Rensselaer &ᶜ Dʳ			
To Cash................................2247	1500	—	—

	£	s	d
June 30 1779 Zephaniah Platt &c. D.r (May 29.th) To Cash Advanced to them a[s] Comm.rs of Conspiracy.....2258	1500	—	—
October 15.th 1779 Sundry Accounts D.r To Cash viz.t Zeph.h Platt &.a on Acco.t 2279	2000	—	—
October 21.st 1779 Jeremiah V. Rensselaer &.c D.r To Cash p.d Matthew Fisher[1] one of the Comm.rs of Conspiracy of the County of Albany.....2281	2000	—	—
November 18.th 1779 Sundry Accounts D.r To Cash viz.t Zephaniah Platt &.c Comm.rs of Conspiracy 2368	2000	—	—
September 23.d 1780 Sundry Acco.ts D.r To Cash viz.t Zeph.h Platt &.a Comm.rs of Conspiracy the Ballance of an Account this day settled.....2503A.......	56	—	11
January 29.th 1781 Cash D.r To Zephaniah Platt &.a a repaym.t of £2000. which they had not Credited in their Account Audited & Settled at Poughkeepsie.............	2000	—	—
To State of N Y re.d of ditto the forfeited Recognizance of Peter Storm.......................	400	—	—
of ditto....D.o....of Ja.s Hammond jun.r................	268	—	—
June 12.th 1781 Jeremiah V. Rensselaer & Co Comm.rs of Con- spiracy D.r To Cash paid them the 16.th December last £ 41 „ N E. at 40. the then Exchange 2611	1640	—	—

[1] Visscher.

	£	s	d
September 17th 1781 Sundry Accounts Dr. To Cash vizt. Jeremiah V Rensselaer &c. Commissioners of Conspiracy in Albany £160.............. N. E...............2783 £160	12000	—	—
November 19th 1781 Joseph Gasherie Cornelius Schoonmaker and Cornelius E Wynkoop Commrs. of Conspiracy Dr. To Cash 2809 £40 „ — „ —	3000	—	—
Jeremiah V. Rensselaer &c. Commrs. of Conspiracy 2812 76 „ — „ —	5700	—	—
January 16th 1782 Jeremiah V Rensselaer & Co. Dr To Cash £73 „ 14 „ — N E — 2823	5527	10	—
March 11th 1782 Jeremiah V Rensselaer & Co Dr To Cash paid Leonard Gansevoort junr. ℔ their Order £350 N Emission 2831	26250	—	—
January 29 1784 Sundry Accounts Dr To Cash vizt. Honeywell, Purdy & Rockwl. Commrs Conspy for W: Chester £20 „ — „ — 2984	1500	—	—
February 20th 1784 State of New York Dr. To Cash pd. Ab. DePeyster Clerk of Commrs Conspy. £50 — 2989	3750	—	—
May 5th 1784 State of New York Dr To Sundry Accounts vizt. To Alexander Webster, Ebenezer Clark, Alexander McNitt and John McClung Commissioners of Conspy in Charlotte County for Amount of their Accots of Contingencies..........say Ball 3027 £ 155 „ 16 „ 2¾......................	11685	17	2

<table>
<tr><td></td><td>£</td><td>s</td><td>d</td></tr>
</table>

May 24.th 1784

Zephaniah Platt &.^c the Commiss.^{rs} of Con-
spiracy at Poughkeepsie D.^r To Cash p.^d
R Harpur one of the Members of that
Board......3165 £100..................

	£	s	d
	7500	—	—

May 24.th 1784

State of New York D.^r To Sundry Accounts vizt
To Zephaniah Platt &.^c for the pay of Robert
Harpur a Member of the Board of Comm.^{rs}
of Conspiracy 3165 £ 156 „ 12 „ —

	£	s	d
	11745	—	—

September 3.^d 1784

Sundry Acco.^{ts} D.^r To Cash vizt
Zep.^h Platt &.^c p.^d R. Harp.^r
3336 £56 12 —

	£	s	d
	4245	—	—

STATE TREASURER

Accounts — May, 1775 to January, 1797

(Archives of New York State Library)

1778			£	s.	d.
Sep.^t 23	By Cash from Egbert Benson &.^c Comm.^{rs} of Conspiracy		47	17	4
April 28	To Cash p.^d Jeremiah V. Rensselaer, Isaac D Fonda &.^c Commissioners for detecting Conspiracies	1933	1000	—	—
July 1	To Cash p.^d Zephaniah Platt &.^c the new App.^d Commissioners of Conspiracy. diff.^t Paym.^{ts}	2002	1500	—	—
July 12	To d.^o p.^d Serg.^t David Mills pay of a party to apprehend disaffected persons	2023	50	—	—
Augt 12	To d.^o p.^d Jeremiah V. Rensselaer &.^c the Comm.^{rs} of Conspiracy in Albany on Account	2037	1000	—	—
28	To d.^o p.^d Platt &.^c the Comm.^{rs} of Con-spiracy at Poughkepsie on Acco.^t	2038	500	—	—

		£	s	d
Sept.ʳ 25	To dᵒ pᵈ Zephaniah Platt &ᶜ the Commiss.ʳˢ of Conspiracy at Poughkepsie on Accoᵗ 2067	500	—	—
Nov. 8	To Cash pᵈ Zephaniah Platt &ᶜ the last Appointed Commissioners of Conspiracy in part of the £3000 C.ʳ by a Late Law 2084	500	—	—
1779 Janʸ 1	Paid Zephaniah Platt &ᶜ the Commiss.ʳˢ of Conspiracy at Poughkeepsie on Accoᵗ 2098	2000	—	—
1	Paid Egbert Benson &ᶜ Commʳˢ of Con-spʸ 2104	4021	17	6
May 31	Paid Jeremiah V Rensselaer &ᶜ Comm.ʳˢ Conspʸ at Albany 2247	1500	—	—
June 30	Paid Zepʰ Platt &ᶜ Commʳˢ Conspiracy on Accoᵗ 2258	1500	—	—
Octobʳ 15	Paid Zepʰ Platt &ᶜ Comm.ʳˢ Conspiracy 2279	2000	—	—
21	Paid Jeremiah V Rensselaer &ᶜ Com. Conspʸ 2281	2000	—	—
Nov.ʳ 18	Paid Zepʰ Platt &ᶜ Commrs Seqⁿ [*sic*] 2368	2000	—	—
1780 Sep. 23	Paid Zephaniah Platt &ᶜ Comm.ʳˢ Conspʸ A2503	56	0	11
1781 June 6	Paid Jeremiah V. Rensselaer &ᶜ Com. Conspʸ 2611	1640	—	—
Sep.ᵗ 17	Paid Jer.ʰ V. Rensselaer &ᶜ Commissioners of Conspiracy £160 2783	12000	—	—
Nov.ʳ 19	Paid Gasherie Schoonmaker & Wynkoop Comm.ʳˢ Conspiracy £40 2809	3000	—	—
19	Paid Jer: V. Rensselaer & Com.Cons: £76 2812	5700	—	—
1781 Janʸ 29	From Zepʰ Platt &ᶜ Com. Conspʸ ¹	2000	—	—
	From dᵒ for Sundry Forfeited Recognizances	668	—	—
1782 Janʸ 16	Paid Jer: V Rensselaer & Com: Consp: N E £73 „ 14 — 2823	5527	10	—
March 11	Paid Jer: V Rensselaer &ᶜ Com: Cons: N E £350 2831	26250	—	—

¹ This item is out of order in the original.

1784			Specie £	s	d	Continental £	s	d
Jan.ʸ 29	To Honeywell, Purdy & Rockwell, Commis̄s Consp. W. Chester	2984	20	"	"	1500	"	"
Feb.ʸ 20	To Dᵒ Ab: Depeyster, Clk of Commiss: Cons̄. £50 "—"—2989		50	"	"	3750		
May 5	To Webster, Clark &ᶜ in part (Commiss: Conspiracy)	3027	34	8	3	2580	18	9
May 24	To Zepheniah Platt &ᶜ Commiss: Consp. at Poughkeepsie pᵈ R. Harpur, a memʳ of that board	3165	100	"	"	7500	"	"
Sepᵗ 3	To Zephaniah Platt &ᶜ pᵈ R. Harpur Conspiracies	3336	56	12	"	4245	"	"
October 11	Paid Gilbert Livingston, Commissʳ of Conspirʸ	3377				163	2	"
12	Paid Rynier Mynderse Comʳ Conspirʸ for Schenʸ	3378				56	"	"
12	Paid Andrew Renex Ditto	3379				2	14	"
12	Paid Hugh Mitchell Ditto	3380				66	10	"
Nov. 20	Paid Jeremiah V. Renselaer &Cᵒ Comˢ Conspirʸ	3449				1949	11	"
25	Paid Rynier Mynderse &Cᵒ Comˢ Conspʸ	3454				62	2	"
1785								
April 12	Paid Egbert Benson &Cᵒ Comˢ Conspʸ	3670				250	"	"
12	Paid Robert Harpur Dᵒ	3671				231	5	"
14	Paid Zepheniah Platt &ᶜ Commiss: Conspʸ	3684				64	16	"
18	Paid Gasherie, Schoonmaker & Wynkoop, the Ballance of their Account C. C.	3688				4	19	"
May 7	Paid Zephᵃ Platt &Cᵒ Comʳˢ Conspiracy	3718				56	5	"
October 21	Paid Joseph Strang, a Comʳ of Conspʸ	3908				29	14	1
Decemʳ 20	Paid Joseph Strang, a Commissʳ of Conspiracy	3974				8	2	6

			£	s	d
1786					
Janua^r 23.^d	Paid Peter Cantine, late Commiss^r. Conspī.	4021	3	15	*u*
1787					
Novem^r 24	Paid Egbert Benson for so much Adv^d by him as Commissioner of Conspiracy	5158	2	*u*	*u*
1791					
November 19.th	Paid Thomas Moffat, as a Commissioner of Conspiracy	7053	9	7	6
1792					
January 14	Paid Thomas Moffat a Ball^{ce} due to Moffat, Wissner & Cooper, Commiss^{rs} of Conspiracy for Orange	7085	42	3	11

APPENDIX III

MISCELLANEA

FIRST GENERAL COMMISSION OF COMMISSIONERS
FOR CONSPIRACIES

THE PEOPLE OF THE STATE OF NEW YORK by the Grace Rev. MSS. of God free and Independant   To William Wills, Soverinas 40 : 156 Cock, and James McMasters of the County of Tryon, John (State Compt.) M Beekman Jeremiah V. Rensselaer, Isaac Fonda, Matthew Vischer Hugh Mitchel Cornelius Humfrey, John McClung and Peter Wynkoop of the County of Albany, Cornelius C Wynkoop, Cornelius C Schoonmaker, and Peter Cantine 1778 Apr. 4. (Son of Matthew Cantine Esquire) of the County of Ulster, Israel Honeywell Jonathan G. Tomkins and Joseph Strang of the County of West Chester, Zephaniah Platt, Egbert Benson and Israel Thompson of the County of Dutchess, Henry Wisner, Thomas Moffat and Gilbert Cuyper, of the County of Orange, and Alexander Webster, Alexander McNitt, and Ebenezer Clark of the County of Charlotte Esquires Greeting,   KNOW YE that pursuant to two certain Acts of the Legislature of our Said State the one entitled: "An Act to appoint Commissioners for detecting and defeating Conspiracies and declaring their powers," and the other entitled, "An Act for encreasing the Number of Commissioners for detecting and defeating Conspiracies within this State." WE HAVE appointed constituted and assigned, and by these presents do appoint constitute and assign you the said

William Wills Soverinas Cock, James McMasters, John M Beekman, Jeremiah Van Rensselaer, Isaac Fonda, Matthew Vischer, Hugh Mitchell, Cornelius Humfrey, John McClung, Peter Wynkoop, Cornelius C Wynkoop Cornelius C Schoonmaker, Peter Cantine, Israel Honeywell, Jonathan G. Tomkins, Joseph Strang, Zephaniah Platt, Egbert Benson, Israel Thompson, Henry Wisner, Thomas Moffat, Gilbert Cuyper, Alexander Webster, Alexander McNitt and Ebenezer Clark Commissioners for enquiring into detecting and defeating all Conspiracies which may be formed in this State against the Liberties of America, with full power and Authority to you and any and every three of you to do and perform the several Acts Matters and Things in the said two several Acts mentioned, which by you or any three of you as Commissioners as aforesaid may be lawfully done and performed. IN TESTIMONY whereof we have caused these our Letters to be made Patent and the Great Seal of our said State to be hereunto affixed. WITNESS our trusty and well beloved George Clinton Esquire Governor of our said State, General and Commander in Chief of all the Militia and Admiral of the Navy of the same the fourth Day of April in the Year of our Lord one thousand seven hundred and seventy eight.

Geo: Clinton

By His Excellency's Command,
    Jnᵒ Morin Scott Secretary
        A true Copy, Examined by me,
           Teunis Tappan Secʸ

Endorsed:
        Appᵗ of Commissioners of
        Conspiracy 4ᵗʰ April 1778.

OATHS[1]

I............... do solemnly swear and declare in the presence of Almighty God that I ought not and do not acknowledge any Allegiance to the King of Great Brittain, his Heirs or Successors or any power or Authority of the Parliament of the said Kingdom of Great Brittain, and that I will bear true faith and Allegiance to the State of New York as a free and Independant State, and that I will in all things to the best of my knowledge and Ability do my Duty as a good Subject of the said State ought to do, So help me God,

[Signatures]

Ebenezar Allen
Adam Vrooman
Daniel Chase
his
Jonathan X Chase
Mark
James X Lake
Daniel Mosher
Ishmel Reynolds
his
John X Van Hining
Mark
Charles Near
his
Nicholas X Boss
Mark
his
Jacob X Finehout
Mark
his
Peter X Finehout
Mark

Joseph Greenman
Benjamin Greenman ju[2]
Mindert Van Hoesan
Jeremije mullr
his
William X Bartel
Mark
his
Mathewis X Pool
Mark
his
Tobias X Salsbury
Mark
John Cobham[2]

[1] From the manuscript minutes, vol 1, pp. 240–243.
[2] These signatures were attached to the oath at various times in 1778 and 1779.

I ——— do hereby solemnly without any mental Reservation or Equivocation whatsoever swear and declare and call God to witness that I renounce and Adjure all Allegiance to the King of Great Britain and that I will bear true Faith and Allegiance to the State of New York as a free and Independant State, and that I will in all Things to the best of my Knowledge and Ability do my Duty as a good and faithful Subject of the said State ought to do — so help me God —

    Sworn 12th Augt 1782⎱   Arch^d McNeil
      before me at Albany⎰   [*Signatures*]
      Saml Stringer Justice.

The above Oath administred by
me to Abner Darling the 10th Abner Darling
Day of October 1782.   [*Signatures*]
    John M: Beeckman Justice

I . . . . . do solemnly and without any mental Reservation or equivocation whatsoever Swear and call God to Witness that I beleive & acknowledge the State of New York to be of Right a free and Independent State and that no authority or power can of right be exercised in or over the said State but what is or shall be granted by or derived from the People thereof and further that as a good Subject of the said free and Independant State of New York I will to the best of my knowledge and Ability faithfully do my duty, and as I shall keep or disregard this Oath so help and deal with me Almighty God.

    John Visger   Duncan MacDougall
    Volckert Van Veghten   Corn^s Van Schelluyne
[*Signatures*]   R^t Bleecker

[*Signatures*]

Robt Clench
John Glen
Hendrick Frey
John Duncan
Barnet Stilwell
Peter W. Yates
Henry Ten Eyck
Gysbert Fonda
Corn^s Glen
Daniel Campbell
James Ellice

I Leonard Gansevoort Junr Clerk to the Commissioners of the County of Albany appointed for detecting & defeating all Conspiracies which may be formed in this State against the Liberties of America do most solemnly swear in the Presence of Almighty God, that I will keep secret all such Matters as shall be given me in Charge by the said Commissioners and that I shall remain under such Injunction till discharged therefrom by the said Commissioners —
Leon^d Gansevoort Junr [1]

CERTIFICATION OF TORIES.

To John Morin Scott Esqr Secretary of the State of New York —

We John M. Beekman, Mathew Visscher and Isaac D. Fonda Esq^rs Commissioners appointed for enquiring into detecting and defeating all Conspiracies which may be formed in this State against the Liberties of America agreeable to the Directions of an Act of the Legislature of the State of New York entitled "an Act more effectually to prevent the

New York
Col. MSS.
101 : 149
(NYSL)

1778
Sept. 22.

---

[1] The entire oath is in Gansevoort's handwriting, and was subscribed to by him on April 24, 1778. For facsimile see Vol. I, p. 292.

Mischiefs arising from the Influence and Example of Persons
of equivocal and suspected Characters in this State" do
hereby certify that in Pursuance of the said Act we have
caused the following Persons to come before us viz.ᵗ David
Van Schaack of the District of Kinderhook on the Thirtieth
Day of August last, Nicholas Stevens of the Township of
Schonectady on the Fifteenth Day of August last, Henry Van
Schaack of the District of Kinderhook on the Seventeenth
Day of August last, and Lambert Burghart of the District
of Kinderhook on the twenty first Day of August last Alex-
ander Campbell of the Township of Schonectady on the
Seventh Day of September Instant and Martin Crom of
Claverack District on the Fourteenth Day of September
Instant and offered to administer to them respectively the
Oath therein mentioned which the said David Van Schaack,
Nicholas Stevens, Henry Van Schaack Lambert Burghart,
Alexander Campbell and Martin Crom severally refused to
take   As Witness our Hands and seals this twenty second
Day of September in the Year One thousand seven hundred
and seventy eight

John M: Beeckman   [Seal]
Mat: Visscher   [Seal]
Isaac D Fonda   [Seal][1]

New York
Col. MSS.
102 : 30
(NYSL)

1783
Feb. 8.

List of the Names of Persons who have refused to take the
Oath prescribed by a Law of this State to be taken by Persons
of neutral and equivocal Characters and who have in Consequence thereof been removed within the Enemy's Lines
or detained by his Excellency the Governor for Exchange.

Richard Cartwright   Richard Minifee
Peter Vosburgh   John Stevenson
Lowrence Goes   Absolom Woodworth

[1] The body of this document is in the handwriting of Leonard Gansevoort, Jr., and is signed by the Commissioners.

Harmen Pruyn   John Cumming
William Rea   Isaac Man
Barent Van Der Pool   John Kortz Jun.ʳ
Andries Huyck   Alexander White
Benjamin Baker   √ Dirck Gardinier
Henry Van Dyck   Mathew Goes Jun.ʳ
James Dole   √ John D. Goes
Marte Van Buren   John Van Alen
David Van Schaack   Henry Van Schaack
Nicholas Stevens   √ Lambert Burghart
John Thurman   Alexander Campbell
Peter Van Schaack   √ Martin Crom
    Andries Ten Eyck

Those marked (√) were to have been sent down with the Van Schaack's but secreted themselves and could not then be found and are now at their respective Homes — they with the Van Schaacks &c had been reserved for Exchange by the Governor.

Albany 8 Feb.ʸ 1783
    Stewart Dean   ⎤ Commiss.ʳˢ
    John M. Beeckman ⎬ for
    Sam.ˡ Stringer   ⎦ Conspiracies[1]

Endorsed: Return of
    the Persons
    banished by
    by Commiss.ʳˢ
    at Albany

AN EXCHANGE.

May it please your Excellency.

Having been a Prisoner on Parole to the Commissioners of Conspiracy for these two years past, & confined to the Town of Schenectady, not being allowed to reside on my Farm, —

New York
Col. MSS.
102 : 19
(NYSL)

1781
Mar. 30.

[1] The body of this document is in the handwriting of Leonard Gansevoort, Jr., and is signed by the Commissioners.

my Property not protected; — These, with other Reasons, induce me to wish for Permission to remove to Canada with my Family.— I have therefor[e] presumed to apply to your Excellency for Permission to be exchanged for some Citizen of this State now a Prisoner in Canada, and that I may be allowed to go under the Protection of the first public Flagg.— I will do myself the Honor to wait personally upon your Excellency at any Hour that may be convenient.— An Answer from your Excellency will much oblige,

Your most obedient
& very humble serv^t

His Excellency   John Stuart.
    Governor Clinton.

Albany March 30th 1781

I hereby signify my Consent and Approbation to the Exchange of John Stuart agreable to his above Request. Given at Albany this 30th March 1781

Geo: Clinton

Addressed: *Endorsed:*
    To   John Stuart permitted to be
His Excellency   exchanged by the Gov-
Governor Clinton   ernor
    Albany   March 30th 1781
                       filed in the Secretary's Of-
                       fice the 30th day of March
                       1781 —

See Analytical Index
Vol. III.

MINUTES OF THE COMMISSIONERS FOR DETECTING AND DEFEATING CONSPIRACIES IN THE STATE OF NEW YORK

ALBANY COUNTY SESSIONS, 1778-1781

VOLUME III
ANALYTICAL INDEX

MINUTES
of
Commissioners
for
Conspiracies

MINUTES of the Commissioners for detecting and defeating Conspiracies IN THE STATE OF NEW YORK

ALBANY COUNTY SESSIONS, 1778–1781
Edited by VICTOR HUGO PALTSITS, State Historian

VOLUME III : ANALYTICAL INDEX

PUBLISHED by the STATE OF NEW YORK, ALBANY, 1910

Reported to the Legislature
May 2d, 1910

Albany, N. Y.
J. B. Lyon Company, State Printers
1910

PREFATORY NOTE

THE general plan for this analytical index was devised by the State Historian, who personally indexed the first one hundred and thirty-eight pages. From this point the work was continued to the end by Dr. Richard E. Day, Chief Clerk of this office, to whose patience and efficiency its consummation is due.

A few words may suffice to elucidate the scheme of this index. It is closely analytical, by persons, places and subjects. The vagaries that occur in personal and place nomenclature, so common to the period, have been preserved in parentheses after the standard entry or are pointed out by cross-references, which have been used freely for this purpose, as well as for calling attention to correlated or synonymous topics. It should be noted that the condensed form "commissioners," when unaccompanied by any other designation, signifies "Commissioners for detecting and defeating Conspiracies in the State of New York;" similarly, "Albany board," "Charlotte county board," "Poughkeepsie board," etc., are short forms for the boards of commissioners for conspiracies in the respective sections of the State. The initials *I* and *J* in personal names are generally written alike in the manuscripts, on the line, and some uncertainty as to interpretation has resulted. Usually, the printed text prefers *J* for unverified names.

This volume completes the set and will, I trust, be an acceptable magnet with which to extract the ore from a rich mine of operations of commissioners for conspiracies during the American Revolution.

VICTOR HUGO PALTSITS,

May 7, 1910.   State Historian.

5

ERRATA

174, foot-note—For "the arrest of" read "fetching up as guide."

296—The text states that the surprise of Baylor's dragoons occurred in New Jersey.   It took place at Tappan, N. Y.

399, line 14 from bottom—For "his" read "this."

533, line 14 from top—The name in the text is erroneous and should read "John M. Dorn."

6

ANALYTICAL INDEX

A ARSE. See Aerse.

Abbot, Joel, lodges information against Jacob Timmerman, 634, 635, 639.

Abeel, David, kidnapped with his son, 704.

Abramse, Anthony, of Rensselaerwyck Manor, yeoman, bailsman for Frederick Boonstel, 459.

Achquetuck (Acquatough, Aquatuck, Auckquetough, Auckquetuck, Hackatough, Hacketock), Albany county, residents of, 568, 570, 577, 581, 583, 741.

Adam, John, deputy-commissary of prisoners at Peekskill, ordered to send prisoners who are officers to New York, 272; asks that officers of New Levies may be sent to New York, 295, 299.

Adams, Elijah, sergeant, apprehends persons refusing to pay fines, 644; his prisoners forcibly delivered, 644–645, 646.

Adams, Jesse, suspicious character apprehended at Stephentown, 738; committed, 738.

Adams (Adems), Robert, of Johnstown, merchant, inquiry regarding his conduct at time of destruction of Caughnawaga, 451; effort to relieve him from

Adams, Robert—continued.
imprisonment by habeas corpus defeated, 458; application for his release denied, 475; released on bail, 493; allowed to visit Johnstown on business, 612.

Adams, William, of Albany, released on bail, 338.

Adgate, Matthew, of Kings district, justice of peace, forwards information touching Daniel Green and others, 452; order to, for arrest of Jonah Case, 453; issues warrant for arrest of Joel Pratt and Hezekiah Hammond, 461; course of conduct suggested to, for dealing with Shakers, 461; writes to Albany board respecting persons committed to jail, 461; forwards examinations respecting Major Zadock Wright, 506–507; sends prisoner to Albany, 507, 517; advises release of prisoner, 518.

Aerse (Aarse), Isaac, of Sir John Johnson's corps, prisoner, 558; released on bail, 668.

Aerson (Arsin), Mathew (Matthew), ferryman at Albany, account for ferrying Ryley's rangers across the Hudson, 49, 233, 810; ordered not to ferry any of

7

Albany, city—continued.

bailed person forbidden to leave, 549; efforts made in, to dissuade persons from bearing arms, 552; Coxsackie militia in, 565; Albany board meets at city hall in, 582; prisoner granted liberty of city hall in, 600, 602–603; inhabitants of, sign petition in behalf of Jane Moffit, 619; suggestion that soldiers be sent from, to Helderbergs, 676; delinquents to be brought to city hall of, 679; prisoner on way to, escapes, 684; person advised to surrender to commissioners at, 695; fort in, marks limit of residence prescribed to bailed person, 703; party of levies detained in, 728; encounter with dangerous tory near, 729; Thomas Chittenden gives pass to, 739; despatches from Canada brought to, 755, 759, 760; capture of resident in neighborhood of, 759; supposed plot to kidnap mayor of, 763; person returning from Canada lurking near, 767.

Albany county, 82; 83; 86; 88; 89; 105; 680; commissioners for conspiracies in, 9, 12, 29, 33, 35, ff., 42, 43, 63, ff., 67, 79; night watch in, 20; representation of grievances from districts of, received by legislature, 27; assemblymen from, 31, 48; only incomplete minutes extant of

Albany county—continued.

commissioners in, 36, 63, 64; meetings of Albany board, where held, 36; secretary, treasurer, doorkeeper of Albany board, 37; deserters from Burgoyne given passes to go at large in, 39, 86, 89, 91, 98, 133, 159, 207, 224, 352; rangers employed by committee of city and county, 47 (note); disturbances by disaffected persons in, 50; correspondence kept up between Poughkeepsie and Albany boards, 51; robberies in, 52, 98; secretary of committee of city and county, 65 (note); officers in regiments of, to report names of men absent from their homes, 139; request to representatives of city and county in assembly, 150; oath of neutrality taken before committee of, 200; committee of, confines tory suspect, 221; officers of militia in, to report names of persons who have joined enemy, 238; person paroled by committee of, 264; court of general sessions of, 265, 274; information sent to representatives of city and county in legislature, 268; negro confined by committee of, 304; restrictions imposed by committee of, 331; committee of, advises that dangerous person be cited before commissioners, 386–387; committee of, advises

Alt, Nicholas — continued.

Albany, 364; charge against, to be examined, 364; released on bail, 385, 386; his bail to be prosecuted, 673.

Ammunition, to be furnished volunteer rangers raised in Manor of Rensselaerwyck, 50, 358; to be provided for company of horse employed by Albany board, 50; taken from prisoners by Albany board, 105; furnished to Indians and tories by persons in Albany, 157; seized on wrong information and restored, 602; Shakers accused of purchasing, 724.

Anderson, Alexander, prisoner, removed from Albany jail to fort, 128.

Anderson, Alexander, sent prisoner by Colonel Alden to General Stark, 241; delivered to Albany board, 242; committed, 242; released on bail, 265; reported to be with enemy, 289; bailsman required to deliver him up, 289; brings information about Brant and Butler at Chemung, 293; receives gratuity from Albany board, 293, 811; letter respecting, written to Colonel William Butler, 293.

Anderson, John, apprehended and committed, 739.

Anderson, Thomas, blacksmith, arrest ordered on charge of encouraging negroes to desert their masters and of forging a

Anderson, Thomas — continued.

pass, 142–143; ordered confined, 146; Albany board seeks information regarding, 152; released on bail, 161.

Andrew, Elisha, gives evidence regarding Amos Moore, 414, 415.

Andrew, John, of Newtown, laborer, apprehended on way to Canada to join enemy, 447; committed, 448; released on bail, 649; order for his arrest, 693–694; confined, 694.

Andrew, Thomas, of Newtown, yeoman, confined by order of Albany magistrates, 456; released on bail, 457.

Angle, Jacob, of the Beaver Dam, sent prisoner to Albany, 255; committed, 255; examined and recommitted, 256; attempted to join Brant, 277; released on bail, 277.

Angle, Peter, bailsman for Jacob Angle, 277.

Annin, Daniel, of Dutchess county, allowed to examine prisoners in jail about stolen property, 243.

Any, George, certificate concerning, 384; liberated on bail, 384.

Any, Godfrey, bailsman for George Any, 384.

Aple. See also Apple, Appley.

Aple, George, Hessian deserter from British army, takes oath of neutrality, 204.

Apple, Hendrick, bailsman for John Scheffer, 218.

14　　　　State of New York

Bail. See Bonds, Recognizances.

Baily, Hugh, witness against Jacob Best, 686, 688–689.

Baker, Mrs., widow, informs Albany board of property stolen from her in summer of 1777, 128, 149.

Baker, Albert, of Charlotte county, justice of peace, sends dangerous persons to Albany, 508.

Baker, Benjamin, released on recognizance and enlisting in continental army, 107; bailsman for Zachariah Overmagh, 127.

Baker, Benjamin, of Rensselaerwyck, cited to appear before Albany board, 177; refuses oath of allegiance, 177–178; committed to jail for contempt, 178; advised of day for removal, 191; his refusal certified to secretary of state, 197–198; in list of persons removed to enemy's lines or held for exchange, 835.

Baker, Deborah, witness against Thomas Blewer, 508.

Baker, Ebenezer, paid by Albany board for services, 94.

Baker, Edward, bailsman for Samuel and John Perry, 97.

Baker, Samuel, of Rensselaerwyck Manor, weaver, examined and discharged, 473; has in his possession British commissions and proclamations, 658; arrested and committed, 658; released on bail, 714.

Baker, William, bailsman for

Baker, William — continued.
James Bruce, 378; required to deliver up Bruce, 773.

Baker, a, 495.

Baldwin, Alexander, of Stillwater, farmer, bailsman for Joseph Carr, 608, 619.

Ball, Jacob, cited to appear before Albany board, 182; goes to enemy, 255; sent prisoner from Schenectady to Albany, 468.

Ball, Jacob, Jr., of the Beaver Dam, farmer, suspect, released on bail, 84; cited to show cause why recognizance should not be forfeited, 163; released on bail, 519.

Ball, John, tory, sent prisoner from Schenectady to Albany, 468.

Ball, John, Jr., of the Beaver Dam, laborer, released on bail, 520.

Ball, Peter, of the Beaver Dam, charged with enlisting men for enemy's service, 611; to be apprehended, 611.

Ball, William. See Bell, William.

Ballard, William, captain, persons apprehended by, examined by commissioners, 208, 211–212; accused of seizing and appropriating private property, 300–301; charge against, referred to General James Clinton, 301.

Ballinger, Peter, of Tryon county, signs instrument committing persons to custody of sheriff, 431.

Bartel, William — continued.
witnesses against, 324, 325; discharged on taking oath of allegiance, 325; his signature, with mark, to oath, 831.

Bartle, John, disaffected person, to be apprehended, 575; allowed to bring evidence to disprove charges, 584.

Bartley, Oliver, cited as witness against persons in Hoosick, 688–689.

Barton (Bartin), William, of Newtown, farmer, bondsman for John A. Concklin, 112, 467; account for conveying him from Coxsackie to Albany, 156.

Bartow, George, of Colonel Gansevoort's regiment, his charge against James Furnwall, 302.

Bartram, Christian, of the Helderbergs, asks for liberation of Hessian deserter, 207.

Bass, Daniel, of Dutchess county, tory suspect, ordered confined, 89; ordered sent to commissioners at Fishkill, 123; sent to hospital at Albany, 126; certificate from committee of Dutchess county favorable to, 130; released on bail subject to appearance before committee of Fredericksburgh, 130.

Bass, Nicholas, tory suspect, ordered confined, 89.

Basset (Besset), Martha, witness against Robert Martin, 352, 354.

Batavia, Greene county, scouts to be sent to, 401.

Batchelor (Batchalor, Batchelar, Batchelder), Zepheniah (Zephaniah), of Tryon county, justice, request to, for placing Albert Van Der Werken under recognizance, 271; complies with request, 283; request to, for placing tory deserters from enemy under recognizance, 284–285; joins in statement of charges against Philip Helmer, 371; writes about removal of prisoners by General Clinton, 381; prisoners from Tryon county to appear before, 382, 383, 386; takes recognizance of Michael Van Cougnot, 388; writes to Albany board, 400; brings prisoner before Albany board, 557; orders arrest of Albert Van Der Werken, 560; makes return of women whose husbands have joined enemy, 560; warrant transmitted to, 563; citation transmitted to, 591; requested to take recognizance of witnesses to appear at court, 593–594; sends information about William Laird and Dr. Tice, 682; warrant forwarded to, 682; informs Albany board of William Laird's enlistment, 707; informs Albany board of John Coppernoll's removal, 750.

Bateau, requested by Albany board for use of rangers, 48, 144; enlistment under Captain Teunis H. Visscher in service

Boom, Matthias (Mathias), guide, ordered to attend meeting of Albany board, 144; express sent to Coeymans for, 174.

Boon, Peter, of Tryon county, to be examined, 628.

Boonstel. See also Bonestel, Bonistel.

Boonstel (Bonestel), Frederick, of Rensselaerwyck Manor, weaver, confined for going to the enemy, 149; examined and released on bail, 149; his bail augmented on account of depreciation of currency, 459.

Borst, Peter, of Schoharie, farmer, bailsman for William Loucks, 500.

Boskerk. See also Van Buskerk.

Boskerk, Lowrence, bailsman for Isaac L. Witbeck, Joachim Collier and John G. Klauw, 160.

Boskerk, Martin, bailsman for Joseph Concklin, 112.

Boss, Nicholas, released on bail and taking oath, 104; his signature, with mark, to oath, 831.

Bottger, Andries, deserter from British army, takes oath of neutrality, 201; allowed to live in Schoharie, 201.

Bought. See Boght.

Bound Brook (Broock), N. J., continental soldier at, deserts to enemy, 412.

Bourn, Thomas, deserter from Burgoyne, apprehended as suspicious character, 553; discharged, 553.

Bovee. See also Bovie.

Bovee, Rykert, of Maple Town, farmer, bailsman for John Hodkison, 675.

Bovie (Bovee), Abraham, of Hoosick district, farmer, ordered to assist in apprehending men who have returned from Canada, 151; bailsman for Jacob Timmerman, 664.

Bovie, Philip, bailsman for Joseph Devall, 106.

Bowen, Timothy, ordered to arrest persons who have rescued prisoner from officer, 372.

Bowen, William, released on bail, 169; his reimprisonment decided on, 473; to be forwarded from Schenectady to commissary of prisoners, 497-498, 506.

Bower, Nicholas, lieutenant, brings prisoner from Livingston Manor to Albany, 653.

Bowman, Andrew, of Rensselaerwyck Manor, accused of intending to join enemy, 475-476.

Bowmans (Bowman's) Kill, Montgomery county, 432.

Boyd, James, bailsman for Janet Clement, 227; bailsman for Alexander Carson, 370.

Boyd, John, bailsman for James Blakely, 148; bailsman for Alexander McAuley, 164; bailsman for John Purves, John Murray, John Howard and Dougall McAslin, 249; receives permission to take Janet Clement to Philadelphia, 320; sur-

Brant, Joseph — continued.
for attempt to join, 277; at
Chemung, 293; deserter from,
confined, 293; despatches for,
from New York, 329; prisoner
who was lately under his command, 349; prisoner supposed
to have been with, 375; follower
of, in border devastations apprehended, 387, 539.

Bratt. See also Bradt.

Bratt, John, of the Helderbergs,
farmer, released on bail and
oath, 512–513.

Brattleboro (Brattleborough), Vt.,
residents of, 312, 549, 559;
petition that paroled tory be
allowed to remove to, 312–313.

Breadfrick, John, of Stone Arabia,
farmer, bailsman for Jacob Merkle, 433.

Breakabeen (Beakabeen), Schoharie county, party of men sent
there to intercept tories, 323;
residents of, 613, 623.

Breise. See Bresie, Brisie.

Bremerman, Frederick, Hessian
deserter from British army, examined and discharged, 172.

Bresie. See also Brisie.

Bresie (Briese), Benjamin, of
Rensselaerwyck Manor, witness
in case of Myndert Van Hoosen
and others, 324, 325.

Bresie, Gabriel, of Rensselaerwyck Manor, summoned to
testify against Myndert Van
Hoosen and others, 324.

Bresie, Hendrick, of Rensselaer-

Bresie, Hendrick — continued.
wyck Manor, witness in case of
Myndert Van Hoosen and
others, 324, 325.

Bresie (Breise), Janake (Janakie),
of Rensselaerwyck Manor, witness in case of Myndert Van
Hoosen and others, 324, 325.

Brevoort, Henry (Hendrick), of
Newtown, farmer, bailsman for
Peter Van Campen, 428, 467.

Brewster, N., money paid to, insert opp. 821.

Brickmakers, 691.

Brisben. See also Brisbin.

Brisben (Brisbin), James, of Saratoga district, farmer, sent prisoner to Albany on charge of
harboring spy, 554; examined
and recommitted, 595; on bail
within prescribed limits, 600,
607, 676; allowed to go to Saratoga, 621, 650, 676; allowed to
live at Saratoga, 727.

Brisben, Robert, of Saratoga,
farmer, tory suspect, on bail
within Saratoga district, 353;
required to renew his bail, 520,
532; goes to Canada, 736; his
bail forfeited, 736–737.

Brisbin, William, given pass, 85–
86.

Brisie. See also Bresie.

Brisie, William, of Rensselaerwyck Manor, his charges against
Myndert Van Hoosen and
others, 324.

Broachim (Broachiam), John, of
Schenectady, farmer, sent pris-

Butternuts—continued.
oners ask permission to go to, to recover papers, 262, 276; persons captured by Oneidas at, discharged, 263; prisoner from, enlists in continental army, 301.

CADOGAN, Barney, of Schoharie, complaint against, discharged, 727.
Cafort, John, arrest ordered for robbery, 144.
Cagnuago. See Caughnawaga.
Caine, John, suspect, confined, 329.
Caldwell, ———, warrant for his arrest on charge of active toryism, 357.
Caldwell, Jacob, money paid to, 814.
Caldwell, James, of Albany, merchant, his bill for writing paper, 184 (note); bailsman for John Cobham, 221; bailsman for John Maginness, 300; bailsman for Duncan McConnelly, 359; surrender of Maginness and McConnelly demanded of, 491; bailsman for Robert Adams, 493; bailsman for Ezekiel Ensign, 604.
Caldwell, Robert, of Schaghticoke, weaver, released on bail, 589–590.
Cambridge, Washington county, residents of, 87–88, 91, 92, 712.
Cambridge district, Washington county, petition from officers of,

Cambridge district—continued.
81; residents of, 82, 87–88, 91, 92, 110, 111, 127–128, 129, 130, 134, 152, 219, 242, 397, 553; supposed spy residing in, 417.
Cammeron, Sarah, of Hoosick district, warned to remove from state, 528.
Campbell (Mrs.), of Cherry Valley, wife of Colonel Samuel Campbell, prisoner in Canada, exchanged, 563; gives information touching John Docksteder, 563.
Campbell, Alexander, of Dutchess county, arrest ordered on suspicion of robbery, 97–98; arrested and confined, 99; Albany commissioners request General Schuyler to secure and send him to them, 100.
Campbell, Alexander (Archibald), of Schenectady, cited before Albany board, 225; refuses oath of allegiance, 225; to go to Canada, 225–226; instructions for his removal, 228; his refusal of oath certified to secretary of state, 240, 833–834; in list of persons removed or held for exchange, 835.
Campbell, Archibald. See Campbell, Alexander, of Schenectady.
Campbell, Archibald, of Cambridge district, farmer, exonerated of disloyalty, 87; released on bail, 88; bailsman for Daniel Marsh, 136, 137; furnishes new bail, 626.

Clinton, George—continued.

commissioners for conspiracies, 12, 777, 782; issues proclamation for reconvening legislature (Dec. 15, 1777), 15; empowered to remove dangerous disaffected persons, 17, 780–781; required to certify data about dangerous disaffected persons to commissioners of sequestration, 17, 781; empowered to detain for exchanges persons attainted, 19, 786; passes granted British military prisoners to appeal for exchange to, 41, 255; his opinion taken as to paroles, 44; requests Albany board to show leniency to certain tory prisoners, 45, 265; Albany board intercedes with, for pardon of accomplice in robbery, who turns State's evidence, 53, 259; pardons robber condemned to death, 53, 279; address of senate to, about suppression of robberies, 54; legislature orders him to issue proclamation against plundering British subjects, 55; legislature requests him to ask governors of New Jersey and Connecticut to issue proclamations against plundering, 55; complaints by Albany board to, against General Stark, 57, 170; names of tories to be removed, certified to, 57, 175, 218, 223, 268; might detain tories for exchanges, 57, 58, 175, 223; tories denied tem-

Clinton, George—continued.

porary suspension of removal to appeal to, 57–58, 184; Albany board interrogated him as to authority in doubtful cases, 58; captured lieutenant given pass to, for arranging his exchange, 58, 255; requested Albany board to assist in arranging certain exchanges, 59, 303; original papers of, in New York State Library, 65, 170 (note), 178 (note), 179 (note), 184 (note), 205 (note), 206 (note), 209 (note), 211 (note), 230 (note), 237 (note), 239 (note), 240 (note), 243 (note), 244 (note), 265 (note), 272 (note), 273 (note), 281 (note), 303 (note), 414 (note), 467 (note), 471 (note), 535 (note), 545–546 (note), 774 (note); correspondence of, with Albany board, 65–66; certain tory suspects arrested upon request of, 87; Poughkeepsie board requested by Albany board to call upon, about charges against certain persons, 92; replies to complaints of Albany board against General Stark, 178; notified that seven persons from Vermont will be sent by General Stark to enemy's lines, 179; asked by Albany board to remove paroled tory and women whose husbands are with enemy, 184; writes to Albany board, 205; asked by Albany board to

Clinton, George—continued.
examinations of imprisoned officers sent to, 765; correspondence of Albany board with 774
(note); authorized to permit
temporary use of unoccupied
frontier farms, 796; authorized to
fortify frontier dwellings, 797;
authorized to remove tories living
on frontier, 798; authorized to
remove or destroy stock, grain
or forage, 798–799; charge
for messenger to, 807; witnesses commission of commissioners, 830; tories held by,
for exchange, 834, 835; application to, for permission to be
exchanged, 835–836; his approval of application for exchange, 836.
Clinton, Henry (Sir), British commander, his proclamation read
at tory meeting, 636, 637, 639,
641, 644, 645, 649, 657, 670;
his proclamations distributed,
638, 645, 653, 658; his offers of
peace, 687.
Clinton, James, general, engaged
in arranging exchange of inhabitants of Cherry Valley,
captive in Canada, 59, 303,
304; charge against Captain
Ballard referred to, 301; asked
to have tories at Peesink apprehended, 323; orders Lieutenant Conine to apprehend
tories, 323; delivers to Albany
board persons captured on way
to join enemy, 329; advises that

Clinton, James—continued.
Zadock Wright be retained in
Kings district until exchanged,
343; unable to aid in apprehending robbers, 355; about to go on
western expedition, 355; delivers prisoners to Albany board,
360; requested to define nature
of crime committed by prisoner,
361; orders that persons confined at Johnstown be sent to
Albany, 364, 371, 380, 381,
382, 385; copy of examination
of robber sent to, 388; information received from Fort Schuyler, conveyed to, 596; writes to
Albany board concerning John
Palmer, 669; orders Dr. Smith
to prepare for exchange, 675;
informed that persons from the
enemy are collecting in Helderbergs, 676; presents to Albany
board information from Catskill, 679; addresses Albany
board in behalf of Dr. George
Smith, 683; Albany board
advizes him to release certain
prisoners, 690; prisoners apprehended by his order, bailed,
697–698, 699; advised of commissioners' approval of Mrs.
Welsh's request, 698; asked
to aid in capture of tory party,
700; deserter delivered to, 700;
his aide-de-camp, 703; con-
sents to liberation of Hazelton
Spencer, 703; suggests removal of tories from Ballston,
724; transfers party of levies

Coenly, John — continued.
bail, 578–579; discharged from obligation to appear at court 617.
Coenradt. See also Coonradt.
Coenradt, Johannis, of Durlach, charge against, 751; committed, 752.
Coenradt, Philip, of Rensselaerwyck Manor, farmer, receives counterfeit money, 544; bound in recognizance to testify in court, 544.
Coeymans (Coyemans), Albany county, party of rangers sent by way of, to neighborhood of Peesink, 144; express sent to, by Albany board, 174; militia party ordered to, 566; prisoners brought from, to Albany, 566–567; hostile persons to be intercepted at, 677; suspicious character at house on road to, 681.
Coeymans Hollow. See Achquetuck.
Coeyman's Patent, Albany county, resident of, 731.
Coffin, William, bailsman for Daniel Folger, 141.
Coffman, David, of Durlach, charge against, 752; committed, 752.
Cogh. See also Coch, Cock, Cough, Kogh.
Cogh, Andries, German prisoner, released on bail, 697.
Cogh, Casper, of Stone Arabia, farmer, bailsman for Daniel Hewson, Jr., 668.

Cohoon, Peter, supposed British spy, 472, 473; physician in Albany charged with aiding, 477; William Pemberton charged with aiding, 488.
Colbreath (Colbrath), William, lieutenant, reward to, for apprehending follower of Brant, 349, 811.
Cole, Mrs., wife of Peter Cole, sent to Albany as accessory to robberies, 199–200; committed, 200; removed to hospital on account of illness, 224; indulgence to, in matter of residence, 237.
Cole, Gerrit, son of Peter Cole, sent to Albany under guard, as accessory to robbery of Henry Van Rensselaer, 121; examined and recommitted, 164; released on bail, 173.
Cole, John, suspected person, request for his arrest, 686.
Cole, Nicholas, warrant for his arrest as dangerous person, 419.
Cole, Peter (Petrus), sent to Albany under guard, as accessory to robbery of Henry Van Rensselaer, 121; examined and recommitted, 147, 164; removed, with his wife, to hospital on account of illness, 224.
Colehamer (Colekamer), Andries, assists in rescuing delinquents from officer, 644.
Colehamer, Coenradt, apprehended for helping to rescue

Comrs. for Consp.— continued.
to keep minutes, 36, 64; minutes of Albany county board, only extant, 36, 63, 64; Albany board's minutes incomplete, 36, 63, 64, 774 (note); meetings of Albany board, where held, 36; sub-boards of the county boards, 36; activities of, revealed by financial accounts, 36; where financial data of, are now kept, 36; expenditures, how conducted, 37; issued warrants to constables against counterfeiters, etc., 38; use good money found upon counterfeiters to reimburse persons defrauded, 38, 282–283, 285; advertise for persons defrauded by counterfeiters, 38, 287; disposal of deserters by Albany board, 39–40; did not exercise extra-judicial authority in murder cases, 40; concerned with arrest of murderers or suspects, 40; could release persons duly acquitted from charges of murder, 40; system of issuing passes by Albany board, 40–41; procedure of, for making arrests, 41; system of, in relation to prisoners, 41–47; Albany board posts notices for appearance of prisoners on release, 42; return of prisoners in confinement procured by Albany board, 43, 80, 127; prevent local committees from exercising functions of, 43, 81; authorize military officers to examine certain

Comrs. for Consp.— continued.
persons and issue recognizances, 43; Albany board objects to conduct of certain whigs against disaffected persons, 43–44, 185, 197; disaffected persons to be brought before them, accompanied by charges, 43–44, 185; issuance and voiding of mittimus by, 44, 155, 188, 230, 231; mittimus issued by, prevented judges and magistrates from bailing persons, 44, 155; 779; disown discharge of negro prisoner of war by General Stark, 44, 232; Albany board orders removal of prisoners from jail to fort, 44, 107, 200; confine prisoners from other states in Albany jail, 45; requisition for apprehension of concealed person near Worcester, Mass., 45, 224; issue pass to prisoner confined by court martial, 45, 231–232; release prisoners captured by the Oneidas, 45, 263, 266, 271, 273; imprison women as well as men, 45; Albany board protests against undue liberty given prisoners, 45; Albany board orders arrest of spy from New York city, 45–46, 147, 150, 152–153; conduct of Albany board toward sick prisoners, 46–47, 191, 224; request sent from General Stark for dangerous prisoners in Albany hospital, 46; order of Albany board about receiving state prisoners at hos-

Comrs. for Consp.—continued.
nish return of their property in
his charge, 214; Albany board
orders removal of sick prisoners
to hospital, 214; persons arrested by Captain Ballard released by Albany board on bail,
217; Albany board inquires into
seizure of cattle by troops
stationed at Cherry Valley, 218–
219; prisoners examined by commissioners at Claverack brought
before Albany board, 220–221;
board at Claverack binds person by recognizance to appear
before Albany board, 222; commissioners at Claverack cite
neutral person to appear before
Albany board, 223; names of
persons to be removed certified
to governor by Albany board,
223; order of Albany board to
director of hospital for care of
sick prisoners and cost of their
maintenance, 224; Albany board
postpones removal to enemy's
lines of important witness, 226;
Albany board directs Captain
Nanning Visscher to superin-
tend removal of persons refusing
oath, 228; report submitted to
Albany board on cattle taken
at Butternuts by continental
troops, 230; Poughkeepsie board
writes to Albany board, 231;
money transmitted to Albany
board by state treasurer, 231,
284; Albany board transmits to
governor information touching

Comrs. for Consp.—continued.
appropriation of cattle by continental troops, 231; Albany
board notified by General Stark
that he will deliver up two
prisoners who have deserted
from Canada, 232; General
Stark asked to deliver prisoners
to commissioners, 232, 242, 245;
persons confined by Albany
board for advising others to
join Indians, 232; Albany commissioners forbid molestation of
tory prisoner's family, 233; Albany board pays bill for ferrying rangers across the Hudson,
233; Albany board entrusts £40
to Isaac D. Fonda, 234; Lieutenant Colonel William Butler
asks release of prisoner by Albany board, 234; Albany board
will furnish wood for use of
prisoners, 235; Albany board
informed of exchange of certain
tories, 237; recommendation to
General Stark from Albany
board to send to Canada women
whose husbands are with enemy,
237–238; Albany board ordered
by governor to hold certain
tories for exchange, 240–241,
310; governor orders Albany
commissioners to place Henry
Van Schaack on parole, 241;
sheriff of Tryon county ordered
to send prisoner to Albany
board, showing cause of com-
mittal, 243; Peter Cantine, Jr.,
writes to Albany commissioners

Comrs. for Consp.— continued.
apprises Albany board of journey of express from New York to Canada, 351; Albany board takes measures to stop robberies in Helderbergs, 354–355; Albany board issues warrant for troublesome tories in Schaghticoke, 357; General Clinton delivers prisoners to Albany board, 360; General Clinton requested by Albany board to define nature of crime committed by prisoner, 361; Albany board returns prisoner to Poughkeepsie board, 363; Colonel Du Bois sends to Albany board persons confined at Johnstown, 364; £100 paid to Charlotte county board for expenses, 365; Albany board sends soldiers to Helderbergs in search of robbers, 366; Albany board proceeds to Helderbergs to direct search for robbers, 367; flour secreted for exportation to be seized by order of Albany board, 371–372; Albany board directs its secretary to give written orders for provisions for prisoners, 375; Albany board recommends raising company of rangers for Helderbergs and Peesink, 377; Albany board inquires into destruction of property on pretense of disaffection, 388; two hundred dollars paid by Albany board for capture of robbers, 392;

Comrs. for Consp.— continued.
request to committee of city and county of Albany not to grant passes except on recommendation of Albany board, 394; request of Albany board to justices, 394; Albany board pays £222 16s. for securing prisoners, 397; Albany board receives intelligence that enemy threatens Catskill and Schoharie, 401; General Ten Broeck advised by Albany board to order out one eighth of militia brigade, 401; persons on recognizance notified to appear before Albany board, 402; General Schuyler informs Albany board of action of tories at Palmertown, 405; Albany board advised by General Schuyler to hold meeting at Saratoga, 405; Albany board asked to make return of prisoners in its charge to deputy commissary of prisoners, 407; expenses of Albany board at Saratoga, 410; £28 12s. paid to Jacob Slingerlandt for services to Albany board, 410; Albany board asks specification of charges against prisoners from Tryon county, 412; Albany board sends deserter to General Washington, 412; Governor Clinton requested by Albany board to send wife of tory to Canada, 414; Albany board informed that disaffected persons are believed to be in league with

Constables — continued.

325; to arrest on charge of aiding prisoner to escape, and advising soldiers to desert, 404; to arrest tory for slander against Washington and congress, 455; citation to be delivered to constable of Livingston Manor, 499; one arrests person returning from Canada, 560; one lays information before Albany board, 574; one arrests person in Hoosick district, 639; any, in Tryon county authorized to arrest William Laird, 643; one arrests Teunis Smith, 644; one arrests Dr. John Tice, 698; one apprehends suspicious characters at Stephentown, 738.

Continental Congress. See United States.

Convention, the. See New York: state.

Conway, Thomas, general, Albany board requests from him detachment to assist in hunting for robbers, 119.

Conyne. See also Conine.

Conyne, Casparus, captain, robbed, 685.

Coock. See also Cook.

Coock (Cook), Philip, of Rensselaerwyck Manor, tailor, examined and released on recognizance, 98; ordered to appear before Albany board, 497; his bail renewed, 502; bailsman for Wilhelmas Dillenback, 503.

Cook, Ichabod, released on bail, 118.

Cook, Joseph, lieutenant, warrant directed to, 466.

Cook, Peter, of Albany, merchant, bailsman for Christian Hartwick, 698.

Cooksburg (Cooksborough), of Albany county, residents of, 494, 543, 672.

Coolman, Gebhard, Hessian deserter from British army, takes oath of neutrality, 204.

Coon. See also Coons.

Coon (Coen), Coenradt, sworn into British service, 629, 630; discharged from confinement, 743.

Coonradt. See also Coenradt.

Coonradt, Frederick, Hessian, to be apprehended for persuading negroes to go to Canada, 455; required to procure surety for good behavior, 457.

Coons. See also Coon.

Coons, Jacob, of Hoosick district, constable, ordered to summon witnesses against Simon Frazer, 185.

Coons, Matthias, tory suspect, order for his arrest, 94.

Cooper, Christian, cited as witness against John M. Dorn, 307; testifies against Dorn, 308.

Cooper (Cuyper), Gilbert, lieutenant colonel, commissioner for conspiracies, Orange county board, appointment, 68; his

Courts — continued.

finds no bill against accused persons, 274, 275, 276, 278, 280; persons apprehended for attempt to join Brant give bail to appear before supreme court, 277, 278; witnesses bound to appear at supreme court, 279, 280, 418, 472, 473, 544, 593–594, 606, 672, 750; bailed persons to appear at supreme court, 280, 378, 391, 403, 413, 415, 434, 436, 437, 462, 479, 492, 493, 504, 531, 537, 562, 578, 605, 607, 618, 650, 651, 660, 663, 664, 665, 666, 669, 671, 673, 691, 693, 702, 712, 741, 749, 751; justice of peace confines suspected person to limits of his farm, 306; person rescuing drafted man from officer bound to appear before court of oyer and terminer, 379; persons guilty of destroying property to be bound over to appear at supreme court, 388; persons discharged from obligation to appear before supreme court, 393, 678; witness bound to appear at court of general sessions, 407; persons bound to appear at court of oyer and terminer, 432, 657; persons confined by order of Albany magistrates, 442, 445, 446, 456, 458, 479; list of prisoners in Albany jail, with names of magistrates who committed them, to be prepared, 443; Albany

Courts — continued.

magistrates order arrest of person on way to Canada, 447; Charlotte county justices send prisoners to Albany, 508; justices of Albany county to receive copies of act of July 1, 1780, 508; justice of peace detains effects of person from New York, 521; justices of peace order removal of tory families, 523, 525, 541, 543, 560–561, 612, 709; justices recommend exemptions from this order, 525, 528–529, 546, 612–613; proceedings in supreme court under confiscation law, 548; witness in robbery case cited before supreme court, 548; Tryon county justices order arrest of person returning from Canada, 560; justice of peace to take recognizance of witnesses for appearance at court, 593–594; persons on bail released from obligation to appear at supreme court, 617; justice of peace orders arrest of disaffected persons, 661; witness directed to attend grand jury, 692; Tryon county justices send prisoner to Albany, 740; tories from Durlach to be tried in supreme court, 752; consent of supreme court to release of prisoner to be sought, 755.

Courts Martial, prisoner confined by, discharged by Albany board, 45, 231–232; trial of spies by,

Courts Martial — continued.
46; insults to, by delinquents on trial, 442, 458; delinquents refuse to pay fines imposed by, 644; supposed spy to be tried by, 732.

Covell, Simeon, tory, his children to be removed from state, 540.

Coventry, Sintie, warned to remove from state, 612.

Cowan (Cowen, Cowin), John, of Saratoga, tory suspect, ordered confined, 89; prisoner in Albany jail, 127; released on bail, 210.

Cowan, Moses, released on bail, 118.

Cowan, Robert, bailsman for Moses Cowan, 118.

Coxsackie (Coocksakie, Cooksakie, Coxackie, Coxsakie), district, Greene county, rangers of Albany board to execute orders at, 48, 120; correspondence of committee of, 103; robbery of Arent Van Schaack at, 108, 250; persons conveyed to Albany from, 156; removal of residents of, refusing oath of allegiance, 203; residents of, 514, 524, 577, 578, 579, 580, 581, 657, 662, 704, 725, 729; tory meetings back of, 564; tories to be seized by militia of, 565; suggestion for sending soldiers from, to Helderbergs, 676; delinquents secreted in neighborhood of, 679; aid from, invited for capture of tory party,

Coxsackie district — continued.
701; robbery committed near, 742, 744, 746, 748, 749.

Crandell (Crandel), Jasper, of Little Hoosick, farmer, confined as disaffected and dangerous person, 660–661; released on bail, 667.

Crandell, Joseph. See Crandell, Jasper.

Crandell, Peter, witness against Jacob Best, 686, 688–689; witness against Jacob Lantman, 690–691.

Crandell, Thomas, of Little Hoosick, farmer, bailsman for Jasper Crandell, 667.

Crankheydt. See also Cronkheydt, Cronkheyt.

Crankheydt, David, tory suspect, order for his arrest, 94.

Crans (Cranse, Crants), Frederick, of the Helderbergs, farmer, asks for release of Johannis Hendersans, 172; bailsman for Andries Loucks, 583; bailsman for Christian Merkle and Michael Merkle, 764; surrenders Christian Merkle, 773.

Cranse, Crants. See Crans.

Crapole, Peter, prisoner, supplied with provisions at cost of Albany board, 457; recommitted, 461.

Cray, Christiaen (Christian), of Rensselaerwyck Manor, farmer, released on bail by committee of Manor of Rensselaerwyck, 84; surrendered by bailsman,

Cumming (Cummings), John, cited to appear before Albany board, 192–193; refuses oath of allegiance, 193; advised of day for removal to enemy's lines, 193; his refusal of oath certified to secretary of state, 197–198; his exchange delayed, 281; on parole within limits of Great Imbocht, 295; in list of persons removed or held for exchange, 835.

Cummings, Thomas, convicted of treason but pardoned by legislature of New York, 60.

Cumpston (Cumstead, Cumsted), Edward, captain, obtains release of soldier belonging to Colonel Greaton's regiment, 345; continental soldiers taken on their way to Canada delivered to, 346.

Cumstead, Cumsted. See Cumpston.

Cuppernul, Cuppernull. See Coppernoll.

Curden, John, of Schaghticoke district, released on bail, 102.

Currey. See also Curry.

Currey, Lidia, imprisoned for harboring and concealing persons from the enemy, 445; released on bail, 446.

Curry, John, of Ballston, farmer, sent under guard from Schenectady, 639; committed, 639; bound to appear before commissioners at Schenectady, 647, 648.

Currytown (Currey Town), Montgomery county, persons charged with assisting in its destruction, 749, 751, 751–752.

Curtis, Joel, bailsman for Zachariah Butler, 379; bailsman for John and Zopher Brotherton, 379.

Cutler, a, 572.

Cuyler, Abraham, tory, letters from, conveyed to Schenectady, 147.

Cuyler, Abraham, colonel, detachment from his regiment apprehends persons rescuing delinquents, 646; men from his regiment to apprehend supposed spy, 682.

Cuyler, Cornelius, of Albany, his account for flour for prisoners paid, 394, 812; bailsman for Thomas Reed, 770.

Cuyler, Harmanus, of Coxsackie, delivers letter to Albany board, 704.

Cuyler, Henry, arrest of person for carrying letter from David Van Schaack to, 99; governor advised to remove, 184; detained at Albany for exchange, 206; exchanged and paroled, 237, 244; to be sent to Poughkeepsie, 239; in charge of Captain Edward Willet, 245.

Cuyler, Jacob, of Albany, merchant, bailsman for Jacob Saltsbergh, 696.

Cuyper. See Cooper.

DAET, Johannis, Jr., of Hoosick district, farmer, bailsman for Jacob Timmerman, 664.

Danby (Charlotte county), Vt.,
tory ensign apprehended at,
committed to prison in Albany,
45, 515.

Daniels (Danials), Cornelia, wife
of Dirck Daniels, warned to remove from state, 523; allowed
to remain at home, 525.

Daniels (Danials), Dirck, tory,
his family ordered to remove
from state, 523; in service of
enemy, 525.

Daniels, Jacob, witness against
Edward McGurkey, 736.

Darling, Abner, of Pittstown,
farmer, disaffected person, apprehended, 609; released on
bail, 610; his oath of allegiance,
832.

Darrow, David, of New Lebanon,
farmer, apprehended on suspicion that he is collecting sheep
for use of enemy, 452; rejects
authority of state and refuses to
do military duty, 452; committed, 453; released on bail, 542.

Davenport, Humphrey, bailsman
for Nicholas Boss, 104.

Davidson, James, deserter from
continental army, apprehended
and committed, 680.

Davidson, Samuel, of Pennsyl-
vania, deserter from continental army, sent under guard from
Catskill, 700; delivered to General Clinton, 700.

Davis, Mrs., pass to Poughkeepsie given to, 222.

Davis, ——, his examination by
Albany board, 396.

Davis, Benjamin, testimony received concerning, 436.

Davis, Evan, of Rensselaerwyck,
released on recognizance, 155.

Davis, John, under suspicion at
Schenectady, 121; Albany board
asks commissioners at Fishkill
about him, 121.

Davis, John, of Tryon county,
sent under charges from Poughkeepsie to Albany, 584; committed, 584.

Davis, Peter, of Tryon county,
tory deserter, surrenders himself to Colonel Frederick Fisher,
284; to be put under recognizance to appear at Tryon county
court, 284–285.

Davis, Robert, of Normans Kil,
schoolmaster, accused of encouraging continental soldiers
to desert, 415; to disprove charge
or surrender himself to jailer
of city and county of Albany,
415; released on recognizance,
with limits prescribed, 439;
gives bail, 506.

Davis, William, gives information
against tory, 469–470.

Davis, William, testifies respecting robbery of Peter Van Slyck,
744.

Dawes, William, of Worcester,
Mass., his account of Thomas
Gleason, 695.

Dewitt, Gertruyd, wife of Evert Dewitt, warned to remove from state, 523.

Dewitt (De Wit), Luke (Lukas), of Great Imbocht, farmer, charged with disaffection, 675; warrant issued for his arrest, 676; arrested and committed, 689–690; examined and recommitted, 699, released on bail, 724.

Dewitt, Luke (Lukas), Jr., of Coxsackie, farmer, arrested and committed, 680; released on bail, 725.

Dewitt (Dewit), William, apprehends suspicious character, 677–678; reports case of depreciation of new money, 707; reports encounter with dangerous tory, 729; to assist in capture of tory, 730.

Diamond, Thomas Smith, bailsman for Joseph A. Concklin, 110.

Dickinson (Dickerson, Dickison), Daniel, major, of Stillwater, consulted by commissioners at Stillwater, 466; sends supposed spy to Albany, 551; money paid to, 812.

Dies, Catharine, wife of Jacob Dies, warrant to remove from state, 523.

Dies, Eva, wife of Mathew Dies, warned to remove from state, 523.

Dies, Jacob, tory, his family ordered to remove from state, 523.

Dies, Mathew, tory, his family warned to remove from state, 523.

Dietz, Adam, ensign, furnishes information concerning tories, 255; bailsman for Lotham Stull, 278.

Dietz (Deitz), William, of Schoharie, captain and justice of peace, sends suspected robbers to Albany board, 109; sends prisoners to Albany under guard, 125–126; forwards proposals of tories to prevent robberies, 341; asks exemption of woman from order for removal of tory families, 528–529; presents charges to Albany board, 727.

Dietz, William, of the Helderbergs, farmer, bailsman for Christian Sea, 485.

Dillenback (Dillenbagh, Dillenbeeck), Wilhelmas, of Rensselaerwyck Manor, farmer, examined and released on recognizance, 98; ordered to appear before Albany board, 497; bailsman for Philip Cook, 502; his bail renewed, 503.

Disaffection. See Neutrals, Tories, Toryism.

Dobs, Daniel, tory suspect, confined in Fleet prison, 249; escapes on way to Hartford, 249; apprehended, and released on bail, 249.

Docksteder, Frederick, bailsman for John Docksteder, 216.

EALIGH, William, tory prisoner, money paid by, for his maintenance, 817.

Earhart, Simon, of Saratoga, released on recognizance, 86; Albany board waives appearance of, at request of General Schuyler, 102.

Earing, Christian, of Albany, merchant, sick prisoners at his house, 758, 761; bailsman for Michael Merkle, 761; released from suretyship, 764.

Earle, Jonas, of Cambridge, released from prison on bail, 91; examination of, respecting Captain John Wood, 91, 92.

East Camp, Columbia county, resident of, 105; pass to, given to a suspect, 151; suspected person at, 686.

Eastern States, contrary to law to transport flour to, 371.

Easton, George, witness in behalf of Jotham Bemus, 305.

Eastwood, Abel, examined and released on recognizance, 152.

Eckert, Jacob, deserter from British army, 86.

Eckler, Maria, wife of William Eckler, warned to remove from state, 523.

Eckler (Eckleer), William, tory, his family warned to remove from state, 523.

Edgar, Jean (Mrs.), widow of David Edgar, of Albany, asks permission to go to Canada, 545.

Edmund, Mathew, gives evidence regarding Amos Moore, 414, 415.

Edwards, Timothy, of Stockbridge, Mass., writes to Albany board about Dr. Tidmarsh, 217; Albany board writes to, about John Van Deusen, 665.

Egbertse, Martin, of Schodack, innkeeper, disaffected person, arrested, 638, 640; committed, 640; released on bail, 651–652.

Eggers, Julis, Hessian deserter from British army, takes oath of neutrality, 204.

Ehl, Peter, writes to Albany board, 391.

Elder, John, released on bail, 118.

Eldrige, James, of Saratoga, farmer, bailsman for John Stiles, 526.

Elizabeth (Elizabeth Town), N. J., enemy's descent on, 356.

Ellice, James, of Schenectady, held on recognizance for detrimental conversation, 102–103; cited to appear before Albany board, 169; refuses oath of allegiance, 172, 175; his removal ordered, 172, 173; his offer to take oath referred to supreme court; 189; advised of day for removal, 189–190; detained at Albany for exchange 206; oath administered to, 344; his oath, 832–833.

Elliot, David, his account, insert opp. 820.

Elliot, Walter, of Harpersfield, bailsman for John Park, 273.

Esselstyne, Richard — continued.
restore arms and ammunition seized on wrong information, 602; orders removal of tory families, 612; asks exemption for certain women from order for removal 612–613, 620; money paid to, 812.

Eusopas, Eusopus. See Esopus.

Evans, ——, deserter from British army, 84.

Exchanges, governor empowered to detain persons for, 19, 57, 58, 175, 223, 240–241, 268, 281, 333, 786; act of Feb. 17, 1779, not favorable to persons held as 21; act of March 20, 1781, relative to, 57 (note); pass given captured lieutenant to Poughkeepsie, for arranging his exchange, 58–59, 255; release of exchanged prisoner from Albany jail, 135; prisoners sent to Highlands to be exchanged, 135; tory woman attempts to effect exchange for her husband, 206; of certain tories held at Albany, 237; exchange asked by bailed person in Albany, 253; applicant for exchange referred to governor, 253; Alen McDonald held for exchange, 258; exchange sought for assistant quartermaster, 296; sought for persons in Canada captured at Cherry Valley, 303, 304; Zadock Wright kept on parole for exchange, 344; Andrew Squire

Exchanges — continued.
released on bail to await exchange, 434; persons on bail to be reimprisoned in order to expedite exchange, 473, 476; persons on parole to be imprisoned to await exchange, 476; prisoners to be forwarded to Fishkill for exchange, 477–478; Dr. George Smith asks to be exchanged, 483; William Bowen to be forwarded to commissary of prisoners for exchange, 498; prisoners in Canada exchanged, 562, 563; Peter Ten Broeck exchanged, 626; Dr. George Smith to be exchanged, 675; correspondence touching exchanges, 774 (note); persons detained for exchange, 834, 835; petition for exchange, 835–836.

Eylers, Johan, Hessian deserter from British army, takes oath of neutrality, 204.

FAGLER (Flager), ——, search for Joseph Bettis to be made at his house, 755, 756.

Fagler, ——, goes to Canada, with Joseph Bettis, 756; returns and offers to surrender, 767; receives assurances, 767.

Fairchild. See also Fairchilds.

Fairchild (Fairchilds, Hainhild), Jesse, of Albany, blacksmith, bailsman for Andrew Liddle, 104; his account for securing prisoners paid, 397, 812; another account of his, 397

Fay, Joseph — continued.
prehended, 726; sends intelligence of Dr. Smith's surrender, 728; his communication replied to, 729; writes again to Albany board, 733.
Felony. See also Treason.
Felony, counterfeiting made a, 37-39; attempting to pass counterfeit bills made a, 37; bringing into New York counterfeit bills made a, 37; raising true bills made a, 37; counterfeiting French crowns in New York made a, 37-38; counterfeiting, raising or passing notes of Bank of North America made a, 38; constitutional methods recommended in cases of, 54; trials by jury before courts of oyer and terminer for, 55; maintaining that king of Great Britain had authority in or over New York, adjudged to be a, 55-56; persons condemned to death for, might be respited to serve on ships, 56; legislature of New York abolished barbarous English laws for punishing, 59; powers of judges in cases of, 60 (note).
Felt, Frederick, sent under guard from Claverack to Albany, 220-221; committed, 221; released on recognizance, 264.
Fences of stolen property. See Robberies, Robbers.
Ferguson. See also Farguson.

Ferguson, Robert, tory suspect, ordered confined, 87.
Feries. See also Ferris.
Feries (Farre, Farries), John, witness against Robert Martin, 352, 354.
Ferris, Peter, prisoner, cost of guarding, 806.
Fiddletown (Fiddle Town), Bacon Hill, Saratoga county, resident of, 766.
Fikes, George. See Fikes, Peter.
Fikes, Peter, prisoner, removed from Johnstown to Albany, 364; charge against, to be examined, 364; released on bail, 385, 386; his bail to be prosecuted, 673.
File, Christian, released on recognizance, 224.
File, Christopher, his bail augmented to offset depreciation of currency, 459-460; assists in rescuing delinquents from officer, 644; apprehended and committed, 646; discharged after giving sureties to court, 668.
File (Fill), Melchert (Melchart), of Rensselaerwyck Manor, farmer, bailsman for Marte Freligh, 134; confined, examined and recommitted, 220; released on bail, 226; bailsman for Christopher File, 460; charged with passing counterfeit money, 544; ordered to appear before Albany board, 544; apprehended for helping to rescue

Fisher, John — continued.
delivered to, by Albany board, 206, 228; his account for removal of persons paid, 262, 810; money paid to, 814.

Fisher, John, of Cambridge, millwright, bailsman for Constant King, 712.

Fisher (Fischer, Vischer, Visscher), John T., of Albany, yeoman, bailsman for Abraham Person, Jr., 713, 720.

Fisher, Matthew. See Visscher, Matthew.

Fishkill, Dutchess county, printing at, 16 (note), 19 (note), 20 (note), 21 (note), 22 (note), 23 (note), 25 (note), 27 (note), 54 (note), 55 (note); Albany board requests Poughkeepsie commissioners to confine suspects about, 99; Albany board writes commissioners at, about suspected person, 121; Albany board sends prisoner to commissioners at, 123; removed persons conducted to, 189 (note); paroled tories to be conducted to, for exchange, 477–478; tories enter into parole to proceed to, 482, 484, 506; supposed spy professes to come from, 492; deserter from bateau service sent to, 505; paroled tory prevented by illness from proceeding to, 512; prisoners ordered sent to, 557.

Fishkill, Saratoga county. See Fish Creek.

Fitch, Joseph, attempts to disperse tory meeting, 313, 326.

Fitch, Pelatiah, commissioner for conspiracies, Albany county board, appointment, 67; active in Charlotte county board, 67; his audited account, 805–806.

Fitzpatrick, Peter, order for his apprehension as dangerous person, 179.

Flaharty, James, prisoner of war, committed for associating with disaffected persons, 370; suspected of knowledge of robberies, 374; released on bail, 375.

Flake, Coenradt, robbed, 335.

Fleet prison. See Prisoners.

Flick, Alexander Clarence, work on loyalism in New York cited, 10–12.

Flinn. See also Flyn.

Flinn, John, of Half Moon, farmer, bailsman for Samuel Burns, 622; allowed to deliver up Burns, 634.

Flint, Asa, of Cambridge district, prisoner, sent from Poughkeepsie to Albany, 93; released on bail, 110–111.

Flintye, Frederick, deserter from British army, 91; allowed at large in Albany county, 91.

Flood, William, committed to jail, 342; released on bail, 395.

Flyn. See also Flinn.

Flyn (Flinn), John, sent to Albany under guard, as accessory to robbery of Henry Van Rens-

Fonda, Isaac D.—continued.
ceives information respecting
attempt to kidnap General
Schuyler, 760; money paid to,
812; his account as commissioner, 814, 820; 824; money
paid to, 814; his commission,
829; his certification of names of
persons refusing oath, 833–834.
Fonda, Jan, his land near Albany,
767.
Fonda, Jellis, major, of Tryon
county, charge against, 628.
Fonda, Jeremiah, money paid to,
812.
Fonda (Fanda), John, of Tryon
county, justice of peace, joins
in statement of charges against
Philip Helmer, 371; certifies
that certain persons may safely
be bailed, 382; prisoners from
Tryon county to appear before,
382, 383, 386; certifies to general
good character of John More
and George Any, 384.
Fonda, John, Jr., £74 paid to,
for beef for prisoners, 439, 812.
Fonda, Lawrence (Lourence, Lowrence), of Claverack, justice of
peace, forwards information regarding robbery, 341, 342; orders removal of tory families,
612; asks exemption for certain
women from order for removal,
612–613, 620; forwards examinations and prisoners, 684.
Footie (Fotie), Lewis, of Albany,
baker, bailsman for Henry J.
Mesick, 138; surrender of Me-

Footie, Lewis—continued.
sick demanded of, 491; renews
his bail for Mesick, 495.
Ford, Jacob, assemblyman, of
Albany county, introduced bill
for repealing commissioners for
conspiracies, 31.
Ford, Jacob, of Kings district,
justice of peace, sends communication relating to Ambrose
Vincent and others, 671, 672;
to serve warrant and put witnesses under bonds, 672.
Forgason, John, bailsman for John
Brock, 125.
Forgery. See also Money.
Forgery, of passes, 41, 143, 154.
Forman, Christopher, deserter
from British army, 83.
Forrister, Benoni Robins, confined on suspicion of being a
spy, 766.
Fort Edward, Washington county,
tories removed to, 267; residents of, indebted to John Cobham, 514; person on bail removes to, 549; resident of, 633.
Fortfuydt, John, money paid to,
814.
Fort Hunter, Montgomery county,
Indian minister at, removes to
Schenectady, 142.
Fort Miller, Washington county,
resident of, 237; John Cobham
allowed to go to, 670.
Fort Montgomery, in the Highlands, New York, reduction of,
by British, 15; effect at Kingston of reduction of, 15.

Frihart, Christian, of Sir John Johnson's corps, prisoner, 556.

Frobert, John, confined, 330.

Fuller, William, of Albany, joiner, bailsman for Daniel McLoud, 616.

Fullerton, Robert, of Niskayuna, suspected of knowing purpose of certain person to join enemy, 727; examined and discharged, 727.

Furnival. See also Furnwall.

Furnival, James, bailsman for Moses Thirsty, 273.

Furnwall. See also Furnival.

Furnwall, James, of Albany, innkeeper, accused of enlisting for British army, 302; committed, 302; released on recognizance, 302.

GALER, Christopher (Stoffel), tory suspect, ordered confined, 87; sick in jail, removed to fort of Albany, 107.

Galer, Martin, Jr., of Rensselaerwyck Manor, farmer, tory suspect, ordered confined, 87; removed from Albany jail to fort, 129; released on bail, 165; furnishes new bail, 463.

Galer, Mattice (Martinus), tory suspect, ordered confined, 87; removed from Albany jail to fort, 129.

Galer, Silvan, tory suspect, ordered confined, 87.

Gansevoort, Coenrad, lieutenant, to apprehend supposed spy, 682; spy escapes from, 682, 683.

Gansevoort, Harmen, asks permission for return of certain persons removed within enemy's lines, 272.

Gansevoort, Leonard, of Albany, asks that John Cobham be allowed to take oath of allegiance, 420; bailsman for Thomas Reed, 770; draft on, as treasurer of Albany county, 821.

Gansevoort, Leonard, Jr., secretary of Albany board of commissioners, 36; takes oath of office, 36, 63, 95; made acting treasurer of board, 37, 195; salary of, 37, 63, 95, 192; his official expenditures, how made, 37; pay-bill of, 63-64; retained manuscript minutes of Albany board, 64; minutes given to state in 1850 by his grandson, Thomas Hun, 64; what minutes of Albany board were written by, 64, 65; ordered to acknowledge delivery of prisoners, 125; accounts of articles purchased by, for use of Albany board, 183-184, 197, 292, 810; money deposited in his hands by retiring treasurer, 195; ordered to pay for arrest of John Myer, 202; continental money taken from suspect delivered to, 204; ordered to pay money to Colonel John Fisher, 206; writes to Albany board, 218; money transmitted by state treasurer delivered to, 231, 284; ordered to pay

Gardinier, Derick — continued.
refusal certified to secretary of state, 197–198; advised of day for removal to enemy's lines, 213, 218; his name certified to governor, 223; instructions for his removal, 228; held for exchange, 241, 244, 835; governor recommends lenient treatment of, 265; to be removed to new place of confinement, 266, 269; paroled, 269, 309; his request to return to Albany on business denied, 314; allowed to go to Kinderhook, 350; required to return to place of confinement, 350; commissary of prisoners writes about, to Albany board, 472; to await exchange in Goshen jail, 476; to be conducted to Fishkill, 477; to be arrested for violating parole, 506.

Gardinier (Gardineer), Jacob, commissioner for conspiracies, Tryon county board, appointment, 68; bailsman for John Van Sela, 380.

Gardinier, Samuel, confined in Johnstown jail, petitions for release on bail, 212.

Gardner, George, of Ballston, aided Burgoyne, 82.

Garnet, Thomas, arrest ordered for robbery, 143, 144; Nicholas Kerglaer cited before commissioners to give information respecting, 151; persons suspected of holding correspondence with,

Garnet, Thomas — continued.
162; goods stolen by, at Freehold, 168.

Garnsey, Isaac, of Half Moon district, farmer, bailsman for David Miller, 126, 276; bailsman for Joseph Meacham, 574; bailsman for Hezekiah Hammond, 574.

Garret, John, of Coxsackie district, farmer, released on bail, 578–579; discharged from obligation to appear at court, 617.

Garret, Simeon, of Coxsackie district, farmer, accused of harboring tory express, 579; discharged on recognizance, 585; bail provided for, 587–588; reports encounter with dangerous tory, 731; his testimony regarding John Ver Plank, 731.

Garth, Lutwig, deserter from British army, takes oath of neutrality, 201; allowed to live in Schoharie, 201.

Gasherie (Gasharie), Joseph, commissioner for conspiracies, Ulster county board, appointment, 68; his audited account, 815; his account with state treasurer, 823, 825, 826.

Gates, Horatio, general, 94; dangerous persons to be forwarded by, to enemy's lines, 170; gives woman pass to Canada, 208; supplies for his army, 686.

Gaul, Jacob, money paid to, 812.

Grant, Benoni—continued.
his examination sent to Governor Clinton, 765; his information touching one Rodgers, 766–767.

Grant, George, suspected person, required to enroll in militia and give recognizance, 369.

Grawberger (Crawberger), Hendrick, warrant for his arrest on charge of toryism, 357; discharged, 361.

Gray, Charles, sent from Albany jail to the Highlands to be exchanged, 135.

Great Barrington, Mass., prisoner brought from, to Albany, 221; examination of prisoner in, 251; commissions and proclamations from enemy concealed in, 665; letter from, 682; letter to person in, 686.

Great Britain, 25; 55; 56; 87; 131; 167; 372; New York abolishes forms of English capital laws, 59; powers of commissioners continued during continuance of war with, 440–441; persons bound to good behavior during continuance of war with, 442, 444, 447, 449, 451, 457, 459, 460, 461, 462, 463, 464, 466, 478, 479, 481, 482, 483, 484, 485, 486, 487, 488, 490, 492, 493, 494, 495, 497, 498, 499, 500, 501, 502, 505, 506, 507, 509, 510, 513, 514, 515, 516, 517, 518, 519, 520, 521, 522, 524, 526, 527, 530, 532, 533,

Great Britain—continued.
535, 536, 537, 540, 547, 550, 559, 562, 563, 564, 569, 570, 571, 572, 573, 574, 575, 576, 577, 580, 581, 582, 583, 584, 585, 588, 590, 592, 593, 594, 597, 598, 599, 601, 604, 610, 613, 614, 616, 618, 622, 623, 624, 625, 626, 631, 632, 633, 635, 640, 641, 642, 643, 647, 648, 649, 651, 652, 654, 655, 658, 659, 660, 661, 663, 664, 667, 668, 683, 684, 685, 691, 692, 696, 697, 698, 699, 709, 714, 716, 718, 719, 720, 721, 722, 724, 725, 726, 741, 743, 744, 745, 756, 757, 758, 768, 771, 772, 773, 774; tory predicts that troops of, will soon be in Albany, 454; tory avows loyalty to crown of, 542; harboring officers of, in Livingston Manor, 624, 633, 644; forces of, commanded by Sir Henry Clinton, 636; person apprehended on suspicion of being officer of, 766; act relating to deserters from army of, 791–793; oaths forswearing allegiance to king of, 831, 832; authority of parliament of, disowned, 831.

Great Imbocht (Great Imboght, Great Imbought, Groote Imboght, Grote Imboght), Greene county, paroled person confined to limits of, 295; residents of, 626, 713, 720, 724, 725.

Greaton (Grating, Greatan), John, colonel, deserter from his regi-

Greaton, John—continued.
ment, 322; soldier of his regiment in confinement, 345.
Green, Daniel, suspected of collecting sheep for use of enemy,
452; apprehended and exonerated, 452.
Green, Edmund, of Rensselaerwyck Manor, gives information
against disaffected persons, 406,
408.
Green, James, of Cambridge, exonerated of disloyalty, 88; released on bail, 88.
Green, James, of Albany, yeoman,
bailsman for William Adams,
338.
Green, James, apprehends Nathaniel Cotton, 662.
Green, Thomas, of Cambridge,
bailsman for James Green, 88.
Green, William, of Saratoga district, bailsman for David Miller,
276.
Greenbush, Rensselaer county,
resident of, 359.
Green Island, Albany county,
resident of, 474.
Greenman, Benjamin, Jr., deserter from British, takes oath
of allegiance, 216; his signature to oath, 831.
Greenman, Joseph, deserter from
British, takes oath of allegiance,
216; his signature to oath, 831.
Gregory, Philip, bailsman for
John Thomas, 120.
Greswold, Mathew, lieutenant-
governor of Connecticut, bailed

Greswold, Mathew—continued
prisoner from Albany ordered
to report to, 132; informs
Albany board of disposition
made of Bethuel Huntley, 281.
Greves, Thomas, his account,
insert opp. 820.
Greykenbom, Hendrick, Hessian
deserter from British army,
takes oath of neutrality, 204.
Griffen. See also Griffin.
Griffen (Griffin), William, of
of Charlotte county, farmer,
committed as dangerous person, 508; examined and recommitted, 595; petition in
his favor, 596; released on bail,
597.
Griffin, Jacob, commissioner for
conspiracies, Dutchess county
board, appointment, 68.
Griffith. See also Griffiths.
Griffith, Joshua, witness against
Robert Martin, 352, 354.
Griffiths, Thomas, of Sir John
Johnson's corps, prisoner, 554;
examined, 555.
Griggs, Alexander, of Half Moon,
yeoman, bailsman for Simeon
Griggs, 447.
Griggs, Simeon, of Half Moon,
yeoman, apprehended on way
to Canada, 447; on bail within
prescribed limits, 447; on recognizance, 449.
Grippen, Reuben, of Kinderhook,
bailsman for Peter Finehout,
170.
Groat. See also Grote.

Hail, Coenraedt, deserter from British army, 83.

Hainer. See also Heyner.

Hainer, Barent, Jr., of Rensselaerwyck, accused of treachery 86.

Haines. See also Haynes.

Haines, Adam, captured on way to join enemy, 329; released on bail, 390.

Haines, Jacob, of Peesink, confined for entertaining robbers, 388; takes oath not to aid robbers, tories, delinquents or deserters, 388–389; released on bail, 389.

Haines, Jacob, of Durlach, charge against, 752; committed, 752; examined and recommitted, 753.

Haines (Hainer), Wilhelmus, paid for apprehending John Myer, 202, 810.

Hale, ——, major, commissary of prisoners, notifies Albany board of exchanged prisoner, 135; prisoners ordered sent to, 140, 153.

Halenbeck. See also Halenbeeck.

Halenbeck, Daniel, of Maple Town, summoned as witness against Simon Frazer, 185.

Halenbeeck, Arent, examined and released, 90.

Halenbeeck, Arie, accused of attempting to join savages, 368.

Halenbeeck, Casper P., tory, his family warned to remove from state, 523.

Halenbeeck, Jacob, of Schaghticoke, lieutenant, charged with disaffection, 357–358; cited to appear before Albany board, 358; discharged on producing certificate of having sworn allegiance, 361; certifies in behalf of wife of tory, 543.

Halenbeeck, Jacob, of Helderbergs, charged with disaffection, 368.

Halenbeeck, Jacob, of Klinkenbergh, farmer, bailsman for Jacob Halenbeeck, Jr., 570.

Halenbeeck, Jacob, Jr., of Coxsackie, farmer, sent under guard from Claverack to Albany 221; committed, 221; released on bail and limited bounds, 236; required to renew his bail, 497, 514; enlisting men at Oniskethau, 564; apprehended and committed, 566; released on bail, 570, 580.

Halenbeeck, Mathew, of the Helderbergs, charged with disaffection, 368.

Halenbeeck, Michael, robbed, 334, 335, 340; his wife testifies respecting robbery, 392.

Halenbeeck, Nicholas, of Albany, carpenter, bailsman for John Blackley, 443; discharged, 464.

Halenbeeck, Rachel, wife of Casper P. Halenbeeck, ordered to remove from state, 523.

Halenbeeck, William, charged with robbery and harboring robbers, 399; discharged on

Hickety, Catharine, cited to appear before Albany board, 252; examined and ordered to reappear, 254.

Hicks, Benjamin, joins in recommendation of Marcy French, 709.

Hicks, George, of Newtown, farmer, released on bail, 610.

Hicks, Thomas, of Rensselaerwyck Manor, farmer, apprehended for being present at tory meeting, 638–639; ordered to appear before Albany board, 639; furnishes bail, 641, 642, 643.

Hicks, Wheater, to appear as witness at supreme court, 606.

Hiedley (Heidley), Johannis, bailsman for Charles Near, 103; cited to show cause why bail should not be forfeited, 163.

Higby (Highby), Flemon (Flemin), testifies respecting conduct of inhabitants of Newtown, 458; summoned before commissioners at Stillwater, 466.

High, William, of Charlotte county, farmer, bailsman for William Griffen, 597.

Highlands, the, New York, British successes in, 15; troops on way from Albany to, 123; exchanged prisoner allowed to go, 135; prisoners sent there from Albany, to be exchanged, 135.

Hill, George, sent from Albany jail to the Highlands to be exchanged, 135.

Hill, Samuel, of Rensselaerwyck Manor, reports that tories are collecting in Bethlehem, 531; witness against James Starks and others, 534; examined, 641; warrant for apprehending Jabez Spencer delivered to, 641.

Hillsdale district, inhabitants of, petition legislature in favor of deported persons, 32 (note).

Hilton, Adam, of Coxsackie, farmer, bailsman for Jacob Halenbeeck, Jr., 514.

Hilton, Jacob, directed to apprehend one Thomas, 655.

Hilton, Peter W., of Albany, cooper, bailsman for Wouter Witbeeck, 578.

Hilton, Richard, apprehends Peter Waley, 587.

Hincocks, John, bailsman for John Sealy, 126.

Hindsauce, Johannis George, ordered confined, 168.

Hoagteling, Hooghtaling, Hooghteeling, Hooghteling, Hoogtaling. See Hoogteling.

Hocknear, John, of Niskayuna, disowns authority of state and refuses to do military duty, 452; committed, 453.

Hocknel, John, of Rensselaerwyck Manor, farmer, released on bail, 571.

Hodge, Samuel, bailsman for Jonas Earle, 91.

Hodkison, John, of Albany, laborer, on bail within prescribed

Hodkison, John—continued.
limits, 675; allowed to work on
Tunnicliff's farm, 711.
Hoff, Hendrick, suspicious char-
acter, order for his apprehension, 728.
Hoffer, Philip, Hessian deserter
from British army, permitted
to go at large in Albany county,
203.
Hoffman. See also Hoofman.
Hoffman, Hendrick, Hessian from
British army, takes oath of neutrality, 204.
Hoffman, Jacob, deserter from
British army, 89; allowed at
large in Albany county, 89.
Hoffman, Robert, his audited account, 820.
Hogan, Henry, his negro slave,
Tom, committed to prison, 104;
his slave charged with inciting
insurrection, 304.
Hogeboom, Cornelius, captain,
receives captured tories, 566.
Hogle, Elizabeth, wife of John
Hogle, warned to remove from
state, 540; allowed to remain
at home on account of good
behavior, 540.
Hogle, Francis, tory, his family
warned to remove from state,
540.
Hogle, Jane, wife of Francis Hogle,
warned to remove from state,
540.
Hogle, John, committed to prison
as accessory to robberies, 252,
276; grand jury finds no bill

Hogle, John—continued.
against, 276; released on bail,
277; his family warned to remove from state, 540; killed at
battle of Bennington, 540.
Hogle, Peter, bailsman for John
Hogle, 277.
Hogstrasser, Jacob, of the Helderbergs, his house robbed, 100,
109.
Hoit. See also Hayt.
Hoit, William prisoner, com-
mended for consideration, 338;
released on bail, 338.
Holly, William (Williams), money
paid to, insert opp. 821.
Holmes, John, of Ballston, farmer,
bailsman for John Boyd, Jr.,
509.
Holsapple, Zachariah, his affidavit concerning Teunis Smith,
633; examined, 635–636; his
charge discredited, 644.
Holt, John, printer at Kingston,
16 (note), 44 (note); printer at
Poughkeepsie, 19 (note), 20,
(note), 21 (note), 23 (note),
37 (note), 38 (note), 43 (note),
46 (note), 54 (note), 55 (note),
56 (note), 60 (note), 777 (note),
780 (note), 781 (note), 783
(note), 786 (note), 787 (note),
789 (note), 791 (note), 793
(note), 794 (note), 796 (note),
800 (note).
Honeywell, Israel, commissioner
for conspiracies, Westchester
county board, a petitioner to
legislature, 30; appointment as

Hoogteling, William—continued.
wyck Manor, declares himself
a king's man, 516; cited to
appear before Albany board,
524.

Hoogteling, William, of Oniskethau, farmer, brought as prisoner from Coeymans to Albany,
566; committed, 567; released
on bail, 581.

Hooper, Christina, gives information about inhabitants of Durlach, 753.

Hooper, John, of Newtown, farmer, tory suspect, detained for
trial, 87; released on bail, 113;
bailsman for Stephen Hooper,
118; again on bail, 466.

Hooper, Stephen, of Newtown, farmer, tory suspect, detained for
trial, 87; released on bail, 118;
again on bail, 466; bailsman
for Joseph Deval, 467.

Hoosick (Hosick), Rensselaer
county, residents of, 151, 686,
688; spy from New York at,
339; Dr. Smith and others met
on their way to, 726.

Hoosick (Hosack, Hosick) district, Rensselaer county, residents of, 82–83, 85, 130, 185,
639, 664, 688; lawless proceedings against inhabitants of,
197; tory families in, warned
to remove from state, 527–528;
certificate from officers of,
694.

Hoosick (Hosick) road, meeting of
disaffected persons on, 651.

Hopper, Coenradt, of Durlach,
charge against, 751, 752; committed, 752.

Hopper, Jacobus, of Durlach,
charge against, 751, 752; committed, 752.

Hopping, Ephraim, deserter from
Canada, receives passes from
Thomas Chittenden and Albany
board, 739.

Hops (Hop), Isaac, of Rensselaerwyck Manor, farmer, bailsman
for John Myers, 104; ordered
to deliver up John Myers, 108;
discharged from recognizance
entered into for John Myers,
109; apprehended for helping
to rescue prisoners, 646; committed, 646; released on bail,
663.

Horn, John, of Rensselaerwyck
Manor, butcher, bailsman for
John Klock, 547; bailsman for
Jotham Bemus, 602–603.

Horses, law against stealing, 54;
stolen in Dutchess county, 92;
stolen in Albany county, 119;
escape of persons apprehended
for stealing, 480; person permitted to go to Tryon county
in search of, 541; person
charged with stealing, sent up
from Poughkeepsie, 584; James
Watson ordered to deliver one
to Berijah Tyler, 695; person
charged with stealing, delivered
to Major Graham, 711.

Horton, David, Jr., money paid
to, insert opp. 821.

Jalley, Hugh, bailsman for William Gordon, 274.
James, Moses, of Kings district, farmer, bailsman for Abner Darling, 610.
James, Nathaniel, warrant to apprehend, 466.
Jansen. See also Johnson.
Jansen, Cornelius J., captain, sends suspicious character to Albany, 705, 708.
Jansen, Cornelius T., captain, of Colonel Van Schaick's regiment, 680.
Jansen, Dirck, major, of Livingston Manor, Albany board requests information from, 152.
Jansen (Johnson), Evert, apprehended for consorting with British emissary, 653; committed, 653; apprehended for harboring emissaries from enemy, 741; committed, 741; examined and recommitted, 750.
Jansen, Johannis, tory, his family warned to remove from state, 523.
Jansen, Maria, wife of Johannis Jansen, warned to remove from state, 523.
Jay, Augustus, money paid to, 815.
Jay, Sir James, senator, only member of senate who voted for assembly resolutions for examining and adjusting public accounts, 23.
Jeram, Augustus, warrant issued for his arrest, 652-653.

Jericho, Albany county, resident of, 614.
Jerseys (Jersies). See New Jersey.
Jessup, ——, tory, induced Americans to join British army, 86.
Jessup's Patent, Warren county, persons arrested at, confined, 147-148, 163; intelligence forwarded to Canada from, 601; order to tory families in and near, 696; suspicious character apprehended at, 705, 708; persons removed from, allowed to return for property, 711, 721.
Johnson. See also Jansen.
Johnson, ——, receives and passes counterfeit money, 545.
Johnson, —— (Dr.), persuades young man to join enemy, 479; goes off to enemy, 480.
Johnson, Mrs., widow, stolen property found at her house, 146; released with her daughter, 176-177.
Johnson, Adam, given pass, 85-86.
Johnson, Coenradt, cited before Albany board for supposed complicity in robberies, 233; dismissed, 237.
Johnson, Jeremiah, of Albany, asks pass to New Jersey, 365; required to produce evidence of attachment to American cause, 365; receives pass, 366; examined in matter of secreting escaped prisoner, 397, 398; witness against John McDole, 413.

Larawa, Peter—continued.
and recommitted, 699, 706; released on bail, 725.
Lary, John, deserter, delivered to
General Stark, 145.
Latham, James, Dr., charges
Thomas Anderson with en-
couraging negroes to desert
their masters and with forging a
pass, 142–143; accused of harboring tories, 222; bound by
board at Claverack to appear
before Albany board, 222; given
time to consider taking oath of
allegiance, 227, 238; letters
concerning, received by Albany
board, 238.
Laughlin. See Loughley.
Lawrence, Isaac, witness for
James Starks and others, 535.
Lawrence, John, witness against
James Starks and others, 534.
Lawrence, Jonathan, senator, reports progress of bill for creat-
ing commissioners for conspiracies, 14.
Lawrence, Mine, witness for
James Starks and others, 535.
Lawrence, Richard, witness for
James Starks and others, 535.
Laws. See New York: state.
Lawson, Isaac, of Tryon county,
tory deserter, delivered to Al-
bany board by General Stark,
232; committed, 232; released
on recognizance, 266; asks permission to return home, 284;
to be put under recognizance
to appear before Tryon county

Lawson, Isaac—continued.
court, 284–285; apprehended
and sent to Albany, 740; committed, 740.
Lawyer, Jacob, of Albany, bailsman for John Summer, 771.
Lawyer, Johannis, of Schoharie,
justice, request to, to inquire
into injuries suffered by Catharine Simpson, 388; asks exemption of woman from order
for removal of tory families,
528–529.
Ledeke, John, Hessian deserter
from British army, takes oath
of neutrality, 204.
Lee, William, of Livingston
Manor, yeoman, apprehended
as disaffected person, 337; retained within limits of Albany
pending inquiry, 338; recommendation in his favor, 339, 340;
released on recognizance, 340.
Leek (Leak), Philip, commissioner for conspiracies, Westchester county board, appointment, 68; his audited account,
806–807.
Lees, William, of Niskayuna,
blacksmith, dissuades friends
of liberty from taking up arms,
469; arrested, 469, 470; committed, 471; released on bail,
569–570; bailsman for James
Whiteacre, 571; bailsman for
Ann Standerren, 592.
Legrange, Arie, of Albany, merchant, bailsman for James Legrange, 533.

Liddle, Ann—continued.
go, with family, to Canada, 234.
Lilley, John. See McCormick, James.
Lincoln, Levy, requested to cause arrest of person concealed near Worcester, Mass., 224.
Linn. See Lynd.
Lister, Benjamin, bailsman for John Dusenbury, 381.
Lister, James, of Rensselaerwyck Manor, farmer, tory meeting at his house, 636, 637, 641, 644, 645, 649, 657, 670; apprehended, 638; ordered to appear before Albany board, 639; furnishes bail, 641.
Litchfield county, Conn., order for arrest of tory from, 453.
Little, Isaac, of White Creek, farmer, bailsman for John Todd, 635.
Little East Hoosick, Rensselaer county, pass given to, 235–236.
Little Hoosick (Hosick), Rensselaer county, residents of, 667, 691.
Little White Creek, Washington county, residents at, 96; charge for express to, from White Creek, 806.
Liverse, William, of Rensselaerwyck Manor, farmer, bailsman for Jacob A. Lansing, 505.
Livingston, Gilbert, commissioner for conspiracies, Dutchess county board, appointment, 68;

Livingston, Gilbert—continued.
his audited account, 805; his account with state treasurer, 826.
Livingston, Henry B., colonel, his regiment, 470.
Livingston, J. H., Rev., brings £500 to Albany board, 231.
Livingston, Jacob, of Livingston Manor, sent under guard from Claverack to Albany, 221; committed, 221; grand jury finds no bill against, for complicity in robberies, 275; released on bail, 275.
Livingston, James, colonel, deserter from his regiment, 679.
Livingston (Livingstone), Peter, Jr., of the Helderbergs, examined and released on recognizance, 98; cited to show cause why recognizance should not be forfeited, 163; ordered to appear before Albany board, 497; warrant issued for his arrest, 582; his recognizance forfeited, 672.
Livingston, Peter R., colonel, justice of the peace, sends prisoner charged with disaffection to Albany, 337, 339; sends examination of Anna Proper, 569; directs Anna Proper to appear before Albany board, 588; writes letter concerning Anna Proper, 588; forwards to Albany board examination of Jacob Cline, 601; orders arrest of persons who obstruct col-

Loucks, William — continued.
harie district, released on bail,
95; to be apprehended for persuading negroes to go to Canada, 455; sent prisoner from
Schenectady to Albany, 468;
released on bail, 500; examined,
563.

Loudon (Lauden, Louden), Samuel, printer at Fishkill, 16 (note),
19 (note), 20 (note), 21 (note),
22 (note), 23 (note), 25 (note),
27 (note), 54 (note), 55 (note);
notice to suspected persons
inserted in his paper, 190, 202,
203, 242; his account for notices,
253; money paid to, 810.

Loughley (Laughlin), Barnabas
(Barney), captured by Oneidas,
266; released on bail, 266; asks
permission to go to Butternuts
to recover papers, 276; permitted to lay request before
General Hand at Cherry Valley,
276; his surrender demanded
of his surety, 491.

Louks. See also Loucks.

Louks, Dedirick, prisoner, removed from Johnstown to Albany, 364; charge against, to
be examined, 364.

Low (Loe), John, of Rensselaerwyck Manor, yeoman, certificate in his favor, 582; released
on bail, 582; apprehended on
suspicion, 740; examined and
discharged, 740; permitted to
reside at Beaver Dam, 743; on
bail, 744.

Low, Nicholas, of Rensselaerwyck Manor, gentleman, bailsman for John Low, 582.

Low, Simon, tory prisoner, money
paid by, for his maintenance,
817.

Loyalism. See Neutrals, Tories,
Toryism.

Loyalists. See Neutrals, Tories,
Toryism.

Lucas, Amos, of Kingsbury, bailsman for William Tyler, 135;
required to deliver up Tyler,
524, 591.

Lucas, Israel, his signature to a
pass forged, 154.

Lucka, George, deserter from
British army, 83.

Ludlow, James, comes from New
York to Kinderhook, 468;
order for his arrest, 468, 475;
discharged, 475.

Luke, Jacob, examinations regarding robberies committed at
his house, 335–336, 353.

Luke, Philip, captain, tories in
his company to be removed
from home, 738.

Lull, Benjamin, of Butternuts,
taken prisoner by Captain Ballard, 208; examined and recommitted, 208; delivered to Albany
board by General Stark, 214;
recommitted, 214; released on
bail, 216; captured by Oneidas,
263; discharged, 263.

Lull, Caleb, of Butternuts, captured by Oneidas, 263; discharged, 263.

McMichin, Thomas, of Schoharie, delivered by General Clinton to Albany board, 360; committed, 360; released on recognizance, 370.

McMullen. See also McMullin.

McMullen, Archibald, brought under guard to Albany for complicity in robberies, 133; imprisoned, 133; left stolen goods in care of John Johnson, 164.

McMullen (McMullin), John, apprehended on suspicion of being a spy, 551; committed, 551; his examination, 552, 556; person accused of aiding, 558.

McNeal. See also McNeil.

McNeal, Mrs. (widow), of Albany, sick prisoner allowed to live at her house, 620–621.

McNeal, Alec, of the Scotch Patent, charged with aiding party on its way to join enemy, 595, to be apprehended, 595.

McNeal, Archibald, liberated from confinement on condition of joining levies, 349.

McNeal (McNeil, McNiel), Archibald, of Saratoga, merchant, accused of corresponding with and aiding enemy, 567; apprehended and committed, 568; on bail within prescribed limits, 603; permission to visit home withheld from, 610, 615; permitted to visit home, 617, 631; to be delivered up for exceeding limits, 769–770; examined and discharged, 771.

McNeal (McNeil), Archibald, of the Scotch Patent, farmer, charged with assisting party on its way to join enemy, 595; to be apprehended, 595; apprehended and committed, 599–600; his request to be admitted to bail denied, 611; on bail within specified limits, 621; allowed to remove his family from the Scotch Patent, 625; allowed to visit home, 638; ordered to remove from frontier, 674; refuses oath of allegiance, 712; committed, 712; on bail within prescribed limits, 719, 721–722; permitted to visit home, 754.

McNeil, Archibald, his oath of allegiance, 832.

McNeil, Neal (Neil), of Rensselaerwyck Manor, yeoman, his arrest and imprisonment ordered, 220; bailsman for James Atkins, 463.

McNight, ——, of Ballston, aided Burgoyne, 82.

McNitt (McNit, McNutt), Alexander, commissioner for conspiracies, Charlotte county board, appointment, 67, 116; signs draft for funds for Charlotte county board, 133; acts on case of Andrew Stephenson, 209–210; forwards petition to Albany, 596; his audited account, 805–806, 807–808, his account with state treasurer, 823; his commission, 829.

Miller, George, deserter from British army, 83.

Miller, Gerrit, released on bail to report to Charlotte county board, 126–127.

Miller, Gilbert, of Ballston, farmer, released on bail, 622.

Miller, Hendrick, warrant for his arrest on charge of toryism, 357; discharged, 361.

Miller, Henry, deserter from British army, 86.

Miller, Jacob, warrant for his arrest as dangerous person, 419.

Miller (Mullr), Jeremiah (Jeremije), of Rensselaerwyck Manor, accused of corresponding with and harboring tories, 324; warrant issued for his arrest, 324; examination of witnesses against 324, 325; discharged on taking oath of allegiance, 325; his signature to oath, 831.

Miller, Johannis, of Livingston Manor, cited as witness against Teunis Smith, 634; examined and discharged, 644.

Miller, John, of Cambridge district, bailsman for William Reside and William McAuley, 82.

Miller, John, committed on evidence of having been with enemy, 414; witnesses give evidence regarding, 414, 416; bail for, refused, 417.

Miller, John, promotes circulation of British proclamation, 645; warrant issued for his arrest, 645.

Miller, John J., of Rensselaerwyck Manor, farmer, promotes circulation of British proclamation, 645; warrant issued for his arrest, 645; released on bail, 649, 651.

Miller, John Ja., of Rensselaerwyck Manor, tailor, bailsman for Nicholas Miller, 649.

Miller (Muller), Nicholas, of Rensselaerwyck Manor, innkeeper, promotes circulation of British proclamation, 645; warrant issued for his arrest, 645; released on bail, 648–649, 650.

Miller, Peter, examined by Albany board, 418.

Miller, Peter I., of Claverack district, wheelwright, released on bail, 573.

Miller, Stephen, arrest ordered for robbery, 144.

Miller, Stephen, of Rensselaerwyck Manor, accused of corresponding with and harboring tories, 324; warrant issued for his arrest, 324; summoning of witnesses against, 324.

Miller, a, 626.

Milligan, James, suspicious character, apprehended and committed, 760–761.

Mills, Abel (Able), of Saratoga, farmer, apprehends person from Canada, 353; bailsman for person apprehended, 353; testimony of his wife received, 574.

Mills, Cornelius, confined in Johnstown jail, petitions for release on bail, 212.

Money — continued.

paper currency, 38–39, 305, 309, 310; depreciated state of, affects renewal of recognizances, 42–43, 459–460; disposal of, when stolen, 52, 134, 137–138; various kinds of, taken from a prisoner, 101; arrests for passing counterfeit money, 114, 136, 282; recovery of stolen, 137, 142; continental money taken from suspect, 204; thirty and forty dollar counterfeit bills passed, 282, 287; good money found on counterfeiters used to reimburse persons defrauded, 285, 287; secreted by robbers near Peesink, 336–337; certain issues exchanged for continental bills by Albany board, 337; taken from supposed deserter, 360; depreciation of, affects value of compensation for public service, 375; paid to spy in British service, 417–418; compensation of commissioners in money issued under resolution of congress, 441; allowance for expenses of commissioners in money issued by congress, 441; £144 in continental money paid for paper, 446; offered for release of persons under arrest, 480; counterfeit bills circulated in Rensselaerwyck Manor, 544; counterfeit money circulated in Albany, 545; money of new emission sent to Albany board,

Money — continued.

599; forfeited recognizance paid in emission of March 18, 1780, 603, 737; person accused of depreciating issue of March 18, 1780, 681; counterfeit money distributed from New York, 686; money of new emission paid to Peter Seger, 688; persons accused of depreciating new continental money, 706, 707; bounty received from class used to pay for stolen horses, 711; Dr. Stringer advances money to express, 726; guinea offered as bounty for enlistment in king's service, 735; depreciation of commissioners' pay, 815, 816, 817, 818, 819.

Monk, William, of the Helderbergs, farmer, cited to appear before Albany board, 182; given time to consider oath of allegiance, 182; discharged on taking oath, 185; bailsman for Christopher Hutt, 521; bailsman for Peter Waley, 594.

Monument mountain, in Great Barrington, Mass., 665.

Moor. See also Moore, More.

Moor, ——, lieutenant, money paid to, insert opp. 821.

Moore, ——, of Catskill, wheat in his possession to be seized, 734.

Moore, Amos, of Newtown, farmer, committed on evidence of having been with enemy, 414; witnesses give evidence regarding, 414, 415; examined by

New York: state *assembly*— cont.
others of manor of Rensselaerwyck to, 28–29; memorial of
Albany board presented in, 29;
petition from inhabitants of
Westchester county against commissioners for conspiracies received by, 20; committee of,
reports in favor of abolishing
commissioners for conspiracies,
30; petition from Westchester
county board received in, 30;
joint committee of legislature
on expenditures of public
money (Jan. 31, 1783) reports
to, 31; bill for repealing laws
relating to commissioners for
conspiracies in, 31; Albany
representatives in, requested to
favor act to raise company of
rangers, 150; Albany representatives in, informed of atti-
tude of certain persons toward
oath of allegiance, 268.
attorney general, Egbert Benson,
85.
auditor general. See also subhead
comptroller.
auditor general, accounting for sale
of effects of tory families by
commissioners for conspiracies
to be made to, 26, 799; to
report to legislature state of
accounts of commissioners, 32,
801; accounts of commissioners
audited by, 36; where early
records of, are now kept, 36,
803; audited accounts, 803–804,
804–820.

New York: state— continued.
commissary of prisoners, prisoner
awaiting exchange to appear
before, 434.
*commissioners for detecting and
defeating conspiracies.* See under that name in main alphabet.
commissioners of sequestration,
governor required to certify to
them data about dangerous disaffected persons removed, 17,
781.
committee of safety, arrest of disaffected by, 11; committee on
suppressing disaffection reports
to, 11.
comptroller. See also subhead
auditor general.
comptroller, financial vouchers and
pay-bills of commissioners for
conspiracies now in custody
of, 36, 64, 141 (note), 146 (note),
156 (note), 174 (note), 184
(note), 188 (note), 189 (note), 192
(note), 195 (note), 202 (note),
210 (note), 215 (note), 221
(note), 233 (note), 238 (note),
250 (notes), 251 (note), 252
(note), 253 (note), 258 (note),
261 (note), 262 (note), 265
(note), 267 (note), 279 (notes),
285 (note), 291 (note), 292
(note), 293 (note), 307 (note),
309 (note), 311 (notes), 314
(notes), 319 (note), 320 (note),
331 (note), 339 (notes), 344
(note), 349 (note), 350 (note),
354 (note), 358 (note), 363
(note), 392 (note), 393 (note),

Oaths—continued.

serters from Burgoyne's army,
213; oath of allegiance taken by
deserters from enemy in Rhode
Island, 216; oath of neutrality
taken by person allowed to go
to Canada, 218; oath of allegiance taken by persons accused
of corresponding with and harboring tories, 325; oath of allegiance may be taken after refusing it, 336, 342, 344, 346,
359, 788; certificates of oath of
allegiance received, 361; oath
of neutrality taken by soldiers
in hands of robbers, 364–365;
oath not to aid robbers, tories,
delinquents or deserters, 388–
389; oath not to aid robbers or
tories, 399; oath of allegiance
taken by former tory, 420–421;
oath taken to disprove connection with tories of Albany
county, 473; spy under oath
charges Albany physician with
aiding him, 477; oath to communicate intelligence to commissioners and withhold it from
enemy, 504, 507, 512–513, 630–
631; oath of allegiance refused
by Archibald McNeal, 712;
oath of allegiance taken by
Lambert Starnbergh and Dirck
Miller, 718–719; prisoner confesses that he has taken oath
of loyalty to king, 735; oath
of allegiance taken by persons
arrested when about to go to
Canada, 747; form of oath of

Oaths—continued.

allegiance to state of New York,
747; oaths of allegiance with
signatures, 831–833; oath taken
by clerk of Albany board, 833;
certification of names of persons refusing oath of allegiance,
833–834; persons removed to
enemy's lines or held for exchange for refusing oath, 834–
835.
O'Brian, Jonathan, deserter, confined, 679.
Odell, ——, warrant for his arrest
as dangerous person, 419.
Odell, Gersham, of Hoosick district, constable, apprehends
Jacob Timmerman, 639.
Odell, Jonas, his examination, 652.
Oliver, Frederick, attacks soldiers
sent to capture deserter, 368.
Oliver, John, of Rensselaerwyck
Manor, farmer, witness against
Edward McGurkey, 736; bailsman for Jacobus Van Valkenburgh, 758.
Olmstead, Noah, cited before Albany board to testify respecting
conduct of John Miller, 414;
gives testimony, 416.
Oneidas. See also Indians.
Oneidas (Oneyda Indians), the,
persons captured by, released
by Albany board, 45, 263, 266,
271, 273; persons captured by,
near Crown Point, 737.
Oniskethau (Niscutaw, Niscuthaw, Nistutaw), Albany county,
rangers employed to ferret out

Petitions — continued.
prisonment of disaffected person, 247; for restoration of goods seized by militia, 270; of Jotham Bemus, 303; in behalf of Zadock Wright, 312–313; in behalf of John Smith, 321; in behalf of Nicholas Kittle, 327; in behalf of John Smith, 334–335; for permission to take oath of allegiance, 420; of John Ratcliffe and Arent Ratcliffe, 424; of Edward Finn, 435; of Dr. George Smith, 503; of Ephraim Knowlton, 537; in behalf of Margaret McCulpin, 546; in behalf of Thomas Yarns and other prisoners, 596; in behalf of Jotham Bemus, 596, 598; of Archibald McNeal and Ezekiel Ensign, 610; in behalf of Jane Moffit, 619–620; of Joshua H. Smith, 624.

Petry (Petrie), William, commissioner for conspiracies, Tryon county board, appointment, 68; signs instrument committing persons to custody of sheriff, 431; witness against tories of Durlach, 752.

Pettit, Dunham, bailsman for George Snyder, 194.

Pettit, Jonathan, of Albany, cordwainer, bailsman for Christopher Bennet, 97; examined with regard to escape of prisoner, 402; bailsman for Robert Brisben, 532; pays forfeited bail, 736–737.

Petzholdt. See Pattshold, Peatzhold.

Pharo, ——, information furnished by, 157.

Philadelphia, Pa., pass to, 308; tory woman to be taken to, 320; pretended journey of suspected person to, 671; residents of, 681, 711; adventure of William Dewitt on way from, 729.

Philips. See also Phillips.

Philips, Philip, of Rensselaerwyck Manor, weaver, charged with dissuading persons from taking up arms, 526, 534–535; released on bail, 581.

Philipstown (Philips Town, Phillips Town), N. Y., 138 (note); residents of, 85, 100.

Phillips. See also Philips.

Phillips, Jacob, released on bail by committee of Manor of Rensselaerwyck, 84; surrendered by bailsman, 84; released on bail to enter continental army, 84.

Physicians, captured British doctors, imprisoned at Albany, 99–100, 100–101; one examines prisoner before Albany board, 236; one attends suspected person from New York, 347; one in Kinderhook put under bonds, 437; one charged with aiding spy from enemy, 477; one on bail allowed to visit patient, 611–612.

Picksen, Jane, wife of John Picksen, warned to remove from state, 523.

Powers (Power), Jacob, of Livingston Manor, farmer, bailsman for Thomas Anderson,
161; makes affidavit concerning Dr. Thomas Thompson,
531; bailsman for Hans Peter
Snyder, 618; arrests suspected
person, 644.

Powers, John, released on bail, 121.

Powers, William, bailsman for
David Wyng and John Powers,
121.

Pownal, Vt., resident of, 185.

Pratt (Platt), Joel, of New Lebanon, farmer, refuses to take up
arms, 461; confined, 461; released on bail, 573.

Prendergast (Pendergrast), William, of Cambridge district,
cited to appear before Albany
board, 220, 235, 242; proof of
service of citation on, required,
286.

Price, Daniel, sent under guard
from Claverack to Albany, 221;
committed, 221; released on
bail because of injury received,
239–240.

Price, David, sent under guard
from Claverack to Albany, 221;
committed, 221; accused of complicity in crimes of Nathaniel
Morgan, 256; released on bail,
256.

Price, Isaac, design of robbers
against, 368.

Price, William, of Schoharie, tory
suspect, ordered confined, 89;
released on recognizance, 116.

Prices, exorbitant, prohibited by
commissioners for conspiracies,
38–39, 310.

Primmer, Elsie, examined and discharged, 164–165.

Primmer, Joe, Ryley's rangers
ordered to search barn of, for
stolen property, 135; stolen
goods buried near his house,
164–165.

Prince, negro, discharged from
confinement by General Stark,
232.

Printup, William, prisoner in
Johnstown jail, petitions for release on bail, 212.

Prisoners. See also Felony, Tories.

Prisoners, commissioners for conspiracies empowered to arrest
or release, 12, 13, 24; subsistence of, 13; judges and magistrates not to bail those committed by commissioners, 13;
deserters from British lines when
confined, how released, 24, 791;
release of, did not excuse from
militia duty, 24, 791; legislature
requests report about, from commissioners, 31; guards placed
over counterfeiters, paid by
commissioners, 38; good money
found on counterfeiters, held
to reimburse persons defrauded,
38; those captured by Brant,
39; one of Burgoyne's German
allies, 40; British military, seek-
ing exchange, granted passes to
Poughkeepsie, 41; system of

Provision—continued.
of Leonard Gansevoort, Jr., 375; not to be furnished to robbers, 388; account for flour for prisoners, 394; to be furnished to prisoner at cost of Albany board, 457; furnished to enemy, 468, 733; wheat at Catskill to be seized, 734; robbers supplied with, 748; purchase of, for enemy, 762; stock and grain on frontier may be removed or destroyed, 798–799; pork purchased for prisoners, 817; pay for transporting and smoking beef, 820; accounts for flour, 820, insert opp. 820; money paid for, insert opp. 821.

Pruyn, Harmen (Harman, Harme) cited to appear before Albany board, 171–172; asks time to consider oath of allegiance, 174; his removal to enemy's lines ordered, 177; advised of day of removal, 189; his refusal of oath certified to secretary of state, 197–198; in list of persons removed or held for exchange, 835.

Pruyn, Samuel, of Albany, yeoman, bailed person confined to house of, 236, 570; bailsman for Jacob Halenbeeck, Jr., 580.

Pulver, Hendrick, offers recommendation in behalf of William Lee, 339–340.

Punishments, barbarous methods of, under English law, abolished in New York, 59.

Purchase, Thomas, of Newtown, farmer, tory suspect, detained for trial, 87; released on bail, 118; enters into new bail, 588.

Purdy, Ebenezer, commissioner for conspiracies, Westchester county board, a petitioner to legislature, 30; appointment as commissioner, 68; his audited account, 806–807, 819; his account with state treasurer, 823, 826.

Purves, John, prisoner, released on recognizance, 249.

QUACKENBUSH, Garret, denounced by disaffected person, 630.

Quackenbush, Walter, presents information against Harmen Haver, 630.

Quakers. See also Shakers.

Quakers, to take oath of allegiance by affirmation, 18, 43, 784; object to wording of oath, 43; petition legislature for relief from wording of oath, 43.

Quant, Coenrad, of the Helderbergs, released on recognizance, 156.

Quant, Henry, from the Helderbergs, prisoner, captured as supposed robber, 109; sent from Schoharie to Albany, 109; confined, 109; released on condition of joining continental army, 127.

Quartermaster general, requested to send deserter from bateau service to Fishkill, 505.

Rangers — continued.

Kinderhook to Albany, 250; account of goods seized by, required, 263; account for conveying company of, with prisoners, 344; request for ammunition for, 358; arrest soldier from Burgoyne's army, 358; required to protect inhabitants of Helderbergs and Peesink, 377; to arrest person in hiding at Peesink, 397; to scout as far as Roe Kill and Batavia, 401; discharge of Captain De Forest's rangers, 413; John Tillman, Jr., invited to raise company of rangers for Albany board, 488.

Ratcliffe. See also Radliff.

Ratcliffe (Radliff, Ratcliff, Rodliff), Arent, required to give account of matters at Unadilla, 424; to give security for good behavior, 424; his bail forfeited by refusal to do militia duty, 490–491; summond to appear before Albany board, 494; released on bail, 497; to be delivered up to Albany board, 723, 728; testimony concerning, 728.

Ratcliffe (Radcliff, Ratcliff, Rodliff), John, required to give account of matters at Unadilla, 424; to give security for good behavior, 424; his bail forfeited by refusal to do militia duty, 490–491; summoned to appear before Albany board,

Ratcliffe, John — continued.

494; released on bail, 497; to be delivered up to Albany board, 723, 728; testimony concerning, 728.

Ratcliffe (Radliff, Ratcliff, Rodliff), Rykert, father of John Ratcliffe and Arent Ratcliffe, 424; asked to show cause why bail of his sons should not be forfeited, 491; denies charge against his sons, 494; renews his bail for their good behavior, 497; required to deliver up sons, 723; examined and discharged, 728.

Rathbun, Valentine (Rev.), writes to Albany board about prisoners from New Lebanon, 554–555.

Rawbottom, John, permitted to go to Tryon county on bail, 533.

Rawworth, Francis, of Johnstown, his testimony regarding Robert Adams, 450–451.

Rea, William, cited to appear before Albany board, 171–172; asks time to consider oath of allegiance, 174; his removal to enemy's lines ordered, 177; advised of day of removal, 189; his refusal of oath certified to secretary of state, 197–198; in list of persons removed or held for exchange, 835.

Recognizances, taken by commissioners for conspiracies, 12, 778; prosecuted, canceled and released by same, 13, 778;

Scharp, George, of Rensselaerwyck Manor, farmer, Christopher Witting in his charge, 715;
bailsman for Christopher Witting, 716.

Scharp (Scherp), Lourence (Lawrence, Lowrence), of Kinderhook, brought under guard to
Albany for passing counterfeit
money, 136; imprisoned, 136;
bail refused for, 165; issuance
of habeas corpus for relief of,
231.

Scharp (Sharp), Peter, of Albany, carpenter, bailsman for
John Hocknel, 571; bailsman
for James Brisben, 607, 621,
676, 727.

Scharpe, George, captain, ordered to arrest tory suspects,
94–95.

Schaver. See also Scheffer,
Shafer, Shaver.

Schaver (Shaver), Johannis, of
Schoharie, tory suspect, ordered
confined, 89; released on bail,
114; bailsman for Johannis
Schaver, Jr., 115.

Schaver, John (Johannis, Jr.),
of Schoharie, tory suspect, ordered confined, 89; released on
bail, 115.

Scheffer, John, released on bail,
218.

Schell, Jacob, of Sir John Johnson's corps, emissary in Helderbergs, 555–556; confined, 556;
examined and recommitted,
556.

Schenck, Abraham, commissioner
for conspiracies, Dutchess
county board, appointment, 68.

Schenectady (Schnectady, Schonectady), night watch in, 20;
prisoner confined by committee
of, 104; suspicious person at,
121; Indian minister at Fort
Hunter removes to, 142; letters
conveyed to tories in, from New
York city, 147; persons confined
to limits of, 158, 169, 396, 410,
422, 427; residents of, 172, 175,
189, 197, 225, 330, 426, 427,
450, 484, 485, 486, 487, 489,
517, 617, 700; account for serv-
ing citations at, 314; Rev. Mr.
Stewart ordered to repair to
371; tories under arrest brought
to, 465; commissioners at, for-
ward prisoners to Albany, 468,
472, 481, 484, 486, 492, 502;
commissioners at, order tory
to remove to Albany, 471;
captured spy professes to have
been on his way to, 492; prisoner to be sent from, to Albany,
497–498; persons cited to appear before commissioner at,
503; prisoners sent from, to Albany, 558; commissioners at,
write concerning delinquents,
612; persons sent under guard
from, to Albany, 639; recognizance furnished to appear before commissioners at, 647;
commissioners at, communicate
with Albany board, 697; aid
of men from, invited for

Sidnam, George, apprehended for harboring emissaries from enemy, 741; committed, 741.

Siekeler, Paul, petitions for restoration of goods seized by militia, 270.

Siemon. See also Simmon, Simmons.

Siemon, Albertus (Albartus), of Livingston Manor, farmer, put under bail, 510, 511; bailsman for Johannis Siemon, 512.

Siemon, Johannis, of Livingston Manor, farmer, put under bail, 510, 512; bailsman for Albertus Siemon, 511.

Sierenger, Jacob, Hessian deserter from British army, takes oath of neutrality, 204.

Sietz, Peter, prisoner in Canada, exchanged, 562; testifies in favor of Albert Van Der Werken, 562.

Sigsby. See Sixby.

Silversmiths, 659; 709.

Silvester, Peter, craves permission for paroled persons at Schodack to come to Kinderhook, 349–350, 352.

Simmon. See also Siemon, Simmons.

Simmon, Charles, sent under guard to Albany, as accessory in robbery of John Van Ness, 125; confined, 125.

Simmons. See also Siemon, Simmon.

Simmons, ——, of Dutchess county, horses of, stolen, 92.

Simmons, Robert, captain, late in British service, examined, 648.

Simpson, Alexander, money paid to, 808.

Simpson, Catharine, of Schoharie, her property destroyed on pretense of disaffection, 388.

Simpson, Hannah, of Hoosick district, warned to remove from state, 528.

Simpson, Henry, of Albany, tavern-keeper on Schenectady road, warrant for his arrest as suspicious character, 443; released on bail, 444; required to report matters prejudicial to United States, 444; reports movements of Joseph Bettis, 653, 654–655; delivers prisoner to Albany board, 704.

Singer, Philip, prisoner, sent from Poughkeepsie to Albany, 93.

Sittamon. See also Cittimon.

Sittamon, George, of the Helderbergs, disaffected person, ordered to furnish bail, 709.

Sixby (Sixbey), Evert, his house to be searched for stolen goods, 396; confined on charge of harboring robbers, 748.

Sixby, Nicholas, denies charge of having been with enemy, 415; enters into recognizance, 415.

Skene (Skeene), Philip, major, sends spy into General Stark's army, 417.

Skenesborough (Skeensborough), Charlotte county, resident of,

Tories — continued.

tory advised to make concessions to inhabitants of his district, 248; tory escapes from guard on way to Hartford, 249; two apprehended for going to enemy, 255; pay-bill for conducting certain, to Poughkeepsie, 258, 262; account of goods taken by rangers from suspected persons to be rendered, 263; removal of, to Fort Edward, 267; application to permit return of certain, removed within enemy's lines, 272; order to send officers in American hands to New York, 272; one deserting from enemy delivers himself to Colonel Frederick Fisher, 284; two confined for corresponding with enemy, 291; two apprehended on way to Canada, 291; Washington orders that officers of New Levies in American hands be sent to New York, 295; commissioners at Poughkeepsie consulted about complying with this order, 299; meeting of, in Rensselaerwyck, 313; warrant for arrest of those attending this meeting, 313; certain, to be removed within enemy's lines unless legislature intervenes, 319; those who have returned to Peesink from enemy's service to be apprehended, 323; those fleeing from Peesink to be intercepted at Schoharie creek,

Tories — continued.

323; correspondence with and harboring of, an offense, 324, 325; wives of those with enemy harbor persons in concealment, 327; party of, captured on way to join enemy, 329; those offering to take oath after refusing not to be removed within enemy's lines, 332–333; one on parole asks extension of his bounds, 339; engage to prevent robberies at Beaver Dam and elsewhere, 341; account for conveying, from Claverack to Albany, 344; certain, take oath after refusing, 342, 344, 359; suspect ordered to appear before Albany board when discharged from militia, 345; certain, on parole at Schodack, allowed to go to Kinderhook to settle estate, 349–350, 352; those in Schaghticoke interfere with orders of officers and secrete enemies of state, 357; cruelties committed by, 377; presence of two on parole at Schodack required at Kinderhook, 381; at Stillwater, 395; oath not to harbor, taken, 399; party of, collected to join enemy, 401; several at Palmertown harbor and conceal enemy, 405; woman imprisoned for harboring, 411; descent of, on western frontiers, 411; removal of wife of one to Canada requested, 414; cooperate with enemy's

Tories—continued.

scouting parties, 416; certain, at Newtown, to be apprehended, 417; bound to good behavior during continuance of war, 442, 444, 447, 449, 459; cause disturbances in Albany county, 443; certain, declare purpose of joining enemy in Canada, 448; order for arrest of one from Goshen, Conn., 453; one on parole dissuades people from taking up arms, 453; one confined for assisting persons to join enemy, 457–458; several confined by order of Lieutenant Colonel Van Rensselaer, 458; conduct of, necessitates meeting of Albany board at Newtown or Stillwater, 460, 466; arrested and taken to Schenectady, 465; apprehended by commissioners at Schenectady while attempting to join enemy, 468; one ordered by commissioners at Schenectady to remove his family to Albany, 471; two on bail to be reimprisoned in order to expedite their exchange, 473; connection with, disproved by oath, 473; party of, from Newtown, attempt to join enemy, 474; several in west district of Rensselaerwyck Manor accused of intending to join enemy, 475–476; certain on parole to be removed to jail to await exchange 476; certain to be conducted to Fishkill, 477–478; one released

Tories—continued.

on bail on account of sickness of his wife, 478; one assists escape of men charged with stealing horses, 480; enter into parole to proceed to Fishkill 482, 484, 506; one guilty of robbery captured, 492; several accused of violating parole, 506; sent as prisoners from Charlotte county to Albany, 508; one allowed to remain in Kinderhook on parole because of illness, 512; one declares himself a King's man, 516; certain, supposed to obtain intelligence from New York, 522; order for removal of wife of one, revoked, 525; exemption from order for removal of tory families refused, 528; collecting in Bethlehem, 531; testimony received against those in New Scotland, 534; circulate counterfeit money, 544; certain, in Cumberland county, in communication with enemy, 549; minister accused of preaching tory doctrines, 551; tory women at Saratoga desire to go to Canada, 558; hold meetings near Coxsackie, 564; enlisted at Oniskethau, 564; certain, at Oniskethau, to be apprehended, 565; enlisted in Livingston Manor, 565; certain, in Livingston Manor, to be apprehended, 565; those detained at Coeymans to be sent to Albany, 566; information about their enlist-

Van Rensselaer, Henry K.— cont.
Archibald McNeal in order that
he may join levies, 349; applied
to for soldiers to go to Helderbergs, 366; drafted men in
hiding delivered up to, 378,
379, 386, 391; explains charges
against Nicholas Kittle and
others, 456; imprisons dangerous persons, 458; dangerous
persons not to be liberated
without his knowledge, 458;
suggests mode of obtaining information concerning Abraham
Ja. Lansing, 470; requested
to furnish witnesses against
Thomas Blewer, 500; furnishes
witness against Blewer, 508;
asks liberation of John Armstrong, 519; gives information
against Nicholas Williams, 550;
gives information of tory meeting in Rensselaerwyck Manor,
636; reports rescue by tories
of delinquents under arrest,
644–645, 646; certifies in behalf of Sander Bulson, 656;
presents information against
Thomas Blewer, 713.

Van Rensselaer, Henry K., of
Rensselaerwyck Manor, farmer,
bailsman for John Rysdorp and
Leonard Rysdorp, 316; bailsman for Samuel Baker, 714.

Van Rensselaer (Van Renselaer),
Jeremiah, commissioner for conspiracies, Albany county board,
wrote part of minutes, 64–65;
appointment as commissioner,

Van Rensselaer, Jeremiah— cont.
67, 79; his attendances at Albany
board meetings, 75–76; signs
oath, 80; signs warrant appointing John Ryley, captain of
rangers, 112; waits on General
Stark in behalf of persons sent
from Bennington to Albany,
169; paid by Albany board for
paper, 173–174; to assist in exchange of Cherry Valley cap-
tives, 304; £95 paid to, on
salary account, 320; applies to
General Clinton for soldiers to
seize tories at Peesink, 323;
furnishes information against
Stephen Van Dyck, 394, 404;
money advanced by, to Albany
board, 410, 812; money received
by, for Albany board, 599;
resigns office of commissioner,
670; money paid to, 811; his
account as commissioner, 814,
820, 821, 822, 823, 824, 825,
826; his commission, 829.

Van Rensselaer (Van Renselaer),
John, major, advises Albany
board of finding of stolen property, 146.

Van Rensselaer, John, Jr., signs
receipt for David Van Rensselaer, 279 (note).

Van Rensselaer (Van Renselaer),
Killian, colonel, men from his
regiment employed as company
of horse by Albany board, 50,
444; detachment from his regiment to arrest in robbery case,
119; bailsman for Robert

Van Valkenburgh, Bartholemewis (Bartholemew), of Kinderhook, farmer, sent under guard from Claverack to Albany, 220–221; committed, 221; released on bail on account of illness, 259–260; his surrender demanded of his surety, 495; his bail renewed, 498.

Van Valkenburgh, Isaac, captain, bailsman for John J. Van Valkenburgh and Mathew McCagge, 515; receives certificate showing that John J. Van Valkenburgh is under bail, 520–521.

Van Valkenburgh, Isaac Joachim, of Rensselaerwyck Manor, farmer, bailsman for Jacobus Van Der Pool, 316.

Van Valkenburgh, Jacob, pay-bill for arrest of robbers, 133, 810.

Van Valkenburgh, Jacob J., of Schodack, cordwainer, bailsman for John Kittle, 658; bailsman for Peter Wyngart, 659; bailsman for Hendrick Kittle, 663.

Van Valkenburgh, Jacobus, of Rensselaerwyck Manor, farmer, confined on charge of harboring robbers, 748; released on bail, 758.

Van Valkenburgh, Jerone, of Schodack, farmer, bailsman for Nicholas Miller, 650; bailsman for John J. Miller, 651.

Van Valkenburgh, Joachim, disaffected person, 313; warrant for his arrest, 313.

Van Valkenburgh, John, of Rensselaerwyck Manor, cordwainer, disaffected person, 313; his arrest, 313; released on bail, 315.

Van Valkenburgh, John J., of Kinderhook, laborer, gives bail at Poughkeepsie to surrender himself to Albany board, 515; liberated on bail, 515; release of his effects dependent on proof that he has furnished bail, 520–521; cited to appear before supreme court, 548.

Van Valkenburgh, ,John J., of Schodack, farmer, cited to appear before Albany board, 637; apprehended, 640; released on recognizance, 640.

Van Valkenburgh, John Jerone, of Schodack, farmer, released on bail, 652.

Van Valkenburgh, Jurry, of Kinderhook, farmer, bailsman for John J. Van Valkenburgh, 515.

Van Valkenburgh (Van Valkenbourgh), Mathewis (Mathew), of Rensselaerwyck Manor, blacksmith, bailsman for Hendrick Skinkle, 131; tory meeting at his house, 313, 326; his arrest, 313; advised to prepare his defense, 314; released on bail 315; avows loyalty to King George, 470; bail renewed for, 501; bailsman for Hendrick Skinkle, 501.

Van Valkenburgh, Nicholas, of Schodack, yeoman, committed for avowing loyalty to king,

Wheeler, Jurie, of Livingston Manor, sent under guard from Claverack to Albany, 221; committed, 221; released on bail to remain within prescribed limits, 254; grand jury finds no bill against, for complicity in robbery, 274; released on bail, 275; advises deserter to go to New York, 708.

Wheeler, Mary, sent under guard from Claverack to Albany, 221; committed, 221; discharged, 254.

Wheeler, Nicholas, of Livingston Manor, farmer, bailsman for Peter Wheeler, 239; put under bail, 509, 511; bailsman for Broer Witbeeck, 511.

Wheeler, Peter, sent under guard from Claverack to Albany, 221; committed, 221; released on bail, 239.

Wheelwrights, 573; 746.

Whigs, in New York, 9; partizan literature of, against toryism, 10; in Westchester county, 29; recommendation from, required for issuance of passes to Vermont, 41; charges by, preferred against suspected or disloyal persons, 41; obliged to reveal disloyalty, 41; conduct of overzealous, objected to by Albany board, 43–44; barbarity of, in plundering tories, 55; called scoundrels and rascals, 56, 454; compelled to procure private guards for security against tory violence, 416.

Whitacre. See also Whiteacre.

Whitacre (Whitaker), Barent, confined for refusing to aid in transporting military stores, 368; committed for disaffection, 369; released on bail, 377.

Whitaker, Whitakre. See Whitacre, Whiteacre.

White, Alexander, applies for permission to appear before Albany board, 193; refuses oath of allegiance, 193; his removal to enemy's lines ordered, 193; released on bail till day of removal, 193; his refusal of oath certified to secretary of state, 197–198; detained at Albany, for exchange, 206, 835; his wife given pass to Poughkeepsie, 206; his wife to solicit exchange for him, 206; exchanged and paroled, 237, 244; to be sent to Poughkeepsie, 239; in charge of Captain Edward Willet, 245.

White, George, captain, assaulted and robbed at house of Nicholas Michel, 119, 120, 149; stolen goods seized upon warrant from, 138; sends John Lary to Albany board, 145; heads remonstrance against privilege granted to Aaron Hammond, 279; requested to support charge against Hammond, 279; withdraws charge against Hammond, 289; brings charge of disaffection against Robert Martin, 325, 351; writes concern-

Woodward, Thomas — continued. 282; committed, 282; good money taken from, to compensate persons defrauded, 283, 285, 287; inquiry about, is made, 287–288, 304; information about, received, 321.

Woodworth (Woodward), Absalom (Absolom), bailsman for Jeremiah Shans, 122; asks time to consider oath of allegiance, 180; refuses oath, 188; advised of day for removal, 191; his refusal of oath certified to secretary of state, 197–198; presents to commissioners objections to oath, 203; in list of persons removed or held for exchange, 834.

Worcester, Mass., requisition for person concealed near, 45, 224; requisition for person confined at, 224; letter from, relating to Thomas Gleason, 695.

Wormer. See also Warmer, Wermer.

Wormer, ——, his daughter's husband attempts to join savages, 368.

Wormer, Frederick, ordered confined, 167.

Worthington, township in Massachusetts, certificate from officers of, 694.

Wrag, Mrs., asks permission to join husband in Canada, 237; granting of request recommended to General Stark, 237–238.

Wrathbone, Joshua, of Cambridge, captured by British, 92; his service for British, 92; released on bail by Albany board and called "an ignorant man," 92.

Wright, Alexander, warrant for his arrest on charge of active toryism, 357.

Wright, Job, of Stillwater, farmer, captain, Albany board takes opinion of court on his case, 106; court recommends his discharge, 106; released, 106; bailsman for Jotham Bemus, 303, 609, 616; warrant to, for arrest of disaffected persons, 395; apprehends Isaac Bryant, 406.

Wright, Moses, of Brattleboro, Vt., captain, bailsman for Zadock Wright, 292; presents petition in behalf of Zadock Wright, 312; surrender of Zadock Wright demanded of, 525.

Wright, Reuben, of Stillwater, farmer, ensign, warrant directed to, for arrest of dangerous persons, 419; bailsman for Jotham Bemus, 609, 616.

Wright, Umfreys, warrant for his arrest for encouraging soldiers to desert and plunder, 419.

Wright, Zadock, of Hartford, Conn., tory, sent under guard from Northampton to Albany, 167; ordered confined, 167; order for his examination, 200; released on bail, to remain within prescribed limits, 292;

Wright, Zadock—continued.
to reimburse Albany board for cost of his removal from Northampton, 292; petition in his behalf not granted, 312–313; recommendation that he be allowed to reside in Cumberland county, 343; obliged to remain in Kings district, 344; professes to be a Shaker, 453; cited to appear before Albany board, 453; to be sent to Fishkill for exchange, 478, 482; evidence respecting, sent to Albany board, 506–507; reported to be in Cumberland county, 524; his surrender by his surety demanded, 525.

Wrymer, Andrew, of Stone Arabia, bailsman for Godfray Sybert, 426.

Wurmer, Frederick, released on bail, 210; testifies respecting John Cittimon, 343.

Wycoff. See also Wykoff.

Wycoff, Abraham, commissioner for conspiracies, Dutchess county board, appointment, 68.

Wykoff (Wickhoffs), John, of Ballston, prisoner, sent from Poughkeepsie to Albany, 93; in Albany jail, 127; released on recognizance, 235.

Wykoff, John, of Niskayuna, laborer, released on bail, 635.

Wyng, David, released on bail, 121.

Wyngart, Johannis, of Albany, yeoman, bailsman for Jacob J. Truax, 507.

Wyngart (Wyngaert), Peter, of Schodack, farmer, apprehended as disaffected person, 640; committed, 640; released on bail, 659.

Wynkoop, Cornelius E. (C. [sic]), commissioner for conspiracies, Ulster county board, appointment, 68; prisoner bailed by Albany board to work at Kingston for, 118; his audited account, 815, 816; his account with state treasurer, 823, 825, 826; his commission, 829.

Wynkoop, Evert, bailsman for George Atkin, 405.

Wynkoop (Wynekoop), Peter (Petrus), Jr., commissioner for conspiracies, Albany county board, appointment, 67, 79; his attendances at Albany board meetings, 76, 106; signs oath, 80, 106; requested to cause arrest of two men charged with robbery, 143; his attendance at Albany board meeting requested, 150, 167; writes to Albany board, 203, 208; asked to serve citations in Livingston Manor, 347; unable to serve citations, 354; his commission, 829.

Wynkoop, Petrus, money paid to, 812; his account, 815.

YAGER, Hendrick, of Livingston Manor, yeoman, arrest of, ordered, for passing counterfeit money, 114; account for